Midwestern Food

Midwestern
FOOD

A CHEF'S GUIDE TO THE SURPRISING
HISTORY OF A GREAT AMERICAN CUISINE,
WITH MORE THAN 100 TASTY RECIPES

Paul Fehribach

THE UNIVERSITY OF CHICAGO PRESS
Chicago and London

The University of Chicago Press, Chicago 60637
The University of Chicago Press, Ltd., London
© 2023 by The University of Chicago
Published 2023
Printed in the United States of America

32 31 30 29 28 27 26 25 24 23   2 3 4 5

ISBN-13: 978-0-226-81949-5 (cloth)
ISBN-13: 978-0-226-81952-5 (e-book)
DOI: https://doi.org/10.7208/chicago/9780226819525.001.0001

Library of Congress Cataloging-in-Publication Data

Names: Fehribach, Paul, author.
Title: Midwestern food : a chef's guide to the surprising history
   of a great American cuisine, with more than 100 tasty recipes /
   Paul Fehribach.
Description: Chicago : The University of Chicago Press, 2023. | Includes
   bibliographical references and index.
Identifiers: LCCN 2023002876 | ISBN 9780226819495 (cloth) |
   ISBN 9780226819525 (ebook)
Subjects: LCSH: Cooking, American—Midwestern style. | Cooking,
   American—Midwestern style—History. | Food habits—Middle West.
Classification: LCC TX715.2.M53 F44 2023 | DDC 641.5977—dc23/
   eng/20230127
LC record available at https://lccn.loc.gov/2023002876

♾ This paper meets the requirements of ANSI/NISO Z39.48-1992
(Permanence of Paper).

This book is dedicated to the women of the greater Midwest, who have nurtured and fed our people, most often quietly and without recognition or thanks. I see you, thank you, and hope that these words do justice to your labors of generations.

Contents

Introduction · 1

1 **On Relishes, Sweets, and Sours: Pickles and Preserves** · 15
Cherry Barbecue Relish · 18
Chili Sauce · 19
Chow-Chow · 21
Piccalilli · 23
Chicago-Style Hot Giardiniera · 25
Sauerkraut · 26
Watermelon Pickles · 28
Cranberry Pear Preserves · 29
Quince Honey · 30
Apple Butter · 31
Cranberry Sweet Corn Relish · 33
Quick Blackberry Jam · 34
Rhubarb Marmalade · 35

Meet the Locals: Justin Dean · 37

2 **A Country Well Lit: Cocktails** · 39
Brandy Manhattan · 46
Brandy Old-Fashioned · 46
Elderflower Collins · 48
Pink Squirrel · 48
Albert Fehribach's Wild Cherry and Blackberry Wine · 49
Three Doyennes Blackberry Cordial · 51

Meet the Locals: Andy Hazzard · 54

3 **Baker's Delight: Breads** · 57
Lincoln Family Frontier Cornbread · 60
Brown County Fried Biscuits · 61
"Everything" Rye Pretzels · 64
Conchas Chocolates · 66

Sorghum Pecan Sticky Rolls · 69

Pumpernickel · 71

Friendship Bread · 75

Apfelkuchen · 78

"Chicago Hardy" Fig Kringle · 81

Kansas Zwiebach · 84

Donuts · 86

Meet the Locals: Titus Ruscitti · 91

4   **Of State Fairs, Tailgates, and Main Street Cafés: Sandwiches and Handheld Food** · 93

Beer Brats (the Real Way) · 95

Fried Cheese Curds · 97

Ranch Dressing · 99

Cold-Pack Cheese · 100

Apple Cider Pecan Cheese Ball · 101

Bierocks, a.k.a. Runzas · 103

Toasted Ravioli · 105

A Tale of Three Tamales · 107

Breaded Pork Tenderloin · 113

Italian Beef · 116

Jibarito · 119

Hot Dog Heaven · 122

5   **Please Pass the Corn: Vegetables and Sides** · 135

Pan-Fried Morels · 137

The Many Colors of Borscht · 139

You Say Knoephla, I Say Knefle · 141

Prepared Sauerkraut · 143

Green Bean Casserole · 144

Candied Yams · 146

Aunt Mary Lou's Pretzel Salad · 147

Latkes, a.k.a. Potato Pancakes, a.k.a. *Rosti* · 149

Go Goetta! · 151

Potato Salad Two Ways · 154

German Fries · 157

Oyster Dressing · 158

Meet the Locals: Rob Connoley · 161

6 **Pull Up a Chair: Meat and Potatoes** · 65
   Booyah · 167
   Duck and Manoomin Hotdish · 170
   Chicken and Noodles · 173
   Fish Fries · 176
   Fried Chicken: Of Church Suppers and June Weddings · 185
   Queen City Chili · 191

   Meet the Locals: Marty and Will Travis · 196

7 **Burgerlandia** · 199
   Cannibal/Wildcat · 202
   Loosemeat Burgers · 204
   Jucy Lucy · 206
   Butterburgers · 208
   Horseshoes · 209

8 **Midwestern Barbecue** · 213
   Kansas City–Style Barbecue · 217
   Chicago-Style Barbecue · 221
   East Saint Louis–Style Barbecue · 223

9 **A Pizza Tour** · 229
   Saint Louis–Style Pizza · 232
   Basic Midwestern Pizza Sauce · 234
   Chicago-Style Deep-Dish Pizza · 235
   Detroit-Style Deep-Dish Pizza · 238
   Tavern-Style Pizza · 240
   Pan Pizza · 242

   Meet the Locals: Stephanie Hart · 246

10 **Sweets: Pies, Cakes, Cookies, and Confections** · 249
   Grandma Fehribach's Strawberry Custard Pie · 251
   Sugar Cream Pie · 253
   Cherry Delight · 255
   Sweet-Potato Pie · 257
   Coconut Cream Pie · 258
   Persimmon Pudding · 260
   Pawpaw Chiffon Pie · 262

Cranberry and Bone Marrow Pudding Pie · 264

Mince Pie · 266

Rhubarb Charlotte · 269

Angel Food Cake · 270

Devil's Food Cake · 272

Banana Caramel Cake · 275

Grandmother Hazel Spence's Black Walnut Spice Cake · 278

Gooey Butter Cake · 279

Spritz Cookies · 281

Springerle · 283

Lebkuchen · 286

Black Walnut Rugelach · 288

Mexican Wedding Cakes · 290

Meet the Locals: Erika Allen · 292

11   **What Next, Heartland?** · 295

Acknowledgments · 303

Notes · 305

Bibliography · 317

Index · 333

INTRODUCTION

Moonshine pours through my window
the night puts its laughter away
clouds that pierce the illusion
that tomorrow would be as yesterday . . .

—**Sixto Rodriguez**

GRANDMA Morelos, riding shotgun, held court while the Sobeleskis and Fehribachs swayed and bobbled down Gratiot Avenue in East Detroit as Dad navigated, weaving the ocher-hued Dodge Tradesman van through mid-morning traffic past a booming downtown before catching the highway to the southwest side. Our destination was a relatively new addition to the Mexican-town enclave, La Gloria Bakery, which would thrive through decades of tumul-tuous change in the erstwhile Motortown to become an institution, an impor-tant stop for anyone looking for a taste of Mexico in Detroit.

The adults had their own agenda—to secure some chorizo, tortillas, and av-ocados at the grocery on the corner—but for me, there was one reason and one reason only to be in Mexicantown, and that was the panes dulces—sweet, rich yeast breads with any number of glazes and toppings in a mind-bending array of shapes and designs, displayed alongside cookies and cakes made with the same marvelous creativity in a long, floor-to-ceiling wood and glass display case. My most rabid obsession was the one smeared with a red jam, raspberry or strawberry perhaps, but to my young palate the flavor was just a delight-ful fruity *red*, then showered with a snow of coconut that reminded me of the dreams that live inside a snow globe. It would yield to my bite with a pillowy softness laced with the tang of fruit, the perfume of yeast, and the heady aroma of coconut. The pan dulce never made it all the way back to Grandma's home in Roseville, the working-class ward populated by a diverse mix of people who powered the city's tool and die factories, providing existential support to the automobile industry.

Summer visits to Detroit were the highlight of the year. There was Grandma, of course, and Grandpa Fernando, and aunts and uncles and cousins from Mom's family, but most alluring was the magnetism of a more diverse Amer-ica than we lived in day-to-day in the WASP-y southern Indiana woods. Mom's family was a curiously American and outrageously fun blend of Grandma's Ulster Appalachian and Florida bush heritage, her Mexican husbands and the children they bore, Uncle John's Polish immigrant whimsy, and the hip, urbane stylings of Uncle Olin and Aunt Carol, who introduced me to the music of Prince years before it percolated to our small town. Most consequential to me today is the early exposure those trips to Detroit gave me to a diverse array of foods deeply embedded in their cultures. To experience these through family is akin to programming your soul.

Back home in the brown clapboard bungalow east of Jasper, I begged a place in the kitchen as soon as I could stand on a chair and reach over the counter. I preferred my twin sister Pam's Easy-Bake Oven to sports or more "masculine" pursuits, attempting every trick I could muster to coax "red" flavors out of everything from cookies to brownies and biscuits as I chased an obsession with strawberries and cherries, though I quickly learned that red food color would not impart the coveted flavor. But somehow I was undeterred, and I would ultimately pursue the culinary vocation, never giving up the mind-set of a tinkerer even in the big city. There is no escaping a youth in the woods, however, and ironically, I am as infatuated with the country as a man as I was with the city when I was a boy.

I first embarked on this book as a culinary memoir, tracing the migration of the Fehrenbach family from the tiny village of Reute in Baden, in the present-day German state of Baden-Württemberg, in 1838. (The Fehrenbach name was misspelled often, and my great-great-grandfather Raymond's last name was spelled at least six different ways during his service in the 65th Indiana Regiment during the Civil War, before it was ultimately spelled "Fehribach" on his marriage records.) They departed during a rare time of relative calm in German politics, so I imagine they came to the United States, like many other rural German émigrés, in search of land after generations of inheritance had parsed the family plots into untenably small farms. Southern Indiana at the time was similar in temperature and terrain to the Black Forest and attracted immigrants from Baden, Swabia, Bavaria, Hesse, Saxony, and Württemberg. George and Anna Fehrenbach traveled down the Rhine and sailed from Amsterdam to Philadelphia, then followed the Wagon Road to the Cumberland Gap, the easiest and safest route into eastern Kentucky. From there they traveled west on the Buffalo Trace, a mammoth pathway hewn out of the forest by buffalo as they migrated from the Great Plains to salt licks near Frankfort, Kentucky, and back. Without the work the buffalo had done, the forest would have been impassable by wagons. After crossing the Falls of the Ohio just east of Louisville and traveling about another sixty miles down the Trace, they settled on the farm that would feed five generations of their descendants.

Many of the foods that would become iconic to the Midwest migrated along the same route; thus, my family may have contributed a stitch or two to the patchwork quilt of Midwestern foods that we'll examine in this book.

* * *

Across the sun-bleached gravel lot from the weathered barn, which housed their rugged John Deere tractor and Swiss Brown dairy cow, was the heavy oak side door to Albert and Frances Fehribach's modest wood farmhouse. Inside my grandparents' home was an expansive kitchen, the centerpiece of which was a large rectangular Formica dining table, like those that graced millions of homes throughout midcentury America, except that this one sat a family of twelve after Frances clanged the iron skillet to summon them.

From the back porch, a cramped landing led to the narrow, creaky wooden stairs to the cellar and basement, where rough-hewn timber walls were lined with skinny shelves laden with all manner of preserved vegetables, fruits, and meats: syrupy candied beets, green beans suspended in smoky brine flecked with carefully cut squares of ham rind, neatly coiled sausages climbing the sides of quart jars and mortared by the rendered fat in which they were cooked, dusty rose–colored watermelon rind pickles. A small room down there held more of the same: sweet bread-and-butter pickles and mouth-puckering dill pickles, pepper relishes, green tomato relishes, blackberry jelly, strawberry and wild cherry jams . . . all to supply a farming family through the cold months into the spring and summer.

The centerpiece of the unfinished basement was an ancient coal-fired furnace, before which stood a wooden rick laden with gallon jugs of Grandpa's renowned wild cherry and blackberry wine, an annual project. The cherries grew abundantly on towering trees behind the farm.

Back up on the back porch sat the sauerkraut barrel—a repurposed whiskey barrel. It was kept out there to shield the family from the odiferous process of fermenting cabbage. Over the winter, the cold would help preserve its crunch until the barrel was empty in early summer. Then the barrel was used to collect water in case of a dry spell. Several steps past the porch was the chicken coop, and to the immediate right of that, a spartan smokehouse where yet more whiskey barrels held pork curing on salt. Beyond the smokehouse was the tomato field, which supplied the family with its main cash crop, and the wild blackberry patch, which flanked the tomato field and forest. Together with the mushrooms, pawpaws, squirrels, rabbits, and deer that could be hunted in the woods, every square foot of the farm played its role in a self-sustaining rhythm of life.

In 2015, on a holiday trip home, Mom and I had been poring over Grandma

Morelos's papers and recipes. I started recounting a visit to the old Fehribach farm in which I was gobsmacked by all the mysterious jars lining that stairway and cellar, the whiskey barrel on the back porch, and the afternoon spent foraging blackberries with my older cousins, after which Aunt Rita and daughters made blackberry pies and other delights.

But my reminiscences spurred a small argument. Mom insisted there was no way I could know anything about the farm because the farmhouse burned to the ground in December 1970. I had been just two years and eight months old when the blackberries had been in season the preceding July. But the recollections were clear as the sky on a frost-burnished morning, and I realized what a tenacious impression that day made in my young mind. I still have warm feelings about it. That day was profoundly influential in shaping the way I think about food—as something that comes from the land and wilds and is shared among family and community.

Industrialization has seemingly made food production and feeding people less personal and more of a commercial pursuit, yet we can find many examples of distinctively Midwestern foodways that emerged and changed as immigrant communities fed one another over generations. The process continues to this day. A generation from now, a book like this one might have many new recipes, and some included here might be relegated to history. I've sought to identify Midwestern foods that currently define our climes and cultures. But while this book will cover a lot of ground, it can't possibly canvas *all* the unique foods of the Midwest. The region is far too large and diverse, with more than two hundred years of modern history and millennia of Native American civilization.

Still, across more than one hundred recipes, we're going to look at the foods through which people all over the Midwest have found identity, celebrate the people who have brought forth innovation and held onto tradition, and see that our foodways are second to none in the United States, or the world. Many of these recipes will be familiar to most readers, such as Chicago-style pizza, fried chicken (which is every bit as Midwestern as it is Southern), and bratwurst. But we'll also discuss many more that are uniquely Midwestern and ready for a fresh look, from breaded pork tenderloin to Cincinnati chili, kringles, casserole culture, fried biscuits and apple butter, coney dogs, rib tip & hot link combos, catfish fiddlers, and barbecued pig snoots. Even as industrialization has changed how we structure our lives and feed ourselves, behind the foods we love are still real people, and the fertile farm-to-table movement, along with insurgent urban farming, makes a connection to the land easier than it's been in two generations.

* * *

The reputation of the Midwest as a land of meat and potatoes has long engendered a bicoastal attitude of derision. Outsiders roll their eyes as they decry our food as bereft of flavor, a cuisine sprung from cans and freezers. This image has never been accurate. We did bring forth the sacred haven of chophouses specializing in mammoth cuts of meat flanked by comically oversized baked potatoes and velvety tranches of creamed spinach, as might be expected from the province of slaughterhouses and fecund land, but since the early twentieth century we have also been home to some of the most influential cookbook authors, among them Bertha Kramer, a.k.a. "Aunt Babette" (*Aunt Babette's Cook Book*), Irma Rombauer (*The Joy of Cooking*), and the fictional but monumentally important Betty Crocker (*The Betty Crocker Picture Cookbook* and many others), without whom modern American cooking would not be the same.

Starting with the whiskey industry that popped up around the old Buffalo Trace and created a new genre of spirits that spread north and west via the Trace and south via the rivers, Midwestern culture has seeded America perhaps more fertilely than any other region has. Building on the great brewing towns of Cincinnati, Milwaukee, and Saint Louis, the Midwest has long kept America's whistle wet. An unusually conducive location on the upper Mississippi River allowed Washburn-Crosby (now General Mills) and Pillsbury to turn Minneapolis into the first flour-milling capital of the United States, and the Twin Cities brought Betty Crocker to life. Chicago used its position as a railroad hub at the crossroads of grain and livestock production to create a nationwide food industry that, for all the criticisms of it, has become the most productive in human history.

For better or worse, fast food as an enterprise began here with White Castle in Kansas, and McDonald's famously took a California concept and refined it in Des Plaines, Illinois, to build a global enterprise. Wendy's got its start in Ohio, Domino's in Michigan, Papa John's in Indiana, and Pizza Hut in Kansas. I'm not sure we should take too much pride in our status as a springboard for fast-food enterprises, but it signals that some element of Midwestern mores permeates the whole United States. Today, our regional chains, such as Runza and LaRosa's, Portillo's and Culver's, Skyline (or Gold Star) Chili and Graeter's, make a higher priority of quality and definitely bring the local flavor.

In spite of a long tradition of fine steakhouses and world-class hotel restaurants, the Midwest stepped onto the global stage of fine dining only in 1973, with Jean Banchet's Le Francais in Wheeling, Illinois. *Bon Appetit* named Le Francais the best restaurant in America in 1980,[1] and it would be held in high regard for another decade. In 1987, Charlie Trotter opened his namesake restaurant on a quiet stretch of Armitage Avenue in Chicago, bringing European-style degustation to the United States. But Trotter's was anything but a European restaurant; he created a distinctly American cuisine with his daring aspiration never to do the same dish twice, and his menus changed daily. It was perhaps the first American restaurant where you could describe dining as "thrilling," and even the stuffy *New York Times* said Trotter's made Chicago "a must." Trotter's changed American fine dining more than any other restaurant up until that time, except, perhaps, Chez Panisse, but another wildly influential restaurant would open in Chicago in 2005: Alinea brought "modernist cuisine" to Chicago and instantly became one of the city's most celebrated restaurants, commonly regarded as one of the best in the world, and in some cases, as the very best.[2] Its influence continues to percolate from Chicago to the rest of the country. Other chefs across the Midwest are reinventing what is possible with food and drink, as we will see with Minneapolis's Sean Sherman and Ann Kim, Saint Louis's Rob Connoley, and Cincinnati's Justin Dean.

Where and Who Is the Midwest?

> Mr. Letterman grew up here, in what show business people, which now includes our best-known politicians and so-called journalists, often call "flyover country." We are somewhere between television cameras in Washington DC, and New York, and Los Angeles. Please join me in saying to the undersides of their airplanes, "Go to hell."
>
> —**Kurt Vonnegut**[3]

Uniquely among the regions of these United States, the Midwest isn't clearly defined by geography. It's not coastal, it's not mountainous, nor was it part of the Confederacy, which largely defines the geography of the South. Only partially framed by the Ohio River to the south and the Great Lakes to the north, you could say that the Midwest has been considered what's left over once the East and West Coasts, South, and Southwest have been demarcated, and that leaves a lot of territory. During the New Deal, the WPA Federal Writers' Project, following the US Census, defined it as Ohio, Indiana, Michigan, Illinois, Minnesota, Wisconsin, Iowa, Nebraska, Kansas, Missouri, South Dakota, and North Dakota.[4]

In contrast, nearly twoscore years later, for the Time-Life Books *Foods of the World* series, esteemed food writer James Beard would christen our domain "the Eastern Heartland" and shift the geography significantly eastward, including almost all of New York State, much of New Jersey, Pennsylvania, Ohio, Indiana, Illinois, and Michigan. To support this definition, he stated, "A great many of the people who settled the more westerly states in the region came from, or at least paused in, New York, New Jersey and Pennsylvania long enough to absorb and carry westward with them, via the waterways or overland, the strong patterns of cooking and eating that the original Dutch, English and German colonists had established."[5]

This analysis runs counter to the general inclusion of Iowa, Wisconsin, and Minnesota in most maps and popular depictions of the Midwest, and the inclusion of New Jersey and New York is especially bold. Even so, if food is a construct of culture, then a shared heritage of national or geographic origin should logically help to unite a region culturally, so Beard was onto something.

From a race and ethnicity perspective, the Midwest, as defined by the census, is the least diverse region in the country, with 79.5 percent of its residents claiming White race only, versus 71.4 percent in the Northeast, 68.2 percent in the South, and 65.4 percent in the West.[6] The Midwest lags all other regions in the percentage of people claiming either Black or Hispanic heritage.[7] We are a diverse province, however. The Midwest's cities have long been destinations for immigrants from all over the world as well as participants in the Great Migration from the South. Many of these groups have contributed substantially to dishes that are distinctly Midwestern, as we will see. However, with more than three-quarters of Midwesterners claiming White ethnicity and more than 24 percent claiming German ancestry (more than double the proportion in the country as a whole),[8] if we were to start mapping the Midwest by common heritage, as Beard suggests, the large prevalence of people of German descent would be a good starting point.

The mark German immigrants have left in Midwestern cities from Cincinnati and Saint Louis north to Chicago and Milwaukee is widely known, yet unique among American regions. Interestingly, focusing on this most populous group together with two obscure religious sects may help us establish some geographic boundaries. New Jersey and most of New York State have no role here, but Nebraska and the Dakotas (all over 30 percent Germanic) do. Critical to our definition are the Amish and Mennonites, two small Anabaptist religious sects from the German-speaking northwest of Switzerland and Alsace. They are concentrated in areas generally considered to be part of the Midwest—we can begin to see reason for including the upstate regions of New York and Pennsylvania (north and west of Philadelphia).[9] The Amish and Mennonites, as the progenitors of the famed "Pennsylvania Dutch" cooking, have been deeply influential in Midwesterners' perception of what constitutes true home cooking and are thus an important part of Midwestern identity, at least for the White majority. Interestingly, and perhaps tragically, what the

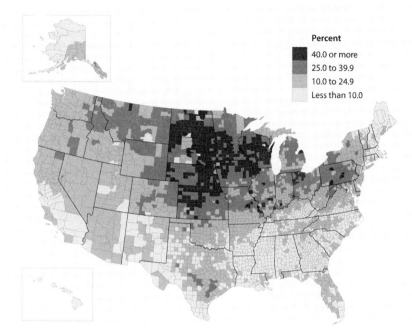

Percentage of the population with German ancestry across the United States, by county.

Source: United States Census Bureau.

general public understands as traditional Amish cooking is a tourist-trap cuisine and almost entirely fictitious.[10] In many cases German-derived Midwestern dishes are nostalgically projected back onto the Amish. Yet the influence, even if it is largely imagined, abounds.

Our Midwest, then, stretches from central and western Pennsylvania and the Finger Lakes of New York west to the Great Plains states—it's a truly diverse region in terms of geography and topography, containing some of the most productive agricultural land in the world. Yet the humid and sticky summers of the river towns Cincinnati, Louisville, and Saint Louis remind us of the Southern influence on Midwestern culture, in stark contrast to the Scandinavian- and French-influenced cultures of the Great Lakes, where the summers are sublime and the winters harsh.

As important as Germanic ancestry is to defining the Midwest, it's only a small part of the picture. Today, nearly as much of the population is non-White (23 percent) as Germanic (26 percent). And that leaves 51 percent of the Midwest's population as non-Germanic White—most significantly Irish, Polish, and British. All other groups come in under 5 percent, but we'll see that Italian, Asian, and Scandinavian Americans have brought significant cultural contributions to Midwestern foodways. Further, Jewish Americans—and in the

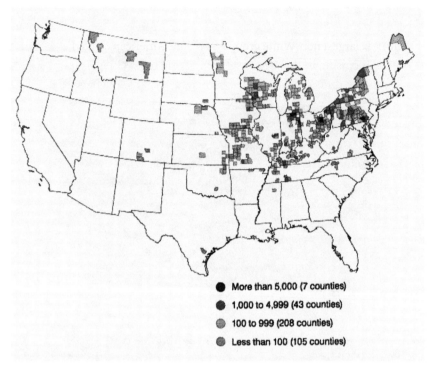

● More than 5,000 (7 counties)
● 1,000 to 4,999 (43 counties)
● 100 to 999 (208 counties)
● Less than 100 (105 counties)

Numbers of Amish across the United States, by county. *Source*: IBRC, using 2010 Religious Congregations and Membership Study data. Reprinted with permission from Indiana Business Research Center.

Midwest we are talking almost exclusively about Ashkenazi Jews—have been key to some of the most significant developments in Midwestern cuisine, despite being just 2 percent of the population.[11]

But let's turn back to that 23 percent of Midwestern residents who identify as non-White. They have made monumentally important contributions to Midwestern foodways, particularly in recent decades. To begin with, the Great Migration, which was one of the largest mass movements of people in history,[12] brought millions of Black Southerners to Northern cities. Blacks in cities such as Minneapolis, Indianapolis, Cleveland, Chicago, and Detroit came primarily from the middle-South states of Mississippi, Alabama, Tennessee, and Kentucky.[13] This is worth noting because Black Southern foodways are regional as well, so Black foodways in the Midwest will be different from those in, say, Philadelphia and New York, where the Black migrants tended to come from the Southeast. The connection between Chicago and Mississippi is especially strong, influencing everything from the Windy City's blues, jazz, and rock and roll scenes to some of our subject matter in this book—barbecue. It is also likely that Mississippians helped entrench Midwesterners' love for dishes such as fried chicken, fried fish and shrimp, and macaroni and cheese through the soul food canon.

The next largest non-White group is Hispanic Americans, and the influence of Mexican cuisine in the Midwest, particularly in its cities, is tremendous. Cook County, Illinois, alone is home to approximately 1 million people citing full or partial Mexican origin.[14] Populations of immigrants from Mexico and Guatemala have popped up in small towns throughout the Midwest, and many formerly all-White towns can now claim at least one Mexican restaurant run by people who learned the cuisine firsthand. Immigrants from the eastern Mediterranean, Persia, and eastern and southern Asia have contributed to a vibrant restaurant culture, such that young people today may be likely to taste ramen before they've had chicken and noodles. Many of the immigrant cuisines are now thoroughly enmeshed in Midwestern dining culture, but other than Mexican, most of them haven't been creolized into mainstream cooking. This may take another generation or two.

It would be impossible to write about our contemporary foodways without acknowledging who and what we have destroyed or lost as well as what remains. The Midwest was, for millennia, home to an astonishing heterogeneity of Indigenous cultures, with over five hundred language groups extant.

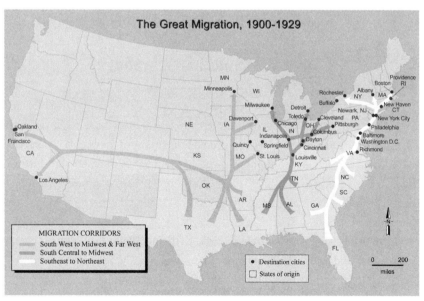

Routes taken during the Great Migration signify regional differences in Black foodways between the Midwest, Northeast, and West.

Source: Arwin D. Smallwood, *The Atlas of African-American History and Politics.* Reprint permission granted by Schomburg Center for Research in Black Culture, New York Public Library. Map by Michael Siegel, Rutgers Cartography, 2005.

Ojibwe, Odawa, Potawatomi, Erie, Ho-Chunk, Kaskaskia, Miami, Cayuga, Oneida, Kickapoo, Peoria, Tamaroa, Wea, Menominee, Meskwaki, Sauk, Sioux, and Wyandott represent only a few of the distinct cultures that were disrupted, subverted, and subjected to a relentless campaign of forced removal and extermination by the colonizers of North America.

It is estimated that over centuries, as they were victimized by a series of genocides and European diseases, 95 percent of the tens of millions of Indigenous inhabitants of the Americas were lost. It is one of history's most atrocious holocausts.[15] One of the Midwest's cultural and economic icons, corn, was co-opted from Indigenous peoples, along with numerous other ingredients: squashes, chilies, dozens of varieties of beans, potatoes, cranberries, huckleberries, juneberries, and more.

The marginalization of Indigenous cultures further constitutes ethnocide, in which the culture itself is threatened and wiped out. While America has long made room for some immigrant communities, that is not what happened with our First Nations, which have continued to be marginalized. Today, however, we can witness a robust Indigenous movement toward reestablishing their food sovereignty, and a growing number of Indigenous chefs are finally finding a dining public that embraces them with gusto. Should these chefs continue to find success, our food culture will be immeasurably richer.

On the Recipes and Methods

In researching this book, I've navigated over twenty thousand miles of road, visited hundreds of bakeries, restaurants, and cafés, pored over thousands of news articles, and read over two hundred books (many of them old cookbooks) to try to see through the lore of our foodways and get to the facts. I'm forever grateful that "Midwestern nice" is truly a thing because it allowed me to get tips and pointers from proud folks everywhere I went, who were eager to share their town's best.

I have tried to keep my sources as close to the people as I could, using local newspapers and books. Perhaps more unconventionally, I sought community cookbooks, spanning more than one hundred years, from every corner of the Midwest, with abandon. I scoured each for corroborating receipts or recipes (a receipt is an older form of recipe, a loose narrative of instructions without defined standardized measurements and ingredient lists), locations, and dates to ascertain how dishes had shifted or evolved around the region.

The conventional cookbooks I consulted span more than four centuries.

Books such as *Aunt Babette's* or *Betty Crocker* are canon, required reading for anyone trying to understand Midwestern food. Most cookbooks, however, were sought for singular reasons. For instance, I was never satisfied with the explanation for the evolution of American fried chicken because it didn't come close to explaining my own experience with it. As a result of this cognitive dissonance, I chased fried chicken recipes backward in time in every single cookbook I could find in English, German, or Spanish. You may find the results astonishing, as I did. In the case of certain recipes, I paged through many dozens of books solely in search of facts. For this reason the bibliography may at times seem haphazard or confusing, but so goes the pursuit of truth!

In selecting and researching the recipes and the stories behind them, I have done my best to approach our subject with a blank slate, using original sources whenever possible in order to bring fresh insight into many of these stories. I wanted to be sure that what Pennsylvania Dutch foodways scholar William Woys Weaver refers to as "foodlore and fakelore" wasn't allowed to shroud the truth about the foods we call Midwestern. In many cases we will find that long-accepted stories are, in fact, quite wrong. But establishing the truth to the extent that we can is essential to telling these stories and recognizing the people who bring them to life. More pointedly, if we want others to take Midwestern food seriously, then we must take it seriously.

Most of the dishes discussed in this book are important today and as popular as ever, but it also presents many archetypal foods that have waned in popularity but are worthy of a fresh look. A few are novel creations incorporating unique Midwestern ingredients, or combinations thereof, that are often overlooked, although I have been careful to keep my own culinary inclinations out of the recipes as much as possible and let Midwestern mores speak for themselves.

I have also had the unenviable charge of selecting which foods or recipes couldn't be included, whether because of space, because their stories are tenuous, or because there isn't really a recipe to speak of. A particularly salient example is corn on the cob. The "recipe" consists solely of ears of (hopefully) just-picked sweet corn, and either boiling or grilling them wouldn't make for much of a recipe. The most important of these omitted foods are mentioned in chapter openings.

In considering what to include, I first put a three-generation (roughly ninety-year) requirement on intact or mostly unchanged dishes from the Old World. While this requirement may seem arbitrary, it affirms the staying power of an immigrant dish. Alternatively, I looked for foods that evolved here in novel ways. As an example, even though tacos have been increasingly popular since the '70s, they don't meet the three-generation threshold, nor could I identify a taco that specifically developed in the Midwest (and has since become popular) or that we could call our own. So, in spite of the perhaps tens of millions of tacos eaten in the Midwest every year, I ceded that topic to the many other excellent books on tacos in America. Tamales, on the other hand, have a history in the Midwest all the way back to the later nineteenth century, and we'll learn what that history is along with their present state. For another example, pizza is a fairly recent phenomenon, and original Italian styles don't meet the three-generation threshold, but we have many styles unique to our climes. Given how popular these styles all are, we'll have a lengthy discussion about why the Midwest is the most exciting pizza region in America.

The recipes in this book have been tested, and I vouch for their deliciousness. It is my hope, first of all, that they will tell the stories held within them but also that they will inspire readers to cook more often at home and perhaps will bring an invigorated sense of place to both the market and the kitchen. Just as importantly, they've been selected to inspire you to take a fresh look at our cities and towns as places where eating can be an epically life-affirming experience and where food culture abounds.

The august importance of Midwestern food in America's national diet cannot be overstated, even though it has been understated to date. Midwesterners, rarely the type to talk about ourselves beyond what's happening in our children's schools, our Big Ten or professional sports teams, or how the corn's looking, have done what we always do, keeping our noses to the grindstone to get the day's work done, building things and feeding people. I'd say there's never a time like the present to reflect on what we have, recognize its value, and talk about it.

1

ON RELISHES, SWEETS, AND SOURS

Pickles and Preserves

Sing of women making grape jelly, watching for the "rolling, tumbling boil that cannot be stirred down" and the juice sheeting from the spoon when the jelly is ready to be taken off the fire, of the filled glasses set in a window where the light can shine through and show the beauty thereof. Sing of paraffin, melted in a small pot, to cover.

—**Rachel Peden, "A Psalm of Grapes"**

WHETHER you are a home cook, chef, or hobbyist, there are few pursuits more worthwhile in terms of reward for effort made than building at least some of your own pantry. In more than a half century eating my way through life, I have yet to taste one store-bought pickle or preserve that is of the quality you can make at home. And let's face it, if you really want to have exciting food on your table, the best thing to do is have an arsenal of sweet, sour, and salty things nearby. The American reflex of reaching for ketchup or ranch dressing is just that: an impulse to push certain buttons on the palate to give food either more balance or more excitement, to our taste. But there is so much more to it, and when you have a pantry full of ways to give that food oomph, the ketchup and ranch start to lose a lot of their appeal.

Barely a decade ago, one might have seen the ancient arts of pickling and preserving as all but dead in the Midwest, and, indeed, the entire country. Fortunately, the decades-long deterioration of these homesteading arts has reversed itself, and it's become easier to find artisanal pickles and preserves at farmers' markets and specialty stores. Many restaurants make at least one of their own pickles, and house hot sauces and preserves are increasingly common. Yet much of our former abundance remains obscured behind a wall of pickled cucumbers, ketchup, and salsa. Salsa is definitely a welcome addition to our store shelves and home-cooking repertoire as so many other options have vanished, but it, too, seems to inhabit a narrow range of possibilities.

By comparing the Midwestern pantry as represented on grocery and even specialty store shelves with what we can find in our old cookbooks, we get a depressing picture of culinary richness lost. Witness today's narrow range of fruit preserves and even narrower range of pickles—there are only endless brands and variations of cucumber pickles, some cucumber-based relish, and perhaps beets, giardiniera, and jalapeños. Preserved fruits appear almost exclusively as bland and nutritionally stripped objects in water or syrup. Jams and jellies come from a narrow range of fruits and are cooked to a mercilessly consistent industrial standard, devoid of character. Such formerly popular (and exquisite) fruits as quince and damson typically aren't represented at all, while preserved fruits such as nectarines and the rinds of melon aren't deemed worthy of sale. So we must make these condiments, request them from retailers, and visit farmers' markets and encourage farmers to grow their ingredients and make them. Many farmers' markets now host at least one artisan specializing in pickle and preserve obscura made with locally grown produce, and they are worthy of our support.

When we scour early Midwestern culinary literature for pickles, relishes, and sweetmeats, it's striking how much of the pickle's story is shared between the South and Midwest, and how different their sauces and fruit preserves are. This makes sense, since fruits differ significantly with climate, and many of our pickles (such as piccalilli and chow-chow) arrived from England via India and spread throughout America quickly via influential publications like Philadelphia's *Godey's Lady's Book*. The most widely circulated magazine on the cusp of the Civil War,[1] *Godey's* included several receipts for chow-chow and one for piccalilli in its 1870 publication *The Godey's Lady's Book Receipts and Household Hints*.[2] While chow-chow appears to be more widespread nationally, piccalilli appears more frequently in Midwestern cookbooks than Southern ones, but both are ubiquitous.

Hannah Glasse's *Art of Cookery* and Maria Rundell's *New System of Domestic Cookery*, the two most popular books during the late Colonial and Federal periods,[3] helped establish a standard range of pickles from cucumbers to green beans to peaches and beyond, which would remain popular in a diverse American pickle repertoire well into the twentieth century and in some cases even today. Their receipts for preserves and conserves remain relevant, even if ingredients such as roses, damsons, and barberries are seldom encountered. Even Irma Rombauer's *Joy of Cooking* includes some forty recipes for preserves and more than two dozen for pickles—some of them calling for damsons, quinces, and currants—as well as recipes for piccalilli, chow-chow, and the once ubiquitous chili sauce, which was used mostly for cold meat.[4] Written in Saint Louis and published in Indianapolis from its first edition in 1931 through 1973,[5] *The Joy of Cooking* sold more than 18 million copies, making it the most popular cookbook in American history.

From a more macro perspective, it is from the Midwest that such powerhouse purveyors of condiments and preserves as H. J. Heinz, Smucker's, and the formerly formidable T. A. Snider's hail. The exploits of H. J. Heinz are well established, but the *Cincinnati Enquirer* once claimed of Snider's, "The company is the largest manufacturer of catsup in the world, and it is to be found on the tables of every first-class restaurant in Europe and America." Most of the company's formulas were adapted from the sauces and preserves one Mrs. Snider served at her boardinghouse.[6] The projection of such a humble host onto a colossal industrial concern surely wasn't an entirely new concept in advertising and PR, but when the food industry was transforming in the late nineteenth century, this was surely one of the first attempts to bring down-home cred to industrial food products.

The coexistence of industry with mom-and-pop businesses and home cooks is a reality of modern foodways pioneered in the Midwest. We are unique among American regions because we have both a strong farmhouse tradition and a strong industrial base. In fact, they largely evolved alongside each other and have long vied for the Midwestern heart and stomach.

Like those throughout the book, this chapter's recipes—some lost to time, some as popular as ever—are based on a census of Midwestern culinary literature over almost two hundred years. Southern recipes for chow-chow and piccalilli appear in my first book, *The Big Jones Cookbook*, but I am providing different, Midwestern recipes for them here. These recipes will demonstrate some explicit contrasts between the regions and illustrate some uniquely Midwestern tastes.

Cherry Barbecue Relish

One of the unfortunate casualties of the past hundred years is barbecue relish, which was a cold condiment to be served with grilled or smoked meats. It was enormously popular midcentury and could be extraordinarily creative—I've seen receipts calling for mangoes, cherries, and guavas—or hopelessly mundane, little more than green pickled cucumber relish gussied up with onions and some extra sugar and vinegar. Perhaps it was those more mundane expressions that led to its demise. A creative and competently made barbecue relish adds another dimension of texture, as well as a host of flavor possibilities, as a topping for hot dogs or sausages, with ribs or pork shoulder, or with more adventurous grilled fare such as smoked duck or lamb.

Makes about 1 quart

1 pound fresh bing cherries
3 tablespoons red wine vinegar

½ teaspoon kosher salt

½ teaspoon crushed red pepper

2 tablespoons extra-virgin olive oil

1 tablespoon spicy brown mustard, such as Koop's

¼ teaspoon ground cloves

¼ cup green onion, very thinly sliced

¼ cup celery, very finely diced

½ cup **CHOW-CHOW** (p. 21), drained and finely chopped

Pit the cherries and set aside. In a separate bowl, whisk together the vinegar, salt, red pepper, olive oil, mustard, and cloves, until combined well. Add the cherries, green onion, celery, and chow-chow, and toss. Serve well chilled with any kind of grilled meat, but cherries have a special affinity for game birds or pork. Store in an airtight container and refrigerate for up to 10 days.

Chili Sauce

Chili sauce has been a mystery, an unsolvable conundrum in my mind for decades. Heinz chili sauce used to be fairly common on grocery-store shelves and still endures, but to be honest, to me it always tasted like a mutant ketchup. I do, however, have to admit my young palate was not particularly well adapted to the subtly spiced nuance of a good chili sauce versus the pure sweet and sour tomato essence of ketchup. It could also be, frankly, that the chili sauce from the grocery store just wasn't very good. Or it could be that when I tasted it, I could only wonder, "Where are the chilies?" The moniker tempts with heat it never delivers.

I recall seeing chili sauce used only in the occasional cocktail sauce recipe, instead of, or in addition to, ketchup. So I always wondered, *What is it for?* Recipes for it are common in Midwestern newspapers beginning in the 1860s, and chili sauce appears in numerous cookbooks from the 1870s to well into the twentieth century. For the last two decades of the nineteenth century, it's in every cookbook, ubiquitous. All the rage. There's still a recipe for it in *The Joy of Cooking*.

I finally found my answer when searching for the earliest printed recipe (winner: *Evansville Daily Journal*, 1867).[7] I wanted to see not only if and how the recipe changed but, more importantly, *why* people made it. Perhaps I should have been clued in by its typical presence right above or below ketchup in cookbooks, but I eventually came across a housekeeping column in the *Boston Globe*

PIGGLY WIGGLY

PRICES GO DOWN

FLOUR		COOKING OILS	
5 Lbs. Gold Medal	25c	Pint Mazola	25c
12¼ Lbs. Gold Medal	52c	Quart Mazola	45c
24½ Lbs Gold Medal	$1.03	Half Gallon Mazola	89c
5 Lbs. Pillsbury	30c	Pint Wesson Oil	25c
12¼ Lbs. Pillsbury	59c	Quart Wesson Oil	48c
24½ Lbs. Pillsbury	$1.17	Pound Snowdrift	17c

CLEANSERS		PRUNES	
Spotless, per can	5c	90-100 size, per lb.	11c
Sunbrite, per can	5½c	70-80 size, per lb.	14c
Old Dutch, per can	10c	40-50 size, per lb.	18c
Saniflush, per can	22c	20-30 size, per lb.	31c
Magic, per can	4c		

CATSUP		CHILI SAUCE	
Arcadia, 8-oz.	16c	Arcadia, 8-oz.	18c
Arcadia, 16-oz.	26c	Arcadia, 16-oz.	29c
Snider's, 8-oz.	17c	Snider's, 8-oz.	21c
Snider's, 16-oz.	27c	Snider's, 16-oz.	32c

Sunmaid Seeded Raisins 20c
Dromedary Dates 23c
Brookfield Butter 48c
Meadowgold Butter 49c
Brookfield Eggs 51c
Granulated Sugar, 25-lb. bag. $1.64
Best Head Rice. 7c

WE WISH TO THANK YOU FOR YOUR SPLENDID PATRONAGE FOR THE MONTH OF OCTOBER. IT WAS THE BEST BUSINESS WE HAVE EVER HAD IN CINCINNATI.

PIGGLY WIGGLY

Chili sauce was once a major staple, often advertised right next to ketchup and other important commodities.

Source: *Cincinnati Enquirer*, November 12, 1921, page 12.

in which the author avers that chili sauce "is lovely with beans or meat and is an old-fashioned recipe."[8] During the first decade of the twentieth century, many competing brands stated in their advertisements that chili sauce is for meats. So, folks used chili sauce like we use ketchup or barbecue sauce. I decided to adapt and make the recipe from the *Evansville Courier*, bringing up the heat somewhat for modern tastes, and it is delightful. The sweet spices give it more complexity than ketchup and an aroma eerily similar to that of Cincinnati chili. You can now revel in a condiment that will excite your adult palate yet is as easy to use as ketchup.

This sauce is delicious with french fries in addition to cold and hot meats of all varieties, including barbecue. It's even delicious swirled into prepared beans or chili. Most early chili sauce recipes don't call for putting the ingredients through a food mill after cooking, yielding a chunky product. I puree it in the blender so it's smooth, but the choice is yours.

Makes 1 pint

> 1 quart ripe Roma tomatoes
>
> 1⅓ cups yellow onion, finely diced
>
> 1 small to medium green bell pepper, finely diced
>
> 6 tablespoons sugar
>
> 1⅓ cups apple cider vinegar
>
> 2 teaspoons kosher salt
>
> ½ teaspoon ground allspice
>
> ½ teaspoon ground Korintje cinnamon
>
> ½ teaspoon ground dry ginger
>
> ¼ teaspoon ground cloves
>
> ½ teaspoon crushed red pepper
>
> ⅛ teaspoon cayenne pepper

Peel the tomatoes by plunging them into rapidly boiling water a few at a time for 20 to 30 seconds, then dropping them into ice water. A few minutes later, the peels will slip off. Cut into ½-inch dice. Place all the ingredients in a medium stainless-steel saucepan and bring to a boil over medium heat, stirring often. Maintaining a low boil and stirring frequently, cook until most, but not all, of the liquid has evaporated or been absorbed back into the fruit, leaving what looks like a chunky salsa, which sloshes back and forth when you shake the pan but isn't watery. This will take about 1 hour. Remove from heat and cool to room temperature, covered, for 2 to 3 hours. Bottle as is if you like a chunky chili sauce, or puree in the blender for smooth sauce. Transfer to bottles or jars. Capped airtight, this will keep in the refrigerator for months, or you can seal the bottles or jars by boiling in a hot water bath according to standard canning methods.

Chow-Chow

Whether you call it chow-chow, chaw-chaw, or simply chaw or chow, it's perhaps the most versatile pickle in our repertoire. Yet it might be considered not merely *a* pickle but an entire genre of pickles. Look up ten recipes for chow-chow and you're likely to find ten completely different vegetable musters to be chopped, diced, or shredded, and there will be still more variations in the composition of the brine and seasoning. Early American recipes from Malinda Russell and Annabella Hill use jarring quantities of horseradish and a very stripped-down ingredient list, while many later recipes serve as repositories for all manner of garden produce.

A co-opted pickle of the Colonial era, chow-chow originated in India, and the name was believed to mean a mélange, or "a medley of anything," in Indian and Chinese commerce and cuisine.[9] Loosely defined, then, chow-chow could be just about anything pungent and delightful.

Chow-chow arrived on American shores no later than 1804,[10] according to an advertisement by Charleston importers McKenzie and McNeill. Like other cultural co-optations from that era, chow-chow (and also piccalilli, as we will learn) came here through trade, in this case with the British. Americans eventually started making their own chow-chow; the earliest written recipe I could find for it was in Malinda Russell's self-published gem from Paw Paw, Michigan, in 1866,[11] beating out Annabella Hill's receipt for "chow," published in Georgia in 1867. Russell's case is an interesting one. A formerly enslaved woman who had escaped to the North, she wrote her book with the hope of earning enough money to return home to the South as a free woman. Because it was self-published, we don't have further information about how well the book sold or even how influential it might have been, but within two decades, chow-chow was a staple in Midwestern and national cookbooks, appearing in such successful publications as *Godey's Lady's Book Receipts and Household Hints* (1870), *Aunt Babette's Cook Book* (1889), and *The Settlement Cookbook* (1903), as well as countless regional and community cookbooks well into the twentieth century. Chow-chow makes a great gift during the holidays.

Makes about 6 pints

1 cup young pickling cucumbers, cut into small dice, approximately ⅜ inch

2 cups yellow onion, very finely diced

2 cups fresh string beans, cut into ¼-inch slices

3 cups green tomato, cut into small dice, approximately ⅜ inch

½ head white cabbage, chopped finely into pieces no larger than ⅜ inch

½ cup green bell pepper, finely diced

½ cup red bell pepper, finely diced

2 tablespoons kosher salt, divided

¼ cup fresh horseradish, grated, or 6 tablespoons prepared horseradish

2 teaspoons turmeric powder

1 tablespoon yellow mustard seed

1 teaspoon celery seed

½ teaspoon ground allspice

¼ teaspoon ground cloves

½ teaspoon cayenne pepper

1 cup granulated sugar

2 cups apple cider vinegar

1 cup water

Toss all the prepared vegetables together with 1 tablespoon of the salt. Cover tightly and refrigerate overnight. The next day, use a fine mesh strainer to drain all the accumulated juices off, pressing gently to squeeze out extra juice. Transfer to a stainless-steel stockpot or a slow cooker. Cover with the remaining ingredients, including the remaining tablespoon of salt. Stir to combine well. Bring to a boil slowly over medium heat, stirring regularly. Once at the boil, reduce heat to a low boil, cover, and cook for 30 minutes. Transfer to sanitized canning jars or other airtight containers while hot. Refrigerate or seal in a water bath to store in the pantry. Chow-chow, which improves with age, is best consumed after 1 month.

Piccalilli

I'm silly for piccalilli. It's easily the condiment in my pantry for which I reach most. The combination of sweet, sour, and pungent hits everything square on the nose and can even rescue a bad plate of food. On a good plate of food, it can induce delirium.

Piccalilli is another recipe we can date back to the East India trade, and it's perhaps more interesting than chow-chow because the recipe has evolved from the same kind of kitchen-sink relish as chow-chow to narrower versions strictly composed of green tomatoes, together with supporting ingredients. Funny thing is, when piccalilli's earliest versions were showing up in English culinary literature, Brits and their colonists were still shy of tomatoes, believing them to be unfit for consumption.[12] Therefore, the earliest version we have, "To Pickle Lila, An India Pickle" from Lady Anne Blencowe, contains no tomatoes at all. Instead, a dizzying array of vegetables and fruits, including cabbage, plums, radishes, french beans, asparagus, long pepper, and celery, along with a heady blend of spices, go through a multiday tour de force of brining, lye curing, and salting. Each vegetable and fruit is processed separately.[13] A century later, Richard Briggs adds melons and apples to the party, but still no tomatoes, in his receipt for India pickle, or "picca lillo."[14] Lettice Bryan includes tomatoes in her receipt for India pickle, also adding radish seed pods, nasturtium pods, peaches, apricots, nectarines, and barberries.[15] I have yet to experience these ingredients in season together, but I always become giddy at the prospect whenever I read that receipt. A clue in these early receipts is that each ingredient is cured or preserved separately, and they are added in sequence until, at the end of the growing season, the pickle is ready. It's a phenomenal way to make something improbably sophisticated while saving an ongoing harvest.

Like chow-chow, piccalilli begins showing up in advertisements long before recipes, such as the one for "piccalillie" in the New York *Evening Post* in 1802, appear.[16] By the time piccalilli shows up in *Aunt Babette's Cook Book*, it manifests as the familiar tomato-cabbage relish with peppers and onions.[17] Although not quite as ubiquitous as chow-chow in Midwestern culinary literature, it is common, and in my mind, it's one of the very best of our pickles when properly made. At Big Jones, we serve the *Big Jones Cookbook* recipe on dozens of dishes. Its fruity-sweet-sour-bitter fugue is beguiling. This recipe goes a little deeper into the woods, with a little more fire and a different kind of finesse.

Makes about 6 pints

6 cups green tomato, cut into ¼-inch dice

2 cups yellow onion, cut into ¼-inch dice

2 cups red bell pepper, cut into ¼-inch dice

2 cups white cabbage, finely shredded

¼ cup kosher salt

2 cups apple cider vinegar

1 cup water

1 tablespoon celery salt

¼ cup fresh horseradish, grated, or ½ cup prepared horseradish

2 tablespoons fresh ginger, grated

¼ cup coriander seed

¼ cup black mustard seed

6 bay leaves

Place the tomato, cabbage, onion, and bell pepper in a bowl and toss with the kosher salt to combine. Cover tightly and refrigerate overnight. The following day, use a fine mesh strainer to drain off all the accumulated liquid released from the vegetables, pressing gently to squeeze out extra liquid.

Transfer to a 4-quart nonreactive pot with a tight-fitting lid, and add the remaining ingredients. Cover and steam at a high simmer for 1 hour, stirring every 10 minutes.

Remove the lid and bring to a boil for 15 seconds. Remove from heat. Transfer to sanitized canning jars or other airtight containers while hot. Refrigerate or seal in a water bath to store in the pantry.

Chicago-Style Hot Giardiniera

When I arrived in Chicago from southern Indiana, giardiniera was as exotic to my taste as were the fish sauce–sodden salads at Vietnamese and Thai restaurants and the hog maws at dim-sum restaurants. Giardiniera isn't unheard of outside Chicago, but in other parts it's likely to be the Italian version, which consists of larger cuts of vegetables preserved in vinegar and can be served as antipasti with cold meats and cheeses. This was the giardiniera I knew, and I wasn't a fan. I usually encountered it by chance on a salad bar or at an Italian restaurant.

But I was immediately smitten by the Chicago style, with its more finely chopped vegetables bathed in olive oil laced with sport peppers, giving it plenty of *heat*. It's a perfect foil for the famed Italian beef or a topping for pizza, giving just enough heat to cut the rich flavors of beef or cheese while also contributing a texture that is both unctuous and biting. The oil causes flavors to linger longer on the palate while slicking everything in its path. The vegetables aren't overprocessed and retain an enchanting bite, adding much-needed texture to thinly sliced roast beef on Italian bread or to a cheesy pie. It's also great with any sausage, on tacos, in sandwiches of all types, and with cold cheeses, meats, and crackers or bread.

Giardiniera in Italian is a catchall term for preserved garden vegetables. When it arrived in Chicago, almost certainly along with the late nineteenth-century wave of immigrants from Italy, it took the city by storm. According to Jeff Johnson, general manager for V. Formusa, a company founded in Chicago in 1898 that now manufactures the best-selling Marconi brand and has several others under contract, company founder and Sicilian immigrant Vincent Formusa "got into the Sicilian method of preserving vegetables in oil."[18] And there we have the beginning of a true Chicago original, a condiment worthy of the big time.

Makes 3 pints

1 cup carrots, quartered lengthwise and sliced on a 45-degree bias, about 2 to
  3 medium carrots

1 cup celery, stalks split lengthwise and sliced on a 45-degree bias, about 2 to
3 ribs

4 cups cauliflower, broken into small, marble-sized florets, stems cut into ½-inch
dice, about half a large head of cauliflower

½ cup serrano peppers, cut into ½-inch slices on a 45-degree bias, or ¾ cup
jalapeños split lengthwise and cut into ½-inch slices on the same bias

3 fresno peppers, split lengthwise, seeds removed, and cut into ½-inch slices on a
45-degree bias, or substitute jalapeños

¼ cup plus 2 tablespoons kosher salt, divided

1½ cups white wine vinegar

6 cups water, divided

1 dried bay leaf or two fresh

1 cup extra-virgin olive oil

1 cup grapeseed oil or other neutral vegetable oil

Place the vegetables in a 4-quart glass container with a tight-fitting lid. Cover with 5 cups cold water; add ¼ cup of the salt. Cover and refrigerate overnight. The following day, drain the vegetables well and rinse under cold running water. Leave in a colander to drain while you prepare the brine. Heat the vinegar, the remaining cup water, bay leaf, and remaining 2 tablespoons salt to a high simmer. The liquid should be shimmering with small bubbles around the edges. Add the vegetables and simmer, taking care not to boil the mixture, which can make the vegetables mushy. Simmer for 8 to 10 minutes, testing beginning at the 6-minute mark; you want to stop cooking when the cauliflower still has a crunch to it but has softened noticeably. Remove the bay leaf, drain the vegetables well, then transfer them to a wooden bowl. Cover them with the oils while still hot, tossing with a wooden spoon. Transfer to jars with airtight lids, being sure to distribute oil evenly between jars to submerge all the vegetables. If the vegetables aren't completely covered, top off with more olive oil. Refrigerate for up to 1 month. If you wish to seal the jars to store in your pantry, you must use the pressure canning method.

Sauerkraut

I was admittedly a bad Chicagoan at first, because I wasn't interested in the local pizza (but I have long since become a convert) or hot dogs (ditto). I ate my hot dogs as I had always preferred them, with sauerkraut and mustard. To me, that was the most effective way to counter the intense richness of the sausage. While I've since become a Chicago-style dog convert (who else gets to eat something as decadent as a hot dog and also check off the salad box for the day?), there is still no accompaniment to sausages that can rival sauerkraut.

The association of Germans with sauerkraut is well established, as evidenced by the derogatory epithet "krauts," and it is believed that the modern process for thus preserving cabbage did originate in Germany in the seventeenth century.[19] But fermented cabbage is an important food for most Northern and Eastern European cultures, from Alsace to Russia and from Hungary to Scandinavia. As these climes may suggest, the needed ingredient for a sauerkraut-laden cuisine is a cold winter, in which growing vegetables isn't an option and cellars can be kept cold, helping to preserve fermented vegetables through the winter. It's a common misconception that *Sauerkraut* translates to *sour cabbage*—in fact, *Kraut* could mean any leafy vegetable, though it did most often refer to cabbage.[20]

Sauerkraut is easy to make, probiotic, and nutritious. Centuries of Central European foodways relied on sauerkraut to prevent scurvy, especially during those long winters, as sauerkraut is rich in vitamin C.[21] I love making it at home as a way to connect with my ancestors, particularly the hausfrau grandma I never knew. When I have a craving and I don't have any of my own on hand, I buy it at the store in the refrigerator section (the shelf-stable canned versions aren't as tasty) and cook it with onions and hard cider. My favorite vegetable dish to this day. And it's a must with the **BEER BRATS** (p. 95) that my dad taught me to make, which might well be the best sausage you ever put in your mouth. In chapter 5, on side dishes, I'll share my favorite way of preparing sauerkraut. For now, here's a fail-safe DIY kraut you can easily make with your homegrown or farmers' market cabbage.

Makes about 3 quarts

5 quarts finely shredded white cabbage (freshly picked is best, store-bought works but may ferment more slowly), two medium heads

2 tablespoons kosher salt

Toss the cabbage and salt in a mixing bowl, then rub the cabbage between your hands for just a few moments to bruise. Pack into a sanitized 1-gallon glass jar with a tight-fitting lid. Add an inch at a time, tamping down firmly with each inch added. All 5 quarts of cabbage should fit, once packed, with about an inch to spare at the top of the jar. Cut out a circle of parchment or waxed paper to fit over the top of the cabbage inside the jar, to prevent too much air from getting into the cabbage. Place the lid but turn it only halfway, to allow gases to escape. Place the jar somewhere with a steady temperature of 60°F to 70°F, away from any high-traffic areas, as it will release sulfur gases, which do not have a pleasant smell.

Check on the jar every couple of days, but it should work on its own. Fermentation will take about 4 weeks; when you no longer see gas bubbles in the rising brine for a few days, it is ready. Remove the waxed paper from the top of the cabbage, place the lid on tight, and refrigerate for up to 2 months.

Watermelon Pickles

Pickled watermelon rind was one of my dad's favorites, and it's an enduring underdog of a pickle, never the most popular, but present throughout our cookbook canon. While it's missing from a lot of important cookbooks such as *Aunt Babette's Cook Book* and *The Settlement Cook Book*, and is spotty in community cookbooks, we find it in a wide range of books over the years, from ambitious pro cookbooks such as *The American Cook Book*[22] to *The Joy of Cooking*,[23] early community cookbooks such as a Presbyterian church cookbook from LaPorte, Indiana,[24] and farm industry publications such as *The Indiana Farmer's Guide New Cook Book*.[25]

Proper watermelon pickles retain a nice crunch, so the cooking should be minimal. In fact, pouring a boiling brine over the pared rind is usually enough to do the trick. They can be sweet or spicy, mild or fiery hot. As with their cucurbit cousin, the cucumber, the only real limit is the pickler's imagination.

Here, I'm sharing a sweet and warmly spiced watermelon pickle that is popular at my restaurant during the fall, after we pickle them in the summer. These pickles are great for snacking on their own or as a relish with poultry, game birds, seafood, or cheese.

Makes 3 quarts

3 quarts watermelon rind, green skin peeled away, cut into ½-by-2-inch strips

2 quarts plus 1 cup water, divided

1 quart white wine vinegar

1 cup granulated sugar

3 tablespoons plus 2 teaspoons salt, divided

1 Korintje or Mexican cinnamon stick

12 whole cloves

12 whole allspice berries

3 bay leaves

One 2-inch strip of orange rind, cut with a vegetable peeler

1 tablespoon thinly sliced fresh ginger

Place the pared watermelon rind in a 1-gallon container with 2 quarts of water and 3 tablespoons of salt. Cover tightly and refrigerate overnight. The following day, prepare a brine by combining the vinegar, remaining cup water, sugar, remaining 2 teaspoons of salt, and spices in a saucepan and bringing to a boil. Maintain a low boil for 10 minutes to infuse. Drain the watermelon rind and rinse it under cold running water, then divide evenly between sanitized canning jars, packing the rind in as tightly as possible, all the way up to the rim. During curing, the watermelon will shrink somewhat and fall back into the brine. You can strain the brine after infusing or leave the whole spices to go into the jars as well. Off the boil, carefully divide the brine between the jars of watermelon, filling to just below an inch from the top—the uppermost watermelon will not be submerged. Cap tightly with new canning lids while still hot. Pickles will be ready to eat in 1 week; they can be refrigerated for months or canned in a standard water bath to store in the pantry.

Cranberry Pear Preserves

Commonly associated with the East Coast because of Pilgrim and Thanksgiving legends and the dominant cranberry concern, Massachusetts-based Ocean Spray, cranberries are native to North America and grow throughout the Great Lakes region.[26] The Indigenous Anishinaabe people of the Great Lakes region used them to make jams with maple sugar, dried them and cooked them together with dried sweet corn and maple sugar, and used both the berries and the leaves in medicine.[27] Cranberries are as Midwestern as corn, black walnuts, and Big Ten football, perhaps even more so.

Cranberries appear in their dried form in salads and pastries in contemporary cooking, but other than that are reserved almost strictly for the Thanksgiving and holiday table. High in pectin, they make great preserves, conserves, and jellies. Since they pack a real bitter punch compared with other fruits, they are often cut and paired with milder fruits, commonly apples, but they are especially complementary to the more fragrant pears.

These cranberry pear preserves are adapted from community cookbooks. You'll find that they're much more interesting than grocery-store preserves. While they're perfect in any situation in which you'd use a jam or jelly, they make an excellent sweetmeat with barbecue or any pork dish, game birds, or cold meat and cheeses.

Makes about 6 pints

1 quart very ripe Bartlett pears, peeled, cored, and coarsely chopped

1 quart cranberries, fresh or frozen

2 blood oranges, chopped into ½-inch or smaller pieces, with rind on

1 tablespoon fresh ginger, grated

½ teaspoon salt

2 quarts granulated sugar

Place all ingredients except the sugar in a 4-quart or larger nonreactive pot and slowly render the juices from the fruit, starting on low heat, stirring frequently, and gradually increasing the heat to medium when you have enough liquid that you can worry less about scorching. Once the fruit is swimming in its own juices, add the sugar, stir to dissolve, and maintain medium heat, stirring often, to bring to a boil. Boil until the preserves reach 220°F on an instant-read digital thermometer. Transfer to sterilized glass jars while hot and cap tightly with new lids. After resting to cool to room temperature, the preserves can be refrigerated for months or sealed in a standard water bath to store in the pantry for a year or more.

Quince Honey

Some years ago, I was intrigued when I came across a receipt for quince honey in a 1950s Appalachian cookbook. We preserve quinces at my restaurant every fall, which is my favorite canning project of the year because the aroma is so heavenly. We always have a fair amount of liquor left after the fruits are served, and we usually use it in cocktails. But this time I reduced some of it by about a third, and voilà! It looked like honey and actually tasted like honey of quince. It's hard to explain, but if you like honey, you have to try it because this is delicious stuff.

I was delighted to find a recipe for quince honey in *The Indiana Farmers Guide New Cook Book*, and quince recipes abound in virtually every community cookbook from the Midwest from the late nineteenth century well into the mid-twentieth century. Quince is a tragically overlooked fruit. It's related to apples and pears, but when cooked right, it's more fragrant than anything you can make with them. This honey is a perfect example. It's delicious on toast or bagels, over ice cream, to garnish many desserts, and as a glaze for pork and poultry dishes, and it's an absolute knockout when used to sweeten tea.

The Indiana Farmers Guide New Cook Book's recipe is pretty plain—quinces, sugar, water. I like to use some additional aromatics to make the quince truly sing.

Makes about 4 pints

- 2 pounds quinces, washed, peeled, cored, and cut into ½-inch or smaller dice
- 2 pounds granulated sugar
- 1 quart water
- Juice and zest (stripped with a vegetable peeler in one piece) of 1 lemon
- One 1-by-2-inch strip orange zest, stripped with a vegetable peeler
- 1 Mexican or Korintje cinnamon stick
- 1 vanilla bean, split lengthwise
- 6 whole cloves
- 6 whole allspice berries
- ½ teaspoon kosher salt

Place all the ingredients in a 4-quart or larger nonreactive pot, stir to dissolve the sugar, and bring to a boil over medium heat. Reduce heat to a high simmer, cover, and cook until the quince has changed color and reddened to a deep rusty hue, 60 to 90 minutes. Strain through cheesecloth or a fine mesh strainer. Cool about a teaspoon in a small bowl or teacup in the refrigerator to test thickness. Once cooled, it should be about the same consistency as honey, but if it's too thin, return to medium heat and reduce by boiling off some water. Check consistency every 10 minutes by again cooling a small amount. Transfer to sanitized canning jars or bottles while hot and cap tightly with new lids. Can be refrigerated for months or sealed in a standard water bath to store in the pantry.

Apple Butter

If there was one way to capture the aroma of the Midwestern harvest moon in a jar, no doubt it would be apple butter. It's perfumed with sweet spices and laden with mollifying Maillard reactions that contribute a deep, withered, raisin-like flavor that is the consummate metaphor for the season of hibernation that approaches with the apple harvest.

Apple butter is often associated with the Pennsylvania Dutch. Early nineteenth-century periodical descriptions certainly reinforce that perception, and in fact make it seem like we modern Midwesterners are missing out on something. My favorite story of apple butter, printed in New Hampshire's

Farmers Cabinet in 1839, states that "to make this article according to German law, the host should in the autumn invite his neighbors, particularly the young men and maidens, to make up an apple butter party."[28] Not that one ever needs an excuse to throw a party, but whipping up a big ol' batch of apple butter sounds as good as any, when conjuring up the myth of Dionysus and Aphrodite could be in the cards amid frosty weather, shimmering fires, and intoxicating aromas. Apple butter parties were actually a thing during the nineteenth century, as it could take 12 hours or more to cook down the barrels of cider and bushels of apples to the desired consistency.[29] Many people would be needed to take their turns stirring the pot and staving off scorching.

One detail that's often missed in apple butter recipes that I regard as key is that the apples should be unpeeled so that the peels' pectin can contribute to the semisolid, buttery texture. Like softened butter, apple butter should hold its shape when cut or dipped yet yield and spread easily. There really is no expression of fruit more luscious. When it's properly made, the water activity level (a key food safety metric that indicates how much free water is available to spoiling microbes) of apple butter is so low that it can be stored virtually indefinitely.

I like to add some additional citric and malic acids to my apple butter to brighten it up, but they are of course not required. If you can find an heirloom apple called Winesap, definitely go for it, but any old-time apple will do. Apple butter is spectacular when used to make crepe cakes, as a donut filling, between pancakes, and on cornbread with barbecue, to name just a few examples. Of course it's a must with **BROWN COUNTY FRIED BISCUITS** (p. 61). This recipe is easiest to make in a slow cooker—you can skip the oven step below and continue to thicken the butter on the countertop in the slow cooker on low for 8 to 10 hours.

Makes about 4 pints

    1 quart sweet apple cider
    5 pounds apples, washed, cored, and coarsely chopped
    Zest of 1 orange, finely grated
    1 pound light brown sugar
    ½ teaspoon citric acid
    ¼ teaspoon malic acid
    1 teaspoon kosher salt
    1 teaspoon ground coriander
    1 teaspoon ground Korintje or Mexican cinnamon

1 teaspoon ground allspice
½ teaspoon ground cloves

Pour the apple cider into a 4-quart or larger nonreactive pot, bring to a boil, and reduce by half. Add the apples, orange zest, sugar, acids, spices, and salt, and stir to coat the apples. Reduce heat to medium low and render the apples, stirring occasionally with a wooden spoon so they cook evenly. When they are thoroughly softened and mushy, in about 1 hour, remove from heat and puree in the blender or food processor.

Preheat oven to 275°F.

Transfer the puree to an enamel or glass roasting pan and place on center rack of the oven, uncovered. Use a rubber spatula to stir the butter and scrape down the sides of the pan as it cooks and reduces, every 20 to 30 minutes. Cook for 4 to 6 hours, until you can stand a small spoon in the butter.

Transfer to sanitized canning jars or bottles while hot and cap tightly with new lids. Apple butter can be refrigerated indefinitely or canned in a standard water bath to store in the pantry.

Cranberry Sweet Corn Relish

Fascinated by descriptions of the Menominee practice of preserving both wild berries and sweet corn for winter by drying, then cooking both together with maple sugar to sweeten the pot, I thought it worth pondering this combination in a new way for our pantry. Whether you've had them together before or not, sweet corn and berries of all types are a dream team, and farm-to-table chefs have been pairing them in both sweet and savory dishes for years. Wherever these modern chefs got their inspiration, we should all recognize that Algonquian peoples were way ahead of us on this one.

This relish is a perfect addition to salads and is great with poultry and fish, especially salmon or grilled trout. It's best made early in the season with the greenest flavor of sweet corn. Dried cranberries from the previous season and the first sweet corn will give you the most explosive flavors in an exciting combination.

Makes about 5 pints

4 cups sweet corn kernels, cut from the cob (about 12 ears)
2 cups yellow Spanish onion, minced

1 cup red bell pepper, seeded and minced

1 cup poblano pepper, seeded and minced

2 cups apple cider vinegar

1 cup water

1 cup maple sugar

2 tablespoons kosher salt

2 cups dried cranberries

Place all ingredients except the cranberries in a large saucepan and place over medium-low heat. Stir every few minutes while gradually increasing the heat as the sugar dissolves. Cook at a low boil for 10 minutes, stir in the dried cranberries, and return to a boil for 1 minute. Transfer to sanitized canning jars while still hot, top with additional vinegar if needed to submerge all the vegetables, and cap with new lids. Can be refrigerated for up to 2 months or canned in a standard water bath to store in the pantry.

Quick Blackberry Jam

I've always loved quick "salvage" recipes like this one, in which you take the by-product of another project (in this case, the blackberry cordial in the next chapter) and turn it into something delicious on its own, essentially turning your kitchen into a zero-waste operation, if only for a couple of recipes. Extractions of fruit for jellies and liqueurs will often leave behind pulp that is both high in pectin and still packed with fruit flavor. So make jam!

To my mind, blackberries have long been the most Midwestern of fruits. They grow wild throughout our region and permeate our culinary literature. Sure, we have apples, but they're also big in New England and the Tidewater. Peaches are also big down South; ditto cranberries out East. Blackberries are mostly ours, and what a treasure they are. I always add a twist of black pepper to brambleberry recipes because I think it helps bring out the bramble flavor and balance the raw fruitiness. If pepper in your jam creeps you out, feel free to omit it.

Makes a little less than 2 pints

Leftover blackberry pulp from **THREE DOYENNES BLACKBERRY CORDIAL** (p. 51), about 2 cups

Granulated sugar, in a volume equal to that of the pulp

Juice of ½ lemon

⅛ teaspoon kosher salt
1 twist freshly ground black pepper

Place all ingredients in a saucepan and gradually bring to a boil while stirring regularly to dissolve the sugar. Stir from the bottom regularly while boiling until the mixture reaches 225°F on a candy thermometer. Transfer to sanitized canning jars and seal at once. Can be refrigerated for months or sealed by the standard water bath method to keep in your pantry for a year or more.

Rhubarb Marmalade

No Midwestern cookbook would be complete without rhubarb, one of the first fresh items we can harvest in the spring of each year. Rhubarb has one of the most interesting stories to tell, too, involving a sprawling early global trade network, industrial espionage, and mistaken identity.

Known since ancient times, rhubarb was used as a medicine until the early modern era. The drug rhubarb came from the root of a unique variety and was primarily produced in the northern provinces of China. It was so prized for its purgative effects that it was listed next to "musk, rubies, diamonds, and pearls" as among the most valuable cargo traveling the Silk Road.[30] By the mid-nineteenth century, it was such a vital product of trade that Chinese official Lin Zexu hatched a scheme in which he would blackmail Queen Victoria by threatening a ban on rhubarb exports, his aim being to "bring a constipated nation to its knees and thus to end British sales of opium in China."[31]

Needless to say, such a valuable commodity created a centuries-long race to discover alternatives or figure out how to grow rhubarb elsewhere. A Siberian variety of wild rhubarb that didn't give the medicinal kick required eventually became what the British called the pie plant, and a recipe for a tart was mailed from England to America in 1739, specifying "Siberian stalks."[32]

By the early eighteenth century, *New England Farmer* was pimping rhubarb by lamenting its neglect, claiming that "many tons of stems are annually sold in the city of London" and that "pies and tarts properly made of this vegetable, are inferior to none"[33]—a claim with which I personally, as a huge rhubarb fan, would not disagree. Finally, by 1897, a German-American cookbook published in the Midwest was calling the most popular use of the plant "*englische Pastete von Rhabarber*," or "English rhubarb pie."[34]

I always make room for rhubarb pies and tarts during the spring—it's such a refreshing jolt after a winter of citrus and storage fruits. This marmalade is a great way to put it to further use and a great way incorporate some citrus fruits before laying them off for summer. The orange peel contains abundant pectin and gives the marmalade structure, and the fruit mellows out the rhubarb's more bitter expressions ever so nicely. I like the additional color blood oranges yield, and their best season is usually wrapping up just as rhubarb pops, but you can of course substitute navel or juicing oranges.

Makes about 6 pints

> 2 pounds blood oranges
> 3 pounds rhubarb, thin membrane peeled away, sliced into ½-inch segments
> 3 pounds sugar
> ½ teaspoon kosher salt

Peel the oranges, and coarsely grind the peels in the food processor. Take the fruit segments and, working over the food processor bowl, squeeze the seeds out and discard, allowing any juice that drips to fall into the bowl with the peels. Add the seeded segments to the bowl and grind a few pulses to break up the segments.

Place the rhubarb, sugar, and salt in a 4-quart or larger nonreactive pot, add the orange peels and juice, stir to combine, and render gently over low heat for 30 to 60 minutes, until the sugar is dissolved and all the rhubarb has fallen back into its juice. Gradually increase heat to a boil. Maintain a medium full but not rolling boil, stirring frequently, until the mixture registers 218°F on an instant-read digital thermometer. Transfer to sanitized canning jars or bottles while hot and cap tightly with new lids. Can be refrigerated for up to 2 months or canned in a standard water bath to store in the pantry.

Justin Dean

———

If you head west out of downtown Cincinnati in search of Carriage House Farm, you'll quickly get a sense of why those of us who grew up in the Ohio River Valley believe it to be as close to God's country as we can get on earth. Rolling hills and bluffs sandwich bigger baby mountains, all of them festooned with lush forest that hides the rich soil underneath, the kind that farmers dream of. Every fall, that forest undergoes a slow-motion transformation from every shade of green to a technicolor riot. When a fresh snowfall lays down a pearlescent blanket beneath shimmering trunks and branches, the forest looks like the most breathtaking array of skeletons.

Carriage House Farm, established in 1855 a stone's throw from the Miami River, is a state-registered Sesquicentennial Farm. Continuously operated by the same family for five generations and going on six, the farm has thrived over 165 years of upheaval in the American farm economy by navigating its own way through our constantly evolving food system. Its adaptations have included a popular Community Supported Agriculture subscription, an on-farm market, farm dinners, and sometimes a live music venue. Over the past two decades the farm has transformed itself into a hub of agriculture-based businesses, with an artisanal vinegar label and an alcoholic-beverage company, an on-farm restaurant, and an "edible schoolyard" to educate schoolchildren about farming and food.

Mad House Vinegar was dreamed up by Chef Justin Dean in 2015, when a friend working in one of Cincinnati's many craft breweries told him that the city was cracking down on breweries for pouring their trub, or leavings from the brewing process, into its aging sewer system. Recalling that during his years as a chef at Cincinnati's lauded Maisonette restaurant, it was difficult to find truly excellent vinegar of any type, but especially of the more commodified types like malt vinegar, a light bulb went off in his head. He bought some fermenters and other specialized equipment and asked his friend if he could pick up his brewery's next dump of trub. The first test batch of vinegar was a resounding success, and Chef Dean proceeded to acquire the necessary permits and paperwork to produce vinegar for sale. He was able to take a literal waste stream and make it into a high-value product that sells so well that he's often scrambling to ramp up production. There are now several different types of malt vinegar coming out of Mad House, characterized by the type of beer at the base: stout vinegar, brown malt vinegar, light malt vinegar, and the list goes on. Being a chef at heart, Dean ferments local persimmons and makes an impossibly delicate persimmon vinegar. He also uses the network of connections he built up as a chef to source wine made from grapes grown in surrounding counties in Ohio and Kentucky. You can make stellar red wine vinegar from Ohio-grown grapes, and white wine vinegar from Kentucky-grown grapes, and there are more varieties in store. The company is just getting on its feet, and demand is brisk.

Another Carriage House Farm project, Lost Bridge Beverage Company, puts more of the farm's produce to direct use, with a little assist from the nearby MGP Ingredients distillery in Lawrenceburg, Indiana. With a freshly producing stand of Norton grapes, historically one of the most promising wine grapes of the Midwest, the company produces a limited quantity of wine, while fruits ranging from grapes to pears to peaches are used to make artisanal brandy. The peach brandy is reserved to make a popular liqueur, which is now an absolute rarity, called peach and honey. A craft of German distillers, many of whom operated clandestine stills on their farms, peach and honey was as often bootlegged as legitimately produced. It was made by infusing peach brandy with peach pits to incorporate their ridiculously fragrant bitter-almond aroma, then swaddling that crowning achievement in a generous dose of honey. It's a dreamy spirit, and one that should see a great rebound in popularity as it becomes available.

The farm's tillable acres and surrounding woodland supply ample botanicals for Lost Bridge's Old Tom gin, a heady quaff started with neutral spirits from MGP and given a kiss of sweetness by the farm's own honey, for which the bees gather nectar from the fruit orchard and herb gardens, imparting a truly mesmerizing aroma. Not to stop there, the oak is added by aging the gin in a rick house on the farm until it is ready for market. One of few gins that is a true joy to drink on its own, it also makes a spectacular Martinez and a very special Tom Collins.

Chloe's Eatery started as a food truck sourcing its produce from Carriage House Farm, and during the COVID-19 pandemic, it parked itself permanently there, cooking for the on-farm market and providing catering for events at the farm. The farm has a strict policy of using exclusively local products for on-farm events, not just when it's convenient or scores PR points. With an on-farm gravel pit providing unusually crystalline acoustics, this place and its values also make it one hell of a music venue. At 165 years in, Carriage House Farm might just be getting started.

Based on a visit to Carriage House Farm (North Bend, OH) and discussion with Justin Dean, co-owner of Mad House Vinegar, September 9, 2021.

2

A COUNTRY
WELL LIT

Cocktails

People must not think that I cast any reflections on the memory of those good men when I assert that I have often seen the decanters and glasses set out after preaching was over, and all would engage in a "square dram" before partaking of the noonday meal. If the German ministers wanted their weekly keg of beer, they had it, and a jug of bitters could be found in almost every house.

—Colonel J. L. Hughes of Huntingburg, Indiana, 1884

Apple brandy, peach brandy, and corn whiskey were not subject to a government tax in the pioneer days. Many farmers made their own liquor, in fact nearly all the Germans did. . . . Nearly every farmer had cows, and a distillery. The posset cup was in every house and liquor was an article that entered into the economy of the home.

—George R. Wilson, *History of Dubois County*

THE Midwest, especially in and around the triangle formed by the historic brewing cities of Cincinnati, Saint Louis, and Milwaukee, which includes much of historic bourbon country and the mammoth MGP Ingredients distillery, has been instrumental in keeping America well lit for more than 150 years.

Once settlement was under way in Kentucky, word quickly traveled back east that its land was particularly good for growing corn, and that its limestone water was good for distillation and "cutting"—the dilution of high-proof distillate to potable strengths—making for a crisp, refreshing spirit that many regarded as a tonic. Many of the earliest settlers moved to the Indiana Territory (which was later divided into Illinois, Indiana, Wisconsin, and parts of Michigan and Minnesota) to get into the distillation business. Andrew Jackson and William Henry Harrison were among the folks turning corn into the devil's nectar in the early days of the region's development.

Even as a legitimate whiskey industry took shape, alcoholic beverages were very much a DIY affair for a good long while, especially among rural and small-town folks. In fact, during the early Federal period, whiskey was used as a form a currency, good for bartering or even paying wages.[1] In witness to the durability of this DIY culture, well into the 1970s my grandpa Albert Paul Fehribach brewed an annual batch of wild cherry and blackberry wine in a reused whiskey barrel, and many friends and family made their own wines out of anything from dandelions to rhubarb to oranges. I didn't know anyone who still distilled their own hooch at home, which had long ago been outlawed, yet I was always deeply awed by the occasional story Dad would tell of my uncle Tom's moonshine running in the '50s and '60s.

While recipes for many types of beer appear in historic cookbooks, they ceased appearing by the late nineteenth century, by which time commercial beer had become readily available. Most home recipes were for ales, but German-speaking people perennially preferred lager, which is harder to make at home because it needs to be kept cool. (Lager yeasts are anaerobic and produce the best flavors when fermented at steady, cool temperatures, doing their thing in the bottom of a cool, full tank.) This may explain why the American style of mass-produced beer became lager. Nevertheless, some of the early ale

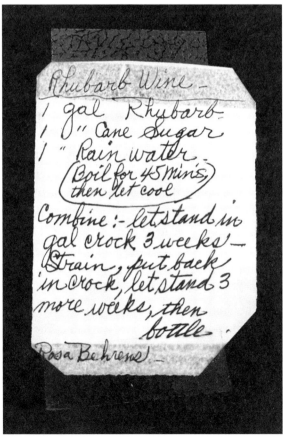

Some community cookbooks are used like scrapbooks.   Photo by Paul Fehribach.
Here, Mrs. Behrens wants to remember this recipe
for rhubarb wine, a popular potable in mid-twentieth-
century Indiana.

42

recipes are elegant, such as Lettice Bryan's receipt for London Porter, which, in addition to an unspecified malt, is fortified with molasses, licorice root, linseed, capsicum, cinnamon, ginger, and cocculus indicus (a preparation of hard multum that produced giddiness, enhancing alcohol's effects)[2] before fining with isinglass.[3] Other recipes for beer are quite crude, consisting simply of molasses and hops boiled and fermented, no barley malt required.[4]

Our tavern culture has long been vibrant and beer-driven. One of my favorite aspects of Midwestern life is that so many small towns still have that family-owned spot that's been doing the same thing for fifty, seventy-five, or a hundred years, serving simple food with local character alongside cold mugs or schooners of beer. I seldom pass through a small town without checking out a spot like the Chicken Place in Ireland, Indiana (open since 1948), or G&R Tavern in Waldo, Ohio (since 1962), both of which feel utterly familiar, like you've been there dozens of times—crowded with locals who all know one another, beer in front of every adult in the bar and soda in front of every child in the family dining room, generations of framed photographs on the wall that serve as a sort of thread, sewing together the stories of everyone who passes through into a big, warm quilt.

With the infamous Schlitz tied houses[5] as a notorious example, urban tavern culture has been heavily beer-driven as well. We'll see later how that culture helped popularize certain distinctively Midwestern foods, notably different regional pizza styles. Over the past several decades, "Irish" pubs have become one of the more vogue tavern styles, even though most are purveyors of fakelore. Meanwhile, German beer halls have faded from memory in most locales save Milwaukee, where the legendary Mader's restaurant and Kegel's Inn, among a host of others, continue to roll out the barrel and keep the beer flowing along with faithfully executed German American fare.

The Anheuser-Busch, Schlitz, Pabst, and Miller breweries established what seemed like a fairly uniform and uninteresting macro beer culture, but things have changed. The openings of Bell's Brewery in Kalamazoo, Michigan, and Summit Brewing in Minneapolis–Saint Paul, Minnesota, in 1985 and 1986, respectively, were shots heard across the heartland. The next thirty years saw an explosion in micro (and not so micro) breweries, which have dramatically changed how Midwesterners drink. As of 2020, the Brewers Association counted more than 2,500 craft breweries in the Midwest, producing over 7.5 million barrels of craft beer annually,[6] ranging in style from light and breezy pilsners to unctuous, brooding barley wines. Every style of sour beer is now being made in the Midwest, too, with the most intrepid pioneers being Indiana's Upland Brewing and Michigan's Jolly Pumpkin.

Before one can brew, grains, primarily barley, need to be malted, or sprouted and cured. The Midwest has long led the country not just in brewing beer but in supplying the trade, as home to industry-leading malt companies like Minnesota-based Cargill and Wisconsin-based Briess. The craft brewing industry is buoyed by a growing contingent of artisan maltsters now popping up in almost every state, from the Ohio-based Rustic Brew Farm to Indiana's Sugar Creek Malt House, Michigan's Fedora Malt House and Mitten State Malt, Illinois's Mammoth Malting, and Iowa's Miller Malting Company, to name just a few. In addition to locally grown base barley malts, brewers now work with malted einkorn, Bloody Butcher corn, Carolina Gold rice, and heritage varieties of rye and oats that haven't graced a mash bill since before the Green Revolution upended grain farming.

The production of fine ciders, spearheaded by Virtue in Fennville and Vandermill in Grand Rapids, Michigan, along with Prima in Long Grove, Illinois, now occurs in almost every corner of the Midwest and promises a truly "old is new again" taste. Virtue and Vandermill have pioneered innovative flavored ciders, using local cherries or blueberries, or honey, or ginger, or even hops. New oak or reused bourbon barrels add heft to some blends, and ciders that draw on wild yeasts or introduced strains such as *Brettanomyces*, or bacteria such as *Pediococcus* or *Lactobacillus*, introduce new (and old) aromatics and acid structure. Prima leads the "old is new" brigade with strictly cask- and bottle-conditioned ciders fermented according to Old World methods, relying on the natural yeasts of the orchard to show the true terroir of the south shore of Lake Michigan, sourcing fruit from Michigan, Illinois, and Wisconsin. Their labors give us ciders as complex and contemplative as any from Normandy in France or the Asturias region of Spain.

Wine recipes provided in Midwestern cookbooks are for fairly typical fruit wines. While as a youngster I certainly had a less developed palate than I do now, my recollection of these homemade wines is that they were customarily syrupy-sweet with an awkward alcoholic burn, although some of the fortified cherry wines made excellent highballs when mixed with cola. In this chapter, I'm sharing an adaptation of Grandpa Fehribach's wild cherry and blackberry wine (you can make it with regular sweet cherries), which is worth making for a mixer. You might even enjoy it, as I occasionally do, on its own.

But oenophiles might be astonished to learn that there is a rich history of wine production in the Midwest that goes far beyond saccharine fruit wines and pallid expressions of European varietals. In terms of raw wine-growing potential, most of the Midwest is cursed with rich organic soils in which grapevines thrive and produce lots of fruit but which fail to punish the grapes with the malnutrition and thirst that European and Californian winemakers have mastered to reduce yields and produce concentrated, aromatic juices. And our natural humidity doesn't help with fruit concentration or with resisting some diseases.

While European winemakers have had millennia to sort out their practices, the Midwestern wine industry is relatively young and has progressed in fits and starts, interrupted by the long, withering abomination known as Prohibition. During the nineteenth century, the Ohio River Valley emerged as the most promising new wine region with the midcentury Catawba craze, followed soon by the Missouri River and the Ozarks. The most promising emerging wine grapes were the American hybrid varieties Catawba and Norton. The Catawba reached its height of popularity and critical acclaim in the business of Nicholas Longworth in Cincinnati.[7] The Norton, which was developed in Richmond, Virginia, by Dr. Daniel Norton during the 1820s,[8] would receive remarkable encomiums in Missouri. The wines made from it were so successful that winemaker M. Poeschel and Sherer won a Medal of Distinction at the Vienna Universal Exposition for their Norton in 1873, followed by another medal at the Paris Universal Exposition in 1878. The most influential wine critic of the day, Henry Vizetelly, declared that "on the strength of Missouri, which is to say, on the strength of the Norton, America was 'destined to become . . . one of the great wine-producing regions of the world.'"[9] This was long before California had a wine industry of note.

Around the historic wine town of Hermann, Missouri, on the south bank of the Missouri River, lies a rare area of the Midwest suitable for making excellent wines, as its well-drained loamy soils produce fruit of excellent concentration. Stone Hill Winery operates on the historic Poeschel and Sherer property, where you can still acquire Nortons grown on the same tract decorated in the 1870s. Many Missouri wineries have taken up the Norton, and at its best it makes a beguiling wine with a nose as Daedalean as a fine Barolo and a structure worthy of decades of aging. Saint James, Hermannhoff, and Augusta make consistently good Nortons, delicious sparkling wines and expressions of Muscat, Riesling, and several other varietals. My advice is to do the wine tour and taste, taste, taste before buying, as vintages can still be inconsistent, but the scenery alone is worth the trip, and the hospitality is excellent.

In recent decades, Michigan has been successful in promoting its wines. While the state overall is too fertile, with warm summer nights and humidity unlikely to produce great wines, a generation of crackerjack winemakers have established a promising wine-growing appellation in Leelanau County, the thumb of the state mitten. This slender, rocky peninsula projecting into Lake Michigan—a great climate moderator—with ideal deposits of sand and loam over a craggy base of granite and limestone has attracted smart winemakers. Larry Mawby makes consistently excellent sparkling wines here, and other wineries to watch (or stop by and enjoy) are Aurora, Soul Squeeze, Bel Lago, Verterra, Blustone, Left Foot Charley, Brys, and Shady Lane. Old Mission Peninsula is worth a look, too.

Around the rest of the Midwest, Norton is popping up with increasing frequency, but most local wineries still specialize in sweetish fruit wines. While peaches could never make a wine with the complexity of Riesling grapes, or blueberries a wine as complex as a cabernet sauvignon, I'd argue that there are a lot of Midwestern fruit wines that are far more enjoyable than a crappy boxed chardonnay or cabernet from California. For everyday drinking we really should drop the pretensions of *Vitis vinifera* wines and embrace our local wineries, talk to them about what we like, and participate in a developing market that is rich with quality Midwestern-grown fruit in a glass.

Recent developments on the distillation front are as exciting as what we see in the beer and wine industries. MGP Ingredients is the largest supplier of rye whiskey in America.[10] Its Lawrenceburg, Indiana, operation, formerly Seagram's, is the source of the "juice" for such famous "craft" rye whiskeys as Bulleit, Redemption, George Dickel, High West Rendezvous, and many, many more. Modern cocktail culture is supported by daring craft distilleries such as North Shore Distillery of Lake Bluff, Illinois; Louisville's Copper and Kings; Chicago's Letherbee, Rhinehall, and Koval distilleries; and Michigan's Journeyman, along with a host of younger upstarts.

The opening of Chicago's Violet Hour bar in 2007 presaged a revival of classic cocktail culture, with an emphasis on carefully crafted drinks and even more carefully crafted ice. The aim was, and remains, to elevate cocktail culture to a fine art, with the crafting of each drink a ritual bordering on the spiritual. The vapid vodka-based martini menus of restaurants and bars alike have disappeared, and even humble neighborhood spots are peppering their cocktail game with local spirits and house infusions. Today any serious cocktail program has a library of house-made bitters, shrubs, and liqueurs.

One of the most peculiar facets of alcohol consumption in the Midwest is the cocktail culture of supper clubs, which are most popular in Wisconsin but also exist in Iowa and Minnesota. Entire books have been written about supper clubs, where one goes to make an evening out of a meal and where time often seems to stand still, in which brandy often stands in for whiskey and Sprite for club soda in otherwise standard cocktails, and where highballs are still a thing. Save for the ubiquitous riffs on the Moscow Mule foisted upon the country, a good highball is underappreciated today. Many supper clubs have embraced the more modern craft cocktail movement, which fixates on pre-Prohibition libations, but the midcentury modern cocktails are where supper clubs hit the sweet spot. As unknown as these potables are in the rest of the country, we're going to take a look at some abiding examples, some long lost, and some re-imaginings of the stalwarts.

Brandy Manhattan

Some twenty years ago, renowned Chicago mixologist Todd Appel bartended a couple of nights a week at one of my favorite local watering holes in Andersonville, on the North Side of Chicago. While I usually drink my whiskey straight during the winter, when in the hands of a good barkeep, I'll order Manhattans or Old-Fashioneds, which Todd, hailing from the Northwoods of Wisconsin, liked making with brandy, because, you know, Wisconsin. It was a revelation, and I've been hooked ever since. Todd now supplies many of Chicago's most famous bars through his company, Appel's Cordials, in which his obsession with local ingredients and seasonal consumption is fully expressed. Manhattans should be a little sweet, especially when going for the Wisconsin style, so use a decent vermouth and don't skimp on it. Neon-red maraschino cherries are de rigueur in supper clubs, but these days I do prefer the widely available Luxardo maraschinos from Italy.

Makes 1 Manhattan

3½ ounces aged brandy, Copper & Kings recommended, or use your favorite

1¾ ounces sweet vermouth

1 dash Angostura bitters

2 or 3 maraschino cherries, speared if you like

Chill a cocktail glass with ice water. Fill a cocktail shaker with ice, the bigger the cubes the better, then add brandy, vermouth, and bitters. Stir vigorously with a bar spoon for 30 seconds. Drain ice water from cocktail glass, add cherries, and strain the cocktail over the cherries.

Brandy Old-Fashioned

I have to admit that even as curious and enthusiastic as I am about old-time recipes and getting to the roots of foods and drinks, one thing I've found jarring is the way barkeepers have returned the Old-Fashioned cocktail to its likely nineteenth-century roots—a simple concoction of liquor with bitters for flavor, and sugar and water to round it out. This treatment is lost on me, since in the nineteenth century most liquors would be rather *rough* by today's standards and needed to be cut and sweetened to be palatable. With distillation science as precise as it is in twenty-first-century America, and most call or top-shelf liquor so pleasurable to consume straight or with a few rocks, why sweeten it unnecessarily? That said, if you're going to make a sweetened cocktail, don't squander your treasure on top-shelf spirits. Use the cheap (but not *too* cheap) stuff.

The historically accurate Old-Fashioned isn't as much fun as the Old-Fashioned I learned to make while growing up in the industry, before the craft cocktail revolution. That Old-Fashioned was a muddled mess of orange, saccharine-sweet maraschino cherries, and bitters topped with bourbon and club soda. It's fun to drink, because it changes all the way down—starting out dry and effervescent from the soda, with some alcoholic heat as the liquor tends to float, and slowly getting sweeter, fruitier, and more bitter all the way down until you find a fruity snack at the bottom of the glass. This is the hallowed Wisconsin supper club way, along with a switch to brandy as the base liquor and, if you like it "sweet," Sprite standing in for the club soda. Best in winter, it's refreshing all year round and a great way to work up an appetite before dinner.

Makes 1 Old-Fashioned

1 slice orange, ¼ inch thick, cut into two half moons, divided

3 maraschino cherries, divided

2 sugar cubes (or 2 packets sugar, or 1 heaping teaspoon)

2 dashes Angostura bitters

2 ounces brandy

Splash club soda or Sprite, to taste (2 to 4 tablespoons)

Use a sturdy 8-ounce rocks glass. Wrap one half-slice of orange around one of the cherries and skewer with a bar pick, and reserve for garnish. Lay the other half-slice of orange in the bottom of the glass, add the remaining two cherries, the sugar cubes, and then the bitters, aiming to soak the sugar cubes with the bitters. Use a muddler to mash the cherries and sugar cubes into the orange, just until sugar cubes have been broken up and "muddled" with the other ingredients, about 15 seconds. Fill the glass with ice—larger cubes are better. Pour the brandy over the ice, then top with soda. Garnish with the reserved skewer.

Elderflower Collins

The formerly universal Tom Collins has all but disappeared from cocktail menus around the country, but thankfully you can still come across this fizzy potion in many a supper club in the Northwoods, along with other lost cocktails of yore such as the Harvey Wallbanger and the Whiskey Sour. I think it's likely these cocktails lost favor because of the way so many bars lazily slopped syrupy sour mix into them, rather than using freshly squeezed juices. Now that many bars across the Midwest are juicing their own citrus for fresh flavors, many of these old classics are worth another look, such as this updated Tom Collins.

Makes 1 Collins

> 2 ounces London dry gin
> ½ ounce freshly squeezed lemon juice
> ½ ounce freshly squeezed lime juice
> 1 ounce elderflower liqueur
> Seltzer water
> Sliced lemon and cucumber, for garnish

Fill a standard 10- or 11-ounce Collins glass with large ice cubes. Add the gin, juices, and liqueur, stir well, and top with seltzer water. Garnish with lemon and cucumber slices.

Pink Squirrel

Maybe the best part of a true supper club experience is an ice cream cocktail, a boozy adult milkshake that combines two treats into one luscious glass. Most of us will know Brandy Alexanders, Grasshoppers, and Pink Squirrels, but all the best supper club barkeepers have their own signature concoctions. Some of them can be quite sophisticated, while others may do something as simple as pouring vodka and Kahlua over vanilla ice cream, blending it, and calling it a White Russian, which it sort of is.

Ice cream cocktails are usually thought of as dowdy and weak, but anyone who likes ice cream *and* drinking (I'm going out on a limb here to say that's most of us) is bound to find something to like. So rethink dessert and break out the ice cream!

Bryant's Cocktail Lounge in Milwaukee claims the original Pink Squirrel cocktail,[11] which for lovers of the bitter-almond fragrance of Amaretto is guaranteed to be a winner. It uses crème de noyaux to achieve both the almond aroma and its namesake color. Being a fan of a little more alcohol burn with any type of sweet drink, I add one part kirschwasser to this. If you don't have kirschwasser you can use your favorite vodka or leave it out entirely. Hurricane glasses are classic for this.

Makes one 12-ounce Pink Squirrel

- 3 scoops vanilla ice cream, approximately ½ cup each
- 1 ounce crème de noyaux
- 1 ounce white crème de cacao
- 1 ounce kirschwasser
- Whipped cream and cookies of choice for garnish (optional)

Place the ice cream in a blender bowl, add the liquors, and put the cap on tight.

Puree until smooth, about 20 to 30 seconds. Serve in a chilled 12-ounce hurricane glass. If it's dessert time, top with whipped cream and garnish with a cookie.

Albert Fehribach's Wild Cherry and Blackberry Wine

As my parents' generation aged, my brothers and I took to picking Dad's brain for his recollections of the World War II era and postwar years. And since our generation has witnessed the subversion of historic Midwestern foodways by supermarket and fast-food cultures, I've also tried to elicit his memories of food and drink culture. From Grandpa's annual sorghum cane crop to hog butcherings to Grandma's gardening and canning exploits, there's a gold mine of information there. One of the most curious recipes from that time is the wild cherry and blackberry wine Grandpa always kept around, which would be imbibed over cigars at the end of the typically long workday.

I had to make some modifications to the recipe because two key aspects of it aren't practical. Grandpa fermented it in a whiskey barrel, which for him, a scarce 90 minutes from Louisville, was easy enough to acquire. In fact, whiskey barrels played a lot of roles on the farm, from wine making to pickle and kraut fermentation to capturing rainwater. Many old-timers swear by rainwater for their homemade wine. However, whiskey barrels aren't as easy to acquire today, and you probably don't want to make a 50-gallon recipe anyway; Grandpa's started with 50 pounds of cherries and half again as many blackberries. So I've pared down the batch size. This recipe also calls for regular bing cherries, as they are much easier to come by than wild ones. Grandpa didn't pit his cherries; the pits can impart a bitter-almond-like flavor, but I recommend using pitted cherries the first time around. Finally, while Grandpa relied entirely on wild yeast to start his fermentation, I recommend using a purchased wine yeast with yeast nutrient just to get you going faster and ensure success.

This is a fairly easy recipe, given the time involved, and it's definitely worth making. It makes an excellent mixer, especially for highballs, but is delicious with lemonade or even on its own when the weather is cold. You can also mull it with spices to drink hot, which is a special delight. The only specialized equipment you'll need to pull it off is a 3-gallon fermenting bucket with an airlock. A siphon tube (available from brewing supply stores) helps make racking the clear wine off the sediment a lot easier but isn't absolutely necessary. Grandpa stored his wine in 1-gallon glass jugs; you can store it in any size bottles or even jars. As long as the containers are filled to capacity and sealed tightly, the wine will keep indefinitely, but I doubt it will improve with age, so enjoy it young.

Makes about 5 quarts

    2 pounds frozen sweet cherries
    2 pounds frozen tart cherries (Montmorencies are the best if you can find them)
    2 pounds frozen blackberries
    3 pounds granulated sugar
    1 gallon distilled water
    1 packet champagne yeast (available at home brewing supply stores)
    1 teaspoon yeast nutrient (available at home brewing supply stores)
    1 American oak infusion spiral (available online or in home brewing supply stores)
    1 bottle (750 ml) young bourbon whiskey (such as Four Roses Yellow Label,
        Benchmark, Evan Williams Black Label, Ezra Brooks, or Wild Turkey)

Sanitize all equipment before use with a mild bleach solution, or you can use Star-San (available in brewing supply stores). Thaw the cherries and blackberries in the refrigerator overnight. Mash them with a potato masher or pulse in the food processor in batches to coarsely grind them. Mix them with the sugar, stirring to incorporate the ingredients and begin dissolving the sugar. Pour this slurry into your fermenter and add the water, yeast, and yeast nutrient. Stir or slosh around a few times to dissolve the sugar and yeast, drop the oak infusion spiral, and cap with the airlock. Put 2 or 3 drops dish soap in the airlock with the water; this makes it easier to monitor fermentation because bubbles will form when gas is passing through the airlock.

Active fermentation should start within 24 hours but may take a bit longer. Monitor the fermentation daily; it will be completed in 7 to 10 days, but I recommend waiting a full month after any yeast activity has ceased (when bubbles no longer form in the airlock).

Now for the first racking—taking the wine off the sediment in the bottom of the fermenter. Use a ladle or siphon tube to transfer to a clean, sanitized, new bucket. Avoid dipping the pull end of the siphon into the sediment—keep it in the center of the wine above, and monitor as the wine recedes. Stir the whiskey into the racked wine. Clean the fermenter and the oak infusion spiral, discarding the sediment, and return the wine and oak spiral to the fermenter, replace the top and airlock, and rest for 1 month before a second and final racking. There will be only a thin layer of sediment at the bottom, so avoid this during siphoning and you'll have a beautiful, gem-colored wine.

Bottle and cap tightly. Rest for 2 months before drinking. This wine is best young, and best enjoyed during the winter months. It adds a wonderful grace to the holiday table.

Three Doyennes Blackberry Cordial

If you take the time to explore old cookbooks, especially those from the nineteenth century, you may be as fascinated as I was to discover the wide range of homemade liqueurs there. The two reasons for their abundance are probably convenience and household economy. If you were an early Midwesterner who wanted to drink at home or entertain even a small party, the only way to guarantee yourself a varied supply of liqueurs and mixers was to make everything, because you couldn't just hop in the car and drive down to the liquor store. You could buy a store of whiskey and brandy (or distill your own), and these would contribute to many further recipes—such as preserves of seasonal fruits and herbs—so making homemade cordials was an economical choice. But I imagine it was also mighty convenient to have something like this cordial on hand on a cold winter night.

I call this recipe Three Doyennes because blackberry cordial appears in all three of the most influential early cookbooks of our region—Lettice Bryan's *Kentucky Housewife*,[12] Bertha Kramer's *Aunt Babette's Cook Book*,[13] and Mrs. Simon Kander and Mrs. Henry Schoenfeld's *Settlement Cook Book*.[14] It's interesting to note that in 1839, when the Ohio River Valley was in its developmental infancy, Lettice Bryan included some eighty receipts for homemade liqueurs, wines, and beers; by 1889, Kramer included eight, and by 1903, Kander and Schoenfeld included only four. The times they were a-changing. Kramer may have been the first Midwestern author to include cocktails in her book along with apple toddies, milk punch, grog, and sherry cobbler.[15] Also interesting to note is that Lettice Bryan begins her receipt by stating that "blackberry cordial is considered good medicine for children in cases of infections of the bowels," a charming reminder of how far medical science has come!

This recipe is adapted from those three receipts. You can make this basic recipe with any summer fruit that yields juice, from strawberries to gooseberries, raspberries to cherries. This cordial is delightful on its own, as a base liquor for sours, or as a flavoring for daiquiris, margaritas, and the like. It's a fun ingredient to play with. For best results, try to get wild-picked blackberries at the peak of summer, but farmers' market blackberries will do fine. Farmers often set aside less-than-perfect fruit for sale at a discount; it never hurts to ask if they have "seconds" available. You'll save a little money, and blemished fruit will still make a lovely cordial.

Makes about one 750 ml bottle cordial

36 ounces ripe fresh blackberries

Cold water (to cover, just under 2 cups)

½ cup granulated sugar

1 small dried bay leaf

3 whole black peppercorns

1½ cups un-aged kirschwasser, or pear or peach eau-de-vie (if you can find blackberry eau-de-vie, even better)

Rinse the blackberries in cold water, then place in a 2-to-4-quart nonreactive saucepan. Add just enough water to almost cover the berries, leaving the top layer partially exposed, around 2 cups. Render the berries over medium-low heat, being careful not to boil and never stirring or otherwise disturbing the berries. Rendering will take 1 to 2 hours; when you see that all the berries are wilted and surrounded by rich, fragrant juice, they are done. Using a jelly bag or cheesecloth, strain the berries, but do not squeeze or force extra juice out—just let gravity give you as much juice as it will. Squeezing may yield a cloudy liqueur. The longer you let the juice drain, the more you'll get. Your yield should be about 2 cups. Set aside the pulp and either use it for **QUICK BLACKBERRY JAM** (p. 34) or discard. Transfer the juice to a clean pot, and add the sugar, bay leaf, and peppercorns.

Over medium-high heat, bring to a low boil, stirring frequently to dissolve the sugar, for 5 minutes. Remove from heat. Stir in the eau-de-vie and cover with a tight-fitting lid.

Allow to cool to room temperature overnight. The next day, strain out any remaining solids through a jelly bag or cheesecloth. Bottle in clean wine bottles with an airtight seal. Be sure your bottles are clean and sanitized, and use a pump-style silicone sealing stopper. Stored in this way, this cordial will keep for a year or more.

Serve chilled in small sherry or cordial glasses, use to top off sparkling wine for a delicious kir variation, or serve over ice with a splash of club soda.

Andy Hazzard

———

Some say the more things change, the more they stay the same. On one small farm northwest of Chicago outside the tiny crossroads of Pecatonica, little has changed in more than 150 years of growing, except some of the heirloom crops grown. Heading west from Rockford and ambling down picturesque country roads over rolling plains platted with farms, hedgerows, and oak and maple trees brings you to Hazzard Free Farm, one of the few farms I've ever known to be owned and run by a single woman.

With her beautiful long golden dreads flopping in the wind, Andrea "Andy" Hazzard tackles a tractor like a chef handles a sauté pan, with a natural aplomb energized by an obsessive passion to feed people. But Andy's mission is larger. Impelled to farm with an ecology-first ethic, she works exclusively with ancient, landrace grains and beans, and farms organically to care for the land that her ancestors farmed. Young and idealistic, and with boundless determination to make her statement, she believes that clean, carefully cultivated land makes for better food. "This is going in your body, it's building your muscles, your bone, your brain. . . . It's so important that we eat good food." To taste the results of her work is the ultimate affirmation of that power.

Her ancestors settled this rich, loamy land in 1847. Hazzard is quick to attribute her passion to the family; she prints the recipe for corncakes she learned from her grandmother on every retail pack of cornmeal she sells. Andy is most animated when she tells of mining the corncrib with her grandfather to select ears of corn, which would be ground by hand by her grandmother and would soon emerge from a cast-iron frying pan as hot little corncakes. In what might be considered a more Southern cultural inclination, that frying pan counts as one of her prized possessions and still works the stovetop today.

Andy is particularly cogent when she speaks of her decision to return to the land and farm as a way to bring her work into line with her spiritual beliefs and, as she puts it, to "counter my frustration toward the role I was playing in the demise of the environment." This spiritual foundation feeds her philosophy of regenerative farming as a rejection of the heritage of conventional farming and its chemical inputs and GMO technology. She devotes herself to seed saving and the restoration of traditional varieties and landrace crops. She knows the old varieties have far more flavor, and she'll tell you that's a clue that there's more nutrition in each grain.

As a small, essentially one-person operation with about fifty acres under cultivation, Hazzard Free Farm has bypassed USDA organic certification. Andy maintains that while the flexibility of remaining uncertified is important, her ideas are bigger than organics. "There was a commitment to farming I needed to make, that was not just about farming without chemicals, but to build the culture of farming, to saving seeds, to working within our community to teach people about farming . . . because the changes we want to see are much, much greater than just eating food that isn't GMO or is chemical free. These are changes that affect every part of our lives—our communities, our culture, our education system."

Andy works with community groups around Rockford to inspire and teach young people about farming. Groups such as Roots and Wings, a youth-run CSA and farmers' market, and Eco Advocates, a Comprehensive Community Solutions academic and environmental program for young adults, bring a steady stream of mentees to Hazzard Free Farm.

One taste of cornbread made with Andy's Bloody Butcher cornmeal, or polenta made with coarsely ground Floriani Red Flint corn or whole-grain emmer wheat, and the taste of the rich land she cultivates comes to life. Personally, I dream of her purple barley, brimming with aromas of fresh mown hay and the sweetness of silage, which I work with each winter at my restaurant in Chicago. These grains are the ambrosia of the soil. Andy is ensuring that these and many more flavors will grace our tables for years to come.

The first time I opened a sack of Althea's White cornmeal from Hazzard Free Farm, I had one of those space-time experiences. The aroma dropped me into my Uncle Rich and Aunt Sue's cornfield east of Celestine, Indiana. On first taste, I was a toddler in their grain barn beneath the mill where they ground corn for feed, sticking my tongue out to catch the fine grist, which would dissolve instantly on it like fine sugar with the minerally perfume of freshly milled corn.

Andy has hand-selected the line she calls Althea's White, named for her grandmother, who showed her how to select corn both for seed and for the baking pan. I work with it a lot in my kitchens both at the restaurant and at home. For Thanksgiving, I've always been torn between the cultural symbolism of hospitality in white bread and the heady harvest aroma of cornbread, so I like to serve both!

Based on a visit to Hazzard Free Farm (Pecatonica, IL) and discussion with Andy Hazzard, owner, September 2, 2022.

3

BAKER'S DELIGHT

Breads

And I won't tell you the name of the delicatessen, but it's in East Rogers Park. As for the rye bread, it is the best in the city, but it's not nearly up to the standards of my cousin Louis. He had a fine old Russian-Jewish bakery in Chicago. It was the Imperial Baking Company and his rye bread was famous. He also made black Russian pumpernickel in huge ovals, each about the size of a three-month-old infant. Carrying it home was hard work. No one makes that kind of pumpernickel anymore.

—Saul Bellow

As I have traveled the Midwest in search of good food, what I have found most remarkable is the baking traditions. A thorough survey of Midwestern baking shows the truth in its designation as "Breadbasket of America." And this status is not only historical; the Midwest continues to be the best place to shop for and consume the leavened fruit of processed grains.

Seeing wheat-based bread as a pillar of the diet is definitely a hallmark of European culture, yet there's a prodigious diversity of ideas that emerged from it as immigrants transmuted it to America. Thus the spectacular array of bakeries the Midwest boasts, as far east as Cleveland, with institutions such as the Farkas Pastry Shoppe, one of the few spots in the country to feature traditional Hungarian linzers, poppy-seed rolls, and the decadent hog crackling–laced *tepertős pogácsa* or lip-smacking *sós stangli*, studded with gruyère and sweating butter from its refined pleats of twisted dough. Cleveland also boasts other Polish and Italian bakeries, churning out everything from paczki and piquant ryes to cassata cakes and crusty Italian loaves, with their crunchy, shattering crusts shrouding a feathery crumb that begs to be dragged through olive oil or gravy.

Cincinnati is a self-styled coffee-cake capital,[1] and if you've been to Graeter's, Busken, Servatii, or any of the other score of excellent bakeries around town, you'll heartily agree. But don't sleep on the pretzels at Servatii—they are a rare expression of the pretzel as a bread of the highest quality. In another river town, Saint Louis, the ancestral German coffee cakes, kuchen and stollen, sing a timeless refrain at Missouri Baking Company. Saint Louis is also one of the best cities for kolaches, stuffed with anything from jams or cream cheese to sausage and onions or barbecue at the Kolache Factory or Saint Louis Kolache, both local chains. Head farther west and you can find Lithuanian Baking Company in Omaha, Nebraska, a true rarity and a source of rye breads deeply rooted in Eastern European cooking. I know many Lithuanian Americans in Chicago who order bread from Omaha for a taste of their Baltic home!

Chicago and Detroit are two of the best cities to shop Mexican *panaderias*, while conchas, churros, and tres leches cake increasingly go mainstream. Milwaukee joins Chicago and Detroit among cities with great Middle Eastern bakeries, not to be missed for fresh pita, lavash, and spinach and cheese pies, in addition to flaky phyllo pastries of myriad varieties. Between Chicago and Milwaukee, the lakefront burg of Kenosha, Wisconsin, channels Danish heritage in its kringles, and Scandinavian influence can be found from Chicago northwest through Wisconsin into the Dakotas and westward to Iowa. Bakeries and cafés with names like Lost Lars, Norske Nook, Krown Bakery, Taste of Scandinavia, Nordic Mill, Smuck's Kringla, and Norsland Lefse dot the landscape, promising luscious potato-scented breads, laminated pastries, and delectable pancakes.

In recent years, Asian baking arts have adventured beyond the Little Vietnams and Chinatowns. Banh mi is leading the advance with its impossibly light bread born of French colonization and brought to the United States, where it promises immigrants a chance at their own business. Bao are on the verge of going mainstream, and both bao and banh mi are being creolized into thoroughly American versions in which the banh mi might serve as a nest for Korean bulgogi or Cajun-spiced fried shrimp, and bao may be filled with smoked brisket and coleslaw or fried chicken smothered in barbecue sauce.

The artisan baking movement has been on fire for a generation, ironically fertilized by chains such as Great Harvest Baking, Corner Bakery, and Panera Bread, which reintroduced mainstream markets to breads beyond the supermarket norms. Bakeries such as Hewn of Evanston, Illinois, Chicago's Floriole, and Minneapolis's Black Walnut Bakery have redefined what is possible with laminated doughs, relegating the flaccid croissants of the '80s and '90s to corporate canteens and grease-sopped drive-through breakfasts. Grand Rapids' Field & Fire, Madison Sourdough, and Chicago's Publican Quality Bread are just a few examples of bakeries reshaping our food culture with organic and locally milled grains, offering Midwestern grain producers a chance to pursue quality rather than quantity.

This baking movement is stoked by the increasing availability of artisan grains. Farms growing heirloom, heritage, and ancient grains number in the dozens, and that number is growing rapidly, supplying a rising contingent of artisan bakers. Janie's Mill in Ashkum, Illinois, started as a grain farm with the idea of milling its own grain and that of its neighbors. Its effort has been so successful that revenues are in the millions of dollars after a few short years, with continuing explosive growth as consumers, bakeries, and restaurants look for certified organic, locally milled flours.

In selecting recipes for this chapter as well as the one on sweets, it was difficult to distill the dizzying constellation of Midwestern baked goods. My intention is, first of all, to pick recipes that are achievable for you at home, but also to tell the story of our people through the recipes, with a healthy look back and an eye on the present. While the Midwest is a great place to eat any type of food, in baking is where we truly slay.

Lincoln Family Frontier Cornbread

Illinois proudly calls itself the Land of Lincoln, but those of us from the southern Indiana woods have always, if quietly, taken issue with that claim. While it's true his career as a shopkeeper, lawyer, and, finally, politician took place in Illinois, his formative years were spent on a small and prosperous farm in Spencer County, Indiana, near the Ohio River. I always enjoyed visiting the Lincoln Boyhood National Memorial there, marveling at the idea of cooking in a hearth with those strange pots and utensils.

As I've grown from a country boy raised in the woods and come into my own as a chef in Chicago, I sometimes ponder Lincoln's move from the woods to Salem, Illinois, then Springfield, and ultimately Washington, DC, and suspect he was full of wonder along the way, too.

In her excellent book *Abraham Lincoln in the Kitchen*, Rae Katherine Eighmey studies his life through food and includes some insightful recipes to re-create Lincoln family foodways. An unusual, and unusually delicious, cornbread recipe that's apparently much like what Abe's mother would have known from her childhood in Lexington, Kentucky, is a standout.[2] I've adapted this crackly cornbread recipe from a source a little closer to my home: Lettice Bryan's 1939 compendium *The Kentucky Housewife*, the seminal culinary text of the Ohio River Valley.[3]

Makes one 9-inch cast-iron skillet of cornbread

1 cup water
1½ cups stone-ground white cornmeal, divided

3 tablespoons bacon grease or lard, divided

1 teaspoon salt

2 large eggs, separated

1 cup buttermilk

Bring the water to a boil in a small saucepan. Place ½ cup of the cornmeal in a stainless-steel mixing bowl with 2 tablespoons bacon grease and the salt. All at once, carefully pour the boiling water over the cornmeal mixture and stir with a wooden spoon until the mix comes together and forms a dough. Beat vigorously for a minute or two more, until the dough becomes very firm and hard to work. Cover the bowl tightly with plastic wrap and set in a warm spot to lighten for a few hours, until a crack forms on top. It should be lukewarm to cool before you proceed to the next stage.

Preheat oven to 425°F. Use 1 tablespoon of bacon grease to oil a 9-inch cast-iron skillet and set it in the oven to preheat as well.

Once the oven is hot, stir the egg yolks into the dough, then the buttermilk, and whisk until smooth. Add the remaining cornmeal. Beat the egg whites until they form soft peaks, then fold into the batter.

Pour the batter into the preheated skillet and place in the center of the top rack of the oven, and turn the oven down to 375°F. Bake for 35 to 40 minutes, until it's springy in the center and the crust is pulling away from the sides of the skillet. Cool until just warm before slicing.

Brown County Fried Biscuits

During my Bloomington, Indiana, days a group of us made regular forays into Brown County and the amiable little hamlet of Nashville. Tucked away in the hills of south-central Indiana and surrounded by old-order small farms and the haunting Hoosier National Forest, Nashville was first settled in 1809 and emerged as an artist colony in the early twentieth century. It soon became a tourist trap targeted at outdoorsy types drawn by unrivaled displays of autumn foliage.

Our stops in Nashville had a clearly defined purpose: to fuel up for hikes in the Charles C. Deam Wilderness south of town, a mammoth stretch of forest carpeting rolling hills and dells. A stop by the Nashville House, a quaint old inn serving home cooking since 1859, would satiate us with simple country cooking—baked ham, roast turkey with giblet gravy, pot roast with carrots and

62

potatoes, and the coup de grâce of Nashville cooking: fried biscuits with apple butter. A brown paper sack of the delicious donut-like confections would provide additional fuel during the woodland ramble.

Fried biscuits aren't quite like what you'd imagine. They're more like a donut, but not quite that either. For one thing, they're pan-fried, not deep-fried. For another, they're not particularly sweet, with only a touch of sugar, and only the worst kind of scoundrel dredges them in powdered sugar. Unlike some traditional biscuits, they are not chemically leavened—the agent is good quick yeast. For additional flavor I like to build up a nice *biga*, a type of starter, to bring a little extra winey perfume to the dough, and buttermilk lends richness and tang.

Fried biscuits probably didn't originate in Indiana; the first description of a receipt hails from Maryland in 1880,[4] and they don't appear in Indiana until the publication of a receipt in the *Indianapolis Star* in 1907, from one Mrs. Charles Bell of Ossian, 150 miles from Brown County.[5] They finally appear in nearby Bloomington in 1917.[6] In subsequent decades, authors suggest sprinkling them with sugar, then cinnamon and sugar, before they appear in an advertisement for the Nashville House in the iconic pairing with apple butter in 1956.[7] Hoosiers have been gorging on them ever since.

Beyond the classic cinnamon-fortified **APPLE BUTTER** (p. 31), I'm also a fan of blackberry jelly or strawberry jam with fried biscuits—just don't tell anyone back home.

BROWN COUNTY'S
NASHVILLE HOUSE
We had a letter from a lady in New Albany who wanted to make sure that we would serve our famous "Brown County Fried Biscuits" when she came up with a party. We told her we "sure would." For we are making these Fried Biscuits a Specialty - of - the - House, and goodness, how folks do take to them, especially when they cover them with our Baked Apple Butter.

Brown County's Nashville House was the first to advertise fried biscuits with apple butter, which has become a Hoosier classic.

Source: The Republic (Columbus, IN), May 18, 1956.

Makes about 2 dozen fried biscuits

FOR THE *BIGA*

> 1 cup warm (100°F to 110°F) spring or filtered water
> 1 teaspoon instant yeast
> 1 cup all-purpose flour
> 1 teaspoon granulated sugar

Mix ingredients in a small bowl with enough room for the *biga* to triple in volume overnight. Cover tightly with plastic wrap and set in a warm spot for at least 24 hours, or up to 36 hours.

TO MAKE THE BISCUITS

> 4 cups all-purpose flour, plus more for flouring the board
> 2 tablespoons granulated sugar
> 2 teaspoons salt
> ¼ cup lard or butter, well chilled and cut into small bits
> 1¼ cups nonfat buttermilk
> The reserved *biga*
> 1 to 2 cups additional lard or vegetable oil, for frying

Sift the flour together with the sugar and salt. Add the lard or butter and work into the flour with your fingers, rubbing between them to incorporate the fat until the mixture resembles a fine meal. Add the buttermilk and mix quickly with a wooden spoon to incorporate, then pause for 1 minute to allow the flour to hydrate. Add the reserved *biga* and mix gently until incorporated, 1 minute. Turn onto a floured board and knead for 6 or 7 turns, just until the dough is able to form a ball. Don't overknead; we're making biscuits, not bread. Turn the dough into a large mixing bowl and cover loosely with plastic wrap, then set in a warm place to rise until doubled in bulk, about 1 hour.

Turn the dough back out onto a floured board and roll out to ½-inch thickness, then cut biscuits with a 2-inch biscuit cutter, setting the cut biscuits aside to rest on a floured surface while you rework the leftover dough from the first cutting, until you have used all the dough. Let cut biscuits rise an additional 20 minutes.

Melt enough lard or vegetable oil to fill a 10-inch cast-iron skillet with ½ inch of fat. Heat to 350°F. Lay the biscuits in the fat, leaving at least ½ inch between biscuits to allow for expansion. Fry the biscuits for 3 to 4 minutes on the first side, moving about to prevent sticking, until golden brown. Gently turn, and cook another 3 minutes on the second side, adding extra oil if needed to retain ¼ inch in the skillet. Pry one of the biscuits open to check for doneness, and cook longer as needed. Place finished biscuits on a platter lined with paper towels to drain while you fry additional batches. Serve at once with apple butter or your favorite preserves.

"Everything" Rye Pretzels

Back home in Jasper, Indiana, with its population of German Catholics from southern Baden and Swabia, pretzels were at every celebration—the choice snack between meals and with whiskey or beer. While I've always liked them, I found it curious that something so mundane as the dry, canned pretzels by Charles Chips could maintain such a deep cultural meaning. For something a little more special, we did have the local Tell City Pretzels, founded in 1858 by a Swiss immigrant who put the art in artisanal long before that was a buzzword. But it was only in the home baking tradition that one could taste the occasional freshly baked pretzel, which is a completely different experience than any pretzel you could buy in a grocery store or snack aisle.

Pretzels have long been considered among the finest breads of southern Germany, Switzerland, and Austria, where they may also pop up as *Bretzels* or *Brezels*. In the High German country, pretzels are the stuff of festivals, processions, parades, and celebration.[8] So, how did a fine bread become a cheap snack-aisle product? Swabian immigrants in Pennsylvania baked the first pretzels during the eighteenth century.[9] We don't yet know who developed the hard pretzel, but it could be easily stored and transported for mass commerce. By 1848, hard pretzels were being consumed in German beer halls and saloons around the United States.[10] Soft pretzels continued to be a specialty of the Philadelphia area and among New York street vendors through the twentieth century, but as an increasingly commodified product without artisanal quality. Well into the 1970s, home-baked pretzels were not unheard of in my home of Dubois County, Indiana, with its substantial population with roots in Swabia and the Palatinate. In her self-published gem of a recipe and story book, *Ferdinand Life: How We Lived and Ate*, Phyllis A. Trout Johanneman includes a traditional *Bretzel* recipe.[11]

When I bake pretzels, which is an annual ritual, I aspire to their fine bread heritage and sometimes wonder why they've been missed by the artisan baking movement. The following recipe is a great deal of fun to make and even more fun to eat with butter, cheese spread, or on its own. These pretzels are perfect with butter for a midafternoon snack on a heavy workday, or with beer during a leisurely sports or movie day.

1½ cups whole milk

2 teaspoons instant baking yeast

1 tablespoon granulated sugar

1 tablespoon sorghum molasses

1 cup whole-grain rye flour

2 cups unbleached all-purpose flour, plus more for dusting

1 tablespoon salt

3 tablespoons unsalted butter, softened to room temperature, divided

All-purpose flour, for kneading and shaping

3 quarts water

¾ cup baking soda

Maldon sea salt, or your favorite flake salt, for topping

Caraway seed, sesame seed, poppy seed, onion flakes for topping

Heat the milk to lukewarm, 100°F to 110°F. Combine with the yeast, sugar, and mo-lasses in a large mixing bowl, cover tightly with plastic wrap, and set in a warm place to bloom for 15 minutes. Add the rye, wheat flours, and salt. Mix gently to wet the flour, and then pause for 5 minutes to let the flour hydrate. Knead for a few turns in the bowl until the dough starts to come together. It will be quite sticky at this point.

Turn the dough out onto a well-floured board, using all-purpose flour, and knead for 12 to 15 minutes, adding flour only as necessary to prevent sticking. As you go along, the dough will become less sticky and require less flour. When the dough is tacky and not sticky, and is smooth and elastic, it is ready.

Butter a mixing bowl with 1 tablespoon of the butter and place the ball of dough in the bowl. Butter the top of the dough with 1 tablespoon of butter, and cover with plas-tic wrap. Set in a warm, draft-free spot to rise until doubled in bulk, 60 to 90 minutes.

Lightly butter two 12-by-18-inch baking sheets with the remaining tablespoon of butter. Return the dough to a lightly floured board and cut into twelve equal pieces. Lightly flour the pieces and rest for 15 minutes to relax the gluten. Using as little addi-tional dusting flour as possible, take each piece of dough and roll out into a long rope about 12 to 15 inches long and ½ inch in circumference. Turn each end back over the center, one under the other, to form a classic, loose pretzel knot. Gently transfer, one by one, to the buttered baking sheets, allowing an inch between pretzels for expansion. Allow to rest and rise for 15 to 20 minutes while you preheat the oven and prepare the boil.

Preheat oven to 425°F.

Heat the water to a medium boil in a 4- or 6-quart dutch oven, and add the baking soda. Gently lift each pretzel with a dough card or bench knife, and turn it, knot side down, into the boiling water. Cook three to four at a time. Boil for 30 seconds on the first side, turn, and boil 30 seconds more. Use a spider strainer to remove each pretzel, tapping gently against the pot to drip off excess water, and return to the buttered baking sheet, knot side up. Sprinkle liberally with Maldon salt, caraway, sesame and poppy seed, and onion flakes while still wet and steamy. Continue until all pretzels are boiled.

Bake for 15 minutes on the top rack of the oven, rotating the pans once for even browning. Serve hot with lots of butter or **COLD-PACK CHEESE** (p. 100).

Conchas Chocolates

Many boys dream of becoming sports stars, firemen, or doctors, but most of what I ever dreamed about was our next family trip to Detroit to visit Grandma Melba Morelos and fam, where we would also pay a visit to La Gloria Panaderia, land of sugar-charged fantasies of pan dulce and tres leches.

One of the breads belonging to the class pan dulce, conchas achieved widespread popularity in Mexico in the twentieth century, relatively recently for a country with such a long and rich history of baking. Slow to take root in a land with complex corn-based foodways, pan dulce was nonetheless widespread enough in Mexico to merit several receipts in Manuel Galvan Rivera's 1845 *Diccionario de cocina*,[12] and the types and variety of pan dulce being made increased greatly during the nineteenth century. According to Salvador Novo in his history of the cuisine of Mexico City, the stunning variety of *bizcochos* and sweet rolls that we find today in Mexican *panaderias* was a natural result of the efforts of Indigenous workers in the seventeenth- and eighteenth-century bakeries. Novo writes that their work gave them "the chance to resume the small creation of edible gods of pigs, of offerings to the dead: ceramics—in the soft clay of the dough, for the infinite opulence of shells, trifles, bread of the dead, sesame buns, chamucos, ties, horns, rings, pinches, picones, campechanas, butter bones, worms."[13] It's a charming passage, but the fact is that Indigenous workers were virtually enslaved, bound by debt peonage, in the bakeries by mostly European owners.[14] By speaking of this enslavement (or simply glossing over it as if it hadn't happened) as a "chance," Novo betrays a hopelessly colonialist point of view, but he nevertheless gives credit to Indigenous Mexicans for what has most often been ascribed to European bakers: the prodigious creativity that would yield an unequaled variety of breads and pastries. Out of this mix, conchas would emerge as iconic during the twentieth century, as pan dulce transitioned from a pricey indulgence of the elite to the bread of the masses.[15]

Mexican immigrants brought their taste (and recipes) for pan dulce to the United States. American cooks and bakeries have taken to conchas as my family did, and they are one of an increasing number of Mexican foods we can begin to call Mexican-American as they take on a life of their own in el Norte. For her own part, over years, Grandma took up making conchas at home for Grandpa. When Mom and I were going through Grandma's kitchen papers a couple of years after her passing, we were delighted to find her conchas recipe, which I've adapted here.

For almost any application of cinnamon, I like to use either Mexican cinnamon or Korintje cinnamon, both of which are true cinnamon and have a mild, sweet fragrance worth seeking out. Typical grocery-store cinnamon is cassia, the bark of a tree with a similar but "hotter" aroma and notably more bitterness. If using regular cinnamon, halve the amount. You can easily find Mexican cinnamon in a Mexican market.

Makes 10 conchas

FOR THE DOUGH

¾ cup whole milk

1 teaspoon instant yeast

½ cup plus 1 teaspoon sugar, divided

1½ teaspoons superfine sea salt

1 tablespoon Mexican vanilla extract

1 tablespoon orange zest, finely grated

3 tablespoons unsalted butter, softened

2 large eggs, plus 1 egg yolk, white reserved for topping

3¼ cups all-purpose flour, sifted before measuring

Gently heat the milk until warm, but not hot, to the touch—110°F; about 20 to 30 seconds in a microwave should do it. Stir in the yeast and 1 teaspoon of the sugar. Allow to rest for 30 to 60 minutes, until the yeast is active and the mixture is foamy. Place the yeast mixture in a large mixing bowl and add the remaining dough ingredients. Mix well with a sturdy rubber spatula, scraping the bottom of the bowl and turning over the top of the mixture. Once the ingredients are incorporated and the dough is a rough mass, let the dough rest for 10 minutes so the fine grains of flour can hydrate.

Resume mixing by kneading with your hands right in the bowl. The dough will be tacky, but use as little flour as possible to knead—you want a soft dough. Knead for 5 to 6 minutes, until the dough is smooth and pliable. Oil the dough ball on all sides. Cover with plastic wrap and allow to rise until doubled in bulk, 60 to 90 minutes.

FOR THE TOPPING

½ cup granulated sugar

¼ teaspoon kosher salt

1 teaspoon Mexican vanilla extract

5 tablespoons unsalted butter, softened

1 teaspoon ground Mexican or Korintje cinnamon, or ½ teaspoon regular
cinnamon

3 tablespoons unsweetened cocoa powder

½ cup all-purpose flour

While the dough rises, make the topping. Using an electric beater or food processor, blend together the sugar, salt, vanilla, butter, and cinnamon until combined but still a little crumbly—the mixture should pack into tight, pasty balls when squeezed. Using a sturdy rubber spatula, stir in the cocoa, then the flour, to form a thick paste. Cover and refrigerate until needed.

SHAPING AND BAKING

Whip the egg white with a fork until frothy, about 2 minutes, and reserve.

Lightly oil a 12-by-18-inch baking sheet, or two smaller ones. Turn the dough out onto a lightly floured work surface and divide into 10 equal pieces, then roll each into a ball. To do this, make your hand into a cup by first making an OK sign with your thumb and forefinger and then aligning the rest of your fingers with the forefinger to create a cup shape. Place this cupped hand over a single piece of dough, with your thumb and pinky flat against the counter. Roll the dough ball around under your hand, applying gentle pressure, to create a taut ball of dough, using the friction from the countertop and guidance from your thumb and pinky to keep the balls rolling smoothly. Be sure to keep your thumb and pinky in firm contact with the countertop so that the ball of dough doesn't get mashed. Space the balls evenly, at least 3 inches apart, on the baking sheet.

Preheat oven to 325°F.

Divide the topping into ten equal parts. Roll each into a ball, then roll each ball out into a flat disk, about 3½ inches round, between two sheets of waxed paper, plastic wrap, or parchment. One by one, brush each ball of dough with egg white and drape a disk of topping over it, tucking the edges slightly. Continue until all rolls are topped. Allow to rise until doubled in bulk and puffy, 30 to 45 minutes. At the 30-minute mark, whether fully risen or not, use a baker's lame or clean razor blade to score in artful designs, such as the classic seashell or "concha." Once fully risen and puffy, place the rolls on the center rack of the oven and bake about 20 minutes, until the center of the rolls registers 185°F on a food thermometer.

Sorghum Pecan Sticky Rolls

Like many other Midwestern foods, cinnamon rolls are a relatively recent invention, which may seem a little difficult to believe. While it's commonly believed that these decadent swirls of spice-perfumed, buttery dough, sugar, and egg were invented in Sweden, there is no evidence that they arrived in the United States from there. However, the absence of evidence does not mean they didn't. In *The Boston Cooking-School Cookbook* of 1896, Fannie Farmer lists a recipe for Swedish rolls, which are glazed with nothing more than a whipped egg white.[16]

The Chelsea bun was the Nashville Hot Chicken of eighteenth-century London, an absolute sensation among royalty and gentry alike, until the eponymous Chelsea Bun House was condemned and demolished in 1839.[17] The Chelsea bun, flavored with cinnamon, rolled, cut, and baked with an exposed spiral shape, was the first publicized roll we would recognize as resembling a cinnamon roll today.[18] Cinnamon rolls weren't named as such until the late nineteenth century, appearing under that name in a newspaper recipe in 1872[19] and as "cinnamon buns" in a cookbook in 1883.[20] Some early recipes call for hot-from-the-oven rolls to be brushed with simple syrup to glaze them, but today the two prevailing ways to glaze them are to slather them with white royal icing, or to coat the bottom of the baking dish with additional butter and sugar to create more of a candied glaze; the latter method gives us the sticky roll.

This sticky roll recipe follows the line of the German *Schnecken*, or snails, named for their spiral shape. The sticky glaze forms on the bottom during baking, and when you turn the rolls bottom-side-up hot out of the oven, you get a sticky butter-and-caramel-soaked crown. The sensation of crispy edges you also get from this technique can be heightened with nuts. Cinnamon rolls, the plain-baked rolls that are glazed with royal icing, claimed by Swedes and American bakers alike, tend to be softer. Both are hearty, textured treats.

Ever since I started working on my own cinnamon roll recipes some thirty years ago, I've experimented with some older-school treatments to the pastry and employed more rustic lamination techniques. I typically use cardamom or coriander in addition to orange peel to flavor the dough, which in home kitchens has almost always been a simple yeast-roll dough with perhaps a whisper of cinnamon in addition to what gets rolled inside.

Kneading cold butter into the dough is easiest in a stand mixer with a dough hook. You can, of course, soften the butter to room temperature and add it with the wet mix before kneading. You'll still get a great sticky roll, just not quite so flaky. I recommend cooler fermentation temperatures for this dough in order to keep the butter from weeping, so allow ample time for the first and second rises.

Makes 12 large rolls, enough to fill a 9-by-11-inch casserole or 12 large muffin tins

FOR THE DOUGH

1 cup plus 2 tablespoons whole milk

1 tablespoon instant yeast

4 cups all-purpose flour, divided

1 teaspoon salt

1 teaspoon ground coriander

2 teaspoons orange zest, very finely grated

2 large eggs

¾ cup (1½ sticks) unsalted butter, chilled and cut into small bits

Heat the milk in a small saucepan over low heat to 100°F to 110°F. Remove from heat, stir in the yeast, and set the mixture aside until the yeast forms a head of foam and is very active, about 15 minutes.

Transfer the mixture to the bowl of a stand mixer with the paddle attachment. Add 2 cups of the flour, the salt, coriander, and orange zest. Mix on low speed until smooth, 3 to 4 minutes. Switch to the dough hook, retrieving any dough that sticks to the paddle attachment. With the mixer running on low speed, add 1 egg and another ½ cup flour, and mix until completely integrated. Add the other egg and another ½ cup flour, turn the mixer up to medium speed, and continue mixing until smooth.

After a few minutes, the dough will be thick and somewhat heavy, but smooth and elastic. Continue running the mixer on medium speed and add the cold butter in bits, alternating with sprinkles of the last ½ cup flour, continuing until all is incorporated and you have a smooth, elastic dough, about 10 minutes. You will need to stop the mixer periodically and scrape down the sides of the bowl. Oil or butter the top of the dough, cover tightly with plastic wrap, and set in a well-ventilated spot at 68°F to 70°F to double in bulk, which will take 60 to 90 minutes.

FOR THE GLAZE

¾ cup (1½ sticks) butter, chilled and cut into small pieces

¾ cup sorghum molasses

Whole pecan halves sufficient to cover the bottom of your baking dish, about
   12 ounces

Place the butter and molasses in a small saucepan and heat slowly, whisking as often as needed to emulsify into a smooth, thick glaze. Liberally butter two large 6-count muffin tins or a 9-by-13-inch casserole. Spread the glaze evenly over the bottom. Add a layer of pecan halves, with the rounded sides facing down so they will face up when turned out after baking.

SHAPING AND BAKING

½ cup (1 stick) unsalted butter, softened to room temperature

½ cup dark brown sugar

1 teaspoon ground cinnamon

½ teaspoon ground allspice

Knead the dough in the bowl for 3 or 4 turns to degas the dough and form a ball. Roll the dough out into a rectangle roughly 12 by 18 inches. Spread evenly with the softened butter. Combine the brown sugar, cinnamon, and allspice and sprinkle the mixture evenly over the buttered dough. From the long side of the rectangle, roll the dough up into a log about 18 inches long, carefully tucking under as you roll. Cut into 12 equal pieces, and evenly distribute them over the glazed baking dish, leaving room between them for expansion. Brush the tops of the rolls with butter and gently tamp down the tops of the rolls to pat them into the nuts. Cover loosely with plastic wrap and leave them at room temperature for their final rise to double in bulk again, 30 to 45 minutes.

Preheat oven to 350°F.

Place the rolls on the bottom rack of the oven and bake until puffy and golden brown and the center of the rolls registers 185°F on a food thermometer, 30 to 40 minutes. Use a sharp knife to loosen around the edges of the pan, and while still hot, invert a sheet pan or serving dish over the rolls, turn the whole thing over, and give a couple of vigorous shakes to loosen the rolls. Tap the bottom of the pan with a wooden spoon to help loosen the rolls if needed. Remove the baking pan to reveal your finished sticky rolls. Serve hot for optimal enjoyment.

Pumpernickel

One true pleasure you can have in the Midwest is shopping in Polish or other Central and Eastern European–style supermarkets, bakeries, or delis. You'll find the most in Chicago and Cleveland, but every Midwestern city has at least one market such as Marina's in Cincinnati, Kramarczuk's Sausage Company in Minneapolis, or the Polish Market in Troy, Michigan, where you can find a range of breads that at first glance appear completely alien to mainstream American tastes, but at second glance look a little more familiar. Even in these markets, however, it's increasingly difficult to find breads like those Saul Bellow describes at the head of this chapter: the dark, rugged 100% ryes that fed nations from the Low German duchies east through Poland, Ukraine, and Russia for millennia. I took Bellow's lamentation as a request and did some digging. I had purchased many 100% ryes over the years at Wally's grocery store in Chicago (RIP) and always loved the taste and rich, cheesy texture. These are easily the most flavorful breads you can sink your teeth into, and infinitely more healthful than white wheat breads as well.

I can't read Cyrillic characters or any of the related languages, so Ukrainian- or Russian-language research was off the table, but I was able to find a fair amount of writing in German, including a book on Westphalian pumpernickel from the late eighteenth century. An amusing and fascinating read, it spends as much time espousing the virtues and civilization of bread, particularly the Westphalian variety, as it does explaining the process of making it. It also contains this cute snippet explaining the origin of the name "pumpernickel," which is a common folktale and almost certainly not true:

> It is said that this bread got the name pumpernickel from a Frenchman travel-ing through Westphalia who demanded bread, and was given it. As soon as he saw it, he felt badly and said: "C'est bon pour nickel," which was the name of his horse. Bonpournickel became pumpernickel.[21]

An irony of this bread is how easy it is to make, the long oven time aside. Of the thousands of recipes I have developed over my career, this was easily the most challenging, requiring almost a dozen formulations. You can count on a full 24 hours, or better yet 2 days, from when the mix is started until you are slicing your loaf, but it is worth every minute because you'll have a rich, tangy, and hearty bread in a quantity sufficient to feed a small army for a week.

Thinly sliced and eaten as is, toasted, or griddled, this rustic rye is great buttered or topped with marmalade, jam, cream cheese, smoked or pickled fish, or cured meats. It's one of my favorite breads to keep around the house because it can be nibbled on for a week or more with little deterioration in quality (one Polish friend's father insisted it tastes best after at least a week); it keeps better than any other bread I know. Simply wrap it securely in plastic wrap and store it at room temperature.

Once baked, the ideal is to leave the bread covered in its pan to cool fully to room temperature. Slice with a serrated bread knife wet with cold water. Don't

use too much downward pressure—count on the back-and-forth sawing motion to do the cutting and you'll get perfect slices as thin or as thick as you like.

Makes one 6-pound pullman loaf

The night before you want to make your bread, make the two starter doughs:

DOUGH 1

> 2 pounds cracked dark rye meal
> 3½ cups boiling water

Place the rye in a heat-resistant mixing bowl and dig a large well in the center. Pour
all the boiling water in at once and, working quickly, mix with a stiff rubber spatula or
wooden spoon until thoroughly mixed with the water distributed evenly throughout the
grain. The mixture won't really come together into a dough or paste, it'll just look like
a lumpy meal. Just make sure it's evenly mixed with no dry grain left and you're good.
Cover tightly with plastic wrap and rest at room temperature for at least 6 but not more
than 8 hours.

DOUGH 2

> 1 pound coarse-cracked dark rye meal
> 1 cup **RYE SOURDOUGH STARTER** (recipe follows)
> 1 cup warm water, 100°F to 110°F

Mix thoroughly. Like dough 1, this mixture will not come together entirely; just make
sure both the starter and water are evenly mixed throughout the grain. Cover tightly
with plastic wrap and rest at room temperature for at least 6 but not more than 8 hours.

TO FINISH THE DOUGH AND BAKE THE BREAD

> 3 tablespoons kosher salt
> 2 tablespoons unsalted butter
> Water as needed for rolling the dough and steaming in the oven

Place two cake pans full of water in the bottom of the oven; you want a very humid
environment. Place a pizza stone on the bottom rack.
    Preheat oven to 250°F for at least 1 hour.
    Place both doughs and the salt in the bowl of a stand mixer with the dough hook

attached. Mix on medium-low speed. At first, the mixture will look as if it will never come together, but your patience will be rewarded. Scrape down the sides of the bowl every minute because it will tend to climb up the sides at first, where it will not mix. Mix for a full 10 minutes, by which time it will have formed a very coarse, yet sticky and firm, dough.

Thoroughly butter a 13-by-4-inch pullman bread pan, including the inside of the lid, with the 2 tablespoons of butter. Fill a small bowl with warm water to wet your hands while you shape the dough—it'll help prevent sticking. Wet your hands and a clean work surface, then remove the dough from the mixing bowl, place it on the wet work surface, and pat it together into a ball. Wet your hands again, and shape the ball into a long log. Transfer to the pan and pat thoroughly into the bottom and all corners, flattening the top. Slide the lid onto the pan.

Place on the pizza stone in the oven, shut the door, and reduce the heat to 210°F to 220°F. Bake for 16 hours, refilling the cake pans with boiling water as needed to keep them full and the oven steamy.

Allow the bread to cool in the pan with the lid on until it reaches room temperature. Wrap tightly and store at room temperature.

RYE SOURDOUGH STARTER

This is an excellent starter for any lean, unenriched sourdough bread. By keeping the ratio of water to flour 50:50, this recipe makes calculating hydration easy. I like to make this starter in 1-quart deli containers, leaving the lid loose during building, so that when I want to refrigerate or freeze it, I simply need to snap the lid shut. As you are building or cultivating the starter over 5 days, do so at room temperature, ideally below 75°F. Using filtered or spring water will make a livelier starter.

It's important to always have the starter in a container that is at least double the volume of the starter, so in case it expands, it doesn't overflow.

Day 1: Mix 1 ounce dark rye flour with 1 ounce water. Place the lid on the container loosely.

Day 2: There may be some evidence of fermentation (bubbles or starter rising up the sides of the container), but probably not yet. Add 1 ounce each dark rye flour and water. Replace the lid loosely.

Day 3: There should be evidence of fermentation, yet it should still be sluggish (small increase in starter bulk or a small number of bubbles). Add 2 ounces each dark rye flour and water. Replace the lid loosely.

Day 4: There should be evidence of the fermentation picking up (more rising or more bubbles). Add 4 ounces each dark rye flour and water. Replace the lid loosely.

Day 5: Give away, discard, or freeze 1 cup of the starter so you are starting again
    with 1 cup. Add 4 ounces each of dark rye flour and water. Place in a 1-quart
    container with a clean cloth secured with a rubber band as the lid.

Day 6: By now, the starter should have more than doubled in bulk overnight. It is
    ready to use.

Freeze any unused starter in 4-ounce portions, tightly sealed. To refresh it, thaw one
4-ounce portion at room temperature for a few hours, then begin the starter process
on day 3 above.

Friendship Bread

When word got around to family and friends that I was working on this book,
one of the recipes I was asked to include was Amish Friendship Bread. A rich,
cinnamon-scented loaf often baked in a bread pan and glazed with a sweet
royal icing, Friendship Bread is unique among what we know today as sourdough breads because it's a fortified dough, one including eggs, milk, sugar,
and other ingredients, as opposed to the lean, flour-only sourdoughs that dom-
inate modern bakeries.

I winced at the notion of including Amish Friendship Bread in a book claiming to shoot straight and tell no lies about Midwestern food, but I decided it
was best to include this recipe for two reasons. First, it's absolutely delicious,
whether slathered in butter straight out of the oven, toasted and drizzled with
honey, or battered and griddled into ridiculously good french toast. Second,
it's a perfect metaphor for the story of Midwestern cuisine as we've known
it versus the reality. Truth is, its story is cute, but someone made it up out of
whole cloth for reasons we can't really know.

When it swept the small-town Midwest by storm during the 1980s, the story
was that this recipe was an *ooooold* Amish tradition and it was called Friendship Bread because as you keep feeding the starter, you eventually wind up
with too much and have to give some of it away to a friend, and then they to
another, and so on, like some sort of culinary chain letter. Amish lore has it
that a starter would be a gift from the mother of a bride to her daughter to help
her begin life in her own home.[22] There is some truth to the idea that a mother
might give her departing daughter some of the homemade yeast she maintained painstakingly week in and week out throughout her life (in the time before commercial baking yeast became available), but the suggestion that this

practice was in any way specific to Friendship Bread, or that this particular recipe is an old-timey Amish tradition, stands on a flimsy basis.

I couldn't find any real evidence of Amish lineage for this specific bread,
or references to it in the popular media, until 1987.[23] The "Friendship Bread"
occasionally mentioned in newspapers around the country before that time is
a generic kind of "Swedish Christmas (Friendship) Bread,"[24] or a catchall term
for sourdough bread,[25] or a biscuit-and-honey construction for New Year's
Eve,[26] or even a prize-winning bread that uses dry active yeast and no sourdough starter at all![27] One tantalizing mention in the Lancaster, Pennsylvania,
Intelligencer Journal on October 27, 1982, describes "Friendship Bread" as "a
delicious concoction of cranberries, raisins and apples in sourdough bread."
In his excellent book *As American as Shoofly Pie*, noted scholar of Pennsylvania
Dutch cooking William Woys Weaver described it as a product of Lancaster
County gift shops and not part of the day-to-day reality of Amish households.[28]
It does appear in a handful of contemporary Amish cookbooks, but this seems
to be due to the feedback loop between what the public is buying and what
those marketing Amish culture can sell them.

Fakelore aside, it's a wonderful bread to keep around the house because it's
excellent straight out of the oven and as much as a week later. Once you've
gone to the daily trouble of making the starter, it's also easy to make the bread,
and the smell of it baking is its own special kind of aromatherapy that'll keep
you in good spirits.

This starter gets a boost with baking yeast straight away and will sour over
time. Distilled or spring water is not absolutely essential, but tap water contains
chlorine and fluoride and will inhibit the friendly bacteria. When maintaining
the starter, keep in mind that *Saccharomyces*, or traditional baking yeast, feeds
on simple sugars, while the souring bacteria feed on more complex dextrins
they get from the milk and flour. If your starter is getting sluggish, or not providing the lift required in a reasonable time, you can up the sugar a day or two
before using it to make your bread.

Makes one 3-pound loaf

FOR THE STARTER

    3 cups all-purpose flour, divided

    ¾ cup plus 1 tablespoon granulated sugar, divided

    1 teaspoon dry active yeast

    1 cup distilled or spring water, warm, 100°F to 110°F

    1½ cups whole milk, divided

Combine 1 cup flour, 1 tablespoon sugar, and the yeast, then stir in the warm water and beat until smooth. Place in a tall 1-quart container and cover with a clean cloth, securing the edges with a rubber band. Place in a warm spot, free of drafts, for 1 day. Then, follow this schedule until the starter is ready:

Days 2, 3, 4, and 5: Stir the starter gently; do nothing else.
Day 6: Add 1 cup flour, ½ cup milk, and ¼ cup sugar; stir; transfer to a larger container.
Day 7: Stir the starter gently; do nothing else.
Day 8: Add ½ cup flour, ½ cup milk, and ¼ cup sugar; stir.
Day 9: Stir the starter gently; do nothing else.
Day 10: Add ½ cup flour, ½ cup milk, and ¼ cup sugar; stir.

The starter is ready once it has a pleasant, winey sour smell and a sweet, tangy taste without a hint of flour.

Stir once a day; once a week thereafter, give away or discard half the starter and feed the remaining half with the following:

½ cup all-purpose flour
¼ cup whole milk
1 tablespoon granulated sugar

Always divide and feed the starter the day before you plan to use it.

To "pause" the starter when you don't plan to use it for several days or more, it may be refrigerated in a sealed container for up to 1 week, or frozen in a sealed container for months. To refresh the starter, thaw 4 days before you want to bake and start feeding as on day 8 above.

MAKING THE BREAD

3 cups all-purpose flour, sifted before measuring, plus more for dusting
3 tablespoons granulated sugar
½ teaspoon baking powder
1 teaspoon kosher salt
1 teaspoon ground cinnamon
1 teaspoon ground cardamom
5 tablespoons unsalted butter, chilled and cut into pea-sized bits, plus more for buttering pan and loaf
3 large eggs
2 cups **FRIENDSHIP BREAD STARTER** (above)

2 teaspoons pure vanilla extract

¾ cup pecans or black walnuts, chopped

¾ cup sultana raisins

Combine the flour, sugar, baking powder, salt, cinnamon, and cardamom, then sift together into a mixing bowl. Add the cut pieces of butter and, after coating your hands with flour, flatten each bit of butter into a disk about the size of a dime. In a separate bowl, beat the eggs, then add the starter and vanilla extract, and combine thoroughly. Pour the starter mixture over the flour mixture and mix until incorporated. Using floured hands, knead the dough in the bowl without adding more flour until it begins to form a rough ball. Knead in the chopped nuts and raisins. Place in a buttered mixing bowl with room for the dough to expand, flour the top, and cover loosely with plastic wrap. Place in a warm spot to rise until doubled in bulk, 1 hour.

Preheat oven to 350°F.

Punch the dough down, knead back into a sticky ball, and transfer to a buttered loaf or large bundt pan. Butter the top of the dough, cover loosely with plastic wrap, and allow to rise until it has increased in size by half. Place on the bottom rack of the oven and bake for 30 minutes. Transfer to the top rack and bake an additional 10 to 20 minutes, until the interior of the bread registers 185°F on a food thermometer. Allow to cool 10 to 15 minutes before unmolding.

FOR THE ICING

3 tablespoons whole milk

Pinch salt

Zest of 1 lemon, very finely grated

2 cups confectioners' sugar

While you are waiting to unmold the bread, make the icing. Stir the milk, salt, and lemon zest into the confectioners' sugar gradually until incorporated, then stir vigorously until smooth. Unmold the bread and spread the icing over it while still warm, so it can melt and form a thin glaze.

Enjoy hot or place in a bread box while still warm.

Apfelkuchen

As we Fehribach kids got into high school, our household was bustling, and the baking gradually devolved into quick breads that were fast and satisfying, but for Christmas Mom would sometimes make a traditional apfelkuchen, for which we would all swoon. It was an edible way to celebrate the German part of our heritage. Kuchen can still be found in bakeries throughout the Midwest, and they appear in multiple forms in two of the most popular and influential cookbooks to come out of the Midwest at the turn of the twentieth century: *Aunt Babette's Cook Book* and *The Settlement Cook Book*, both of which were written by Ashkenazi Jewish women and successful enough to go through several editions.[29] The extra time required for fermentation and proofing of these delectable yeast cakes caused them to decline in popularity during the twentieth century as chemical leavening became the favored way to give lift to cakes of all kinds. True kuchen may yet seem familiar to those who purchase yeast-raised coffee cakes at supermarkets or bakeries: kuchen and the related stollen are the original versions.

If you're adventurous, you can make this recipe with 1 cup **FRIENDSHIP BREAD** starter (p. 76) in place of the yeast and milk. Add extra flour a tablespoon at a time until the dough comes together. To do a simpler, long fermentation, make the kuchen dough, put it through one rise, punch it down, and refrigerate it, in a covered airtight container, for 3 to 5 days. Allow an extra 2 hours for it to come to room temperature and double in bulk.

As far as cooking apples go, my favorites in Chicago are Northern Spies, Calville Blanc d'Hivers, Gravensteins, Red Cortlands, Empires, Macouns, and Esopus Spitzenburgs. Pippins and Arkansas Blacks are great, too. Northern Spies and Calville Blanc d'Hivers in particular are good because they'll soften nicely but also retain their shape. Widely available Granny Smiths work, but the ones you'll find in the grocery store may not fully soften by the time the rest of the kuchen is done.

Makes one 10-inch kuchen

FOR THE PASTRY

¼ cup plus 2 tablespoons whole milk

2 teaspoons instant yeast

2 tablespoons granulated sugar, divided

2 large eggs, beaten

2 teaspoons pure vanilla extract

½ teaspoon kosher salt

Zest of 1 orange, finely grated

1 teaspoon ground cinnamon

2¼ cups all-purpose flour, plus more for dusting

½ cup (1 stick) unsalted butter, chilled and cut into very thin slices

Heat the milk to lukewarm, 100°F to 110°F. Dissolve the yeast and 1 tablespoon sugar in the milk. Rest until the yeast activates and forms a thin, foamy head on the milk. In a mixing bowl, combine the milk mixture with the remaining sugar, eggs, vanilla, salt, orange zest, and cinnamon. Whisk to combine, then add all the flour at once, and mix by hand until the dough comes together and forms a rough ball. Turn out onto a lightly floured board and knead for 4 to 5 minutes, working in a slice of cold butter every 30 seconds. Once all the butter is incorporated and you have a soft, springy, and tacky dough, put it back in the mixing bowl, cover with plastic, and let rise until doubled in bulk, 45 minutes to 1 hour.

SHAPING AND BAKING

3 tablespoons melted butter, divided

2 to 3 cooking apples, peeled, cored, and thinly sliced on the pinwheel to obtain identical half-moon slices

2 tablespoons good bourbon whiskey

Juice of ½ lemon

½ cup plus 1 tablespoon dark brown sugar, divided

1 teaspoon ground cinnamon, divided

1 tablespoon butter, softened, to butter pan

1 large egg, beaten and strained

Melt 2 tablespoons butter in a sauté pan. Cook the apple slices in the butter over medium heat just to blanch them, 3 to 4 minutes. Look for the edges of the apples to turn translucent and tender, but don't cook all the way through. Add the bourbon, lemon juice, ¼ cup of the brown sugar, and ½ teaspoon of the cinnamon. Toss to dissolve the sugar and glaze the apples, then remove from heat to cool while you shape the cake.

Butter a 10-inch tart pan. Roll out the dough into a disk to fit, and tuck it into the buttered pan, massaging the dough into the corners and leaving a little extra around the edges to raise them, like a pizza or a shallow pie. Whisk together the beaten egg, 1 tablespoon brown sugar, and 1 tablespoon melted butter until smooth. Brush the mixture over the dough, covering all areas evenly.

Beginning in the center, arrange the cooled apple slices in a fan, overlapping each slice by ¼ inches, spiraling away from the center until the entire kuchen is covered but leaving ½ inch uncovered around the edges. Reserve the remaining syrupy glaze in the pan. Gently tamp the apples down into the glazed dough. Rest for 20 minutes.

Preheat the oven to 325°F.

Reheat the remaining glaze from cooking the apples over medium heat, add the remaining ¼ cup brown sugar and ½ teaspoon cinnamon, and stir until smooth. Add bourbon a few drops at a time if the mixture is too dry—you want a thick glaze like a caramel or chocolate sauce.

Place the kuchen in the center of the top rack of the oven. Bake until the kuchen is browning nicely, about 30 minutes. Brush the bourbon and brown sugar glaze over all the apples and cake every 5 minutes beginning at the 30-minute mark. Bake until the apples are soft, golden, and shiny and the cake base registers at least 185°F on a food thermometer, about 50 minutes total. Serve warm or store covered at room temperature for up to 1 day.

"Chicago Hardy" Fig Kringle

Only a small handful of states have shown enough devotion to a pastry to designate one as a state symbol, and one of them, Wisconsin, has chosen something special. The kringle is the official state pastry of Wisconsin, and the kringle tradition is strong enough that the legend has spread to nearby states, and its notoriety is on the rise.

Kringle culture centers around the southeastern Wisconsin town of Racine, on the western shore of Lake Michigan, populated by waves of Danish, German, and Czech immigrants. In Europe, kringles are traditional in all the Nordic states, from Norway to Estonia and west to Denmark. Wisconsin is home to people of Swedish, Norwegian, and Danish heritage, but in Racine, the kringle is widely attributed to the Danish, and its dough is quintessentially Danish: a sweet yeast dough laminated with dozens of layers of butter, yielding a feathery crumb that is rich yet light.

Like the king cake of New Orleans, the kringle has been subjected to the never-ending imaginations of generations of bakers, and bakeries such as Racine's O&H Danish Bakery and Bendtsen's offer numerous flavors, from the simple and traditional almond or apricot fillings to more whimsical, modern types such as turtle cheesecake or caramel pumpkin spice. You can use any type of fruit compote or preserve you desire in this recipe. I decided to celebrate the revival of the Chicago Hardy fig, a delicious specimen bred in the Great Lakes region during the nineteenth century, then forgotten. In recent years, an increasing number of orchards have been planting these figs, and they are divine. You may find them available from your local orchardist at a farmers' market, and if not, you can certainly ask about them—they may be willing to plant a few trees! To make the filling below, you can use any fresh fig.

When making laminated dough like this, I always find it easiest to prepare the dough and butter on day 1, then do one turn each subsequent day to ensure it is deeply chilled. This makes the time commitment much more manageable, and importantly, on baking day you can go straight to shaping, proofing, and baking over a couple of hours, rather than trying to manage the long process in one day. To do this, start 5 days before you want to bake.

Makes 1 kringle approximately 12 by 16 inches, serves 6 to 12

FOR THE FILLING

2 pints fresh figs

½ cup clover honey

Zest of ½ orange, grated

½ teaspoon salt

Place figs in a heavy-bottomed stainless-steel or enamel saucepan and add the honey. Over low heat, slowly render the figs to bring the juice out, then increase heat to medium and bring the figs to a low boil. This step could take ½ hour or more. Use the back of a wooden spoon to mash the figs against the side of the pot, reduce heat to a simmer, and, stirring often, simmer until excess liquid is gone and you have a thick paste, up to 3 hours. Stir in the orange zest and salt. Cover and cool to room temperature before using, or refrigerate for up to 1 month.

FOR THE PASTRY

¼ cup plus 2 tablespoons whole milk

2 teaspoons instant yeast

3 tablespoons granulated sugar, divided

1 large egg, beaten

½ teaspoon kosher salt

Zest of 1 lemon, finely grated

½ teaspoon ground cardamom

1¾ cups all-purpose flour, sifted, plus more for dusting

½ cup (1 stick) unsalted butter, softened slightly, plus more for buttering pan

Heat the milk to lukewarm, 100°F to 110°F. Dissolve the yeast and 1 tablespoon sugar in the milk and rest until the yeast activates and forms a thin, foamy head on the milk.

In a mixing bowl, combine the milk mixture with the remaining 2 tablespoons sugar, egg, salt, lemon zest, and cardamom. Whisk to combine, then add all the flour at once, and mix by hand until the dough comes together and forms a rough ball, but don't overknead. Cover tightly with plastic wrap and refrigerate overnight.

Soften the butter slightly at room temperature, until just soft enough to work but still somewhat firm. Lay a 12-by-12-inch piece of waxed paper on a board, lightly flour, and place the butter in the center. Lightly flour the top of the butter, cover with another piece of waxed paper, and, using a rolling pin, carefully roll the butter out into a rectangle about 8 by 4 inches, pausing to flour the butter if necessary. Wrap in plastic wrap and refrigerate overnight.

The following day, on a lightly floured board, roll the dough out into a rectangle about 16 by 8 inches, or a little more than twice the size of the butter. Place the butter on the right side of the dough, leaving a little room around the top, bottom, and right edges. Fold the left side of the dough over the right, and tightly crimp the bottom and side to seal the butter in. Turn the rectangle 90 degrees so that the longer side runs left to right. Fold the right third of the dough over the center, then the left third over that, as if it were a brochure. Wrap in plastic wrap and refrigerate at least 30 minutes, or overnight. You now have three layers of butter.

If dough was refrigerated overnight, allow it to soften for 15 minutes before rolling out, so the butter is pliable but not squishy. Slowly roll out the dough to its 16-by-8-inch pre-folding size, being careful to maintain a rectangle shape. Fold in the same manner as before, for nine layers of butter. Refrigerate at least 30 minutes, or overnight. Repeat once again, for twenty-seven layers. I think twenty-seven is optimal, but if you want to go into super-feathery croissant territory, repeat one more time, for eighty-one layers. Refrigerate for 30 minutes or overnight.

Slowly and patiently, roll the dough out on a lightly floured board, working only lengthwise, to obtain a long rectangle about 6 by 24 inches. Spread the fig paste evenly over the center 3 inches of the dough, leaving an inch or so on each long side clean. Fold one of the long edges to just slightly over the middle, covering half of the fig paste to the center. Wet the other long edge with a little cold water and dust very lightly with flour, then fold it over to overlap the other edge at the center of the what is now a long, flat log. Press down firmly along the joined edges into the center of the log, making a slight V down the middle, to seal tightly.

Bring one end around to meet the other, wet that end with a little cold water and dust very lightly with flour, then insert the dry end into the wet end, and press all the way around to seal. You should now have a ring or oval.

Line a 12-by-18-inch baking sheet with well-buttered parchment and gently transfer the kringle, leaving room around the edges of the sheet for it to expand. Cover loosely with plastic wrap and let rise at room temperature for 1 hour to 90 minutes, or until doubled in bulk.

Preheat oven to 375°F.

Place the kringle on the top rack of the oven and bake for 25 minutes, until puffy and golden brown. Cool to room temperature before icing.

FOR THE ICING

2 tablespoons freshly squeezed lemon juice

1 cup confectioners' sugar

Beat vigorously with a fork until smooth. Spread over the center of the kringle.

Best served on baking day.

Kansas Zwiebach

These delectable rolls, one of the distinctive foods of German Mennonites, aren't to be confused with the hard, crunchy rusk of the same name you'll find on the dry-goods shelves of grocery stores. The rough translation of the name, often spelled *Zwieback*, is "two bake," or perhaps "double bake." In the case of the "other zwiebach"—crusty biscotti-like treats—the reference is clear: the breads are baked, cut, and baked again until hard and dry. In the case of Mennonite zwiebach, the name refers to the shape: a stack of two rolls, one atop the other, like a tiny snowman without a head. The stacked roll is as cute as a button when executed well; keeping that shape during proofing and baking is one of the challenges a baker faces in mastering these rolls.

There are several recipes for zwiebach in Maria Sophia Schellhammer's *Brandenburgische Koch-Buch*,[30] most of which are elaborately flavored, twice baked, and frosted rusks incorporating rosewater, anise, citrus, coriander, and other flavorings. But it includes at least one, "*Gemeine und schlechte Zwiebach zu backen*" (common and poor zwiebach), that is a simple beer yeast–leavened sweet bread given a single bake, without the flourish and snowman-like shape of the Mennonite zwiebach. Mennonite author Norma Jost Voth traces the origin of that tradition to the Prussian port city of Danzig, where rolls were dried by toasting for ship rations and a larger roll called *Zwiebacke* was also made.[31] Thousands of Mennonites emigrated from the environs of Danzig and West Prussia to modern-day Ukraine, then part of the Russian Empire, at the invitation of Empress Catherine the Great. When the political winds in Russia changed, threatening the Mennonite exemption from military service, tens of thousands would depart for North America beginning in the 1870s.[32]

Mennonites constitute a small religious sect, and their zwiebach is scarcely known outside Kansas, but it's a truly fine bread and worth taking the time to make and enjoy among family and friends.

Makes about 16 to 18 zwiebach

1½ cups whole milk

1 small Russet potato, peeled and diced, about ½ cup

⅓ cup granulated sugar

2 teaspoons instant yeast

¾ cup (1½ sticks) very cold unsalted butter, cut into bits, plus more for buttering pans

1 tablespoon kosher salt

2 large eggs, beaten

5½ cups all-purpose flour, sifted before measuring, plus more for dusting

Egg wash (1 large egg and 1 tablespoon cold water whisked together, for brushing before baking)

Put the milk and potato in a small saucepan and scald the milk, heating to a high simmer. Maintain simmer until the potato pieces are tender, 20 minutes or more. Remove the cooked potato from the milk, mash through a fine mesh strainer, and return it to the milk. Allow to cool to about 130°F, still hot but not so much as to burn you, and stir in the butter to melt it, which will also have the effect of cooling the mixture. Continue stirring until the mixture is lukewarm, 100°F to 110°F. Stir in the sugar, yeast, salt and eggs.

Transfer the milk mixture to a large mixing bowl and sift the flour over the wet mix. Use a heavy spatula or wooden spoon to mix into a tacky dough, then knead in the bowl for 6 to 8 minutes (you can use a stand mixer for this) until the dough is smooth, elastic, and shiny. Cover loosely with plastic wrap and set to rise in a warm place until doubled in bulk, 60 to 90 minutes.

Preheat oven to 325°F.

Degas the dough by kneading in the bowl for 4 or 5 turns while reshaping into a ball. Use a sharp knife to cut (do not stretch or pull) small, clementine-sized (about 2 ounces) pieces of dough, each matched with one smaller walnut-sized (1 ounce or 2 tablespoons) piece of dough. Shape each piece of dough into a ball using the method described for **CONCHAS CHOCOLATES** (p. 66). Arrange the large balls evenly spaced on a buttered or parchment-lined baking sheet, and reserve the small balls on a separate parchment-lined plate or sheet pan dusted with flour to prevent sticking. Cover the rolls loosely with plastic wrap and allow them to rest at room temperature for about 10 minutes to partially proof and relax the gluten.

Use the tip of your thumb to press a well into the center of each large ball all the way to the pan beneath, making a fat donut shape. Wet the inside of the donut hole with a few drops of cold water and place a smaller ball on top. Continue until all rolls are shaped, brush all with egg wash, cover loosely with plastic wrap, and allow to rise at room temperature for another 30 to 45 minutes, by which time they should have doubled in size. When you gently press your finger into one of the rolls, it should spring back, but very slowly.

Bake on the center rack of the oven for 25 minutes, or until golden brown on all sides. Enjoy warm with butter and honey or jam.

Donuts

One of the few things in life that brings joy equally to children and adults is a donut. Simple cake donuts; funnel cakes and churros; the entire range of stuffed donuts from fastnachts to paczki, which we mostly know today as jelly or cream donuts; glazed rings, old fashioneds, crullers, apple fritters . . . donuts are an entire lexicon in themselves. While today we would certainly look upon them as wholly American, their roots are in High German cooking and the Austro-Hungarian Empire. They came to America with German, Polish, Bohemian, and Scandinavian immigrants and under the influence of some important cookbooks.

Amazingly, many forms of donuts we would recognize today were already established in the culinary literature of Reformation-era Germany, including the kitchen manuscripts of Philippine Welser, wife to Archduke Franz Ferdinand II of Austria. These manuscripts include a fried boiled dough that eerily resembles the Mexican churros of today and quite likely pre-dates the churro's alleged origin in Spain. There are also fruit fritters, cheese fritters, and pastries called Krapfen, made from dough stuffed with sweet or savory filling and deep-fried.[33]

The first American printing of Hannah Glasse's popular *Art of Cookery Made Plain and Easy* in 1805 includes a receipt for "dough nuts," which probably represents the first widely published use of the term in English.[34] In 1842, a recipe for "doughnuts" appears in what may be the first cookbook specifically targeted at Midwesterners, yet the method seems derivative of Glasse's.[35] By 1856, ring-shaped fritters called "German dough-nuts" show up in a cookbook published in Philadelphia, next to a recipe for "simple dough-nuts," which may be cut into any shape.[36] As the nineteenth century progressed, doughnuts were included in many cookbooks, including *Aunt Babette's Cook Book* and *The*

Settlement Cook Book. A cookbook for German-speaking Americans published in Milwaukee lists several doughnut recipes, including one for Berlin crullers, which may be the first appearance of a prototypical jelly donut in America.[37]

Today, there are many donut chains nationwide, and new-guard artisan donut shops are popping up from Maine to California. In cities with Polish American populations, paczki are highly sought after for Fat Tuesday and year-round. As with many foods you can easily acquire at a grocery store, it's definitely worth your while to add donuts to your personal repertoire. When you make your own, you can experiment and make them to your exact taste. And you'll impress your family and friends.

Since the possible variations are endless, I'm going to provide a basic yeast donut recipe, and since I was always a junkie for cream-filled chocolate-covered fastnachts, I'll provide an easy pastry cream recipe. You can use any of your favorite jams or jellies as well, and I'll provide a couple simple glaze recipes.

POTATO DONUT DOUGH

Makes about 2 dozen large donuts

> 1 medium Russet potato, approximately ¾ pound, baked, peeled, and riced
>   through a mesh strainer
> 1½ cups buttermilk
> 1 package dry active yeast
> 3 tablespoons granulated sugar
> 1 teaspoon kosher salt
> ¼ teaspoon ground Mexican or Korintje cinnamon
> ½ teaspoon ground coriander
> 1 egg, plus 3 egg yolks
> ½ cup (1 stick) unsalted butter, melted
> 4½ cups all-purpose flour
> A large cast-iron or enamel dutch oven with 2 inches of oil or lard, for frying

Place the riced potato in the bowl of a stand mixer. Heat the buttermilk to warm, 110°F. Add the warmed buttermilk, yeast, sugar, salt, and spices to the bowl and whisk well to combine. Allow to form a sponge for 15 to 30 minutes. The yeast should form a foamy head on the mixture; if not, check every 15 minutes until it does. Whisk in the egg, egg yolks, and butter until smooth. With the dough hook, mix on low while adding all the flour at once and continue until it has been evenly incorporated. The dough will be sticky with a rough appearance caused by the potato. Mix on low speed for 5 more minutes. The dough will still be sticky and mostly hold its shape, but be somewhat slack. Cover and let rise to double in bulk, 45 to 50 minutes.

Mix the dough with the dough hook for 1 minute on low speed to degas it, then form it into a flat disk about 1 inch thick and let it rest to relax the gluten for about 15 minutes while you prepare the frying oil.

Heat the oil or lard to 325°F, monitoring the temperature with a clip-on thermometer.

On a well-floured surface, roll out the dough to about 3/8 inch thick, slightly less than 1/2 inch. Cut into 3-inch squares for stuffed donuts or use pastry rings of different sizes to cut concentric circles for ring donuts. Allow the dough to rest and rise for 20 minutes, then gently transfer the donuts to the hot oil in batches, using floured hands or a floured dough card, leaving 1/2 inch or so between the pieces so they have room to expand.

After adding the shaped donuts to the oil, you will need to turn the burner up slightly because the addition of the dough will cause the temperature to drop. Maintain the 325°F temperature during frying. Fry until golden on the first side, about 5 to 6 minutes, then gently turn and cook the second side until golden, about 3 to 4 minutes. Drain on a wire rack and allow to cool to lukewarm before glazing, or cool completely to stuff. For stuffed glazed donuts, glaze while they are still warm, then cool further before filling.

These donuts are delicious just dusted in powdered sugar, or you can use a pastry bag to inject your favorite jam, jelly, or pastry cream from one of the corners, about 2 tablespoons filling per piece. Then dust or glaze with your topping of choice. Custard donuts must be eaten within 4 hours if kept at room temperature; otherwise, refrigerate right away and allow to warm up to room temperature before eating.

RICH DOUBLE CHOCOLATE GLAZE

2 pounds confectioners' sugar

1 cup cocoa powder

1/2 pound dark chocolate, 65% to 70% cocoa, as chips or cut into small bits

1/4 cup (1/2 stick) unsalted butter, cut into 1/2-inch pats and softened

1 tablespoon pure vanilla extract

1/2 teaspoon kosher salt

1 1/2 cups strong coffee, piping hot

Sift the sugar and cocoa together and reserve. Place the chocolate, butter, vanilla, and salt in a stainless-steel mixing bowl. Pour the hot coffee over and stir constantly until the chocolate and butter have melted into a smooth mass. This will take a minute or two. Sift the sugar and cocoa mixture over the melted chocolate mixture and, using a sturdy rubber spatula, stir constantly until it is incorporated and the mixture is smooth and thick. Heat in a double boiler, or transfer to a glass bowl and microwave 15 seconds at a time, to soften the glaze until it is the consistency of a thin milkshake. Glaze by dipping or pouring over the donuts. Dipping is by far the cleaner method. Excess glaze may be refrigerated or frozen and heated in a double boiler before using again.

PLAIN DONUT GLAZE

1 pound confectioners' sugar
⅓ cup cold buttermilk
1 teaspoon vanilla extract
½ teaspoon kosher salt

Sift the sugar into a small mixing bowl. Add remaining ingredients and stir with a rubber spatula until smooth.

LEMON DONUT GLAZE

1 pound confectioners' sugar
Zest of 1 lemon, finely grated
Zest of 1 orange, finely grated
¼ cup freshly squeezed lemon juice
2 tablespoons heavy whipping cream or buttermilk
½ teaspoon kosher salt

Sift the sugar into a small mixing bowl. Add remaining ingredients and stir with a rubber spatula until smooth.

BLUEBERRY DONUT GLAZE

1 pound confectioners' sugar
1½ cups blueberries, fresh or frozen, coarsely pureed
1 tablespoon freshly squeezed lemon juice
Pinch freshly ground black pepper
½ teaspoon kosher salt

Sift the sugar into a small mixing bowl. Add remaining ingredients and stir with a rubber spatula until smooth.

VANILLA PASTRY CREAM

1 cup heavy whipping cream

1¼ cups whole milk, divided

½ cup granulated sugar

½ teaspoon kosher salt

6 egg yolks

2 tablespoons cornstarch

¼ cup (½ stick) unsalted butter, cut into ½-inch pats

Place the heavy cream and 1 cup of the milk in a small saucepan and gently bring to a low boil. In a medium stainless-steel mixing bowl, mix together the remaining ¼ cup milk, sugar, salt, egg yolks, and cornstarch, whisking until smooth. Whisk in the boiling cream mixture in a slow, steady stream to combine without cooking the egg yolks. Return to the saucepan and place over medium-low heat. Whisking constantly, gradually raise to a low boil to activate the cornstarch and thicken the eggs. Maintain a low boil, whisking, for 15 seconds. Remove from heat and whisk in the butter until thoroughly incorporated. Cool to room temperature for 30 minutes, whisking every few minutes to prevent curdling. Transfer to a clean, airtight container and refrigerate fully before use, overnight is best.

Titus Ruscitti

———

"Anywhere you go in Wisconsin you can find a dope little baker and a great local butcher shop. That's why I always say Wisconsin is the best burger state, because so many spots are using that fresh product." These words were spoken by one of the few people I would trust to know, who also happens to be the only food blogger I've read steadily over many years. Titus Ruscitti, a.k.a. Chicago Chow King, the guy behind the blog *Smokin' Chokin' and Chowing* (chibbqking .blogspot.com), is a must-read for Roadfoodies because of his combination of careful sleuthing and erudite analysis. In a world in which everyone thinks they're a food critic and hyperbole is dished out like swag at a trade show, the rare writers who stand out do so because of a combination of curiosity, which begets knowledge, and the sincerity to bring an open mind and get the story right. Titus and I had a long, meandering afternoon discussion in which those qualities came to the fore.

A lifelong Chicagoan, Titus was born of an Irish mother and Italian father, a classic "Chicago mix," and grew up in the Lincoln Park–DePaul neighborhood, which gave him a front-row seat to gentrification and a lot to reflect on as he matured. His mom's side of the family was into the Chicago working-class aesthetic; his dad's side was a clan of gourmands, but in a more populist sense and without pretense. "My grandpa was a real foodie and cooked more than anyone else in the family, and his favorite thing to cook was the peanut butter egg roll, that Chicago egg roll." His family's embrace of diverse city life instilled in him a curious palate and an open mind.

He first got a sense of how regional American food was when he left Chicago for the University of Tampa and was dismayed to learn that there were no Italian beef or hot dog stands to be found. But there was the Cubano, the local specialty of roast pork, ham, swiss cheese, pickles, and mustard on Cuban bread, pressed flat and cooked on a griddle. Moving on to grad school at the University of Wisconsin–Madison, he was exposed to cheese curds and the Church of Bratwurst. He set out to find the best examples, and his pursuit of regional foods and foodways was under way.

Back in Chicago, and fortunate enough to have work that allowed for travel, he began blogging on the Chicago gourmand board LTHForum and plugged into the Roadfood forum as well. The Chicago Chow King blog started in 2008 and has over 1,200 posts—perhaps the greatest treasure trove of information on eating locally you can find anywhere in the United States.

"I don't make a lot of money on the blog," he said. "It's something I do out of love. I just enjoy traveling, and a lot of my posting was for my own recollection but I also realized how much this could help people eat better. . . . I like to say eat locally, not necessarily as in locally grown, but as in, eat like the locals when you're somewhere. . . . The road food life is about going the extra two or five miles to find that local café with a breaded pork tenderloin or the best kebab instead of just doing Culver's again."

Titus is a fount of knowledge about food throughout most of the United States and in many cities around the world, but particularly the Midwest. "There's good food everywhere if you look for it, and I like to find it, and the Midwest is as interesting as anywhere." Besides touting Wisconsin as a great burger state, Titus brags on Detroit as his second-favorite food city in the Midwest (after his hometown). Of course, Detroit and its suburbs are fertile ground for coney dogs and pizza, but "Dearborn is one of the best places in the country for Iraqi and Lebanese food, it's just incredible. Everyone will tell you to go to Dearborn Meat Market, and you should because it's probably the best restaurant in Michigan, but don't skip the Iraqi Kabob house. They're using charcoal, so you can be pretty sure they're not cutting corners elsewhere, and there they are actually chopping the meat by hand, and adding sheep fat to it, which renders on the fire, drips, and you can watch these flames rise from the coals and char the meat. That is my favorite dish anywhere in the Midwest."

Even though Chicago boasts an impressive breadth of global cuisines, he's motivated to "chase what you can't get where you're from." He says, "I look at local populations before I travel somewhere, and then I know if I am traveling through Fort Wayne or Indianapolis, I should look for good Burmese food, they have some of the largest Burmese communities in the United States. Or recently when I was in South Florida, I found great Caribbean cuisine, Bahamian, West Indian, Chilean, and Peruvian." Or sometimes it's just a local specialty, as with *suadero* tacos in Mexico City.

As we often see in the big city, local flavor is driven by immigrant communities, and the local culture can get squeezed out when it's "Americanized," or consumed by chain restaurants, or bowled over by gentrification, and that is a lot of what motivates Titus. "When I was a kid [in Lincoln Park], there was a place like Wiener's Circle on almost every block, every corner had a local bar, an Italian ice shop . . . they're almost all gone. I want people to be able to experience the local culture and uniqueness wherever they go."

Based on a telephone discussion with Titus Ruscitti, blogger at chibbqking.blogspot .com, April 13, 2022.

4

OF STATE FAIRS, TAILGATES, & MAIN STREET CAFÉS

Sandwiches and Handheld Food

Corn sex starts, as most things do, with male and female parts: the tassel at the top of the stalk and the protokernels along the cob. The two are separated by three or four feet, an insurmountable obstacle unless wind and weather collude. When pollen is about to rain down from the tassel, each protokernel sends up a single silk in anticipation. A few days later, a Rapunzel-like spray of blond silky hair emerges from the top of the ear precisely when the pollen is ready to drop. Then each sticky and receptive silk catches one single, crucial grain of pollen.

—Terra Brockman, "Green Corn Moon"

MIDWESTERN state fairs are legend for the multifarious stuff-on-a-stick creations that line the thoroughfares and byways. The point of food on a stick is easy enough to understand: when you are ambling about and enjoying the sights and exhibits, solid food impaled on a skewer is far less messy than sandwiches, tacos, or stuffed foods. Deep-fried candy bars, fish and chips, hotdish, falafel, cheesecake, and more on a stick also promise the liberty of eating with one hand, leaving the other free to tote souvenirs, tap away at a smartphone, or hold the hand of your sweetie.

Food on a stick doesn't much percolate into Midwestern daily life, but it is an apt metaphor for one cardinal tenet of Midwestern foodways: we love to eat with our hands. It's such a fundamental aspect of our way of eating that the majority of foods, from pizza to barbecue and fried chicken, are eaten that way, or with minimal assistance from utensils.

This custom is very much a twentieth-century adaptation of workaday folks who, busy between shifts or tired after a long day of work, embraced sandwiches as an unpretentious dinner, and the cafés and commissaries that fed them surely appreciated having a little less tableware to deal with. Depending on the ingredients, sandwiches could be cheap, quick to make, packable for travel, and easy to consume on the go as industry, both in urban factories and on increasingly mammoth grain farms, made a leisurely, sit-down lunch a thing of the past for most Americans—a major cultural departure for people from many immigrant communities. We'll date hamburgers and hot dogs on bread to the late nineteenth century, along with tamales, and tenderloins and coney dogs to the early twentieth century, all of them heralding a more casual way of eating.

Even as handheld food may seem less than cuisine-y to some, the reality is that as an embodiment of culture, foods like tamales and hot dogs are significant markers of identity and sense of place, arguably the very definition of "cuisine." There's a lot to love about eating out of hand. It can make food preparation and consumption more enjoyable. Eating becomes a tactile experience: the sensation of a hot tamale in your palm, the ritual of unfurling its robe of corn husks, holding the entire steaming ingot to your face, taking in the aroma; the primal elation of biting steak between two pieces of bread; the giddy anticipation as your hands cradle an exquisitely warm, pillowy egg bun pocked with poppy seed before hoisting a hot dog to your lips; the smoky miasma of sauced rib tips as you peck around looking for choice bits or nabbing that bulbous hot link. When the sensual qualities of eating out of hand are fully appreciated, dining with flatware comes off as exceedingly priggish.

Handheld food doesn't have to be dowdy, nor should it be looked down upon. Countless European and American texts support it as the ultimate way to amuse the eyes and palate. Making a good coney sauce, bierock, or tamale is a multifaceted culinary operation requiring patience and skill. Just because we're starting with affordable cuts of meat that the fine-dining set may eschew doesn't make it any less delicious or nourishing. This isn't grubby food, it's high cuisine.

Beer Brats (the Real Way)

The classic jingle by Midwestern scion and ad man James Hartzell may go, "As American as baseball, hot dogs, apple pie, and Chevrolet," but in Wisconsin, it's off by a sausage. At the Milwaukee Brewers' stadium, Miller Park, bratwurst outsells even hot dogs.[1] Also known as the meat that made Sheboygan famous,[2] the humble brat, grilled over charcoal, is iconic for many Wisconsinites. As someone raised on brats in another German American community a few hundred miles to the south, I'm down with that.

Bratwurst stems from the High German word *braten*, of which the most common culinary translation is "roast" or "roasted"—hence *Bratwurst* is a *Wurst*, or sausage, made with roasting meat. Finer cuts were ordinarily preferred for roasting, rather than the normal sausage trim or lesser cuts. The term bratwurst thus implies a sausage made with finer cuts of meat. In German sausage craft, it was also common to combine different kinds of meat, as we see from Sabina Welserin's 1753 receipt:

If you want to make a good bratwurst

Take four pounds of pork and four pounds of beef, have it chopped small, then take two pounds of bacon into it and chop it together. Add about three seidel of water, and also add salt and pepper, as you like to eat it, or if you like to have herbs in it, you can take a little sage and a little marjoram, and you will have good bratwurst.[3]

Known as *Mettwurst* in Low German, bratwurst developed a variety of styles based on meat composition, grind, seasonings, casings, and the like. The ones in my childhood were always made of pork, so when I moved to Chicago and walked into a German restaurant to order bratwurst, I was perplexed when I was served a fat, white, emulsified sausage that looked and tasted more like a *Weißwurst* than what I thought of as a bratwurst. It turned out that veal was commonly used to make brats in Chicago, and further, that the sausage was emulsified to give it a finer texture. I was dumbstruck. Who could call this bratwurst? Well, at least a couple million people or so. When I first tried Wisconsin bratwurst, I was relieved to find the familiar natural pork casing, finely chopped and well-seasoned pork, not overmixed, so that it still had some texture to it, and just a wee bit peppery. But a real brat is all about the meat. You don't take a fine cut of meat and grind it up only to mask the flavor under a wreck of seasonings and smoke.

The pairing of beer and brats is legend, and a common liturgical rite in Wisconsin is to poach the bratwurst in beer before grilling it, especially when tailgating before a Badgers or Packers game. It's definitely a tasty way to go, but it's always vexed me ever so slightly because I am forever haunted by the elegant technique my dad used. It starts with a dab of coffee-can grease, the reserved leftover grease Grandma kept on the back of the stove in a coffee can, which would be scented with whatever you'd been frying recently, be it ham, bacon, chicken, or pork chops. He'd smother the brats in beer and cook it down, yielding a heavily caramelized bratwurst redolent of beer, with a toothsome crusty char that surpasses what can be achieved over charcoal. Be careful with these, though, because they will literally squirt hot beer-infused juice when you bite into them! Always let them rest for a spell before diving in.

Have plenty of sauerkraut and spicy brown mustard handy, and don't forget the cold (lager) beer. Get top-notch brats from your best local butcher, not from the supermarket sausage case. This isn't low-brow food.

A 10- or 12-inch, well-seasoned, heavy-bottomed cast-iron skillet

2 tablespoons coffee-can grease, lard, or vegetable oil

8 best bratwurst (pork or pork and beef, chopped, not emulsified), about
    4 ounces each

Two 12-ounce lager beers, ice-cold (Miller High Life is classic, but German lagers
    such as Weihenstephaner or Dortmunder are fantastic. OK, truly only one of
    the beers needs to be ice-cold; that's for drinking while you use the other one
    to cook the brats.)

Generously oil the bottom and sides of the skillet with your fat of choice. Evenly distribute the bratwurst over the bottom of the pan and pour one 12-ounce beer over them. Turn the heat up to medium high, bring the beer to a boil, then turn down the heat to maintain a low boil, turning the brats at least every minute or two. Even cooking is key to avoiding splits, cracks, or popped casings on your sausages. Eventually, the brats will begin sizzling in their own drippings and the syrupy leavings of the beer. Turn them even more often, every 30 to 45 seconds, to coat them well in the beer syrup and get a full char on them. This entire process will take about 15 minutes. Handle them gently and let them cool for 8 to 10 minutes before digging in. Enjoy as the center of a plate with potatoes or dumplings and kraut, or on buns dressed with kraut and spicy brown mustard.

Fried Cheese Curds

Wisconsin continues to be the largest cheese-producing state in the country[4] in spite of being only the twentieth most populous, outproducing even California.[5] Wisconsin has accomplished this with some of the richest farmland and pastureland in the country, and with steady innovation in an industry that is always developing new products and new ways to use cheese, earning Wisconsinites the name Cheeseheads—a term of endearment to most Midwesterners or, in the heart of Big Ten football season, a cheery sort of derision.

Scanning our culinary literature for examples of fried cheese curds, it's striking how few there are for a dish that is so popular today; in fact, cheese curds appear to be a very recent phenomenon. We have at least one recipe from 1750 in England that is unmistakably fried cheese curds any Wisconsinite would recognize, if a bit eccentric by Midwestern standards.[6] Eliza Smith's receipt calls for dipping the little squeakers in a flour and egg batter laced with saffron and sweet spices, followed by a crisping in deep beef tallow and a dust-ing in sifted sugar. Strangely, the sweet treatment didn't seem to have legs, and fried cheese curds disappeared from the Western culinary literature for more than two centuries. Perhaps Miss Smith should have tried a savory treatment with a ketchup-based dip and an accompaniment of cold beer instead.

Oddly, the first printed recipe I could find for fried cheese curds appears in a beer advertisement from 1966 in which Figi's Certified Beer of Marsh-field, Wisconsin, published a simple recipe submitted by Marshfield's Howard Sullivan.[7] A 1976 ad for Dave's Burger Shanty of Oshkosh calls out the "New Taste Sensation" of fried cheese curds on its menu,[8] and a few weeks later, a write-up of the Minnesota State Fair avers that "you can get something called a deep-fried cheese curd for 50 cents a basket."[9]

In the few decades since, fried cheese curds have become a fixture on pub menus throughout Wisconsin and increasingly outside the state. It might be a cardinal sin to visit the Minnesota State Fair without partaking of them. The flavor of fresh cheese slays, and the texture has a chew to it that fried mozza-rella sticks can't dream of touching. And they're easy to make at home. Many

This ad for Figi's Certified Beer features the earliest known printed recipe for cheese curds.

Source: *Marshfield News-Herald* (Marshfield, WI), July 21, 1966.

recipes call for an egg-based batter, but I dissent, as the eggs yield a batter that is soft and not all that crispy. Best to stick to beer or hard cider.

Serves 4 as an appetizer or 2 for a cheese-curd knockout

- 1 pound cheese curds, separated into individual curds
- 1½ cups dry hard cider or light lager beer (cider is best, but beer's no slouch)
- 1 cup all-purpose flour, plus more for prepping the curds
- ¼ cup cornstarch
- 1 teaspoon baking powder
- 1 teaspoon kosher salt
- ¼ teaspoon cayenne pepper
- Beef tallow or vegetable oil for deep-frying

Place the cheese curds in the freezer for 10 minutes while you heat the fat or oil and prepare the batter. Heat 2 inches of fat or oil in a dutch oven or countertop fryer to 350°F. In a medium mixing bowl, combine the cider or beer, flour, cornstarch, baking powder, salt, and cayenne pepper. Whisk until smooth, but don't overmix. Remove the curds from the freezer and dust with 1 to 2 tablespoons of flour, just to lightly coat, then plunge them, a large spoonful at a time, into the batter. Use a large slotted spoon to transfer them to the hot oil, dropping them in quickly but one at a time so they don't clump. Fry in 2 or 3 batches, about 6 minutes each, until golden brown and delicious. Drain on wire racks or paper towels and serve hot with ranch dressing.

Ranch Dressing

Since we're on the subject of deep-fried foods, I'll share my recipe for ranch dressing, the National Everything Dressing of the Midwest.

Makes about 2 cups

- ½ cup top-quality mayonnaise, such as Hellman's
- ½ cup low-fat sour cream
- ½ cup low-fat buttermilk
- ½ teaspoon dried dill leaf (not seed)
- 2 teaspoons granulated onion
- 1 teaspoon dried chives

¼ teaspoon ground sage

1 teaspoon kosher salt

½ teaspoon freshly ground black pepper

Juice of ½ lemon

1 teaspoon Worcestershire sauce

Whisk together in a mixing bowl and refrigerate overnight before serving.

Cold-Pack Cheese

In the middle of the country, especially the closer you get to Wisconsin, cold-pack cheese is synonymous with holiday celebrations, parties, good vibes, and cheer. Sold in the once ubiquitous sausage and cheese cart at the mall and now in supermarkets across the country, cold-pack cheese is affectionately known as "squeeze cheese" among acolytes for its spreadability. Some think it's like Cheez Whiz and therefore a guilty pleasure, but cold-pack cheese is actually two or more fresh or aged cheeses blended together without using heat. Good ones are minimally processed with few added ingredients or preservatives. It's just another way to enjoy cheese; who's got a problem with that?

While Wisconsin cheesemakers didn't invent the idea of making a spreadable delicacy with cheese, I found sparse evidence of its lineage. It's possible to find references to "crock cheese" (cheese packed in crocks, that is) in the nineteenth century, especially among county fair entries.[10] In fact, crock cheese was considered "a typical delicacy of the Pennsylvania Dutch."[11] However, without accurate descriptions, we're left to assume that this cheese was *Schmierkase*, a cottage cheese–like product popular with the Dutch and Germans alike,[12] which was indeed packed in crocks but doesn't meet the definition of cold-pack cheese.[13]

The common legend that cold-pack cheese was invented by a Wisconsin tavern owner to serve as a snack for his patrons is unsubstantiated. Therefore, it is what it is—a legend. It's more likely that a Swedish immigrant made the first cold-pack cheese in Wisconsin (indeed, possibly a tavern owner). Going back centuries, Swedes have preserved leftovers or scraps of cheese by beating in butter to smooth it out and adding aquavit or beer to aid in preservation.[14] The bulk of Swedish migration to Wisconsin occurred from 1860 to 1890,[15] which dovetails with the emergence of "pub cheese" around the turn of the century.

As with many Midwestern foods, what began as a culturally ingrained foodway has become a formidable industry. The pub-cheese industry was spear-headed by Hubert Fassbender, founder of Kaukana, still one of the best brands of cold-pack cheese, and has grown into dozens of labels throughout the United States, though the best are in Wisconsin. Merkt's is another widely available and excellent example, while my personal favorite is made by the artisanal Fayette Creamery, a label of the Brunkow Cheese Company of Darlington.

With this recipe, even skeptics can see that cold-pack cheese is, in fact, real food with Swedish roots. I strongly advise you not to use pre-shredded cheese; purchase block cheese and shred it yourself on the large holes of a box grater. It should go without saying that you should seek out Wisconsin cheese. Once you master the basics, you can experiment quite widely with different flavorings, seasonings, and crusts. For this recipe, I'm using a favorite combination: horseradish and beer.

Makes a bit more than a pound

- ½ pound (8 ounces) sharp cheddar cheese, shredded
- ¼ pound (4 ounces) baby swiss cheese, shredded
- ¼ cup (½ stick) unsalted butter, chilled, cut into ½-inch pats
- ½ cup pale lager beer
- 2 tablespoons Worcestershire sauce
- 2 tablespoons freshly grated or 3 tablespoons prepared horseradish
- 1 teaspoon kosher salt
- ¼ teaspoon cayenne pepper

Place the cheese and butter in the food processor and pulse to combine coarsely, then puree while adding the beer in a thin, steady stream. Continue pureeing until the mixture is smooth and has the texture of creamed butter. With the food processor running, add the seasonings and puree to combine well, another minute. Store in a glass jar or bowl tightly covered. Refrigerate right away. Remove from refrigerator and allow to temper for 15 to 20 minutes before serving. Serve with crackers, crudités, sausage, and pickles, or use as a base for rarebit.

Apple Cider Pecan Cheese Ball

The pairing of cider and cheese is classic. This is my favorite combination—baby swiss cheese tempered with buttery brie or camembert, sweet apple cider, and toasty pecans, lightened up with a little lemon zest and fresh parsley.

If you don't intend to serve this within a day, it'd be best to skip the parsley; your cheese ball will still be a hit.

Makes 1 ball (or it's fun to shape it as a football on game day), about 1½ pounds

¼ cup (½ stick) plus 1 tablespoon unsalted butter, divided

1 cup pecan halves

1 tablespoon cold water

1½ teaspoons kosher salt, divided

⅜ teaspoon cayenne pepper, divided

12 ounces baby swiss cheese, shredded on the large side of a box grater

4 ounces brie or camembert curd, rind removed (weigh after removing rind)

2 tablespoons fresh tarragon leaves

¾ cup sweet apple cider

2 tablespoons Worcestershire sauce

¼ cup minced fresh curly parsley

Zest of 1 lemon, finely grated

Celery, cut into thin strips to make lacing for football shape (optional)

Preheat oven to 325°F.

Butter a cookie sheet with 1 tablespoon of butter. Place the pecan halves in a small bowl, wet them with the cold water, toss to coat evenly, and drain off the excess—this is to help the seasonings adhere. Add ½ teaspoon of the salt and ⅛ teaspoon of the cayenne and toss to combine evenly. Bake the pecans on the center rack of the oven until well toasted and aromatic, 15 to 18 minutes depending how dark you like them. Cool to room temperature and pulse in the food processor to grind coarsely. You want the largest pieces of pecan to be the size of a pea, the rest smaller, but don't overdo it—you want the pecans to add a crispy, crumbly texture to the cheese ball. Refrigerate to help them stick to the cheese later.

Cut the remaining ¼ cup of butter into thin slices and place it, along with the cheeses, remaining teaspoon salt, remaining ¼ teaspoon cayenne, and tarragon leaves, in the food processor. Pulse to combine coarsely, then puree while adding the cider in a thin, steady stream. Puree until smooth and creamy like creamed butter. Add the Worcestershire sauce and puree for 1 more minute. Turn out into a bowl, cover with plastic wrap, and refrigerate for at least 1 hour or overnight.

Combine the ground pecans, parsley, and lemon zest evenly in the bottom of a pie dish, and distribute in a thin layer. Shape the well-chilled cheese into a ball or football shape, and roll it in the pecan mixture, applying just enough pressure for the coating to adhere in a thick layer that leaves little cheese visible through it. Roll to coat all sides, and use all the coating mixture. If shaping into a football, press it down to flatten the bottom, so your football is essentially the top half. Cut 8 thin strips of celery about 3 to 4 inches long and arrange them as the crosslaces of the football, stacked a little more than ½ inches apart and parallel. Cut one thin strip of celery 6 inches long and use it to "tie" the cross laces of the ball up the center. Cover tightly in plastic wrap to secure the coating and refrigerate for at least 1 hour (overnight is better). Serve with crackers, crudités, apple slices, and summer sausages. Can be refrigerated up to 1 week.

Bierocks, a.k.a. Runzas

The Midwest is full of well-kept secrets, and one of the best is the meal-in-one-hand delicacy of the Plains states, alternately called bierocks or runzas. These pillowy, sweet yeast rolls loaded with ground beef, cabbage, and onions, and sometimes also sauerkraut, give you your meat, carbs, and vegetables in one delectable bite. They're incredibly scarce outside their Kansas and Nebraska habitat, which stretches ever so slightly into Colorado, the Dakotas, and Iowa around the periphery, but at home they are so popular that restaurants thrive by specializing in them, including the Runza chain, with over eighty locations, which admonishes hungry folks, "Get your bunzas to a Runza."

For all I can tell, bierocks and runzas are the same thing. "Runza," a coined term that stuck, has a deep family history with the closely held Runza chain. Sarah "Sally" Everett coined the name and gave her recipe to the members of her family who founded the first Runza in 1948.[16] Mrs. Everett's son Donald Everett Sr. and her grandson Donald Everett Jr. have kept the company in the family and have vigorously defended the Runza name in the marketplace.[17] "Runza" is the trademarked name of the roll served in their restaurants; the public-domain term for the same type of roll is "bierock."

It's generally assumed that the word "bierock" derives from the Russian word *pirog*, "pie," and that the recipe was picked up by ethnic Germans living in Russia. During the late nineteenth and early twentieth centuries, many of those Germans left Russia for the United States as growing religious intolerance in Russia, combined with rising nationalist sentiment throughout Europe, made the fertile American plains more appealing than the Russian steppe.[18] Even though these Russian German immigrant communities existed in relative isolation in the Plains states, bierocks were being promulgated by home demonstration clubs in the area within a few decades.[19]

Bierocks are superbly delicious and deserving of a wider following, and they're easy to make. Like most stuffed breads and dumplings, bierocks can easily be stuffed with just about anything. The ground beef, onion, and cabbage filling is an adaptation to place and time in the Great Plains—ground beef and cabbage were cheap, nutritious, and available to people of any economic means. I'm sticking to the basics here; no need to get fancy when the traditional recipe is so damn delicious.

Makes 12 bierocks

1½ cups whole milk

⅓ cup granulated sugar

2 teaspoons instant yeast

5 cups all-purpose flour, plus more for dusting

3 teaspoons kosher salt, divided

¼ cup (½ stick) unsalted butter, cut into pats and softened, plus more to butter
 the pan

3 large eggs, divided

1 tablespoon bacon grease or vegetable oil

1 pound ground beef, 80% lean

1 teaspoon freshly ground black pepper

1 cup yellow Spanish onion, finely diced

3 cups green cabbage, very finely shredded

1 cup cold water

2 tablespoons Worcestershire sauce

Warm milk to 100°F to 110°F and place in a medium mixing bowl. Whisk in the sugar and yeast. Using a stiff rubber spatula, stir in 2 cups of the flour, then add 1 teaspoon of the salt, the butter, and two of the eggs. Stir in until roughly incorporated. Add the remaining flour and stir until it's too thick for the spatula, then start kneading in the bowl with your hands until it comes together in a ball, just a few minutes. It will be fairly sticky. Using as little extra flour as possible, knead until the dough is soft, smooth, and pliable, about 6 to 8 minutes. Shape into a ball, cover, and allow to rise until doubled in bulk, about 45 minutes, while you make the filling.

　Coat the bottom of a large cast-iron skillet with the grease or oil. Add the ground beef, and over medium-low heat, break up the beef while slowly rendering it. As it breaks into smaller pieces and gives up its juices, gradually increase the heat. When you've got fine pieces the size of a pea or smaller, increase the heat to medium high, add the pepper and the remaining 2 teaspoons salt, and brown the meat well, about 8 to 10 minutes total cooking time. Using a slotted spoon, remove the beef to a bowl, leaving its fat in the pan. Sauté the onion in the beef drippings while stirring constantly until the sulfur smell is gone and it smells sweet, about 4 to 5 minutes over medium-high heat. Add the cabbage and continue sautéing until the cabbage wilts and releases its smell, about 4 to 5 minutes.

Return the beef to the pan with the vegetables, add the cold water, and boil the water out, stirring and steaming the vegetables and meat together. When the water has boiled out and you have a thick and damp, but not wet, mixture, about 10 minutes, add the Worcestershire sauce, remove from heat, and cool to room temperature.

Preheat oven to 325°F.

Butter a cookie sheet. Divide the dough and filling each into 12 equal parts, shaping the dough into balls. Flatten each ball of dough into a disk about 6 inches around, place the filling in the center, dividing evenly between rolls, and wet the edges of each disk with cold water. Bring the outsides of the dough up and over the filling, coming together in the center, and seal with a little twist. Make sure any seams in the dough are pinched shut. Turn the bun over and place it smooth side up on the cookie sheet. Leave at least an inch between buns to allow room for expansion.

Beat the remaining egg with an equal volume of water, and use this egg wash to brush each bun around the sides and over the top. Allow to rise until increased 1½ times in bulk, about 20 to 25 minutes, before baking on the center rack of the oven until deep golden brown, 25 to 30 minutes.

Toasted Ravioli

Toasted ravioli are a local curiosity seldom seen outside Saint Louis until recently. These delectable bites from the Gateway City, often little more than ravioli breaded and deep-fried, are supremely delicious with many different sauces. The stiff competition among peddlers of the delicacy in Saint Louis, however, has caused the local toasties to evolve into more corpulent dumplings, distended with copious amounts of beef and cheese, spiked with herbs to keep them from cloying.

Cooks in Saint Louis have been toasting ravioli since at least the 1940s, and there's no reliable record of them existing earlier, so they are very much a modern phenomenon that unquestionably originated in that city, which still guards them with a sense of local pride.[20]

There are three main competing narratives for the origin of toasted ravioli, all from the 1940s and all centered around a restaurant cook who accidentally dropped raw ravioli into the deep fryer instead of the pasta cooker, and voilà! An instant classic was born.

Claimant 1, with perhaps the best story, is Mama Campisi's, formerly Oldani's. That story has the accidental dish finding its way to the bar, where it was enjoyed by Mickey Garagiola, older brother of Baseball Hall of Famer Joe Garagiola, and his entourage. They loved the deep-fried pockets, and toasted

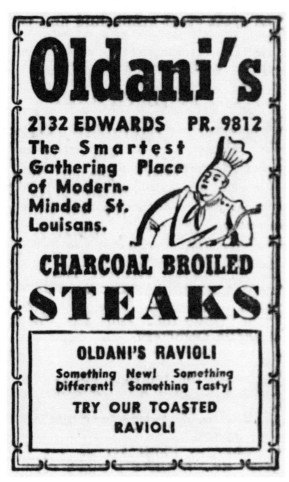

Was Oldani's the first to serve toasted ravioli?   *Source*: St. Louis Star and Times, February 13, 1943.

ravioli were soon on the menus of restaurants all over the Hill, Saint Louis's historic Italian American neighborhood. Claimant 2 is Angelo's, now known as Charlie Gitto's, whose story is fuzzier on the details. Claimant 3 is Lombardo's, whose owner, Tony Lombardo, suggests that he has menus from the 1930s listing toasted ravioli,[21] but it's unclear whether these menus are accurately dated.

In looking for hard proof, I found a newspaper ad for Oldani's hawking toasted ravioli in early 1943.[22] I found no other evidence in the public record for even a few years after the ad. Feuds over the origin of delicious treats aren't uncommon, and they can be a lot of fun. When it's time for dinner, though, such treats are something to enjoy, and quarrels are best left aside.

In Saint Louis, toasted ravioli can become quite elaborate, pushing into entrée territory. In my experience, the most approachable and easy to enjoy are stuffed with a simple ricotta filling, at most with herbs or spinach to cut the richness of the cheese, but most you'll find in Italian restaurants are pregnant with ground beef. They're delicious straight out of hand, or served with a snappy marinara sauce if you like a dip.

Makes 2 dozen ravioli, an appetizer for 4

- 2 inches of vegetable oil in a dutch oven or deep fryer
- 2 large eggs
- ½ cup evaporated milk
- 24 fresh, uncooked ravioli of your choice
- 8 ounces unseasoned French or Italian breadcrumbs (*not* panko)
- ½ cup parmesan cheese, finely grated, divided in half
- 2 teaspoons kosher salt
- 2 teaspoons freshly ground black pepper
- 3 tablespoons finely chopped curly parsley
- 1 cup marinara sauce, for dipping

Heat the oil to 350°F. In a medium mixing bowl, beat the eggs well, then stir in the evaporated milk. Add the ravioli, toss to coat, and marinate for a few minutes while the oil heats.

Toss the breadcrumbs with ¼ cup of the parmesan, the salt, and the pepper. Spread half of this mixture in a thin, even layer on a sheet pan or large casserole dish. One by one, take the ravioli out of the egg mixture, tapping to shake off excess, and lay them on the breadcrumbs in a single layer, edge to edge, just about ⅛ inch apart. Sprinkle the remaining half of the breadcrumbs over the ravioli to coat, then gently press with your flattened hands.

Drop in batches of 8 to 12 into the hot oil, and fry until crisp and golden brown on both sides, about 6 minutes. Remove with a slotted spoon to drain on wire racks or paper towels. While still hot, transfer to a serving platter, arrange in a pyramid, and shower with the remaining ¼ cup of parmesan and the parsley. Serve with warm marinara for dipping.

A Tale of Three Tamales

The folklore of tamales in the Midwest, which orbits Chicago, has been told over generations without much basis in facts beyond the sensation that they, along with chili con carne, caused when they allegedly debuted at the 1893 Columbian Exposition.[23] In parts of the Midwest with substantial Latin American populations, tamales are now part of everyday life. But there's more to the story, as tamales in the Midwest have taken at least three forms over the past 130 years.

Today, the Mexican tamale has become the standard, with its variations lying mostly with the skill and taste of the cook, but what we have is a pone bread made from corn masa, steamed inside corn husks with a filling that is usually pork or chicken in red or green chili sauce, although beans, cheese, and chilies are also common.

The twist in the story of tamales in Chicago is the Mississippi Delta tamale, which shares some distinguishing characteristics with the Mexican one. Both are wrapped in corn husks and employ a corn-based dough with a usually spicy meat-based filling, although the Delta variety is generally spicier. But the similarities end there. While recipes vary, the Delta tamale is usually much thinner, almost cigar-shaped, using less dough but about the same amount of filling, for a higher filling-to-dough ratio. Delta tamales use cornmeal, while Mexican tamales use masa—a flour or dough made from nixtamal, or corn hominy. Mexican tamales are invariably steamed, Delta tamales boiled in a spicy broth. Both are part of the Chicago tradition.

The Mississippi Delta's African American population developed Delta tamales, which undoubtedly came to Chicago during the Great Migration.[24] Yet this foodway, with its deep roots and tons of flavor, languishes in obscurity on the South Side, thanks to cultural discrimination and a history of segregation. The original source of the Delta tamale is commonly thought to be migrant Mexican farmworkers who moved to the Delta in the early twentieth century as the first wave of the Great Migration took tens of thousands of Black sharecroppers and farmhands north. Another theory is that they originated with Native Americans, who were enslaved for a time early in the colonization of Mississippi.[25] All of the Five Nations inhabiting the pre-Columbian Southeast had pone breads wrapped in corn husks or leaves and roasted in coals or boiled,[26] at least some of which used cornmeal.[27] This always seemed like a promising direction for investigation, because the surface differences between Delta and Mexican tamales seem hard to reconcile. Were Delta tamales a lingering foodway of the Five Nations adopted by African Americans, an import from Mexico, or a hybrid?

A piece of correspondence sent from Fort Worth, Texas, to the *Grenada* (Mississippi) *Sentinel* in 1886 refers to tamales as "an article of food that the new arrival from the trans-Mississippi country never saw or heard of."[28] Some months later, the *Vicksburg Evening Post* ponders the question "Isn't This a Dish Worth Importing?"[29] So at least in certain communities, tamales were unheard of. Restaurants serving tamales were opening in the greater Delta region as early as 1880, when Ellen Price, a cook "famed especially for the Mexican delicacies," opened one in Natchitoches, Louisiana, serving "tortillas, tamales, etc."[30] From the available public record, the most logical conclusion is that tamales arrived in the Delta region from Mexico, but at the end of the day, Delta tamales are not a Mexican food; they are a food of Black America. African Americans adopted the tamale and made it their own, and it is one of America's great distinctive regional foods and part of the Midwestern fabric as well.

Tamales first appear in Midwestern media no later than 1867, when a Chicagoan stationed in Querétaro, Mexico, during the French Intervention corresponded with the *Chicago Tribune*, describing breakfasts of chocolate and tamales (sounds dreamy to me) and ruminating over how these tamales would "take" if they were sold at Fulton Market.[31] He didn't think their prospects would be good, but clearly he was wrong. By the 1880s, tamales were getting some good press nationally. Although they were not documented locally, the *Tribune* reported, "They are sold steaming hot on the streets of San Francisco daily, and are very relishing."[32]

By 1892, a California entrepreneur named Robert Putnam was infiltrating the Chicago market with the wares of his California Chicken Tamale Co., and he created a sensation, soon employing five hundred tamale men in Chicago. That's a lot of tamales. One of his workers left the company and started selling a tamale called the San Antonio.[33] The competition became fierce, and soon the *Tribune* was describing "an internecine war that was hotter than the peppery food they served."[34] Enthusiasts formed hot tamale clubs and threw tamale parties, and newspapers printed recipes using masa[35] or cornmeal.[36]

Before wrapping up our tamale story, we need to visit a peculiar sandwich and an equally peculiar tamale variant. There is some speculation that the Delta tamale was the tamale that was first nestled in a hot dog bun and smothered with chili, creating Chicago's most infamous sandwich, the mother-in-law, a preposterous combination that nonetheless continues to have its acolytes. Today's standard mother-in-law counts as its filling the one tamale truly invented in Chicago, a cornmeal-based tube filled with a spicy meat mixture that is mechanically extruded and packaged in chubs that look like dainty little rolls of breakfast sausage. These are palatable in the factory-food way of salt, carbs, and grease and are sold in fast-food restaurants throughout the city.

Despite the speculation that this "Chicago" tamale was inspired by the Delta variety, the size and shape seem to emulate the Mexican tamale.

The plumper, masa-based tamale from Mexico is the dominant one in the Midwest today, but don't miss out on the svelte, fiery Delta version. I'm providing recipes for both.

MEXICAN-STYLE TAMALES

Makes about 2 dozen tamales

PORK, CHICKEN, OR MUSHROOMS IN RED CHILI SAUCE

- 2 pounds chicken thighs, bone-on pork blade steaks, or sliced cremini mushrooms
- 4 teaspoons kosher salt, divided
- 4 to 5 cups cold water, just enough to cover the meat
- 4 ounces guajillo or New Mexico red chilies
- 2 pieces chili de arbol
- 1 cup tomato juice
- 2 teaspoons extra-virgin olive oil
- 1 small yellow Spanish onion, minced
- 3 cloves garlic, minced
- 1 teaspoon Mexican oregano or epazote
- Juice of 1 lime

Place the pork, chicken, or mushrooms in a braising or casserole pan with a tight-fitting lid, cover with the water, and season with 2 teaspoons of salt. Cover with the lid and cook over medium heat until rendered and easily shredded with a fork in the case of the pork or chicken, about 90 minutes. The mushrooms should be ready in about 45 minutes and don't need to be shredded—just cooked well and aromatic. Drain, reserving the liquid, and shred the meat as soon as it is cool enough to handle. Discard any skin or bones.

Preheat oven to 325°F.

Remove stems and seeds from all the chilies, spread on a cookie sheet, and toast in the oven until aromatic but not browning, about 12 minutes. Puree in a blender until smooth, using just enough tomato juice to get things going. Mix in the remaining tomato juice and 1 cup of the reserved broth.

Using a medium saucepan, sauté the onion and garlic in the olive oil just to sweat, then add the oregano or epazote and sauté to release its aroma, just a few seconds. Add the pork, chicken, or mushrooms, and the chili puree. Bring to a low boil, mixing well, and cook down until thick, but not quite pasty. When you pull some meat away from the sides of the pan, liquid should not bleed. Stir in the lime juice and the remaining salt, check for seasoning, and refrigerate until well chilled before using.

MAKING THE DOUGH AND ASSEMBLING THE TAMALES

1 package corn husks for tamales

4 cups masa flour

3 teaspoons baking powder

2 teaspoons kosher salt

1 cup lard, or for a vegan option, non-hydrogenated palm oil

3½ cups warm (100°F to 110°F) reserved pork, chicken, or mushroom cooking
    liquid

Soak the corn husks in very hot water. Mix the masa flour with the baking powder and salt. Then work in the lard or palm oil with your hands, rubbing it into the flour until incorporated and the mixture resembles a coarse meal. Gradually stir in the reserved cooking liquid, working in well with each addition, until you have a soft, pliable dough. Allow to rest 15 minutes.

Have a dish of plain cold water nearby to keep the masa from sticking to your hands. Place a large, intact corn husk concave side up with the pointed end away from you. Wet the fingertips of your working hand, and scoop about 5 to 6 tablespoons (⅓ cup) dough into the center of the husk, closer to you than to the pointed end. Wet your fingers again and swipe the dough into a boat shape, working toward the wider end of the husk (toward you), leaving about 1 inch to spare at the wider end and about 3 inches to spare at the pointed end. Use a spoon to scoop 2 tablespoons of filling into the masa boat. Use one hand to wrap one long side of husk over the filling, pulling the masa around it, creating a tube with the husk, with the grain of the husk lengthwise. Crease the pointed end just below the masa filling, and turn it inward to form a fold, which will be the bottom during cooking. (Optional: Use a thin strip of husk to tie a knot around the tamale and secure it.)

Cover the bottom and sides of the steam basket of a *tamalera* or other steamer with soaked corn husks—this is a good use of ends and pieces and husks that aren't of a good shape for making tamales. Cover evenly over all steam holes to help create an even, gentle cooking vessel for the tamales. Place the tamales upright, open end up, folded bottom down, in the steamer. Steam, covered, for 4 hours over water at a low boil. Enjoy out of hand, or plate with guacamole and crema, or serve with salad.

DELTA-STYLE HOT TAMALES

Makes 3 to 4 dozen tamales

RED HOT CHICKEN FILLING

1 medium fryer chicken, about 3 pounds

3 quarts cold water

1 medium Spanish onion, quartered top to bottom

6 cloves garlic

2 bay leaves

1 teaspoon crushed red pepper

2 tablespoons lard or chicken drippings

4 tablespoons chili powder

½ teaspoon cayenne pepper

2 teaspoons freshly ground black pepper

1 teaspoon ground cumin

1 teaspoon oregano

Juice of 1 lime

2 teaspoons kosher salt

Cover the chicken, onion, garlic, and bay leaves with the cold water and bring to a boil. Simmer until the chicken is fall-apart tender, about 90 minutes. Reserve the cooking liquid and vegetables. Pull the chicken and shred finely, discarding skin and bones. Mince the boiled onion and garlic.

Heat the lard or drippings in a small saucepan over medium heat. Add the boiled onion and garlic, and the crushed red pepper, chili powder, cayenne and black pepper, cumin, and oregano. Sauté until aromatic, 3 to 5 minutes. Add the chicken, toss to mix well, and add 2 cups of the cooking liquid. Cook down until all liquid is absorbed and the chicken is moist and tender. Stir in the lime juice and salt, check for seasoning, and refrigerate before use.

MAKING THE DOUGH AND ASSEMBLING THE TAMALES

2 packages corn husks for tamales

4 cups stone-ground white cornmeal

2 teaspoons baking powder

2 teaspoons kosher salt

1 cup lard

3½ cups reserved chicken cooking broth, boiling

Butcher's twine for securing tamales, cut into 2-inch pieces, 2 per tamale

4 quarts water

¼ cup kosher salt

¼ cup chili powder

1 teaspoon cayenne pepper

1 teaspoon Mexican oregano or epazote

Soak the corn husks in very hot water. Mix the cornmeal with the baking powder and salt. Then work in the lard with your hands, rubbing it into the flour until incorporated and the mixture resembles a coarse meal. Pour the boiling broth in all at once and stir in with a wooden spoon, then beat until everything is well combined and free of lumps. Allow to rest 15 minutes.

Fill the tamales in the same manner as for **MEXICAN-STYLE TAMALES** (p. 110), but use only 3 to 4 tablespoons of dough and 2 tablespoons of filing per tamale, and roll each tightly into a cigar shape, longer and thinner. Fold the thin end of the husk toward the center, and simply twist it and secure it with butcher's twine or a strip of corn husk. Tie the top of the tamale as well, securing both ends and making a cigar shape with knots on the ends. Many Delta vendors further tie them in bundles of three.

Stand tamales on ends in a large pot, cover with the 4 quarts of water, and add the spices. Boil for 1 hour, or until an opened tamale pulls away cleanly from the husk and stands firm. Eat 'em while they're hot.

Breaded Pork Tenderloin

The gilded, crackly crust manifests heady aromas of fried bread and vegetable oil, then yields to luscious, sweet meat before they fall into step together, soon joined by a pillowy, sugary bun, the sour, al dente bite of sandwich pickles, and the bitter tang of mustard. I can say this as someone who's eaten around the country in high-end cheffy properties, dives, diners, cafés, and bars: A well-made breaded pork tenderloin sandwich is unmatchable for its symphonic harmony of textures, aromas, and flavors. It's one of the most epic sandwich experiences to be had in America.

Descended from the Wiener schnitzel, the pounded and breaded veal cutlet that is a specialty of the High German country, breaded pork tenderloin sandwiches (known among groupies as BPTs) are often comically oversized, the bun constituting a little welt in the center of a flat slab of golden brown and delicious. The breading is usually breadcrumbs or cracker meal, although batter-dipped tenderloin isn't unheard of. Toppings may vary slightly but usually include mustard, pickles, tomato, lettuce, and onion. Maybe it's my German blood, but I like to dress the sandwich solely with a spicy brown mustard, lots of thinly sliced Spanish onion, and a few bread-and-butter pickles. I like lettuce and tomato, but BPT time is not salad time.

The generally accepted but unverifiable story for the origin of the pork tenderloin sandwich is that a son of German immigrants, Nick Freienstein, began serving them at Nick's Kitchen in Huntington, Indiana, starting in 1908. According to the Nick's Kitchen's website, Freienstein got his start in 1904, selling hamburgers from a pushcart on the town's courthouse square, and did well enough to open a brick-and-mortar hamburger business. A few years later, he would relocate and open Nick's Kitchen.[37] A great story, American entrepreneurism at its best.

Many affectionately embellished versions of the story have Freienstein selling his version of Weiner schnitzel from the cart in 1904, but I've never seen a food pushcart that could churn out Weiner schnitzel. If Freienstein did serve BPTs from that cart in 1904, then no doubt he was the innovator. In researching BPTs, I was surprised to find that a short spot in the Huntington paper has Nick's Kitchen opening not in 1908 but in November 1909,[38] and we can see sharp ads hawking Nick's "hot sandwiches, hamburgers, and short orders" beginning that December.[39] We could presume that his pork tenderloin sandwich was among these offerings, but since it's not advertised, there is no evidence it was.

Further scanning the public record, we have a tantalizing offer of "something new, pork tenderloin sandwich, at Wylie's and only 5¢"[40] in Kansas in 1906, and while we could presume it was breaded and fried, the ad doesn't explicitly say so. Likewise, in Indianapolis in 1908, we see a pork tenderloin sandwich advertised by Keller & Sons,[41] but without further description. Interestingly, a few months earlier, Keller & Sons was advertising fried pork tenderloin with cream gravy,[42] so it's possible to guess that pork tenderloin sandwiches were indeed becoming a thing by 1908, although we can't be sure that they had yet evolved into the epic pork party we know today. Whether or not Nick's was first, Nick's Kitchen is the oldest restaurant continually serving BPTs, its version is excellent, and I consider it ground zero for BPT country, which stretches from west-central Ohio through Iowa, with Indiana and Iowa the hot spots.

Many versions call for a buttermilk soak, but I prefer a salt brine to get the meat to soak up extra juice before being breaded and fried. It makes an insanely juicy BPT. And to my palate, the best crackle and crunch is yielded by panko breadcrumbs. Use your favorite vegetable oil for this, but I recommend canola oil for its faint whiff of mustard. Especially at state fairs, cheap fast-food buns are de rigueur, but I go for something more buttery and substantial; get a brioche bun or weck if you can, but you can settle for a Kaiser roll.

Makes 4 tenderloin sandwiches

   3 cups ice-cold water
   1 tablespoon cider or distilled vinegar
   2 tablespoons granulated sugar
   1 teaspoon celery salt
   1½ teaspoons kosher salt
   4 filets of center-cut pork loin, 5 to 6 ounces each
   4 cups all-purpose flour
   4 whole eggs
   1 pound panko breadcrumbs
   2 inches vegetable oil in a 12-inch cast-iron skillet or dutch oven
   Buns, spicy brown mustard, bread-and-butter pickles, thinly sliced Spanish onion

Make the brine in the pan you will soak the pounded pork in—a casserole or large cake pan works well. Mix together the cold water, vinegar, sugar, and celery and kosher salts. Stir to dissolve, and refrigerate until well chilled before proceeding with the meat.

One at a time, place each filet on a 12-by-12-inch piece of plastic wrap on a sturdy, heavy counter or butcher block. The grain should be vertical: you should be looking down on a round piece of pork filet sitting upright and not on its side. Cover with another large piece of plastic wrap. Pound out first with the textured side of a meat mallet, until you get it down to about ½ inch thick, then switch to the smooth side, and use gentler and longer strafing strokes to flatten and smooth it out to ¼ inch thick, at which point it may be 10 inches around.

Gently nestle the pounded pork cutlets in the brine, massaging them to get them under the brine to soak it up. Cover tightly and refrigerate overnight.

In a 12-inch-deep cast-iron skillet or dutch oven, heat the oil to 350°F, monitoring with a clip-on thermometer. Set up a breading station nearby, using three large cake pans or casseroles that will fit the tenderloins. In the first pan, spread all four cups of flour in a thin, even layer. In the second, beat the eggs until smooth and then double their volume by adding an equal amount of cold water. Mix well. Spread the panko breadcrumbs evenly in the third and final pan.

One at a time, take each tenderloin out of the brine. Let the brine drain off it for 10 seconds, but do not shake off excess. Then gently lay it in the flour, flip and lay the other side in the flour, and check that all sides are coated with a thin, transparent layer of flour, patching any bare spots. Pass the tenderloin through the egg mixture, coating all sides evenly, then lay it in the breadcrumbs, turning a couple of times and pressing very gently to help the panko adhere on both sides. Gently lay in the oil to fry. Monitoring the oil temperature to maintain 350°F, cook until golden brown on side one, 4 to 5 minutes, then flip and finish side two until golden, 2 to 3 minutes more. Transfer to a wire rack or platter with paper towels to drain. Place in a very low oven while you finish frying all the tenderloins. Warm the buns in the oven along with the tenderloins and build sandwiches with your condiments of choice.

Italian Beef

The Italian beef sandwich is emblematic of the modernization of Midwestern foodways and the speed with which novel creations can grain traction and explode in popularity. The Italian beef was a Depression-era invention of economic necessity intertwined with good taste, and in the decades after World War II, it emerged as an icon of the Second City. While the Italian beef's would-be cousin, pizza, has definitive Italian roots, even if most Midwestern versions bear only passing resemblance to Italian pies, there is no such thing as Italian beef in Italy. Of course, the seasonings are those associated with Italian cuisine, and in the first half of the twentieth century, labeling anything "Italian" in Chicago was a great way to surf the wave of Italian food's rapidly increasing popularity. As hard as it might be to believe today, less than a hundred years ago, Italian cuisine was *the* exotic emerging ethnic cuisine in Midwestern cities.

The genesis of the Italian beef is fairly clear-cut: it was invented by Italian Americans and quickly creolized across ethnic lines until it abounded across Chicago and its suburbs. Al Ferreri, along with his sister Frances and her husband, Chris Pacelli Sr., began making the sandwiches in 1938, delivering them to factory workers for lunch. The Depression called for economical foods, and an inexpensive cut of beef sliced thin[43] and served on an ample piece of bread to make it filling fit the bill.[44] The three would go on to open Al's in 1940, and the imitators piled on.

A proper Italian beef lives on an Italian-bread hoagy roll; Turano is the most ubiquitous brand. The bread is filled with a generous bundle of thinly sliced beef, reheated and held in its own cooking juices, neatly coiled in the fold. Typically, you can order your Italian beef "dry," "wet" (given a dip or quick trip through a pan of the beef's juices), or "dipped" (submerged in juices). The resilience of the bread against this onslaught of meat juices is key, and the combination of the crust's chew with the sop of juices in the crumb is brilliant. You can add sautéed sweet peppers (sometimes with or without onion), and of course there is the cardinal hot giardiniera. The sandwich can be topped with cheese, mozzarella being the most common, but a well-made Italian beef's meat and juices are a masterpiece of richness all their own. Adding cheese always seems like putting a blanket on a beautiful work of art best left naked.

Like most Chicagoans, I love a good Italian beef (for me, dipped and with extra hot giardiniera) but don't indulge often. I do love to drive to the Near West Side to get one at Al's #1 on Taylor Street, which is like walking into a time capsule—a spartan room with no seating (who has time for that?), decorated with many decades' worth of faded newspaper and magazine accolades and a galleria of luminaries who have stopped by during its eighty-year reign. When ordering from the glossy walnut-grain counter under the ancient backlit red, white, and black channel-letter menu boards, and scanning the narrow countertop that wraps around the inside of the restaurant's plate-glass facade for a spot to partake, it's easy to imagine Nelson Algren or Studs Terkel in that timeless space, engaged in "the stance" (bent forward to avoid dripping on one's clothes, elbows stilting on the counter, hands cradling the beef), and feel closer to the heart of Chicago with each bite.

The Italian beef remains virtually confined to Chicago and environs, and I often wonder if an ambitious entrepreneur will try to take it on the road. As of this writing it seems inevitable, in the wake of the hit FX/Hulu series *The Bear*, in which a talented young fine-dining chef returns to Chicago to save his family's failing Italian beef stand.

This recipe is a very easy preparation, the only real challenge being to slice the beef thin enough, sheer like a lampshade. It's perfect to make for small parties, or to stock in the freezer—the meat freezes well sliced, pre-portioned, and wrapped tightly in plastic wrap. Freeze the juice separately in small containers, and reheat together for a quick taste of Chicago.

Makes up to 16 sandwiches

   1 medium Spanish onion, very thinly sliced

   1 (14-ounce) can diced tomatoes in juice

   2 bay leaves

   3 teaspoons kosher salt, divided

   2 teaspoons celery salt

   2 teaspoons crushed red pepper

   1 teaspoon freshly ground black pepper

2 teaspoons granulated garlic

2 teaspoons oregano

1 teaspoon thyme

½ teaspoon ground anise

One 5-pound beef eye of round roast

1 tablespoon extra-virgin olive oil

3 cups beef stock

Italian hoagy rolls, Turano brand if available

CHICAGO-STYLE HOT GIARDINIERA (p. 25)

Sautéed red and green peppers, shredded mozzarella (optional)

Preheat oven to 425°F.

Place the sliced onion and tomatoes in a medium roasting pan or enamel dutch oven and mix together. Add the bay leaves. In a separate bowl, mix 1 teaspoon of the kosher salt, the celery salt, red pepper, black pepper, garlic, oregano, thyme, and anise and combine well. Working over a platter, rub the roast with the olive oil, coating evenly on all sides. Coat on all sides with the spice mixture, rolling to coat it evenly. Any spice mixture you can't get to stick, add to the tomato and onion.

Place the roast in the pan on top of the tomato and onion mixture. Cook on the top rack of the oven until just starting to brown, about 15 minutes. Reduce heat to 275°F. Remove the roast, add the beef stock and remaining 2 teaspoons kosher salt to the bottom of the pan, and place on the bottom rack of the oven. Cook until the roast registers 130°F, 1½ to 2 hours. Allow to cool on the counter for 1 hour. Wrap roast tightly in plastic wrap and refrigerate. Remove bay leaves from pan juices and discard. Pour the juices into an airtight container and refrigerate overnight.

Once the roast is thoroughly chilled, remove and discard any accumulated fat that congeals on the surface. Puree the reserved juices—the onion, tomato, and all—in a blender and strain through a basket strainer. Place in a large saucepan over medium heat and bring to a medium simmer, about 170°F to 180°F. Taste for seasoning and dilute with unseasoned beef broth if too salty or too thick (you're looking for a thick broth or very runny gravy consistency) or season with more salt and pepper if it fits your taste.

While the broth is heating, slice the beef as thin as you can. I find it helps to not try to slice straight down at a 90-degree angle. Try a 15- to 30-degree angle, sloping down the end of the roast, always using long, steady strokes and always cutting away from the hand you're using to hold the roast.

Reheat the beef in the juices, only for a few minutes. The beef will drop the temperature of the juices, so heat until the juices are at 165°F again. Then use long-handled tongs to twist each portion of beef (depending how thin your slices are, 6 to 10 slices for a 6-ounce portion) into a coil, lift it out of the juices, and (holding the roll over the pot) nestle the beef in the roll. Ladle a few tablespoons of juice over the beef if you like it wet, or, using long-handled tongs, submerge the whole roll if you like it dipped. Garnish with desired dressings and eat at once, while still hot.

Jibarito

If most Midwestern food can't really be described as exotic, there are definitely exceptions, and Chicago's West Side neighborhood Humboldt Park is home to one of the most recent newcomers to our cuisine, thanks to the Puerto Rican community that has long called the neighborhood home.

Juan Figueroa's Borinquen restaurant was struggling amid fierce competition for customers in a tight-knit community that wasn't in need of more places to eat out, when one day he read in the Puerto Rican newspaper *El vocero* about a sandwich in which fried plantains stood in for bread.[45] Even though what would come to be called the jibarito wasn't his original idea, in the continental United States it has become known as a Chicago original, even as some claim the sandwich was originally invented as Venezuela's *patacon maracucho*. Regardless, within a few years, jibaritos were on offer at dozens of restaurants in and around Chicago, and they are increasing in popularity around the country. If you taste one, you'll understand why.

Figueroa's jibarito first nestled thinly sliced steak between planks of savory plantain, but soon he and his competitors were stuffing them with pork, chicken, and ham as well. More or less standard condiments are creamy mayonnaise, tomato, and iceberg lettuce. When I first tasted a jibarito at Figueroa's restaurant during the early 2000s, it was stuffed with sliced *lechon*, Puerto Rico's iconic whole roast pig, and I was smitten. Easier for you to produce at home will be a variation, roast pork shoulder picnic, or *pernil*.

This is where it pays to know a good butcher. You'll want a cut of the Boston butt or collar of pork, with a nice fat cap on it and, ideally, the skin intact. You can call it a plantain sandwich, but probably not a jibarito, without crispy pork skin. I'll walk you through making a serviceable *pernil*, then we'll make jibaritos.

TO MAKE THE *PERNIL*

Yields 3 pounds after cooking, about 8 to 10 portions

> 1 skin-on pork shoulder roast from the Boston butt or collar, 4 pounds
> 2 tablespoons fresh garlic, minced

¼ cup shallots, minced

¼ cup green bell pepper, minced

¼ cup parsley, minced

2 tablespoons fresh oregano leaves

1 tablespoon freshly ground black pepper

2 tablespoons adobo seasoning

2 tablespoons kosher salt

2 tablespoons extra-virgin olive oil

1 to 2 tablespoons lard or vegetable oil

Place the pork roast on a heavy cutting board with the skin side down. The fatback is the layer of fat between the skin and the meat. Use a butcher knife to cut the fatback and skin away from the meat in one piece, leaving a thin layer of fat with the meat but cutting most away with the skin. Working your knife parallel to the cutting board makes this easier, Lift the meat away from the fatback.

Turn the fatback over, skin side up. Using a very sharp knife, score the skin diagonally with slits 1 inch apart. These slits should fully penetrate the skin without completely cutting through the fat, only exposing it. Turn the fatback sideways and repeat, so that you have scored 1-inch squares over the fatback. Set this aside and work on the meat. Set the meat fat side up and score it ½ inch deep in the same pattern as the skin. Turn it over, fat side down, and use a paring knife to cut four evenly spaced holes straight down into the meat almost deep enough, but not quite, to pierce all the way through to the cutting board. The holes should be small but just wide enough to fit your finger in snugly.

Place the garlic, shallots, bell pepper, parsley, and oregano in the food processor and grind until well integrated and paste-like. Add the remaining ingredients and grind just long enough to incorporate fully. Use your fingers to stuff 1 tablespoon of this mixture into each of the holes in the roast. Evenly slather the rest of the mixture over the roast and the skin and fatback. Place the roast fat side up in a roasting pan, replace the fatback skin side up, cover tightly, and let rest overnight in the refrigerator.

The following day, fill a large Pyrex or enamel casserole pan with an inch of water and place on the floor of your oven.

Preheat oven to 220°F.

Add ½ inch of water to the bottom of the roasting pan and place it on the bottom rack of the oven. Cook for 4 to 5 hours, refreshing the water in both of the pans as needed. The one on the bottom will maintain a humid oven, and the water in the roasting pan will prevent drippings from burning. After 4 hours, begin monitoring the internal temperature. Cook to 185°F. Take your roast out and rest for 15 minutes before cutting. Prepare the fatback while the meat rests.

Carefully remove the fatback and skin. Place a heavy cast-iron skillet large enough to fit the fatback on a large burner, turn the heat to high, and add a very thin layer of lard or vegetable oil. Once a breadcrumb tossed in sizzles fiercely, gently lay the fatback in the pan, skin side down, to crisp the skin. Be careful of splatter. Turn the heat down to medium high or even medium if necessary to prevent excess smoking, but cook as hot as you can until the skin has crisped nicely, 6 to 8 minutes or more. Transfer to a platter skin side up, season with salt and pepper, and leave to cool to room temperature. Separate the crisped skin into pieces where it is scored, and serve with the roast as a garnish.

Slice the roast ½ inch thick, then arrange the slices evenly in the roasting pan with the juices, and return to the oven. Turn the oven off. Residual heat will keep the roast warm while you prepare the plantains.

TO MAKE THE JIBARITO

Makes 1 jibarito; scale up for more

> Vegetable oil sufficient for 1 to 2 inches in a 4-quart enamel or cast-iron dutch oven, or if you have a deep fryer, to fill it
> 2 unripe fully green plantains, peeled
> 1 tablespoon mayonnaise
> 3 or 4 slices *pernil* (5 to 6 ounces) with crispy skin and pan juices
> 2 or 3 slices ripe tomato
> ½ cup shredded iceberg lettuce

In each of the plantains, cut a shallow slit, just enough to reach the flesh inside, the length of the concave curve. Soak them in warm water while you prepare your hot oil, about 15 to 20 minutes. Peel the soaked plantains by pulling the peel back from the slit you cut. Pat thoroughly dry before frying.

Monitoring with a clip-on thermometer, heat the oil to 325°F, then fry each plantain whole until cooked through and tender, about 3 to 4 minutes on each side. Remove and allow to rest for a few minutes until they are still hot but not dangerously so. They do need to be hot to mash well.

Place each fried plantain on a piece of plastic wrap on a cutting board, then cover each with another sheet of plastic wrap. Use the bottom of a very sturdy plate or another cutting board to press each plantain into a flat plank ¼ inch thick. The planks will have a little bit of a curve to them because of the plantains' shape.

Increase the oil temperature to 350°F and fry your plantain planks until crisp on the outside and chewy but soft on the inside, about 4 to 5 minutes. Drain on paper towels.

Working quickly, build your sandwich. This is best eaten when the "bread" is still hot. Slather the mayonnaise evenly across both plantain planks, lay slices of *pernil* the length of the sandwich on one plank, moisten with pan juices, and dot with crispy skin. Lay a layer of tomato, then lettuce, over the *pernil*, then crown with the other plantain slice.

My favorite spot for jibaritos, Logan Square's Punta Cana, serves these with a side of pigeon peas and rice, and that's always a good idea. You can make any rice and bean preparation you like to go with a jibarito if you can't find pigeon peas, but they're worth seeking out for their sweet, earthy flavor and creamy texture that dances merrily with rice.

Hot Dog Heaven

After a long trudge back up the snowy slope of a sledding hill, I caught a whiff of sweet spices and the unmistakable scent of *Brühwurst* cut with the sharp tang of yellow mustard, which warmed my chilly face and brought a pang to my belly. The hot dog man had schlepped his cart out to Milliken State Park on the Detroit Riverfront to peddle his sausages to frosty folks using the hill for sledding after a splendid lake-effect snow. The standard hot dog cart fare was always upstaged by the wafting aroma of coney sauce, a heady chili-flavored topping spiked with sweet spices and cumin, not unlike Cincinnati chili, but definitely surfing its own wave. Until my arrival in Chicago many years later, the coney dog peddled on the streets of Detroit was my gold standard for hot dogs. More on that later.

Americans eat more than 20 billion hot dogs a year, supporting an industry worth nearly $8 billion annually of sausages alone.[46] While almost every American family eats hot dogs regularly, we do some unique things with them in the Midwest. Midwesterners have led the hot dog industry from its arrival from Germany to the present day. Hot dog manufacturers founded here include Eckrich (Fort Wayne, Indiana), Hillshire Farms (New London, Wisconsin), Armour (Chicago), Oscar Mayer (Chicago), and Ball Park (Livonia, Michigan). In Chicago, we especially treasure the products of Vienna Beef. How wieners, a.k.a. frankfurters, became synonymous with America and a staple of the commoner diet is a most unlikely story.

In spite of its name and the common association of Germans with sausage, this type of sausage—originally made by finely grinding and emulsifying high-grade muscle meat, which was also coveted for roasting or curing whole— undoubtedly originated in Italy in the sixteenth century with the creation of mortadella bologna.[47] Germans were quick to take up the method and expand on the possibilities of fine sausages. By the late seventeenth century, examples of these types of sausages appeared in German cookbooks, and the Germans were doing what they do and the Italians don't: mixing meats. Here we have a later edition of Maria Sophia Schellhammer's receipt first published in 1697:

Belonische Würste

The fat of pigs and the lean meat of the loin of beef must be chopped together very small and there must be the same quantity of each. Then you must take of fresh bacon [fat] that is not yet smoked and cut it in cubes, boil slightly in water, and add it to the meat together with whole peppercorns, ground cloves, salt, and a little sheep's blood, and put it into guts.[48]

Filet mignon ground into sausage makes for some pricey wurst! Even the comedians of the late seventeenth century made light of these luxury novelties for the rich. The second edition of the humorous *Wurstologia* recounts a funny story in which a workingman delivering goods to a merchant's house that doubles as a hostel encounters the fancy sausage, orders several plates, and eats to his content, only to learn that the cost of the meal has drained his pockets.[49]

By the nineteenth century, mentions of Belonische Wurst are rare, and among the hundreds of local sausage styles common in Germany at that time, two emerge on the recipe list in an ad for a sausage maker's manual in Regensburg in 1825: *Wiener Wurst* and *Frankfurter Wurst*.[50] Naturally this raises a question: What is the difference between a wiener and a frankfurter, and how do they relate to hot dogs? F. Eppner's 1870 *Die deutsche Wurstfabrikation* helped to answer the question. Conventional wisdom states that frankfurters were pure pork or pure beef, while the Viennese mixed their meats, using pork and beef or veal. Consequentially, then, Herr Eppner lists only pork in the Viennese sausage, and pork and veal in the Frankfurter; otherwise the seasonings vary in inconsequential ways, and the Vienna wurst receipt concludes with an admonition that they be "treated exactly" as Frankfurter sausages, except for a shorter cooking time because they are smaller.[51] It's funny that a question I asked my dad when I was a little boy would be answered years later by an old German book in exactly the same manner: "Frankfurters are bigger than wieners." Both, however, can be hot dogs.

The early American history of hot dogs is commonly associated with New York, but the earliest mention of its progenitors in popular media seems to be in a German-language newspaper in Saint Louis in 1866, which informs readers that the proprietor of the Chouteau Ave. Brauerei Salon "will offer his guests an excellent glass of young beer with Viennese sausage and sauerkraut."[52] A couple of years later and a few hundred miles away, the Lancaster *Intelligencer* heralds the arrival of Frankforter [*sic*] sausages at the "famous 'Eagle Saloon'" and advises readers that they can obtain "the new luxury, served up in the best style" there.[53] Similar examples of both sausages can be found in popular media, indicating that they infiltrated the American palate via the tables of people with money. It would take a few more decades, an increasingly industrialized meat production system, and American ingenuity to take the erstwhile luxury food to the common man via street carts and roadside stands.

The evolution and wider adoption of the term "hot dog" is usually credited to various Easterners around 1900 or so, but by 1883, the Chicago *Inter-Ocean* was reporting, via the Fort Wayne *Daily Gazette*, that saloonkeepers were giving away a "hot sausage known to Germans as 'Wiener wurst' and to Americans as 'boiled dog.'"[54] It is as likely that this name came about because the shape of the sausage was reminiscent of a dachshund, a popular German dog breed at the time, as that it came from rumors of the sausages containing dog meat. No later than 1886, we can quote the Nashville *Tennessean* deriding street vendors:

> "Hot stuff," "hot pup," "hot dog," sings out the fiend who carried in one hand a tin cooking arrangement, and on the other arm a basket. He is the wiener wurst fiend. It is his cries that greet you as you enter the theater and regreet you as you come out.[55]

and reporting on another occasion when the police were called to hush a vendor:

> "Weener Wurst!" "Hot Poodle!" "Hot Dog!" "Hot stuff!" "Hot sausage!" "Right here!" The persistency with which he repeated over and over those words, would be, if not such a nuisance, worthy of admiration.[56]

The name "hot dog" eventually caught on, and anti-German sentiment around World War I surely accelerated the switch. We've known both wieners and frankfurters as hot dogs for more than a hundred years, even as the sausages don't always conform to their mid-nineteenth-century German formulations. The influx of Central European Jews to American cities played an important part in the switch from all-pork or mixed-meat sausages to all-beef products (as did the rapidly growing supply of beef from the West); thus, we have had, since at least the 1890s, a thoroughly American product.

A lot is said about Coney Island in hot dog history, and it is notable that sausages were a booming business there by the 1880s. However, without detailed descriptions of the sausages, it seems more likely that they were bratwurst or mettwurst than the more labor-intensive frankfurters and wieners. Perhaps the most important contribution to our modern hot dog from Coney Island is the bun. By 1882, sausages were being "inserted into a huge roll" for service,[57] an innovation credibly attributed to Ignatz Frischmann, who had arrived in New York by 1850 and died in 1904. Nevertheless, I'm always down for an S. Rosen poppy-seed bun made in Chicago.

CHICAGO-STYLE HOT DOGS

A riot of color and old-world custom transplanted, amidst a bedlam of sound. Into the heart of Chicago. Such is the Maxwell Street market . . .

Here one finds as cosmopolitan a crowd as can be found anywhere. There is a Burly Russian, looking like one of Tolstoy's characters, dressed in his peasant garb. Here is an old Jewess, clinging to the customs and dress of the old world, and beside her stands her daughter, dressed in the fashion of the American girl of today. Italians, Austrians, Greeks, Hungarians, all are here, and still more color is added to the scene by the appearance of a society man with several society buds, out adventuring.[58]

It's always been amazing to me that such a recent phenomenon as the Chicago-style hot dog would leave the story of its creation clouded in a shroud of the din and clang of a busy urban market, but it's generally agreed that the sausage with a salad on top emerged out of the diversity of the Maxwell Street Market on the Near Southwest Side of the city. Just as amazing is that from that market would emerge the first enduring Jewish American contribution to our food-ways, one that changed how we all eat to this day.

Between 1880 and 1924, 2.5 million Jews immigrated to the United States from Eastern Europe.[59] Even before this influx, 300,000 Jews already called the United States home. Perhaps the longest-lived hot dog manufacturer in the nation was formed by David Berg in Chicago in 1860. His company was followed by another, founded as the Vienna Sausage Mfg. Company in the 1890s by Jewish immigrants Emil Reichl and Samuel Ladany, that would come to be central to the hot dog trade in Chicago. Reichl and Ladany first served their sausages at the 1893 Columbian Exposition before taking up shop near the Maxwell Street Market.[60] Over the next several decades, their sausages would become synonymous with Chicago hot dogs, and by the 1950s, the all-beef frankfurter would become the standard in the Chicago market.[61] Vienna

Beef's frank is made using a natural casing, yielding a signature snap and pop, which is an essential part of the tactile experience of eating a hot dog in Chicago.

Abe Drexler, founder of the legendary Fluky's, claimed to have served the first Chicago-style hot dog at Maxwell and Halsted Streets in 1929. And while even Drexler admitted he had no hard evidence to back up his claim, the *Chicago Tribune* seems to agree.[62] Whether or not his story is true, it's easy to imagine Depression-era vendors scrambling among a cacophony of competition to provide the most value, adding toppings to make a full meal out of a humble sausage sandwich. No later than 1953, that sandwich was called the "meal on a bun" in an advertisement for the grand opening of Suzie's Corner department store at Sixty-Third and Cottage Grove. A customer could choose either a Polish sausage or a Vienna kosher red hot to be served "on Rosen's superfine poppy-seed buns with our own grilled onion, sweet relish, mustard, and Mexican peppers" for 1 cent.[63] Today's standard Chicago-style dog also includes sliced tomato and a whiff of celery salt. We'll get to Coney Island dogs next, but it's notable that the ad offers "Coney Island style for 5 cents extra."

Speaking of that superfine bun, the poppy-seed bun is one of the hallmarks of authenticity of a Chicago-style hot dog. Sam Rosen, a Polish Jew who immigrated to the United States as a young boy and opened his own bakery in New York at the age of sixteen, moved to Chicago and opened his namesake firm in 1909.[64] The company is now owned by conglomerate Alpha Baking but continues to produce millions of the buns each year in the exact style developed by Sam Rosen. Vienna Beef's vice president Bob Schwartz, author of *Never Put Ketchup on a Hot Dog*, believes the poppy-seed bun coalesced with the now standard "Chicago Seven" toppings in the 1980s.[65]

When I first encountered a Chicago-style dog, I thought it was one of the most preposterous things I'd ever seen, but I was an instant convert. Sweet, sour, salty, spicy, bitter, chewy, crunchy, crispy, hot, cold, rich, refreshing, it has it all. It's the sort of thing one might call a symphony of flavors and textures, but it goes beyond that—it's positively operatic. You may enjoy ketchup on hot dogs in any one of a number of other, inferior combinations, but the Chicago dog is perfect. Dare thee not defile it with that syrupy red stuff, for the delicately grand balance will falter and your Chicago dog will fail.

I don't advocate making your own hot dog sausages at home—I've done it enough times to tell you it might be worth the effort if you have the equipment and time, but most of us don't. Fortunately, high-quality hot dogs are widely available, but definitely go out of your way to get the Vienna Beef or Red Hot brand. They must be all beef and they must be made with natural casing—

that's not optional. Go online if you must to get S. Rosen poppy-seed buns. Once you have those two fundamentals in place, Chicago-style dogs are easy to make, and a joy to consume. You can grill or griddle them, but the true Chicago way is to steam them. I always plan on two per person, because if you're going to have hot dogs, you may as well live a little.

Serves 4 to 8

  3 quarts water
  8 natural-casing all-beef frankfurters
  8 poppy-seed hot dog buns
  8 tablespoons yellow mustard
  4 small ripe tomatoes; you'll need 8 slices ⅜ inch thick
  Celery salt
  8 tablespoons **PICCALILLI** (p. 23) or green pickle relish
  8 dill pickle spears
  4 tablespoons finely minced onion
  16 pickled sport peppers (2 per hot dog)

Place the water in a stockpot or large saucepan and bring to a high simmer, 190°F to 200°F. Drop the hot dogs in and simmer for 10 to 15 minutes. The room should start to smell of hot dogs. Perch a colander or strainer over the pot, but without any part of it submerged in the water. Place the buns in the strainer and cover with a clean towel or a piece of aluminum foil to trap steam. When they are warm and soft throughout, in about 5 minutes, they are ready.

1. Line the buns up on a tray with the slit side up.
2. Drain the hot dogs with the strainer, and cradle one in each bun.
3. Along one side of the sausage, draw a long streak of mustard with a squeeze bottle, between the sausage and the bun.
4. Cut each slice of tomato in half to form half-moon shapes, then insert two pieces, cut side down, between the sausage and bun, opposite the mustard. Place them end to end so they line up along the entire sausage.
5. Sprinkle a whisper of celery salt over the tomatoes.
6. Sprinkle 1 tablespoon of piccalilli atop the mustard on one side of the sausage, evenly along its entire length, partly covering that side of the sausage.
7. Tuck 1 dill pickle spear in between the sausage and tomato. Sprinkle 1 tablespoon of onion over the length of the sausage, tying the piccalilli side to the tomato and pickle side.

8. Place the sport peppers end to end over the top of the onion.

9. If you wish, draw one more streak of mustard lengthwise along the top (optional).

10. Enjoy with gusto. French fries (on which ketchup *is* allowed) are a typical accompaniment, but potato chips or potato salad are also perfect sides.

CONEY DOGS

The hot dogs I grew up on, made by Merkley and Sons in Jasper, Indiana, were a perfect representative of the German-style mixed meat, pork and beef wiener with natural casing. Even from a young age, I took them with yellow mustard and kraut. But my first regional hot dog obsession was a coney dog of the Detroit variety. Grandma Melba proselytized me, and the coney dog became my go-to when I could find it, or when kraut wasn't available as a topping. A good coney dog is a thing of wonder. As a slurry of meat shrouds a succulent sausage, its thick, lugubrious constitution coats your palate with lightly spiced essence of pure beef, effecting a dark, sensual tango with the sausage—it's a masterpiece of meat manipulated for maximum pleasure, and on a lean budget at that.

The first thing we need to understand about coney dogs, Coney Islands, or simply coneys, as they're called in Cincinnati, is that they have nothing to do with Coney Island. They are a regional family of hot dog styles dominated by entrepreneurs of Macedonian descent and distinguished by their chili sauce topping. The original creator of the coney dog, whoever it was, made an astute move in the early twentieth century, when both chili con carne and hot dogs were quite fashionable.

There are at least four regional coney dog styles—from Detroit, Flint, and Jackson in Michigan, and from Cincinnati. Some would add Kalamazoo, Michigan, where Coney Island Kalamazoo has allegedly been topping franks with chili since 1915. Some Midwestern drive-ins that serve otherwise excellent food will serve a "coney dog" topped with a sweet slurry that closely resembles a sloppy joe. I am definitely not a fan—stick to coney dogs in restaurants that specialize in them. Beyond the Midwest, coney shops can be found as far away as Minnesota and Texas, and coneys are common in Tulsa, Oklahoma.[66] But really, where coneys are concerned, all roads lead to Detroit.

Much of the lore of the Detroit coney dog surrounds Lafayette Coney Island and American Coney Island, two gems set side by side on Lafayette Boulevard downtown near the Detroit River. Their quintessentially American rivalry, which began with Greek immigrant brothers William and Constantine Keros in the 1930s, has now spanned almost a century. Both are excellent restaurants with proper coney dogs, so it's odd that one of the points of the rivalry is who opened first, and many followers are left believing that the winner of that debate served Detroit's first coney dog. While some claim that Lafayette opened in 1914 and American in 1917, I was able to find at least three different claims of dates in newspaper records. Katherine Young and Joe Grimm, who did the deep dive in their book *Coney Detroit*, found in city directories that the Keros brothers opened Lafayette Coney Island together in 1923. That version didn't last, and after a falling out between the brothers, the present restaurants opened in 1931 and 1936, respectively,[67] some two decades after the likely establishment of the first Coney Island shops in Detroit. Older coney shops still operate in Flint and Kalamazoo, and two of Jackson's beloved spots, Jackson Coney Island and Virginia Coney Island, had set up shop by the mid-1930s.

Lafayette and American do occupy that central spot downtown from which all radii of the coney wheel emanate. From Lafayette via Gratiot, Woodward, Grand River, and Michigan Avenues, coney culture pulses out from the Motor City to Flint to the north, Jackson to the west, and Fort Wayne to the south. We'll discuss Cincinnati's coneys when we discuss Cincinnati chili, which is distinct from that in Michigan. In fact, some Michigan coneys are served not with chili per se but rather with a meat "sauce." What, then, makes a Detroit Coney Island a Detroit Coney Island? We need to take a look at three primary distinguishing factors: the bun, the sausage, and the "sauce."

The bun: Since a proper Coney Island bun is steamed, it takes a piece of bread more substantial than a standard grocery-store hot dog bun. Detroit Coney Island buns are what a lot of people would call old-fashioned, a true milk bread given a longer fermentation for a yeastier, richer bread flavor. Their other unique characteristic is a slightly more resilient crumb; they're going to be steamed and sauced, so they need to be able to stand up under some juicy conditions, yet like any other hot dog bun, they're plenty soft. The favored bakers are Brown's and Metropolitan, but you may be able to find Ball Park buns farther afield; they are a perfect example of a Michigan-style hot dog bun. If none of these can be obtained, "brat" or sausage buns usually do the trick.

The sausage: Michigan's regional hot dogs are distinguished from Chicago-style hot dogs in that they are a beef and pork combination, which makes for a rounded-out meat flavor and a lighter color. The most popular packer in Flint far and away is Koegel's, which started as a tiny meat market downtown and has cornered the market there for a good hundred years. A Flint dog is made with natural casing, as is a Detroit-style dog, where you might also find a Koegel's sausage in your bun or, just as likely, one by Dearborn Brand. The one outlier here is Jackson, where a skinless sausage isn't a nonstarter, knocking that city's dogs down a notch on my scorecard. Wherever you are in Michigan, your dogs will probably be griddled, and ready to serve on a moment's notice.

The toppings: Mustard and finely chopped onion are fairly standard across the state; where the regions differ is the meat sauce. Detroit's is a beanless chili with a consistency like a viscous gravy, varying in spiciness, but even the spiciest are nonthreatening to all but the most timid of eaters. Flint goes all the way in the other direction, making a spicy, assertive "sauce" that is primarily finely ground beef heart or a beef heart–ground beef combination cooked down with spices into a dry, crumbly topping. Done well, it's positively mouthwatering, and easier to eat on the go. Both lean and high in protein and minerals, the beef heart is also a healthier option. Jackson straddles the two, making a sauce that is closer to Flint's in flavor and consistency, although it has a little higher moisture content; its consistency resembles a sloppy joe, but it has that chili spice. A proper Jackson Coney Island sauce is made with finely ground beef heart, and with just the right amount of juice kissing it, this might be my favorite Coney Island sauce. Finally, Michiganders agree with Chicagoans on a key aspect of hot dog culture: save that ketchup for your fries!

Contrary to what you've read and heard in the relentlessly bloviating popular media, Detroit is a beautiful and historic city, and today it is probably the most creative large urban center in the country. Plan a Coney Island trip to Detroit (and don't skip the pizza), and have a little jaunt out to Flint and Jackson—they're worth the trip. And take the local Coney Island as it comes, as one does.

Since every place that serves Coney Islands either serves a packaged sauce or jealously guards the recipe, the best I can do here is use my thirty-nine years of culinary experience to reconstruct the sauces for you. These sauces all freeze well, so they can be reheated for easy enjoyment. Koegel's franks are available online, or use your local natural-casing pork and beef combination wiener or frankfurter. Steam the buns as for **CHICAGO-STYLE HOT DOGS** (p. 125). For each of the three styles, the dress is the same: a smear of mustard inside the bun, then the sausage, then a heap of Coney Island sauce (to your taste), followed by a sprinkling of chopped raw onion and a stripe of mustard. Make any of these sauces a day before you plan to use them so that any congealed fat can be removed. Reheat gently in a skillet to serve.

DETROIT-STYLE CONEY ISLAND SAUCE

Makes about 2 quarts, enough for 2 dozen coney dogs

1 cup beef tallow (preferred), lard, or vegetable shortening
3 pounds lean ground beef

1 pound finely ground beef heart (or substitute ground venison, bison, or more
  beef)

2 cups Spanish onion, very finely diced

1 cup cracker meal or finely crushed saltine crackers

1 (14/15-ounce) can tomato puree

1 quart chicken stock

3 tablespoons chili powder

2 tablespoons Spanish paprika

¼ cup prepared yellow mustard

2 tablespoons ground cumin

2 tablespoons granulated onion

1 tablespoon granulated garlic

1 tablespoon dried Mexican oregano

1 tablespoon freshly ground black pepper

¼ teaspoon ground cloves

¼ teaspoon ground coriander

¼ teaspoon cayenne pepper

2 tablespoons kosher salt

In a 4-quart or larger cast-iron or enamel dutch oven, melt the cooking fat over low heat, then add the ground beef and beef heart. Use a potato masher to break up the meat into fine crumbs while mixing it with the melted fat, gradually increasing the heat to medium as you break it up, until the largest pieces are the size of a pea. Continue cooking over medium heat while stirring from the bottom regularly until all the beef is cooked through and frying in the hot fat. Add the onion, stir to combine, and cook until the onion is translucent. Do not drain off the fat at any time; it is critical for the next step. Continuing over medium heat, add the cracker meal and stir until the fat is absorbed by the meal and the whole mass takes on a pasty appearance. Add the tomato puree and chicken broth and stir well to break up the paste in the stock to form a smooth soupy mixture. Add the remaining ingredients and stir well.

Reduce heat to medium low and bring to a low boil, stirring regularly from the bottom to prevent scorching. Cover the pot and maintain a very low boil for 2 hours, periodically stirring from the bottom. The sauce should tighten until it is the consistency of a thick gravy or loose milkshake; it should flow, but not run. If it gets too thick, add a little stock or water to loosen it up, or if you're approaching the end of 2 hours and need to tighten it, sprinkle with a little cracker meal.

After 2 hours, if you are happy with the consistency, check for seasoning. Then put the pot in a clean and sanitized sink full of ice water to cool as quickly as possible before refrigerating overnight or up to 1 week. After refrigerating, skim any congealed fat that rose to the top. Will freeze well in tightly sealed containers for months.

FLINT-STYLE CONEY ISLAND SAUCE

Makes just under 2 quarts, enough for 18 coney dogs

> ¼ cup pork lard
>
> ¼ cup (½ stick) unsalted butter
>
> 2 pounds ground beef, 80% lean
>
> 1 pound finely ground beef heart (or substitute ground venison, bison, or more beef)
>
> 1 cup Spanish onion, very finely diced
>
> 1 tablespoon crushed fresh garlic
>
> 4 tablespoons ground cumin
>
> ¼ cup plus 2 tablespoons chili powder
>
> 1 tablespoon freshly ground black pepper
>
> 2 tablespoons spicy brown mustard
>
> 2 tablespoons Worcestershire sauce (optional)
>
> 1 teaspoon kosher salt

In a 4-quart or larger cast-iron or enamel dutch oven, melt the lard and butter over low heat, then add the ground beef and beef heart. Use a potato masher to break up the meat into fine crumbs, gradually increasing the heat as you break it up into smaller and smaller pieces, until the largest pieces are smaller than a pea. Then increase the heat to medium high and stir constantly as you brown the meat lightly in the fat. Brown to a uniform light brown. When you are happy with the color, add the onion and garlic, stir, and render the onion and garlic until translucent and aromatic. Do not drain off the fat at any time. Add the cumin, chili powder, and pepper and cook, stirring constantly, until the spices are toasted and quite aromatic. Add the mustard and Worcestershire and combine thoroughly. Add about a cup of water and gradually cook it off, stirring regularly, until the mixture is completely dry. Remove the mixture from the heat as soon as it's dry so it doesn't burn.

Turn out onto a sheet pan to cool quickly, then transfer to an airtight container and refrigerate overnight. Remove any congealed fat from the top of the sauce before serving or freezing.

JACKSON-STYLE CONEY ISLAND SAUCE

Makes just under 2 quarts, enough for 18 coney dogs

> ½ cup pork lard
>
> 3 pounds finely ground beef heart; or a combination of beef heart and venison, bison, or lean ground beef

3 tablespoons chili powder

2 tablespoons granulated onion

1 tablespoon granulated garlic

1 tablespoon ground cumin

1 tablespoon Spanish paprika

1 tablespoon kosher salt

In a 4-quart or larger cast-iron or enamel dutch oven, melt the lard over low heat, then add the beef heart. Use a potato masher to break up the meat into fine crumbs, gradually increasing the heat as you break it up into smaller and smaller pieces, until the largest pieces are smaller than a pea. Then increase the heat to medium high and stir constantly as you brown the meat lightly in the fat. Brown to a uniform light brown. Add the spices, but not the salt, and fry all together until the spices are well toasted and highly aromatic, 4 to 6 minutes. Slow the cooking by adding a cup of cold water, stir to coat everything, then cover and simmer for 30 minutes. Stir well, and if the mixture is too wet (runny juices), increase heat to cook off some of the liquid, until the grains of meat are all coated in syrupy juices, not completely dry like Flint sauce. You can always add a few tablespoons of water if needed to loosen. Add the salt toward the end, tasting and adjusting seasoning if needed.

Turn out onto a sheet pan to cool quickly, then transfer to an airtight container and refrigerate overnight. Remove any congealed fat from the top of the sauce before serving or freezing.

5

PLEASE PASS THE CORN

Vegetables and Sides

We may live without music, poetry, and art;
We may live without conscience and live without heart;
We may live without friends, we may live without books;
But civilized man cannot live without cooks.
He may live without books—what is knowledge but grieving?
He may live without hope—what is hope but deceiving?
He may live without love—what is passion but pining?
But where is the man who can live without dining?

—**Presbyterian Church of LaPorte,** *Many New and Reliable Recipes*

A T the table of Rita and Lee Gress, it was always a struggle to put my head down to say grace as my stomach rumbled for the spread before us. With nine kids of their own and always blessed with the company of friends or family, my aunt and godfather would have at least a dozen people at the table. Besides a main dish (or two) of roast or fried meat or poultry, there would be biscuits or yeast bread, eggs scrambled or hard-boiled from the yardbirds, buttered or creamed corn, green beans perfumed with smokehouse ham and pregnant with the savory tang of onion, rivvels or dumplings, salad, macaroni and cheese, mashed or fried potatoes, pickles and relishes, and always a little something sweet for dessert. We all knew to save plenty of room for dessert because Aunt Rita was a master pie baker, and in her deep freezer she always kept a stash of blackberries from the patch next to the horse pasture, and you never knew when there'd be ice cream whipped up from their own old-line pastured dairy cows. The cylinder of sweetened cream would be buried in rock salt–spiked ice and cranked by hand in the White Mountain ice cream bucket.

Aunt Rita was always, in my mind, the apogee of American home cooks, the high priestess of domestic arts. In the extended Fehribach family, she was always known as the keeper of Grandma Frances's best-kept secrets. One of those, which I gleaned over many years, was that the spread is more important than the main dish. It's all about sides, relishes, little touches, and gathered tastes of the season.

When we peel back the layers of modern side-dish trappings, dominated by the french fries and austere side salads that cast a monotone over all of our nation's cooking, Midwestern community cookbooks are filled with vegetable dishes of all sorts: salads of various beans, cucumbers, tomatoes, or asparagus; soups of okra, peas, onions, turnips, mushrooms, or celery; roasted or sautéed beets, artichokes, carrots, parsnips, cauliflower, or broccoli; stews of cabbage, sauerkraut, eggplant, dandelion greens, spinach, or summer squashes. No vegetable is a stranger to the Midwestern table.

An entire book could be written on Midwestern vegetable and side dishes alone, but we'll cover a lot of territory in twelve recipes. Naturally, many dishes we consider iconically Midwestern, such as corn on the cob, are surely a holdover from Mesoamerican foodways. They are so simple that it would be gratuitous to provide a recipe, as with any vegetable, pasta, or grain simply steamed and buttered or sauced.

Many dishes that have recently been considered foreign will doubtless join the club of Midwestern side dishes as immigrant cuisines continue to be prepared, loved, and adopted by the macro culture. We've creolized versions of kimchi and fried rice, *mezze* dishes such as hummus and falafel, and Latin American standards such as red rice, elotes, and quinoa, which appear on menus from fine-dining establishments on down to dirty neighborhood bar-and-grills. In another generation, some of the standbys I share here will endure, but we'll also have a new set of dishes to look forward to.

Pan-Fried Morels

When the leaves on the oak trees are the size of a squirrel's ears, it's time to keep an extra-close eye on the weather. For the trees to sprout, there must have already been some spring weather, a handful of sunny days in the seventies, and, just as important, a quenching rain that tells the tree to begin its new year. Watch the weather and the trees for bud break; there's a certain rhythm to it. The best time for maximum harvest is an early morning after an overnight rain, followed by plenty of sunshine to warm the ground up and encourage the *Morchella* fungus to send its fruit (yay, delicious mushrooms!) toward the sky. Yellow morels have an affinity for deciduous trees, especially oaks and poplars, while my favorite, black morels, favor conifers or more acidic soils. Look on south-facing slopes and open meadows first—they're the first to warm up in spring—and keep checking those cooler spots in the dells or north slopes. The total window for morels in most climes is little more than two weeks, four max.

The Fehribach family used to fan out into the woods, carrying empty bread bags to transport the precious mushrooms back to the kitchen. After careful cleaning, we'd bread them and chicken-fry them in the manner described in

The Big Jones Cookbook. This simpler, more elegant version gives a nod to Wisconsin's dairy industry and its excellent butter. That said, just because they're not chicken-fried doesn't mean they're light in calories. Mushrooms *want* butter, and we use a lot of it here. This is my absolute favorite side dish for spring, but it may be even better used to smother egg noodles. Shower the whole thing with some Wisconsin pecorino cheese and garden herbs, and you have a spectacular main dish.

Morels are increasingly available in gourmet grocery stores in season, but you'll pay dearly for them, and they probably won't be very fresh—though they are without a doubt worth the splurge. If you know anyone who knows where you might find a patch, hunting morels is always a great excuse for an early spring hike.

Serves 4 to 6

1 pound fresh morel mushrooms

1 tablespoon extra-virgin olive oil

6 tablespoons unsalted butter, cut into ¼-inch pats and chilled, divided

½ cup shallots, sliced very thinly lengthwise

¼ cup crisp, dry white wine such as Alsatian or Austrian riesling

½ teaspoon kosher salt

¼ cup finely shredded pecorino cheese

Freshly ground black pepper, to taste

2 teaspoons freshly picked thyme or tarragon leaves, or a combination, minced

Lemon wedges to garnish (optional)

Split the morels in half lengthwise and use a Q-tip or lint-free cloth to clean them inside and out. In a 10- to 12-inch cast-iron frying pan, heat the olive oil and 2 tablespoons of the butter over medium-high heat until the butter foams but doesn't brown. Add the shallots and sauté just to sweat, stirring constantly, 1 to 2 minutes. Add the morels, stir and toss them to coat with the butter, and sauté, tossing often to cook evenly, until they have softened noticeably and the aroma of mushrooms rises richly. Add the wine and salt and boil hard to reduce the liquid until there are only 1 to 2 tablespoons of syrupy mushroom and wine liquor in the pan. Remove from heat and allow to cool for a moment, then throw in the remaining butter pats and stir constantly as they melt to form a creamy emulsion. Toss the mushrooms to coat well.

Use a slotted spoon to arrange the mushrooms on a serving platter, pour the butter sauce over, then shower with the pecorino cheese, a few twists of freshly ground black pepper, and the herbs. If you like, garnish with a few lemon wedges and serve at once, while the butter sauce is still hot.

The Many Colors of Borscht

I'd be remiss in writing about Midwestern food without doing something with beets, one of the most popular garden and farmers' market crops after sweet corn and tomatoes. Borscht quickly came to mind because, well, I love borscht. A better reason to include it is that it's representative of cultures from Poland east through the Baltics, Ukraine, and Russia, including those of Ashkenazi Jews, who use beef in their borscht instead of the pork or pork sausage often included by non-Jewish cooks.[1]

The name "borscht" comes from the Ukrainian and Russian *borschch*, a type of parsnip that was originally used to make the soup. Contrary to my own long-held assumptions, borscht doesn't usually include sauerkraut, as I discovered when I scoured Polish markets and delis on Chicago's Northwest Side for it. It can, of course, be red, pink (with sour cream added), white (with parsnips or potatoes and hard-boiled eggs), yellow or orange (with yellow beets and maybe carrots), or even green (classically, with sorrel). Today, the name "borscht" is a catchall for any sour soup. What makes it sour is up to the cook, but I'm always looking for more excuses to use sauerkraut.

VEGETARIAN BORSCHT

I learned to make borscht the way most American-born cooks did, with red beets, sauerkraut, and sausage. My adult taste likes it either without any meat or with bacon or beef (or both) instead of sausage. This recipe is my vegetarian (vegan, actually) borscht, which I make when I can find overwintered beets at spring farmers' markets; they're the sweetest beets you can get. The bonus is that those spring markets will also have watercress, whose brininess adds an essential savory flavor to the soup, making any kind of meat an afterthought. I always serve red borscht with sour cream, which makes it vegetarian and not vegan, but you can of course leave it off. If you want to make this borscht with bacon, beef, or sausage, simply dice and brown the meat in the oven (toss lean beef in oil first to prevent sticking) before adding to the soup with the beets.

Makes about 2 quarts

 1 tablespoon vegetable oil

 1½ cups yellow Spanish. onion, very thinly sliced

 1 tablespoon fresh garlic, minced

 2 cups red beets, peeled and very finely diced

1 cup carrot, very finely diced (peeling optional)

½ cup celery, very finely diced

2 cups sauerkraut with juice

4 cups **RICH VEGETABLE STOCK** (recipe follows)

2 bay leaves

1 teaspoon freshly ground black pepper

1 tablespoon kosher salt

Leaves from 2 bunches watercress (save stems for stock)

1 to 2 tablespoons fresh dill, minced, to your taste

Sour cream and rye bread to accompany

In a 4-quart heavy-bottomed stockpot, heat the vegetable oil just up to the smoking point and add the onion. Stir constantly to prevent scorching while sautéing the onion until it just begins to caramelize around the edges and smell sweet and not at all spicy or sulfurous. Add the garlic, beets, carrot, and celery, reduce heat to medium, and sauté until the vegetables release their aroma and you can smell them only by standing over the pot. Add the sauerkraut, vegetable stock, bay leaves, pepper, and salt, and bring to a low boil. Reduce heat to a high simmer and cook until vegetables are tender, 30 to 45 minutes. Remove from heat. Transfer ⅓ of the soup to the blender and puree, then return to the pot. Stir in the watercress leaves and dill. Serve at once or chill to serve cold.

RICH VEGETABLE STOCK

This stock makes an excellent rich base for almost any soup. Save your stems and trimmings from mushrooms, cooking greens, and broccoli and the cores of cabbages or cauliflower. I save quart deli containers and their lids and use them to freeze these items so they're always ready to go.

Makes about 1½ quarts

1 tablespoon vegetable oil

2 cups yellow Spanish onion, cut into ½-inch slices

2 tablespoons garlic, coarsely chopped

1 cup carrot, cut into ½-inch dice

1 stalk celery plus several celery leaves from the bunch

2 or 3 very ripe tomatoes, sliced (this is a great use for tomatoes that haven't completely turned but are too soft for other uses)

2 cups cabbage or cauliflower cores, diced, or sliced stems from cooking greens

2 cups mushroom stems or trimmings

Stems from 2 bunches watercress

A few sprigs fresh thyme

2 or 3 sprigs Thai basil

3 bay leaves

6 cups water

Preheat oven to 325°F.

Toss the onion, garlic, and carrot in the vegetable oil and spread in a thin layer on an oiled baking sheet. Brown on the top rack of the oven until the onions are golden and aromatic, about 30 minutes.

Place all the solid ingredients in a 4-quart stockpot with a tight-fitting lid, and add the water. Tamp down the ingredients, but don't worry if they don't all submerge at first. Cover the pot and bring to a high simmer over medium heat. By the 20- to 30-minute mark, you should be able to coax all the vegetables underwater with the back of a wooden spoon. Cover and simmer on medium-low heat for 2 to 4 hours. Cool to room temperature, covered, before straining. Freeze stock in quart containers if you're not using it right away.

You Say Knoephla, I Say Knefle

One of the quirkiest foods I knew growing up, yet took for granted because it was on the table so regularly, was an obscure dumpling from the southwest of Germany and the German-speaking part of Switzerland called knefles (pronounced "k'-nəff-lees"), knephflas, or knoephlas. I've never been able to get to the root of the spelling variations, although it's clear that "knoephla" is more common in the Plains states, while "knefle" holds out in the German parts of southern Indiana and Ohio. Knefles are a poverty dish made from flour enriched with egg and milk, and steamed; they are substitutes for meat[2] or are eaten on fast days.

Most of my siblings would just as soon forget knefles, since Mom would simply steam them in a finished pot of great northern beans when money was tight. But I reveled in knefles. I mean, sure, the dish overall was bland, but the texture of well-cooked northern beans disintegrating into gravy, napping those chewy nuggets of dough that tasted so purely of flour, milk, and egg while taking on a resilient bite and chew reminiscent of meat, is a reveille of cooking fundamentals. Showered with ample black pepper and perhaps even parmesan cheese, this dish is poverty cooking at its best.

Today, knefles are usually an addition to soups or stews that contain meat or even cream, so the poverty cooking aspect is left to history. Here I'll share the simple preparation I grew up with, which never fails to slake my thirst for honest nostalgia. Knefles are also great in chicken and dumplings, pan-fried and sauced like gnocchi, or as a "noodle" in chicken soup, in beef stew, or next to a roast.

BASIC KNEFLES

Serves 3 or 4

 2 large eggs

 ¼ cup plus 1 teaspoon whole milk

 2 cups all-purpose flour

 1 teaspoon kosher salt

 2 tablespoons butter for sautéing, optional

 Croutons or toasted breadcrumbs, optional

 Grated parmesan cheese, optional

In a large mixing bowl, whisk the eggs until frothy, then stir in the milk. Add the flour and salt all at once and stir with a wooden spoon to combine. When the mixture becomes too difficult to stir, work with your hands to form a stiff, coarse dough. Once it comes together into one mass, the dough is ready, no need to knead it or work it into a smooth mass. Cover and let rest at least 20 minutes before cooking.

Drop dough by teaspoon-sized nuggets into boiling salted water, or into soup or stew at a high simmer. Cover to cook under steam. The dumplings are cooked when they float but are best when allowed to rest in a hot soup or stew until they fall back under, soaked in the soup or stew.

For pan-fried knefles, remove from boiling salted water with a spider or strainer as soon as they float. Sauté briefly in butter with optional onions or scallions. Serve smothered in croutons or toasted breadcrumbs and parmesan cheese.

BEANS AND KNEFLES

Serves 6 to 8

 3 cups Spanish onion, minced

 4 cups great northern beans or navy beans

 3 quarts cold water, plus more as needed

 3 bay leaves

 2 tablespoons kosher salt, divided

 1 teaspoon freshly cracked black pepper

1 recipe dough for **BASIC KNEFLES** (above)

Parmesan cheese and extra black pepper (optional)

Place the onion, beans, water, and bay leaf in a large stockpot or slow cooker and bring to a boil over high heat. Reduce to a low boil and cook until the beans are tender, 60 to 90 minutes. Add water along the way to keep the beans covered with liquid, but keep in mind the end goal is a thick soup/thin stew consistency akin to gravy.

Once the beans are tender, continue at a simmer and add 1 tablespoon of the salt. Then use the back of a wooden spoon to mash some of the beans up against the side of the pot, releasing their starch. As the stew takes on a milkier appearance, add the remaining tablespoon salt and the cracked pepper. Maintain a high simmer until the stew tightens somewhat to a light gravy consistency. Drop in the knefle dough in teaspoon-sized nuggets, stir to distribute them evenly, cover the pot, and steam until they float.

Remove the pot from the heat and rest for 20 to 30 minutes, covered, until the knefles sink back into the beans when stirred. Serve with freshly grated parmesan cheese and a pepper grinder nearby.

Prepared Sauerkraut

Sauerkraut is easily the most underappreciated vegetable preparation in the United States today. Perhaps our taste for it soured as generations of German restaurants and bars left some dubious versions on their steam tables all day. What was often delivered to the table was a strangely bland mush. Perhaps it's because we have learned to associate sauerkraut with mediocre sausage sandwiches at hot dog stands, where, again, the kraut died a second death on a steam table, utterly deprived of any chance at realizing its full potential to thrill the palate and nourish the soul.

Quality sauerkraut, fermented at low temperatures and preserved under cold conditions, is a fantastic foil for countless dishes, not just sausages. Over generations at the Fehribach farmhouse, spareribs were braised with sauerkraut. When done right, with plenty of cider and onions, and with rolls to sop up the drippings, that preparation rivals the best barbecue as a way of cooking spareribs, especially with the cartilaginous tips attached. Here's a quick and delicious way to prepare sauerkraut to go with anything from fried chicken to roast beef to any kind of dumplings. Especially if you're serving mashed potatoes, this is the singular best vegetable to nestle alongside them.

A couple of notes: Nearly all prepared sauerkraut recipes call for the kraut to be drained and rinsed before use. My personal taste is to simply drain and not rinse it. Use your best judgment, but I definitely like it on the sour side. Finally, instead of a dry hard cider, you can, of course, use a lager beer; just be sure to go with something that's not too hoppy. The bitterness of a heavily hopped beer will destroy anything you cook with it. Sliced or diced potato, rutabaga, turnip, parsnip, or celery root are all delicious additions to this; just increase the cooking time in the oven until the vegetables are tender. You can also toss smoked sausages and fingerling potatoes into the casserole and have a full ready-made dinner in under an hour. Just add spicy brown mustard and prepared horseradish.

Serves 4 to 6

2 tablespoons coffee-can grease, bacon grease, or vegetable oil

1 cup yellow Spanish onion, very thinly sliced into ribbons lengthwise, top to bottom

1 quart **SAUERKRAUT** (p. 144), drained

1 cup dry hard cider

½ teaspoon kosher salt

A few twists freshly ground pepper

1 bay leaf

Preheat oven to 350°F.

On the stovetop, heat your cooking fat in a stainless-steel or enamel casserole with a tight-fitting lid until a sliver of onion tossed in sizzles. Add the rest of the onion and sauté over medium-high heat, stirring constantly, until the onions have sweated, the sulfur smell has turned into a sweet aroma, and they have just begun to brown. Add the sauerkraut and cider and stir to combine. Add the remaining ingredients, stir a touch more, and bring to a boil. Turn off the stovetop, and add other vegetables and/or meat to the casserole if desired. Place the lid on the casserole and place it on the center rack of the oven.

Braise the sauerkraut for 30 minutes, longer if needed to finish any added vegetables or meat. Enjoy hot at once or reheat gently in its own juice to dress hot dogs or sausages, or serve with roasts, fried chicken, or game.

Green Bean Casserole

Often disparaged, mocked, scoffed at, and scorned, this heavyweight of modern American home cooking is nevertheless served in an estimated 20 million homes during the winter holidays each year,[3] proving that it still gets a lot of love. Invented by Dorcas Reilly in the Campbell's Soup Test Kitchen in 1955, it epitomizes the emerging industrialized food of the postwar period, which incorporated everything from Jell-O to Campbell's soup, Cool Whip to Tater Tots, Kool-Aid to canned salsa.

Green bean casserole has a couple of attributes that make it an easy target for elitist snobs: its ingredients are easy to find and inexpensive, and it's easy to make. It's a veritable treasure for working folk who have so much going on during their holidays that a simple and easy recipe is a hot ticket—especially because *if you do it right, it's damn delicious.*

I'm not going to denounce anyone who decides to make this casserole exactly according to Campbell's original recipe, although I do think it's possible to develop a deeper flavor by substituting QUICK CREAM OF MUSHROOM SOUP (p. 171) and using Worcestershire sauce instead of the soy sauce. French's french-fried onions are hard to improve on, unless you want to create a long, extra step of prepping, dredging, and frying onions at the exact temperature that will desiccate them to a light golden crispness without burning. So we're going to embrace a bit of our Midwestern heritage and use a processed ingredient from the dry-goods shelf at the supermarket. Likewise, frozen cut green beans can't be beat for this recipe—they invariably have more flavor than what you'll find fresh at the grocery store, especially during the winter, and they are processed just to the point that they are perfect to add to the recipe. Do be sure they are fully thawed before adding them—even partially frozen green beans will throw the time and temperature measures off. Finally, while you can make this any time of year, as a hot casserole it's best during the cool months.

Makes one 13-by-9-inch casserole

2 cups QUICK CREAM OF MUSHROOM SOUP (p. 171), refrigerated

1 teaspoon Worcestershire sauce

4 cups frozen cut green beans, defrosted completely

2 cups French's french-fried onions, divided

1 cup Wisconsin baby swiss cheese, shredded

Preheat oven to 350°F.

Butter a 13-by-9-inch casserole dish. In a mixing bowl, toss the mushroom soup, Worcestershire, green beans, and 1 cup of the onions until combined well. Spread the mixture out evenly in the casserole and use a spatula to gently tamp it down into the dish. Bake on the bottom rack of the oven for 30 minutes. Remove from the oven and sprinkle the swiss cheese evenly over the top, followed by the remaining cup of fried onions. Bake on the top rack of the oven for an additional 10 to 15 minutes, or until the cheese is melted and the top layer of onions is a rich golden brown. Serve hot.

Candied Yams

The omnipresent candied yams at Thanksgiving dinners might be one of the more divisive dishes in America. Some folks love them and some folks hate them. I hadn't tasted them in years because as a youngster, I loathed them, perhaps because when I'd see them on a table in Dubois County they were inevitably secreted away beneath a tranche of marshmallows. To my young mind, that was a truly diabolical thing to do to marshmallows. Or perhaps it was because the glaze was supermarket-fake maple syrup, something that even my insatiable sweet tooth always thought tasted a little suspect.

I've long wanted to revisit this dish because something haunts me every time I roast sweet potatoes in their skins: when they start to ooze glistening amber nectar, signaling that the sugars inside are caramelizing, their intoxicating smell—the hypnotic twin aromas of vanillin and caramelizing sugars—never fails to echo the aroma of toasted marshmallows in my head. Whoever had the idea to crown a raft of syrupy sweets with marshmallows may have actually been on to something, but I still won't do it myself.

The earliest recipe I could find for our modern candied yams (which are actually sweet potatoes) was in Annabella Hill's *Mrs. Hill's New Cook Book*, a domestic manual for post-Emancipation Southern homemakers who no longer had enslaved cooks to do the work for them—meaning candied yams were almost certainly the creation of Black cooks.[4] There the sweets get the full treatment of butter, sugar, cinnamon, and nutmeg. The recipe brings to mind a traveler's account of enslaved Africans on sugar plantations in the French Antilles cooking their sweet potatoes in pots of boiling molasses in the early 1800s.[5] Given the ruthlessness and mobility inherent to the slave trade, it's likely that the taste for sweet potatoes cooked in cane sugar began in the Caribbean and spread to the American South with trafficked human beings.

By the turn of the twentieth century, candied yams were a staple in the South, and Fannie Farmer included them in the 1896 edition of *The Boston Cooking-School Cookbook*. Soon they were a Thanksgiving must. In urban soul food culture, their enjoyment isn't limited to one holiday a year.

Three things can be done to balance the cloying qualities of candied yams by adding savory notes. One is simply to increase the salt. Or you can add cooked crispy bacon to the dish. A sure winner is to use sorghum molasses instead of brown sugar and maple syrup; it's less sweet from the start but has a savory tang as well. It's a great choice of sweetener when you want something rich, not too sweet, and a little savory to balance it all out.

My favorite sweet potatoes are Beauregards, and jewel or garnet "yams" are also good choices, but if you ever get a chance to pick up elusive white or yellow heirloom varieties, go for it!

Serves 4 to 6

4 cups sweet potatoes, peeled and cut into ½-inch slices (cut larger slices into half moons)

½ cup sorghum molasses or maple syrup

1 teaspoon kosher salt

½ teaspoon ground Korintje or Mexican cinnamon

⅛ teaspoon ground cloves

¼ cup (½ stick) plus 2 tablespoons unsalted butter, cut into small bits, well chilled

Arrange the sliced sweet potatoes in a few shallow layers in a large skillet and just barely cover with water. Bring to a boil and cook at a low boil, turning and rotating the potato slices regularly for even cooking. Don't add water; simply let it cook away and reduce. Move the potatoes around to cook evenly. Once the water has subsided by about half, add the sorghum molasses or maple syrup and continue cooking down. Remove and reserve slices of sweet potato as they cook through.

Once the liquid has been reduced back to a syrup and the potato slices are all done, add the salt and spices, and melt the butter into the boiling syrup. Turn the heat up to medium high. Pile the potatoes in the far side of the skillet, leaving enough room on the near side for the syrup to pool in front of you as you tilt the back of the pan upward. Use a large spoon to constantly baste the pooling syrup over the potatoes while it continues to cook and reduce. Reduce heat as needed to prevent burning, but some caramelization is nice. Once the syrup has thickened into a glaze and coats the potatoes instead of pooling in the bottom of the pan, your yams are candied. Serve while hot as is, or, if you dare, cover with marshmallows and quickly toast them in the oven.

Aunt Mary Lou's Pretzel Salad

Congealed salads are often attributed to the Midwest, but in truth they were a nationwide fancy during the mid-twentieth century, occupying the imaginations of cookbook and magazine editors for decades. The variations are limitless, whether you begin with Jell-O brand gelatin or Knox unflavored gelatin. Today we can look back on this trend for a bit of comic relief and sometimes horror. Canned fruit cocktail, shredded carrots, and shrimp suspended in to-mato gelatin molded into the shape of a fish? Absolutely. Lime Jell-O mottled with cottage cheese and onions, topped with salad greens and seafood salad? Coming up! Worcestershire-seasoned lemon Jell-O studded with stuffed olives in a baked cheese-flavored pie shell topped with tuna salad? We've got that one too!

We could spend the rest of this book making light of the many unfortu-nate amalgamations of gelatin and random ingredients, but the appeal of a time-saving and portable one-dish meal was real. Congealed salads began in-nocently enough, if we look back to the 1905 original. Knox was looking for novel uses for its gelatin product and co-sponsored a recipe contest with *Better Homes & Gardens*. No one remembers the first-place or second-place recipes, but third place was taken by Mrs. John E. Cooke of New Castle, Pennsylva-nia.[6] Her combination of cabbage, celery, and pimiento quivering in lemon- and vinegar-seasoned unflavored gelatin sounds reasonably palatable, if odd by today's tastes. Serendipitously, Fannie Farmer was one of the judges, and clearly her imagination was set afire by Cooke's dish: the 1911 edition of *The Boston Cooking-School Cookbook* has several recipes for congealed salads, in-cluding one called "Moulded Russian Salad," in which she cleverly sets cooked beets, carrots, and potatoes in molds with concentrated consommé as the jelly, to be served with mayonnaise dressing. Another recipe, mysteriously called "East India Salad," sets American and cream cheeses in whipped cream with unflavored gelatin, to be served on lettuce with curry dressing.[7] The congealed salad phenomenon was off the chain and running wild.

Occasionally, recipe developers got some things right. Having been turned off by congealed salads as a kid, as an adult I was delighted to try this gem by my partner Mark's aunt Mary Lou Lentz. She made it every year for Christmas dinner, ostensibly as an accompaniment to the ham, and by golly, she kind of nailed it! Sweet, salty, crunchy, and fruity, it sets off a baked ham nicely. If you like gelatin salads, you've probably already had a variation of this salad. If you haven't been a fan, give this one a try—it'll make you a believer!

Makes one 9-by-13-inch casserole; serves 8–12

2 cups pretzel crumbs, crushed in the food processor or with a rolling pin

1 cup (2 sticks) unsalted butter, melted

1 cup plus 3 tablespoons granulated sugar, divided

8 ounces cream cheese

1½ cups heavy whipping cream

1 large box strawberry Jell-O

2 cups boiling water

2 cups sliced strawberries, fresh (best) or frozen

Preheat oven to 350°F.

Combine the pretzel crumbs, the melted butter, and 3 tablespoons of the sugar. Press into a 9-by-13-inch casserole and bake on the center rack of the oven for 12 minutes to lightly toast and release pretzel aromas. Cool completely before proceeding.

In a stand mixer with the wire whip attachment, cream the remaining cup sugar and the cream cheese until smooth and fluffy. With the blender running, add the heavy cream in a thin, steady stream until the mixture is smooth and creamy like a milkshake. Proceed to whip until stiff peaks just form. Spread in an even layer over the baked pretzel crust and refrigerate for at least 1 hour while you prepare the strawberry topping.

Place the Jell-O in a mixing bowl, pour boiling water over, and stir to combine. Allow to cool, without stirring, until lukewarm to the touch. Add the sliced strawberries and refrigerate until it thickens slightly, about 20 to 30 minutes. Gently pour over whipped cream and refrigerate until set, several hours or overnight.

Latkes, a.k.a. Potato Pancakes, a.k.a. *Rosti*

Probably the most famous potato pancakes today are the Ashkenazi Jewish latkes, which are now eaten year-round but are most popular during Hannukah. The original latke of central Europe was made with cheese, but the expense of cheese during the winter months caused it to eventually be replaced with wheat flour or buckwheat and eventually potatoes.[8] Similarly, butter was replaced by schmaltz, which in Yiddish cooking means rendered poultry or beef fat (in secular German it could mean any rendered fat, commonly lard).

During one of the waves of German and Jewish immigration to the United States, an important cookbook targeted at German immigrant communities included recipes for potato pancakes: Henriette Davidis's *Praktisches Kochbuch für die Deutschen in Amerika*[9] includes several versions, many laden with flour and milk, some simple potato-and-egg affairs. I've seen hundreds of recipes for latkes and potato pancakes, or what you'll sometimes see called *Rosti* by people of Swiss or High German ancestry. Some of them use flour or cracker meal; the best use neither.

Any recipe worth calling latkes will start with raw potatoes, whereas recipes for potato pancakes and *Rosti* often start with baked or boiled potatoes. So, I'll say this: Starting with cooked potatoes makes a croquette, however you shape it, not a latke, potato pancake, or *Rosti*. The resilient crunch of the outer edges of an expertly pan-fried latke lures you further into the patty, where a fine crisp crust yields to a steamy, creamy interior of loosely bound shreds of potato, just barely cooked through, tripping lightly upon your palate with moves like an adroit jazz dancer, unleashing layers of potato aroma with onion, egg, and that schmaltz. This you cannot achieve starting with cooked potatoes.

Speaking of schmaltz, poultry renderings are the best here. Pork lard and butter have their own, very special allures, but there's something about that hint of chicken or duck in a schmaltzy potato pancake. Goose fat, too. If you want to use coffee-can grease, pork lard, or butter, try cutting them with vegetable oil, say 50:50, or blending the pork lard with clarified butter. Do not attempt this recipe with unclarified stick butter; it will burn before your dear pancakes have any prayer of crisping.

Serve these with anything you might serve with potatoes, but up in America's Dairyland they are put to special use. In Wisconsin, potato pancakes at a fish fry are "a local tradition dating back to the state's origins."[10] Even as french fries continue to encroach, many folks still seek out those events advertising potato pancakes, considering them as important as the fish. For dressing the pancakes themselves, sour cream and fresh herbs are classic; some say applesauce, but if you go that route, make it a high-quality one because grocery-store applesauce makes a cloying dressing. **APPLE BUTTER** (p. 31) is perfect if you'd like a sweeter touch.

Serves 4 to 6

    3 cups raw Russet, Kennebec, or German Butterball potatoes, shredded on the
        large side of a box grater
    2 teaspoons kosher salt
    4 to 6 tablespoons schmaltz or clarified butter
    2 large eggs, lightly beaten
    ⅓ cup green onion, very thinly sliced
    ¼ teaspoon freshly ground black pepper, with more for topping

Toss the potatoes in a bowl with the salt and allow to rest 10 minutes.

Drain the potatoes in a colander in a clean sink. Press vigorously to squeeze all the juice out. If you feel daring and heroic, put them in cheesecloth or a clean kitchen towel, squeeze, twist, and bleed them until they can give up no more liquid. Put them back into a dry bowl.

Place a large, 10-inch cast-iron skillet (or nonstick is ok) on the stovetop and add a layer of schmaltz ⅛ to ¼ inch deep. Heat on medium high until a piece of potato tossed in sizzles furiously, 400°F to 420°F.

Working quickly, toss the beaten egg, green onion, and pepper with the drained potato. Form into loose patties of about ¼ cup each, and arrange in the skillet, tamping them down gently to about ⅔ inch thick and 3 inches around. Don't worry too much about making them pretty—irregular edges lead to more crispness and texture. Maintain a high sizzle but turn the heat down if burning them becomes a threat. Cook on the first side until a hard, rich brown crust forms around the edges and the underside is nicely browned, 5 to 6 minutes. Gently turn over, and tamp the tops slightly so the raw side hugs the hot skillet better. Cook on the second side until a nice brown, another 4 to 5 minutes. Drain on paper towels or wire racks while finishing the batch, and hold in a low oven in a single layer until ready to serve. Serve piping hot.

Go Goetta!

A most peculiar food that shouldn't be, goetta is a type of grain-bound pudding or sausage akin to scrapple, boudin, or ponthaus. The unique property of goetta is that it's bound with pinhead oats, rather than the cornmeal that's used to bind scrapple or livermush, or the rice that's used in Cajun boudin. Like much of Cincinnati's food culture, it's owed to German immigrants who flooded the city from the 1830s into the early twentieth century.

Its purpose as a meat extender—an offal extender in particular—is indicative of goetta's roots in the peasantry; moneyed folk had ample meat for fine cuts and sausages made only with high-quality meat. Oatmeal sausage as a vehicle for less desirable animal products can be traced to sixteenth-century Germany,[11] and there is no reason not to assume the practice was ancient even then—it's little more than a congealed porridge that is sliced and fried or broiled. Humble as it is, one well made will bring mirth to your table.

As is typical of commoner food, not a lot has been written about this oatmeal mush–turned–sausage or, notably, how it came to be called goetta. The nearest analog you can reliably find at market is the *Knipp* of Bremen in northern Germany. The migration of Germans to America and Cincinnati is well documented; how you get from *Knipp* to goetta is not.

In spite of the long history of porridge-based sausages, goetta didn't really gain traction in Cincinnati until the 1950s, when advertisements described it as a new product "similar to scrapple," which was favored by German households.[12] An article in a recipe-sharing column finds one reader decrying another's recipe for goetta by citing their own as "third generation," while another reader requests a recipe for a regional version that uses buckwheat, saying the recipe is "very old."[13] I'm more than a half century late answering her request, but I did find a recipe for what appears to be goetta in a cookbook targeted at German immigrants in America:

Grüzewurst (Sausage with Oatmeal or Buckwheat Meal)

The rubbish meat and just as much pork belly are cooked together, meat and rinds are minced, the bacon is cut in cubes. You then take 2 pounds of oat or buckwheat grits for every 5 pounds of meat and bacon, which is cooked in meat broth in a special pot. Then you put everything together, add some fat that has been skimmed off from the meat broth. It is seasoned with salt, pepper and, if necessary, mace. This well-mixed filling is put into tight intestines, cooked and the sausage hung up later to smoke.[14]

These days you won't find goetta in a sausage casing, nor will you find it smoked, but we can see its roots in this receipt. Neighborhood butchers continue to market it, and the most famous brand, Glier's, can be found in any grocery store in Cincinnati or across the Ohio River in Covington, Kentucky. Glier's still uses offal in its product, which many goetta purists insist is definitional. To me, that's a stretch, but there's no doubt that organ meats bring a specific flavor to the mush that is on the money. Avril-Bleh in downtown Cincinnati makes an outstanding goetta for the offal-averse, as does A&J Comfort Foods under its Rheinland label.

If you've never tried goetta, put it on your bucket list now. Of all the peasant meat-and-grain quasi-sausages we have, this one may be the best if you like toasty whole-grain flavors. At worst, it rivals Cajun boudin as a meat stretcher. Be sure to give it a hard sear, preferably in coffee-can grease, bacon grease, or beef drippings. The way the oats crisp up around the edges and toast all over is everything. The pearlescent texture of the oats, a serf's caviar, mingles with bits of well-cooked meat to do a tactile two-step on your palate while heady aromas of toasted whole grain and meat waft about your head.

Goetta is easy to make, though it does take a little time. It freezes well, so you can make a decent-sized batch like this one and have a few breakfasts ready to go at a moment's notice. Don't be tempted to use rolled oats; you absolutely must go for the steel-cut. This recipe calls for 8 ounces each pork kidney and ground pork heart; feel free to substitute a rich red meat such as grass-fed beef or bison in its place. I won't call the goetta cops on you.

This is excellent for breakfast griddled or pan-fried and sauced with **APPLE BUTTER** (p. 31) or with peach or cherry preserves melted over. Serve with eggs. The oats play well with hash brown potatoes if they're crisped nicely. You can also make a fantastic sandwich on rye with Jarlsberg or Emmentaler cheese melted over the goetta, slicked with apple butter or peach preserves, or pepper jelly if you like heat. Be sure to slice the goetta at least ½ inch thick (¾ inch is better) to make it easier to handle during cooking. And because a thick slab of goetta is just better than a thin one.

Makes 2 loaves approximately 2½ pounds each

- 2 tablespoons coffee-can grease, meat drippings, or vegetable oil
- 2 cups Spanish onion, very finely minced
- 2 tablespoons garlic, very finely minced
- 4 cups water
- 4 bay leaves
- 2 pigs' feet
- 2 pounds pork shank
- 8 ounces pork heart
- 8 ounces pork kidney
- 5 cups beef broth
- 3 cups steel-cut oats
- 1 tablespoon plus 2 teaspoons kosher salt
- 1 teaspoon ground white pepper
- 1 teaspoon dried sage
- 1 teaspoon dried marjoram
- ½ teaspoon ground nutmeg
- ¼ teaspoon cayenne pepper

In a 4-quart or larger saucepan or stockpot with a tight-fitting lid, heat the cooking fat just until smoking, then add the onion and garlic. Sauté over high heat, stirring constantly, until they sweat and begin to take on just a little color on their edges, but don't caramelize or brown heavily. Add the water, then the bay leaves, pigs' feet, shank, heart, and kidney. Cover the pot and maintain a low boil for 2 to 2½ hours, when all the skin, tendons, and meat on the feet and shanks are completely soft. Strain the cooking liquid but reserve it; add water sufficient to bring it back up to 4 cups if any water has evaporated. Reserve the meats in a shallow pan and allow them to cool until you can handle them with your bare hands. Discard the bay leaves.

Return the pork cooking liquid to the stove and add the beef broth, the oats, and all remaining ingredients. Bring to a boil and reduce heat to a high simmer. Cover the pot and maintain a simmer, but do not boil, for 60 to 90 minutes, until the oats have soft and creamy centers when chewed. In the meantime, once the meats are cool enough to handle, clean all the skin, meat, and gelatinous material from the feet and shanks, and mince it all finely. Discard only the bones. Once the meats are minced, add them to the pot. Likewise, mince the heart and kidney finely, or grind in the food processor by pulsing. Add these to the pot as well. Stir to combine well with the oats. Take a big whiff: *aaaaahhhhhhhhhh!*

Once all liquid is absorbed, stir the pot for 2 to 3 minutes to work the oats so that they stick together somewhat, but be sure that they retain some of their individual grain separation. This step is key to optimal goetta enjoyment. There should be no weeping liquid when a spoonful is dropped on a plate and tilted.

Grease two 9-by-5-inch loaf pans, then line with enough plastic wrap to have extra draping over the ends and sides. Press the wrap against the greased sides and bottom of the pan, working out creases, until the plastic wrap is smooth. Divide the goetta-to-be between the two pans, pressing in well, and wrap the excess plastic wrap over to cover it. Tamp it in until level and without air pockets. Refrigerate overnight, then slice it, fry it up, and enjoy. Refrigerate for up to 1 week or freeze for up to 3 months.

Potato Salad Two Ways

To the extent the Midwest may live up to its meat-and-potatoes reputation, it's true that we do love potato salad. It's probably the most common potluck dish throughout our region, especially during the summer, when cool side dishes also lend a touch of relief from the heat. As with many of our favorite foods, we'll find a history in Germanic culture and wide adoption by all in the United States.

Potatoes were first planted in Germany and Ireland between 1588 and 1600, along with the sweet potato, another New World vegetable that arrived around the same time, if not slightly earlier.[15] Potatoes were first considered an exotic delicacy, and it would take some time before they became staples. In 1712, the *Frauenzimmer Lexicon* lists only five potato recipes, including one that looks tantalizingly like our modern warm potato salad: *Erdapffel* roasted with butter and napped in a sauce of meat stock and vinegar bound with roux.[16] Add a little mustard and onion, and it could be my grandmother's recipe. In 1736, N. Bailey's *Household Dictionary* uses potatoes only twice, both times in savory pies.[17] By 1778, Dubliner Charlotte Mason's *The Lady's Assistant* lists only four dedicated potato recipes,[18] but potatoes are called for in dozens of other receipts throughout the book, from roast beef to dessert puddings. The book gives a great glimpse into why potatoes were often distinguished from sweet potatoes in American and British recipes by calling them Irish potatoes.

Potato salad, however, originated with Germans, and by the nineteenth century the association had become strong enough that the dish was often a cudgel used in racist screeds against Germans in British newspapers, such as this one:

> Tummult and hubbub. An indescribable odor of tobacco, cumin [caraway], and potato salad. A variety of hustled blouses. Sunburnt and haggard faces. Ragged beards and unkempt locks. A strong pipe hanging from every lip; beer, or kümmil (a spirit prepared with cumin) at every hand. . . . Such is the inside of a German trade traveler's room.[19]

Mustard appears in potato salad by 1870 in Annabella Hill's *Mrs. Hill's New Cook Book*,[20] so it was probably the innovation of an enslaved Black cook. Mentions of mayonnaise and potato salad pop up in the late 1870s and increase in frequency in the 1880s. At the same time, we see potato salads with creamy boiled dressing appearing. By the 1880s, using both mayonnaise and mustard was definitely a common treatment, and by the turn of the century, potato salad was well on its way to becoming an iconic American dish.

Hot potato salad isn't so common these days, but it should be. Are we all to eat french fries every day? (Don't actually answer that.) I'm always looking for an excuse to meditate over the perfume of onions cooking in bacon fat on the stove. Add to that the exhilarating aroma of wheat flour toasting over the flame, lance it with a splash of apple cider vinegar and infuse it with abundant free amino acids with a little meat stock, toss in perfectly cooked fingerling potatoes, and you have one of the most soulful fall and winter side dishes.

I like potato salad to have discrete pieces of potato, so I use a waxy variety, favoring fingerlings or small reds, cooking them whole in their skins and never boiling, only simmering, then cubing them afterward, so that they will hold their shape nicely under the weight of dressing and friction of tossing. If you like more of a lumpy consistency, which does have its virtues, use a starchy variety such as Russets or Kennebecs, peel and dice them before cooking, and boil them at a brisk but not a rolling boil. These will crumble a little bit under the pressures of dressing and tossing, making for a potato salad with a soothing, plush texture.

WARM GERMAN POTATO SALAD

Serves 4 to 6

1½ pounds fingerling or small "C-size" red or Yukon Gold potatoes

4 strips smoked bacon, 18/22 count cut

2 tablespoons all-purpose flour

¼ cup Spanish onion, finely diced

1 cup chicken stock

2 tablespoons apple cider vinegar

2 tablespoons fine mayonnaise, Hellman's or Duke's

½ teaspoon freshly ground black pepper

½ to 1 teaspoon kosher salt, to taste

¼ cup green onion, very thinly sliced

Cook the potatoes in their skins in unsalted water at a high simmer until easily pierced with a fork, about 30 minutes. Allow to cool in their cooking water until they are still warm but easy to handle. Drain and cut into bite-sized chunks to your taste, up to 1 inch square; a little smaller is best.

In a heavy-bottomed skillet or dutch oven, cook the bacon strips over medium to medium-high heat until nicely browned and crisped all the way through. Remove and drain on a clean paper or cloth towel. Chop finely, ½ inch or smaller.

Add the flour to the bacon drippings in the pan and cook over medium heat, stirring constantly to prevent scorching, until the floury smell is cooked out and it smells toasty, 3 to 5 minutes. Add the onion and stir constantly until thoroughly sweated and soft but not browned, 3 to 5 minutes.

Add the chicken stock and vinegar and bring to a boil for 15 seconds to thicken. Remove from heat, add the cubed potatoes, and toss to coat. Add the mayonnaise and black pepper and toss to combine thoroughly. Taste for seasoning and add salt ½ teaspoon at a time, incorporating thoroughly after each addition and tasting before adding more. Transfer to a serving platter or bowl, top with the green onions, and send to the table.

CREAMY POTATO SALAD

Serves 4 to 6

1½ pounds large "A-size" red potatoes

½ cup fine mayonnaise, Hellman's or Duke's

¼ cup spicy brown mustard, such as Koop's or Plochman's

2 tablespoons apple cider vinegar

2 teaspoons kosher salt

⅛ teaspoon cayenne pepper

½ cup Spanish onion, very finely diced

¼ cup bread-and-butter or dill pickles, minced (optional)

3 hard-boiled eggs, thinly sliced (optional)

¼ cup green onion, very thinly sliced

Peel the potatoes if desired. Dice into bite-sized pieces of about ⅔ to ¾ inch. Place in a small stock pot and cover with water. Cook them at a high simmer, or if you like softer potato salad, a brisk but not rolling boil, until easily pierced with a fork. Drain in a colander, then set the colander in a drip-proof pan and allow to cool to room temperature, about 30 minutes, turning the potatoes every so often.

Meanwhile, make the dressing by combining the mayonnaise, mustard, vinegar, salt, and cayenne and stirring until smooth. Add the Spanish onion, and pickles if desired, and stir to combine. Place the dressing in a large mixing bowl, add the potatoes, and toss by turning the bottom over the top with a sturdy rubber spatula or wooden spoon, coating the potatoes evenly. Add the eggs if desired and toss to integrate, then refrigerate at least 1 hour or overnight before serving.

Just before serving, garnish with a generous sprinkling of the green onion.

German Fries

Here's a quirky side dish that I didn't know was obscure until I left home for college. In Dubois County, "German fries" are everywhere, and they're a major talking point when comparing local restaurants. Good German fries are highly coveted, and for years the reigning champion has been the Chicken Place in the hamlet of Ireland, a few miles west of Jasper. Theirs are thinly cut yet toothsome, light on the fork, rich with the smell of bacon and the aroma of onion.

I have no idea why they're called German fries. In fact, a search of the public record turns up almost as many hits in southern Indiana as in the rest of the United States combined. It is likely that boiling in salted water and frying in schmaltz with onions is an old traditional German way of cooking potatoes. The simplicity of preparation may be why I've been unable to find recipes in German cookbooks, because who needs a recipe for something so simple? Done right, this is still one of my favorite ways to eat potatoes. German fries are also a salient example of the simplest of foods being key manifestations of cultural identity.

Serves 4 to 6

1½ pounds A-size (large) red or Yukon Gold potatoes
2 quarts water
1 tablespoon kosher salt
4 strips hickory-smoked bacon, 18/22 count cut
¼ cup Spanish onion, very thinly sliced

¼ teaspoon freshly ground black pepper

2 tablespoons very thinly sliced green onions

Cook the potatoes in their skins in a large saucepan with the water and salt—the water should cover the potatoes. Boil them at a low boil until they can be lanced with a knife but are not fully tender—they should still have a bite to them—about 30 to 40 minutes. Remove the potatoes and cool them thoroughly under cold running water.

In a large, 10-by-12-inch cast-iron skillet, cook the bacon over medium heat, turning regularly, until crisp throughout. Be careful not to burn or overheat the rendering fat. Remove the strips from the pan, but leave the rendered fat.

Use a clean towel or vegetable peeler to peel the potatoes, and discard the skins. Quarter them lengthwise, then slice very thinly—¹⁄₁₆ inch is a good goal, but ⅛ inch will do. Add the potatoes and onions to the bacon fat and toss to coat, increasing the heat to medium high. Turn regularly with a spatula so they cook evenly and don't stick to the pan. In the meantime, cut and crumble the bacon as finely as you can—¼-inch bits are ideal. Once the potatoes are evenly just browned on the edges but still creamy and tender in the center (we are not making potato chips here) and the onions are cooked through and translucent, season with freshly ground black pepper, turn out onto a serving platter, sprinkle with the green onions, and serve while hot.

Oyster Dressing

Seemingly an unlikely Midwestern ingredient, oysters have actually been an extremely important regional food over the years, especially during the formative years of our cities. This was particularly true in river towns, where fishmongers tried to get their products into the hands of hungry consumers. In the planning and development of the Baltimore and Ohio Railroad, extending the market for the Chesapeake Bay's bounteous seafood to the Ohio River was a prime motivator, and developers were keen to stay one step ahead of New Orleans fish merchants in the trade's expansion into the interior.[21] Oysters were abundant, cheap, and easy to ship, especially during winter, when the climate would help extend their shelf life. The Baltimore and Ohio became the first railroad to reach the Ohio River Valley on Christmas Eve, 1852,[22] and by 1860, the railroad was shipping 3 million pounds of oysters west each year.[23] By 1874, the B&O had connected all the way to Chicago and Saint Louis.[24] In Midwestern culinary literature, a wealth of oyster recipes ensued.

By the 1870s, *Buckeye Cookery and Practical Housekeeping* had dozens of recipes for oysters stuffed into game fowl, stewed, scalloped, fried, and turned out into dressing.[25] Community and mainstream cookbooks would continue to offer oyster receipts well into the twentieth century, although they became scarcer as oysters did, victims of both overfishing and the rampant pollution of early to mid-twentieth-century America. Today, even though they can be found in restaurants and taverns across the Midwest, especially in the cities, they're not ingrained in our home cooking like they were from the late nineteenth century into the early twentieth century.

My favorite Midwestern oyster recipe is a hand-me-down from my partner Mark's mother, Glennadene Hamel, née Reitz, of Evansville, Indiana. One of her signature holiday recipes was a simple dressing of crackers, oysters and their liquor, butter, Worcestershire, and cream. Basically a "scalloped" oyster recipe, it harkens back to the early American cookbooks *The Carolina Housewife* and *The Virginia Housewife*, both of whose recipes descend from Hannah Glasse's "Scollop of Oysters." Glasse laid shucked oysters with their liquor in scallop shells, added butter, and strewed them with toasted breadcrumbs,[26] then broiled them; each shell yielded a single forkful of buttery, briny deliciousness.

You'll still meet folks who will call variations of this dish scalloped oysters, and they wouldn't be wrong, but as an accoutrement to roasts, it's more aptly called dressing. This mixture can of course be stuffed into a bird and baked; this treatment is common in Midwestern cookbooks published before 1900. Knowing what we know today about food safety, it's definitely a better idea to bake it in a casserole—you'll have much more control over the outcome, and you'll enjoy the bonus of extra toasty brown crispy edges!

Serves 6 to 8

4 cups oyster crackers, crumbled

1 cup (2 sticks) unsalted butter, cut into ½-inch pats and softened

2 pints shucked oysters with liquor, divided

2 tablespoons Worcestershire sauce, divided

1 cup heavy cream

½ teaspoon kosher salt

½ teaspoon freshly ground black pepper

¼ teaspoon cayenne pepper

¼ cup finely grated pecorino or parmesan cheese

Preheat oven to 325°F. Butter a 13-by-9-inch casserole.

Work the softened butter into the cracker crumbs, rubbing it in with your hands and fingers until the crumbs are evenly coated with butter. Use your fingers to "fluff" the cracker crumbs so they are loose and not compacted.

Spread ⅓ of the crumbs evenly over the bottom of the casserole, then evenly spread ½ of the oysters over them, and evenly drizzle ⅓ of the oyster liquor over it all. Dot with 1 tablespoon of Worcestershire sauce. Repeat the layering, and then cover with the last ⅓ of the cracker crumbs.

Mix the last ⅓ of the oyster liquor with the heavy cream, salt, and black and cayenne peppers. Drizzle this mixture evenly over the entire casserole. Allow to soak in for 5 minutes, then cover the casserole with plastic wrap and use your hands to make an even and lightly compacted top. Sprinkle evenly with the grated cheese.

Bake on the center rack of the oven until nicely browned and bubbling and the center of the casserole registers 185°F. Rest for 15 to 30 minutes before serving. May be made ahead and refrigerated. Be sure to reheat to an internal temperature of 165°F before serving.

Rob Connoley

In an unassuming storefront on Washington Avenue in midtown Saint Louis, tucked between a neighborhood theater and Urban Chestnut, one of the Midwest's finest craft breweries, Chef Rob Connoley is rewriting what we know about Midwestern cuisine by taking a deep dive into historic Ozark receipts and ingredients, establishing a rare sense of place with one of the country's most ambitious foraging programs. Here, provenance matters, and if an ingredient's roots don't run deep in the Ozarks, it won't make the cut at his tasting menu venue, Bulrush.

Rob Connor took an unpredictable path to his vision of a cuisine rooted in its own environs. Raised in Saint Louis, he obtained a PhD in social psychology focused on sports and exercise from Purdue University, married his love Tyler Pauley (their last names were wedded to become Connoley), and moved to rural New Mexico, where Tyler worked in hospice and Rob in nonprofit management in methamphetamine recovery.

Wanting something different, Rob opened a gourmet food store, Curious Kumquat, in tiny Silver City, New Mexico. He soon found out that in order for the local folks to be able to use the ingredients he was selling, he'd need to put on cooking demonstrations, and the business proved sustainable enough that he started serving lunch. He eventually learned that a restaurant could do better than a gourmet food store. Inspired by Grant Achatz's *Alinea* cookbook and Michael Pollan's *The Omnivore's Dilemma*, he decided to introduce a tasting menu. In 2010, he put on his first dinner for eighteen guests: twenty-four courses for the absurd price of $35 per person. The abundant foraged ingredients Connoley was finding in the New Mexico outback inspired him to write the beautifully conceived book *Acorns and Cattails*, and his voice as a leading chef-forager was established.

After nine years, Tyler's hospital phased out hospice, and the couple plotted to move back to Saint Louis. A short stint in another restaurant while he searched for a space of his own opened Connoley's eyes to the enormous amount of food waste endemic in restaurants, and he decided that Bulrush would get as close to zero waste as possible. Bulrush opened to acclaim in 2019, making all the city's Best New Restaurants lists and ensuring a full reservation book.

One early diner was the lead archivist of the Gateway Arch, and he invited Connoley to a dinner with a group of archivists. Through people he met there, Connoley was able to obtain the inventory of a Saint Louis seed store, which listed 95 specific seeds, many of which he'd never heard of—Rohan potatoes, Marrowfat peas, cowhorn okra, white spurd cucumbers, oxheart cabbage—along with the inventory of Treemont Coffee House from 1837. This glimpse into another time sent him looking for the seeds in those inventories that were no longer on the market (about a third of them). Through the Seed Savers' Exchange, he was able to obtain all but one of them. These crops have been grown through the past two seasons by farms that supply Bulrush, bringing a taste of Saint Louis history to his guests. Just as important, he's preserving a part of Ozark heritage.

Connoley's foraging program is supported by the Bulrush Land Partnership and includes several privately held farms and estates totaling almost ten thousand acres of pristine forest and countryside. His searing passion for wild edible plants ensures a steady supply of ingredients you simply won't find on other restaurant menus—spiceberries, blue chanterelles, yaupom tea, cattail pollen, and a thrilling array of more familiar wild edibles such as ramps, pawpaws, persimmons, and chokecherries.

At Bulrush, the bar is a soothing space of clean lines and earthen contrasts, from the concrete floor to the rich wood tones of the counter and the textured walls, which change like a chameleon as you move through the space, highlighting a wall-length painting created by the Bulrush team from colors evocative of persimmon. It's reminiscent of a freshly browned-out briar patch filtering an early December Ozark sunset.

You can enjoy a beer, made in collaboration with Earthbound Beer, of malted kernza, a perennial wheat at the forefront of the regenerative farming movement, given a refreshing zip with gooseberries. The cocktails, too, are as unique as the food. They might consist of tequila sweetened with the tropical perfume of pawpaw and given acid tang from mulberries, a simple persimmon shrub laced with cinnamon, or a Black Manhattan given a dizzying perfume and exquisite bitterness by house-made nocino, a liqueur made from unripe black walnuts picked at a very particular time. A spirit-free cocktail might consist of local heirloom cucumber juice spiked with fermented tomatoes and blueberries, given a refreshing twinge of heat with guajillo chili, and topped with a delightful froth of aquafaba.

To call Connoley's cuisine unique is an understatement. If there's a single "signature" dish on the ever-changing menu (repeats are rare because ingredient supplies are dynamic), it's a savory acorn-flour donut that often begins the meal and might be filled with anything from fermented cabbage to whipped potato, sweet-potato caramel, or persimmon and spiked with seasonings from goldenrod to spicebush or wild ginger. A venison and pork bologna slider resides on pillowy *shokupan* bread, a Japanese milk bread that evokes those of the Germans who found their way to the Ozarks during the nineteenth century. Crowned with house-made American cheese and blistered turnip pickles, it's a beguiling and complete reimagination of the iconic bologna on bread. A rhubarb-poached walleye arrives nestled on silky celery-root puree with a rhubarb salsa dressed in pawpaw vinaigrette. A fried chicken breast cleverly hides beneath a sumac and spicebush waffle with a black-walnut-sap sorghum sauce.

Connoley combines this boundless style of cooking with erudite scholarship, using sources ranging from those old archives to old church cookbooks, which provide unique insights into foodways frozen in time. He also consults oral histories and ties them to printed sources. It takes time to make inroads with historically abused communities of color, and Connoley understands that sincerity is the key to opening people to your vision. He works with the local African American community and the Osage, who have managed to defy the odds by staying and surviving in the Ozarks. It is his deeply held belief that the only true Ozark cuisine must include three pillars: the Osage, Black Ozarkans, and the White immigrant cultures that marginalized the first two. Reconciliation will come only through trust and equity. It's a tall order to bring everyone together, but Connoley continues to see a future with everyone at the table together as equals, celebrating shared and unique heritages.

Based on a conversation with Rob Connoley, chef and owner of Bulrush, Saint Louis, October 19, 2021.

6

PULL UP A CHAIR

Meat and Potatoes

When the baseball game has died away and the whiskey has been downed, dinner is ready and the entire clan assembles. The meat platters are the first to move—chicken rolled in flour and fried in shallow fat to a rich, crisp brown, baked ham, beef roasted thoroughly to a heavy, tender darkness, gravied meatloaf kept hot for serving on a big camp-range. . . . The vegetables which follow include potatoes—creamed, scalloped, and chopped into salad—baked beans, green beans, lima beans, scalloped corn, sliced tomatoes, and fresh or pickled beets. Flanking them are deviled eggs, cole slaw, cottage cheese, and an endless variety of homemade pickles, sauces, relishes, jellies, jams, preserves, butters, and savories.

—Nelson Algren, "Festivals in the Fields"

IF there's one time of day when Midwesterners kinda-sorta live up to the stereotype, it's when the dinner bell rings, or when momma clangs that pot out on the porch to call the kids to dinner. While there's more to Midwestern food than meat and potatoes, it does have a lot of meat and potatoes—a trait it shares with the cuisines of central Europe, Ireland, Peru, and Argentina, and even French bistro fare, with its *steak frites* and *boeuf bourguignon* with *pommes duchesse*. What counts as dowdy and what counts as cuisine is in the eye of the beholder, and there is much to behold in middle America.

When I talk food memories with Midwestern folks, the nostalgia isn't as schmaltzy as you might expect, but many find common ground with my recollections of my southern Indiana youth—vegetable gardens linked by well-worn paths to the kitchen door; big pots of stew at church suppers and turkey shoots, and spectacular pie and cake tables there, too; florid displays of homespun candy at school fundraisers; and funnel cakes at the county fair. Some recall fry cones filled with cheese curds or breaded mushrooms or french-fried zucchini, or spaghetti suppers, or the heady aroma of fried perch.

The Midwest gave America the chophouse, with its glistening monoliths of dry-aged beef and comically sized side dishes like 1-pound baked potatoes, creamed spinach, and perfectly arranged pyramids of asparagus draped with lemony hollandaise. Our regional barbecue styles outside of Kansas City, although largely unrecognized, are worthy of an international audience. Church supper and backyard fish fries serve as pop-up community centers. Macedonian immigrants who hopped on the white-hot chili parlor bandwagon have captivated one of America's great cities for a hundred years and counting. And Black Americans' culinary roots from Africa to the American South found common ground with hundreds of years of culinary tradition from the south of Germany to create a dish that has become an American icon: fried chicken.

These memories and recipes tell a story of the Midwest that most Midwesterners won't tell you. For most of our history, the Midwest has been a place of progressive ideas, culinary innovation, and blending of cultures that made America what it is today. Even though we haven't expelled a lot of air talking about ourselves over generations, we've always been great cooks, entertainers, and hosts, as good as they come. Yet what we treasure most is a home-cooked meal among our own.

Booyah

One of a family of American stone-soup community pots, booyah is the Great Lakes cousin of coastal Georgia's Brunswick stew and the Ohio River Valley's burgoo. The communal repast might be a church fundraiser or supper, a political rally, family reunion, or other large social gathering, but any booyah is cooked and, weather permitting, eaten outdoors. The best ones are cooked over a wood fire, which invariably imparts a whiff of smoke to the pot, which some would call the signature of true booyah.

Engineered to feed large groups of people with maximum efficiency and adequate nutrition, booyah, booya, boo-yahs, boolyaws, or booyaw will usually consist of chicken, although other meats, from beef to venison to turtle, may be added, along with beans, tomatoes, potatoes, onions, carrots, and virtually any other ingredient the cook deems worthy of the pot. Rutabaga, cabbage, green beans, and even barley and lima beans aren't unheard of. As the booyah kettle is often massive, over 50 gallons, the cooking takes a long time, up to a full day, and the resulting stew is thick, teeming with free amino acids released by the long cooking, and altogether harmonious. Many a booyah master adds aromatic seasonings by wrapping them in a cheesecloth pouch to infuse whole spices and herbs, which are more flavorful than dried, into the stew. As a chef, I'm well versed in the technique, but I tip my hat to the community cooks exacting enough to pick it up.

Little is written about booyah in cookbooks, and there is a dearth of scholarly writing on this important cultural phenomenon. There are varying theories about the name "booyah," with some suggesting Dutch, Flemish, or even Bohemian origins, but the overwhelming likelihood is that it is a bastardization of the French *bouillon*, as we can see in this tantalizing quote from an Iowa newspaper in 1891:

> It was noon when we reached the Menominee River, and it was while standing on the log platform of a sort of half-way house on the homeward side of the river that I ate my first venison. It was done up in sort of an Irish stew, which the landlord, a French Canadian, called "booyah," or something that sounded like that. It was served in a big stamped iron dishpan set on the head of a beef barrel, and it was not long till our twelve spoons had it empty and were clattering for more.[1]

That quote reminds me of something I learned early in my studies of Louisiana's country cooking. If you've ever heard a rural Louisianan pronounce the Cajun dish *court-bouillon*, you'll pick up on this reference immediately. *Bouillon*, when spoken in the regional patois, becomes *booya, booyaw, booyah*, or what-have-you. *Court-bouillon* is a bouillon-based stew, which makes a meal in one pot.

We have earlier references to booyah, but they are sparse, though with a few riveting clues to its emerging cultural value. Our first mention is in the Junction City, Kansas, *Weekly Union*, and simply states that "'Boo-Yah' is a very popular soup among the boys on Humboldt Creek."[2] This doesn't tell us anything about the soup itself, but a few years later, the same paper tells us, "Our Humboldt correspondent speaks of a very happy and successful 'Booyah' Party in his region, with dancing and chicken soup. 'The beauty and chivalry of Humboldt, chased the lazy hours with flying feet,' &c."[3] Now we're on our way! During the twentieth century, mentions of booyah explode in popular media, and we see booyah most often in Minnesota and Wisconsin. The Northwoods League baseball organization, dedicated to developing elite college baseball players, even had a team called the Green Bay Booyah for a while.[4]

With my exhaustive experience making soups and stews, the best advice I can give you when embarking on a project like booyah is to watch, and carefully control, your flame. The easiest way to destroy a stew is to boil it to death. If you're able to cook it on your grill over charcoal refreshed with wood chips every so often, you'll be able to impart a little of that live-fire flavor. Maintain a very low boil, just above a high simmer, and you will be a booyah legend.

Makes about 3 gallons, serves 15 to 20

5 pounds veal shank, on the bone; use group-raised, pasture-fed veal such as that
   from Wisconsin's Strauss Meats

5 stewing hens, or 6 medium fryers

1 pound red kidney beans, soaked overnight

6 medium Spanish onions, peeled and cut into ½-inch dice

12 cloves garlic, minced

2 heads celery with leaves, cut into ½-inch slices

2 pounds carrots, cut into ½-inch slices

1 medium head green cabbage, finely shredded

1 (28-ounce) can whole peeled tomatoes

1 (48-ounce) can tomato juice or, if you feel like an adventure, V8

1 pound frozen sweet corn

3 pounds red potatoes, cut into large dice with skin on

½ cup pickling spices, tied in a cheesecloth sachet

½ cup kosher salt, or more to taste

1 tablespoon freshly ground black pepper

½ teaspoon cayenne pepper

½ cup Worcestershire sauce

Place the veal shanks and chickens in the bottom of a 5-gallon stockpot and cover with cold water by 1 inch. Bring to a boil over high heat, removing any scum that rises. At the boil, immediately reduce heat to a very low boil and cook until both the chickens and veal are fall-apart tender, about 2 hours. Use a spider or long tongs to remove the chickens and veal from the pot, and place on a large tray to cool until you can handle them. Skim any grease that rises to the top of the broth.

Drain the soaking water off the beans, and add the beans to the pot. Add the onions and garlic and cook at a slightly increased boil until translucent, about 10 to 15 minutes. Add the celery, carrots, cabbage, tomatoes, tomato juice, corn, and potatoes, along with just enough cold water to cover by 1 inch if the broth isn't high enough. Use long-handled tongs to insert the spice sachet into the center of the pot. Simmer, but do not boil, for 2 hours, when the potatoes will be fork-tender but firm. Continue adding water as needed to top off the vegetables, and continue to skim off any oil or scum that rises.

Clean the veal and chicken meat from the bones, and shred with a fork, discarding skin, bones, and gristle. Add the shredded meats to the pot, add 1 inch of water to cover, and bring to a low boil. Cook for 1 hour or more, scraping the bottom of the pot often to ensure the stew doesn't stick and scorch. Continue to add cold water as needed to maintain the consistency you want. You can stand a spoon in a good booyah, but we're not making baby food either. One hour before you want to serve, add the salt, pepper, cayenne pepper, and Worcestershire, taste for seasoning, and adjust if needed. Serve from the pot with a long-handled ladle.

Duck and Manoomin Hotdish

A square meal in a rectangular pan and an icon of the Land of 10,000 Lakes, hotdish is an apt metaphor for Midwestern home cooking in the twentieth century, a time when it evolved from a primarily rural, farmstead style of cooking into one of urbanization, industrialization, and suburbanization. Busy families were primed to adopt casserole and slow-cooker dishes, which could pack in all the food groups and be put in the oven or on low and forgotten about while homework, chores, and extracurricular activities were tended to.

Midwesterners can be self-deprecating in a playful way around the topic of casseroles, especially those composed entirely of processed ingredients, as indicative of their supposed lack of culinary refinement and good taste. While it's true many casseroles can be little more than a salty yet impossibly bland amalgamation of industrial food ingredients, the potential for creative constructions is boundless. Since its beginnings as a ground beef and Creamette brand macaroni concoction submitted by Mrs. C. W. Anderson to a 1930 church cookbook,[5] hotdish has become a genre that mostly lives off the chain, pushing creative boundaries with each household that takes it up.

Casseroles had been gaining popularity for some time before Mrs. Anderson gave hotdish its name, but it became its own specialized genre. Many speculate that the name derives from the USDA's push for a "hot dish" to be included with school meals during the early twentieth century, and many of the guides it published through extension offices were pretty specific about it. One such guide suggests that a hot dish could be used to sneak both milk and vegetables into a school lunch.[6] Cream of mushroom soup and green beans, anyone?

By the definition that evolved from this purpose of forming a square meal out of a single dish, a proper hotdish includes a starch base, a protein such as poultry, meat, or fish, a canned or frozen vegetable, a canned soup, and a crispy or crunchy topping. In the modern gourmet hotdish lexicon, the requirement that the components need to be canned or frozen is cast aside.

In the Gopher State, hotdish is such a cherished tradition that in 2010, Senator Al Franken inaugurated an annual hotdish cookoff to bring Minnesota's congressional delegation together, partisan differences aside. The competition became an institution until the COVID-19 pandemic began in 2020. One of the most popular hotdish ingredients, Tater Tots, featured in the winner of the first competition, Senator Amy Klobuchar's "Taconite Tater Tot Hotdish."[7]

One of the most distinctive Midwestern ingredients you can cook with is manoomin, or wild rice. And since most true Native American wild rice is grown in Minnesota, it makes an appropriate, as well as a delicious and nutritious, grain base for hotdish. As Heid E. Erdrich explains in her excellent book *Original Local: Indigenous Foods, Stories, and Recipes from the Upper Midwest*:

> *Manoomin*, often translated as "good seed," is what Anishinaabe people call wild rice. Dakota call it *psin*, and other tribes had their own names for this important food source derived from an aquatic grass.[8]

Erdrich goes on to explain the very significant differences between true manoomin and the "wild rice" you are likely to find in the supermarket. True manoomin is gathered only by traditional methods and hasn't been subjected to any mechanized planting or harvesting equipment. The same goes for commercial plant breeding: It's not allowed. According to Erdrich, true manoomin varies greatly in color, texture, and aroma. To me as a cook with a passion for special ingredients, this is an even greater reason to seek out manoomin; it can make each meal yet another adventure in discovery. Manoomin is truly a wild food of the upper Midwest.

Erdrich further tells the story of Ojibwe rice harvester Ron Libertus, who spearheaded an activist drive during the 1980s that led to the first laws governing the cultivation and marketing of manoomin. Many continue Ron's work, since laws don't go far enough to protect manoomin from contamination from GMO "wild" rice genes. Moreover, climate change is a dire threat to preservation of this crop, which has adapted to very specific water levels in lakes and streams.[9] The best we can do to help is to purchase true manoomin from Indigenous farmers who are preserving this crop as their heritage and birthright. In many ways, we can help save a food by eating it.

While you can certainly use canned cream of mushroom soup concentrate for this recipe, the following quick, thick soup will make it a little special and be a better accompaniment for the rice and duck. You can even use your own wild-picked edible mushrooms to make it still more Midwestern. To enjoy the soup on its own, reheat and dilute with skim milk, re-season, and enjoy!

QUICK CREAM OF MUSHROOM SOUP

Makes 6 cups

¼ cup (½ stick) unsalted butter
4 tablespoons vegetable oil, divided
½ cup plus 1 tablespoon all-purpose flour
1 cup yellow Spanish onion, finely diced

4 cloves garlic, minced

1 pound cremini mushrooms, finely chopped

1 teaspoon dried thyme

1 teaspoon dried oregano

1 teaspoon freshly ground black pepper

8 ounces maitake or other "wild" mushrooms, coarsely chopped

2 cups strong chicken broth

1 tablespoon Worcestershire sauce

1 cup half-and-half

⅛ teaspoon nutmeg

1 teaspoon celery salt

2 teaspoons kosher salt

In a small saucepan, make a roux with the butter, 2 tablespoons of the vegetable oil, and the flour, cooking over medium heat and stirring constantly to prevent scorching. Cook to a medium-blond color; most importantly, cook until the pasty flour smell cooks out and the roux smells buttery and lightly toasty. Remove from heat, set aside, and allow to cool.

Heat the remaining 2 tablespoons of oil in a medium stockpot and sauté the onions and garlic until they are translucent and smell sweet, not sulfurous, about 6 to 8 minutes. Add the chopped cremini mushrooms, thyme, oregano, and pepper and stir often while the mushrooms cook and render. Cook until the mushrooms are all tender and the pot is aromatic with their scent. Add the roux and stir to combine well, then immediately add the maitakes, chicken broth, and Worcestershire, and bring to a boil to thicken. Maintain a low boil for 5 minutes before stirring in the half-and-half, nutmeg, and celery and kosher salts. Return to the boil once more for 15 seconds, then remove from heat. Serve hot or refrigerate before using in hotdish.

FOR THE HOTDISH

Makes one 13-by-9-inch hotdish

⅔ cup manoomin wild rice

2 cups cold water

5 teaspoons kosher salt, divided

6 tablespoons unsalted butter, divided

Whites of 3 leeks, very thinly sliced

8 ounces maitake mushrooms or other "wild" mushrooms

2 tablespoons Worcestershire sauce, divided

¼ cup dry white wine

3 cups Corn Chex

1 cup pecan halves

3 cups deboned duck confit (available online or in specialty food stores)

1 (10-ounce) package frozen broccoli, thawed

6 cups **QUICK CREAM OF MUSHROOM SOUP** (above)

Preheat oven to 350°F.

Rinse the wild rice under cold water and place in a small pot, then cover with the water. Add 2 teaspoons of the salt, bring to a boil, and maintain a low boil for 40 to 50 minutes, when the rice should be tender but retain a nice chew. Drain any excess water and reserve. You should have about 3 cups of rice.

Pull the maitake mushrooms apart into meaty but manageable pieces. Use 2 table-spoons of the butter to sauté the leeks and maitakes in a large skillet to sweat them, then add 1 teaspoon salt, 1 tablespoon Worcestershire, and the wine. Toss to coat the vegetables well, then boil out all the liquid while continuing to toss, being careful not to scorch or burn.

Pulse the Corn Chex a few times in the food processor until they are broken into pieces about half their original size. Melt the remaining 4 tablespoons of butter, use 1 tablespoon to butter a 9-by-13-inch casserole, and toss the remainder with the Corn Chex. Put the pecans in a Ziploc bag, seal it, and pass over it once or twice with a rolling pin to coarsely crack the pecans. Toss the pecans with the Corn Chex, then season the mixture with 1 teaspoon salt and 1 tablespoon Worcestershire sauce.

Season the duck with the remaining teaspoon of salt. Spread half of the duck across the bottom of the buttered casserole in bite-sized chunks. Cover with half the broccoli, half the maitake mixture, then half the rice, spreading each ingredient evenly. Ladle half the soup evenly over the rice, then tap the entire casserole pan on the counter a few times to settle everything. Repeat the layering with the remaining half of your ingre-dients. Spread the Corn Chex and pecan mixture evenly over the top and bake on the center rack of the oven for 40 to 50 minutes, when the filling should be molten and the cereal topping brown and crispy. Serve at once or cover tightly for the journey to your covered dish event.

Chicken and Noodles

I tip the lid gently to let the savory vapor escape and lean in just as close as I can, but not so close that I steam my face. I'm breaking an unspoken rule of the finishing stages of chicken and noodles, a dish usually finished uncovered, but I'm humoring my own superstition that if I leave the pot uncovered, all the beautiful smells will escape. So, lid on for me. The scent I seek is the unmistakable bouquet of fully cooked egg noodles, a rounder, milder scent than the one given off by al dente ones.

Anyone who grew up in the Midwest who's had chicken and noodles, and I don't know anyone White in the Midwest who hasn't, knows the smell and the soft, squishy texture of the finished noodles innately and primally—it is in our genes, in our blood. It was ingrained so deeply into my own family's cooking that I make it periodically as a meditation when I want to feel close to family and to home, or to imagine myself cooking and eating with the grandmother I never knew. Standing over a pot of chicken boiled nearly to mush to extract as much glutamic acid from the carcass and collagen from its bones and joints as possible, I can feel her there with me, telling me *es ist Zeit, die Henne auszuruhen und die Nudeln zu machen*, in that singsongy Dubois County German patois. *It's time to rest the chicken and make the noodles.*

What we might imagine to be an ancient home-cooking tradition is surprisingly hard to sleuth out, because recipes for chicken and noodles are nonexistent in the early cookbook canon. There are abundant recipes for noodles, but for boiled chicken no recipe is required. Sarah Rutledge provides a recipe "To Make Nudeln" in *The Carolina Housewife* (1847), which she calls "A German Dish."[10] She instructs us to boil them in broth until very soft, but then we have, at best, chicken noodle soup.

Although a multitude of chicken noodle soup references pepper nineteenth-century American newspapers, primarily in the modern Midwest, it is not until June 26, 1890, that the *Scranton Republican* sports an ad for Kennedy's Restaurant offering Stewed Chicken with Noodle.[11] Then the March 10, 1897, *Dixon* (Illinois) *Evening Telegraph* describes an "Annual Pennsylvania Dinner" by the Grace Evangelical Church ladies, headlined by chicken and noodles.[12] The number of news references to chicken and noodles in Pennsylvania itself points to the Amish or the larger community of "Pennsylvania Dutch" as the likely progenitors of this dish.

Like my forebears, I have made a pot full of free glutamic acid, the most abundant (and most needed) amino acid in the body, together with bountiful collagen, a water-soluble, freely available protein, and noodles made with wheat, a carbohydrate and protein powerhouse, and eggs, rich in both protein and essential dietary fats, all cooked to their readily digestible peaks. Whether you are the plate or bowl type when helping yourself to chicken and noodles, the impulse is the same. Your body knows, your nose knows, your tongue knows. Partake of this, and you will thrive, as did generations before you.

Makes between 3 and 4 quarts, serves 6 to 8

   1 medium fryer chicken, about 3½ pounds

   2 to 3 quarts water

   2 cups all-purpose flour

   2 large eggs

   2 tablespoons whole milk

   3 teaspoons kosher salt, divided

   1 teaspoon freshly ground black pepper

Rinse the chicken under cold running water in a clean sink. Place in a 4-quart sauce-pan or small stockpot and add enough of the water to just cover. Bring to a boil over high heat, skimming any foam or scum that rises. Once it boils, immediately reduce heat to medium or medium low to maintain a low boil. Cook for 1 hour or more, until the chicken is starting to fall apart. Remove from heat and use a spider to remove the chicken to a platter and allow to cool for a few minutes.

While the chicken is cooling, make the egg noodles. Place the flour in a medium mixing bowl, and make a little well in the center big enough to hold the eggs. Crack the eggs into the well, along with the milk and 1 teaspoon of salt. Using a fork, beat the eggs, then gradually begin pulling flour into them little by little. When the mixture becomes too thick to work with a fork, finish the mixing with your hands. Continue mixing until all the flour is incorporated, then knead inside the bowl, adding small amounts of flour if needed to prevent sticking, for a minute or two until you have a smooth ball. No need to knead longer than that. Cover with plastic wrap and rest for 15 minutes.

On a well-floured surface, roll out the noodles to the desired thickness; about ⅛ inch is usually ideal. Use a pizza cutter to cut them into the desired shape. I usually cut them about ½ inch wide and the full length of the rolled dough. But make them any width and length you like. Leave them liberally floured to prevent sticking while you pull the chicken and finish the broth.

Pull the meat from the chicken bones, removing and discarding the skin as well. Shred the chicken with a fork and reserve on the platter. Return the cooked broth to the heat, making sure you have 2 quarts or slightly more. Add a little extra water if needed. Add the remaining 2 teaspoons salt and the pepper, and bring to a rolling boil. Drop the noodles in at once and give a quick stir to make sure they don't clump. Reduce heat to medium low and cover the pot. Steam the noodles for 5 minutes, add the chicken, stir, replace the lid, and steam for 5 more minutes. Remove from heat, stir, and allow to steam off the heat, covered, for 10 more minutes. Then serve!

Fish Fries

For anyone raised Catholic in the Midwest, Friday fish fries have long been a
fixture of community life. No later than 1865, Wisconsin cafés were serving
fish fries on Fridays during the Lenten season, and today they are ubiquitous
in the Badger State's tavern and supper club cultures.[13] And many African
Americans have their own fish-fry traditions going back generations.[14] There
are some similarities: fish is fried; members of the community gather; there is
bread, a few sides, and probably tartar sauce and lemon wedges; but beyond
that framework, they differ significantly.

Black folks brought their fish-frying traditions from the South, whereas the
Midwestern fish-fry tradition was born here when German and Polish immigrants brought the Catholic practice of abstaining from meat on Fridays. When
they found themselves surrounded by rivers and lakes teeming with whitefish,
perch, walleye, bluegill, smelt, and catfish, their abstinence Fridays became an
excuse to indulge in a big ol' plate of fried seafood.

Interestingly, our modern techniques for frying fish can be traced back to
Sephardic Jews from Spain and Portugal, who fled persecution there during the
sixteenth and seventeenth centuries, some settling in England and others farther into Europe. By 1715, Germans were frying fish in a similar manner, with
semolina for the dredge and butter as the hot fat.[15] Hannah Glasse included a
recipe for fried carp in her popular 1747 *Art of Cookery*.[16]

It's likely that Germans brought their own fish-frying traditions to the Midwest. Bertha Kramer (a.k.a. "Aunt Babette"), an Ashkenazi Jew, included receipts for several different fried fish in *Aunt Babette's Cook Book*, which echo the
Frauenzimmer Lexicon's simple method of salting the fish, dredging it, and frying
it in very hot butter.[17] Like frying chicken, this was a popular way to prepare fish
for people of means, and something to aspire to for more workaday folks. Rye
bread is still a common accoutrement at Wisconsin fish fries, along with coleslaw. German potato pancakes are still popular, and you might see potato salad,
although french fries continue to encroach as a preferred accompaniment.

Black folks' traditions from the South were influenced by the White Anglo-
Saxon Protestant kitchens of England and Scotland, but along the way a
crunchier, more flavorful cornmeal dredge gained favor, probably because it
was less expensive than wheat and more common in slave rations. Informal
fish fries became a common way for enslaved Blacks to kick back during what
little free time they were afforded, and the fish were free—all you had to do
was catch them. Catfish were, and still are, the big prize. Hush puppies came

Catfish fiddlers at Knob Hill Tavern.   Photo by Paul Fehribach.

along for the ride, as well as Louisiana-style hot sauce, which is a must at any Black fish fry. Especially at Black fish-fry restaurants, french fries are a preferred starchy side, as is white bread, but at informal backyard gatherings there is just as likely to be potato salad, macaroni salad, macaroni and cheese, or collard greens.

The two parallel fish-fry traditions in the Midwest serve to underscore the persistent problem of segregation, as opportunities to blend cultures are overlooked at best and at worst, avoided. In both Black and White cultures, fish-fry traditions carry much with them to highlight the good that human beings can do: come together to feed one another, to raise funds for churches, schools, or other dear causes, to connect anew with one another and weave together the fabric of society. Tilting into the wind for a moment, we can at least be thankful for the diversity of our fish-fry traditions.

WISCONSIN-STYLE FISH FRY

In Wisconsin, there are probably as many recipes for fried fish as there are cooks, but beer batters are especially revered. The treatment of the fish should vary somewhat depending on the kind of fish, the size of the filets, and so forth. Cod has been a popular fish alongside the local ones, and its thicker filets should be dipped in batter and deep-fried, as should meatier filets of whitefish and haddock. I would caution against Atlantic wild-caught cod, as most of the fisheries are depleted. There are fisheries certified sustainable by the Marine Stewardship Council, but most fishmongers aren't yet bothering to vet sustainably caught Atlantic cod. Consult Monterey Bay Aquarium's Seafood Watch for up-to-date information on fisheries sustainability and management. Our local lake whitefish are considered sustainable, and they fry up beautifully; that's my first choice for a fish fry, unless of course I'm doing the fishing myself, then I'm going to catch all the bluegill I need. Fish with thin filets should be done with the dip-and-dredge method, not battered, because they are more delicate and their meat can get lost in a thick pillow of crispy fried batter. For these fish fries, the fish is always fileted and cut into portions, off the bone. Here's a guide to see you through.

DIP-AND-DREDGE METHOD

Recommended for fish such as bluegill, smallmouth bass, river or brook trout, carp, crappie, and smaller walleye (2 pounds or less). It also works on oysters or smaller shrimp. Plan on 5 to 6 ounces of fish per person.

Serves 4 to 6

> Vegetable oil for frying, optionally seasoned with clarified butter, lard, or bacon grease, ¾ to 1 inch in a large skillet or dutch oven
> 4 cups all-purpose flour
> 3 teaspoons kosher salt, divided
> 1 teaspoon baking powder
> 1 tablespoon granulated onion
> 1 teaspoon granulated garlic
> 1 teaspoon ground white pepper
> ¼ teaspoon cayenne pepper
> A shallow pan (a 13-by-9-inch cake pan or casserole is perfect) filled with ½ inch of lager beer or dry apple or pear cider
> 2 pounds fileted fish

Heat the oil, and use a clip-on thermometer and a keen eye to maintain it at 325°F. Mix the flour, 1 teaspoon salt, and the other dry ingredients together in a shallow pan, combining thoroughly. Spread the fish out on a sheet pan and sprinkle 2 teaspoons salt evenly over both sides of the fish. This will be a very thin layer but will begin drawing some moisture out of the filets to help the dredge adhere. Rest fish for 5 minutes.

Working in batches to give the frying fish plenty of room in the pan, gently swipe each side of a filet through the dredge, giving it a thin, even coat. Then swipe it through the beer or cider, being careful to wet both sides evenly, then swipe it through the dredge again, giving a slightly thicker coat to each side. Gently lay it in the hot fat and cook golden brown on both sides. Hold in a low oven on a platter lined with paper towels while you finish the remaining batches. Serve with **TARTAR SAUCE** (p. 183) and lemon wedges.

BEER BATTER METHOD

Recommended for thicker filets (½ inch or more) of whitefish, walleye, sturgeon, catfish, lake trout, cod, or sea bass. It also works on larger shrimp, prawns, and lobsters. Plan on 5 to 6 ounces of fish per person.

Serves 4 to 6

> Vegetable oil for frying, optionally seasoned with clarified butter, lard, or bacon grease, 2 inches in a large skillet or dutch oven
> 2½ cups all-purpose flour
> ½ cup corn starch
> 2 teaspoons kosher salt
> 1 teaspoon celery salt
> 1 tablespoon baking powder
> 1 tablespoon granulated onion
> 1 teaspoon granulated garlic
> 1 teaspoon ground white pepper
> ¼ teaspoon cayenne pepper
> 1½ cups club soda or seltzer
> 12 ounces lager beer or dry apple cider
> 2 pounds fileted fish

Heat the oil, and use a clip-on thermometer and a keen eye to maintain it at 325°F. Mix dry ingredients together in a medium bowl, combining well. Add the soda and beer and fold in with a rubber spatula until smooth.

Use a clean towel or paper towels to thoroughly pat each side of a filet dry before dipping. Stir the batter from the bottom to even it out, lay a filet in the batter, and let it sink, tamping it gently if needed. Pick it up by the thinnest edge with the tips of your thumb, index, and middle fingers, and let the batter run off for a count of three. The next step is important: Go straight to the oil and lay half of the filet in, as if you are going to float it. Continue holding the thin edge out of the oil. After a few seconds, the baking powder in the batter will act on the submerged portion, the batter will start to expand, and the filet will float. Now, gently let go of the edge onto which you have dutifully held. This is the most effective method I know for batter frying without worrying about sticking to the bottom.

Fry for 4 to 5 minutes on the first side, 3 to 4 minutes on the second side. Work in batches so as not to overcrowd the pot. Hold in a low oven on a platter lined with paper towels while you finish the remaining batches. Serve with **TARTAR SAUCE** (p. 183) and malt vinegar.

CORNMEAL-CRUSTED CATFISH

Serves 4 to 6

2 eggs, well beaten

½ cup skim milk

¼ cup Louisiana-style hot sauce

3 teaspoons kosher salt, divided

2 pounds catfish filets, 4 to 6 ounces each

Vegetable oil for frying, optionally seasoned with clarified butter, lard, or bacon
   grease, 2 inches in a large skillet or dutch oven

4 cups stone-ground yellow cornmeal, finely ground

1 tablespoon granulated onion

1 teaspoon granulated garlic

1 teaspoon Spanish paprika

½ teaspoon cayenne pepper

In a casserole dish, combine the beaten egg, milk, hot sauce, and 1 teaspoon salt. Layer the catfish filets in the egg mixture coating all sides of each filet. Cover tightly and refrigerate at least 1 hour, or overnight.

Heat the oil, and use a clip-on thermometer and a keen eye to maintain it at 375°F. If you're using white cornmeal, reduce the temperature to 325°F and increase cooking time by 2 minutes. Mix the cornmeal with the remaining 2 teaspoons of salt and all the spices in a shallow pan, combining thoroughly.

Working in batches so as to give the frying fish plenty of room in the pan, lift each filet out of the egg mixture, first swirling it around a bit to coat it. Then hold it up by the thin end, letting the egg drip back into the pan, for a count of three, but do not brush off any excess. Lay the filet in the cornmeal mixture and pile some extra cornmeal dredge on top of the filet, effectively burying it. Press firmly up and down the length of the filet to help the cornmeal adhere, turn it over, and repeat. Inspect to be sure the filet is evenly coated with cornmeal on both sides, and if not, patch it with more egg mixture, then cornmeal. Give a gentle brush with your fingers to smooth each side. Gently lay it in the hot fat and fry to a nice brown on both sides, about 6 minutes total. Hold in a low oven on a platter lined with paper towels while you finish the remaining batches. Serve with hot sauce, **TARTAR SAUCE** (p. 183), and lemon wedges.

CATFISH FIDDLERS

Nestled amid a few bends in the Ohio River around Evansville, Indiana, and Owensboro, Kentucky, institutions such as the Knob Hill Tavern, Windy Hollow Restaurant, the Moonlight, and Waverly Inn (RIP) have served up a delicacy you won't find in other parts of the Midwest: catfish fiddlers. Owensboro might be able to claim the most restaurants serving fiddlers, but Newburgh, Indiana, is the self-declared ground zero, hosting a Catfish Fiddler Festival each September. The Ohio River Valley's answer to fish fries, a catfish fiddler isn't a fish that fiddles (although many a tavern's signage makes use of the pun) but rather a small, approximately ½-pound catfish breaded and fried whole, sans head and guts. When the favored channel cats, with their broad midsections, are used and the tail fanned out before frying, the finished dish bears a striking resemblance to a tiny fiddle.

Catfish fiddlers are on many dinner menus in the Valley throughout the week and year-round, but they are mandatory on Friday nights, especially during Lent. Newburgh's Knob Hill Tavern goes for broke, serving its famous plate with old-fashioned corn sticks baked in heavy cast-iron pans. Pillowy in the center, the corn sticks sport a strong crunch around the edges, and buttering them only adds to the fun. Some form of white bread or roll is the most common accompaniment, in addition to potatoes, but on the south side of the river, cornbread reigns supreme. Naturally, potatoes are most often seen as french fries, but it's worthwhile to seek out the spots that serve breaded and deep-fried potato wedges, another favorite of the area, or the locally endemic **GERMAN FRIES** (p. 157).

Serves 4

- 2 eggs, beaten well
- ½ cup skim milk
- ¼ cup Louisiana-style hot sauce
- 4 teaspoons kosher salt, divided
- 4 whole catfish fiddlers, approximately 8 to 10 ounces each
- Vegetable oil for frying, optionally seasoned with clarified butter, lard, or bacon grease, 2 inches in a large skillet or dutch oven

2 cups stone-ground yellow cornmeal, finely ground

2 cups all-purpose flour

1 tablespoon granulated onion

1 teaspoon granulated garlic

1 tablespoon freshly ground black pepper

½ teaspoon cayenne pepper

In a casserole dish, combine the beaten eggs, milk, hot sauce, and 1 teaspoon salt. Layer the fiddlers in the egg mixture, coating all sides of each one. Cover tightly and refrigerate overnight, turning a few times before going to bed. The following day, turn the filets in the egg mixture each hour until cooking time.

Heat the oil, and use a clip-on thermometer and a keen eye to maintain it at 375°F.

The famous Knob Hill Tavern in Newburgh, Indiana, open since 1943. Photo by Paul Fehribach.

Mix the cornmeal and flour with the remaining 3 teaspoons of salt and all the spices in a shallow pan, combining thoroughly.

Working in batches so as to give the frying fish plenty of room in the pan, lift each fiddler out of the egg mixture, first swirling it around a bit to coat it. Then hold it up by the tail end, letting the egg drip back into the pan, for a count of three, but do not brush off any excess. Lay the fiddler in the cornmeal mixture and pile some extra cornmeal dredge on top of the fiddler, effectively burying it. Fill the stomach cavity of the fiddler with dredge, tossing to coat all sides of the interior. Press firmly up and down the length of the fiddler to help the cornmeal adhere, turn it over, and repeat. Inspect to be sure the fiddler is evenly coated with cornmeal on both sides, and if not, patch it with more egg mixture, then cornmeal. Give a gentle brush with your fingers to smooth each side. Carefully fan the tail for show, and double-check that it is well dredged. Gently lay it in the hot fat and fry to a nice brown on both sides, about 5 to 7 minutes on the first side and 4 to 6 minutes on the second side. The interior of the catfish should be at least 175°F. Drain on wire racks or paper towels. Hold in a low oven on a platter lined with paper towels while you finish the rest. Serve with **TARTAR** or **COCKTAIL SAUCE** (both below) and lemon wedges.

TARTAR SAUCE

Tartar sauce needs no introduction as a popular accoutrement to fried fish and seafood. It's not evident how it got to the United States or where it originated, but it was probably inspired by the French remoulade, and it began to appear more commonly in the United States in the 1870s. By the 1890s, it was everywhere, a veritable darling of the dinner (or lunch) table.

What's remarkable about early mentions of tartar sauce is that it was used for meat just as often as fish, in one case even being served with lamb fries (testicles) en brochette at an elaborate 1876 banquet at the Lindell Hotel in Saint Louis, alongside sweetbreads à la Marechale, escalop of pheasants à la Perigeaux, potatoes dauphine, omelets with truffles, Clos de Vougeot, champagne, Amontillado sherry, and other delights.[18] With seafood, an 1874 banquet at the Lochiel in Harrisburg, Pennsylvania, honored the Army of the Potomac with sea bass accompanied by tartar sauce, served alongside Westphalian ham glazed in madeira, jellied veal loin, young chicken with watercress sauce, an array of ice creams, and champagnes by Veuve Clicquot, Mumm, Roederer, and Piper Heidsieck, as well as a selection of clarets and sherries.[19] These weren't your cheap Long John Silver's seafood fix or even a greasy night out at the pub; these were elegant celebrations, as one early printed recipe shows:

Put the yolks of four eggs into a basin, with salt and mustard to taste, and stir olive oil into them one tablespoonful at a time; after each tablespoon of oil put in one teaspoonful of tarragon vinegar. Keep on doing this until the sauce is of the desired consistency; then add pepper, the least bit of cayenne, and a few pickled onions chopped very finely.[20]

Tartar sauce is now a cheap condiment, but we could show it a bit more love. We have the luxury of starting with high-quality prepared mayonnaise, which they couldn't do in 1879. I've made enough of these sauces to tell you that using olive oil will almost always leave an overpowering flavor, and we definitely don't want that with our fried fish (or lamb fries). If you do try the 1879 recipe, I recommend using a neutral oil such as grapeseed or rice bran oil for the bulk of it, finishing with a touch of olive oil for that perfume. But here's my recipe.

Makes about 1½ cups

1 cup Duke's or Hellman's mayonnaise

3 tablespoons freshly squeezed lemon juice

¼ cup **PICCALILLI** (p. 23) or diced bread-and-butter pickles

1 tablespoon chopped fresh dill or 1 teaspoon dried dill

1 tablespoon very finely sliced green onion

1 tablespoon Worcestershire sauce

2 teaspoons spicy brown mustard

⅛ teaspoon cayenne pepper

Additional salt, to taste

Mix all ingredients except for the salt together in a nonreactive bowl. Refrigerate for at least 1 hour before tasting and adjusting seasoning. Will keep for up to 10 days tightly covered in the refrigerator.

COCKTAIL SAUCE

Like tartar sauce, cocktail sauce has been part of our restaurant, fast-food, and supermarket culture for so long that it's rarely thought of as anything more than tepid red-flecked dip in a plastic to-go cup, or an accompaniment to a prearranged shrimp cocktail from the grocery store. Unlike tartar sauce, cocktail sauce does not enjoy the cachet or prestige of lofty origins. Its ascendancy took a different track, from commoner condiment to occasional fine-dining accoutrement. Today it occupies both realms, differentiated by the quality and freshness of the ingredients used to make it.

Cocktail sauce appears to have already had some legs when, in 1868, someone named Muller allegedly sold 217 oyster cocktails at a debate in Oakland,

California, between gubernatorial candidates George C. Gorham and Wm. T. Wallace.[21] Some twenty years later, a Californian offered up a tip on "a cocktail we get in San Francisco that knocks out any of the cocktails you get here":

> Put half a dozen to a dozen small oysters into a goblet or beer glass, with enough of the liquor to cover them. Salt, pepper, catsup, a dash of Tobasco [*sic*] sauce, half a spoonful of Worcestershire, two or three teaspoons of vinegar, and sometimes a pinch of horseradish. Stir it up with a spoon and drink it down.[22]

So apparently the modern oyster shooter was invented in California! During the oyster craze of the late eighteenth century, oysters remained the seafood cocktail of choice. Even by 1906, Chicago's celebrated seafood house, Rector's, was still serving clam and oyster cocktails in this fashion.[23] Shrimp cocktail began showing up on menus during the 1910s. Cincinnati's mammoth condiment processor Snider's was engaged in nationwide advertising campaigns for its "oyster cocktail sauce" into the twentieth century, though we don't know when someone first dipped a nugget of fried fish in it.

As dowdy as the stuff may seem, try to forget all the syrupy, bland bottled cocktail sauces you've ever been served and make this one. It'll open your eyes to why seafood cocktail became a thing in the first place.

Makes about 1½ cups, serves 6

    1 cup ketchup
    ¼ cup grated fresh horseradish
    3 tablespoons freshly squeezed lemon juice
    3 tablespoons original Tabasco sauce
    2 tablespoons Worcestershire sauce
    ½ teaspoon celery salt
    Additional salt to taste, if desired

Combine ingredients in a small mixing bowl. Cover tightly and refrigerate at least 1 hour or overnight before serving.

Fried Chicken: Of Church Suppers and June Weddings

As a thinking man, I was befuddled by fried chicken for years because I couldn't make sense of the difference between my own personal experience and the accepted history and lore that have grown up around this dish like the vines of morning glories over a trusty old toolshed. The South has long claimed fried chicken as its own, but it has also been an essential part of the Midwestern experience.

Like many Americans, I grew up with fried chicken as a totemic food deeply ingrained in our local culture, yet not routine. It was a food of celebration, jubilee, and joyous times. I cannot recall a single June wedding during which the newlyweds were not regaled with an expansive buffet with fried chicken as the centerpiece. Yet because fried chicken was held in such high esteem, it just wasn't something you'd go out for on a Tuesday, much less cook at home, save for the occasional Sunday dinner.

The conventional narrative is that fried chicken is a Southern dish, that it came from the South and moved north and westward with the changing population and, particularly, the Great Migration. This explanation never really satisfied me, because while many early nineteenth-century pioneers to the Midwest came from Virginia and Kentucky, two states that subsequently became famous for fried chicken, I couldn't find any evidence that fried chicken came to the Midwest with those pioneers. While there is a definite fried chicken connection between the South and the North via the Great Migration, many Midwestern communities were feasting on the birds before that movement brought hundreds of thousands of Southern Blacks to the Midwest.

My hometown of Jasper, Indiana, came to be populated almost exclusively by German immigrants from Baden, in the southwestern corner of Germany, and it was frankly never particularly welcoming to outsiders of any kind. So how did fried chicken become sacramental *there*? Asking the question from a different angle, in his excellent book *Fried Chicken: An American Story*, Southern Foodways Alliance founding director John T. Edge visits a fried chicken dinner at Saint Paul's Parish in New Alsace, Indiana, and describes a long tradition of such suppers centered around the outer reaches of Cincinnati.[24] Once again, I scratched my head and asked, "How did fried chicken take hold there?" The assumption that some folks moved from the South and brought fried chicken to New Alsace and poof! it took over some German Catholic parishes seemed dubious to me. Noting that the cooks and parishioners who spoke with Edge all had German names, like the folks in my hometown, I decided to look into the German literature, and it turns out that a culture of fried chicken in a town called New Alsace makes perfect sense.

The most commonly cited "first" fried chicken recipe, titled "To Marinate Chickens," is from Hannah Glasse's 1747 edition of *The Art of Cooking Made Plain and Easy*.[25] This book was wildly popular and went through multiple editions over decades, undoubtedly influencing authors Mary Randolph of *The*

Virginia Housewife (1824) and Lettice Bryan of *The Kentucky Housewife* (1839), both of whom threw in with their own fried chicken receipts.

But if we look through a wider lens, we find that the earliest mention of fried chicken in the West comes from the physician and minnesinger Heinrich von Neustadt early in the fourteenth century, when he chastises Viennese women for drinking wine and eating fried chicken before church, "so they will feel better in head and stomach."[26] This is the first known mention of Austria's national dish, *Backhendl*, which bears a striking resemblance to American fried chicken, only it's strewn with breadcrumbs before its pass through boiling beef tallow. *Backhendl* was specific to Vienna, and the early German receipts for fried chicken demonstrate various approaches, but it's likely that in the 1300s a fried chicken would have been simply rolled in flour or batter, as we see in recipes beginning in the Reformation era.

Our earliest known published fried chicken receipt is also by one of the earliest published female cookbook authors, Eleonora Maria Rosalia, in her curiously titled 1699 book *Freiwillig auffgesprungener Granat-Apffel des Christlichen Samaritans* (Willingly Cracked-Open Pomegranate of the Christian Samaritans):

Fried Chickens and Pigeons

When the chickens and pigeons are dismembered / one should remove the little legs / and put in salted water overnight / then sprinkle with fine vinegar / and let them soak again for a while / then dust them in flour / and fry them in lard / throw nice green parsley into hot lard / and take it out right away / and put it on top / it will stay nice and green.[27]

In 1712, the mammoth *Frauenzimmer Lexicon* offers up two different ways to fry your chicken, one following Rosalia's lead with a little salt marinade and a roll in flour before a trip through hot fat (*Hüner junge gebacken*), the other with a batter made of sweet milk and flour in which the pieces of chicken are dipped before frying (*Hüner gebacken andere Art mit einer Klare*).[28]

In the 1718 *Neues saltzburgisches Koch-Buch*, Conrad Hagger offers up two receipts for fried chicken, *Hünlein im Schlaffrock* (Chicken in a Gown), which suggests a beer batter for the bird's dress, and *Hünlein aus geschlagenen Eyern gebackenen* (Chicken Fried from Beaten Eggs),[29] which is the famed Viennese *Backhendl*: chicken rolled in flour, dipped in egg wash, strewn with breadcrumbs, and fried in hot beef lard.

By the nineteenth century, various treatments of fried chicken are ubiquitous in the High German culinary literature. In his 1826 memoirs, the famed

Irish tenor Michael Kelly recounts living in Vienna from 1783 to 1787, perform-ing for the royal court. Describing nightlife on Vienna's great promenade, the Prater, he recounts that locals would "in the evening, *immediately after dinner*, proceed thither to regale themselves with their favorite dish, fried chickens, cold ham, and sausages; white beer, and Hofner wines."[30]

The growing popularity of fried chicken in southern Germany was concur-rent with German emigration to the American colonies. We know that Ger-mans arrived as early as the settlement of Jamestown in 1608,[31] and were specifically sought for skilled trades, and that over the seventeenth century, they scattered throughout the colonies.[32] The historical record makes it more likely than not that Germans cooked the first fried chicken in the colonies, yet the waning of the trade in indentured servants and an increase in the slave trade in Virginia during the late seventeenth century means it was probably an enslaved African who cooked the first documented dishes of fried chicken in Virginia, as stated in William Byrd's diary of 1709.[33] Somewhere in the long intervening century, knowledge had been passed along, although it is certainly possible that West Africans themselves had a tradition of deep-frying birds. The story from there on is well documented.[34]

Fried chicken doesn't appear in American popular media until the early 1800s, first popping up in an ad for a New York restaurant called the Refec-tory.[35] At least some writers pegged fried chicken as a Pennsylvania Dutch phenomenon, pining for the "fare of Berks and Reading counties," including fried chickens, veal cutlets, schnitts, schmeerkaes, and doubled and twisted donuts, among more common fare.[36]

In southern Germany during the nineteenth century, fried chicken was en-joying another moment ensconced in Viennese culture with the silly moniker *Die Backhendlzeit*, meaning "the time of fried chicken." Following the end of the Napoleonic Wars and the Congress of Vienna in 1815, Germany would ex-perience a time many came to consider the "good old days," a time of depolit-icized public discourse and literary censorship, and a complacency that lent itself to carousing in taverns with wine, beer, and *Backhendl*. The conserva-tive politics of the era caused many liberal and educated dissidents to depart for the United States. Some put the end of the *Backhendlzeit* in 1848 with the failure of that year's revolution, which sought democratic reforms, but others place it with the stock market crash of 1873. Both of these tumultuous events would lead to further waves of Germans emigrating to the United States.

In the southern German duchies, fried chicken was a dish of the petite bourgeoisie, something for aristocrats and the merchant class to enjoy, and for all, represented aspiration, abundance, and success. As I contemplate this, I ponder the African American women entrepreneurs who took to hawking fried chicken at Eastern railway depots during the late nineteenth century, a business phenomenon that lasted well into the twentieth century.[37] German immigrants of the merchant class who were greeted at a railroad depot by outstretched Black hands offering fried chicken wouldn't have seen it as an exotic, strange new food: they would have known exactly what it was, and perhaps it would have given them some comfort. To an immigrant working stiff, an offering of fried chicken for a few pennies would surely have been a sign that they had arrived in the land of plenty.

The High German affair with fried chicken followed emigrants to the United States in cookbooks targeted specifically at them. In the 1879 edition of her German-language cookbook *Praktisches Kochbuch für die Deutschen in Amerika*, Henriette Davidis includes the most elaborate receipt for fried chicken I have seen from the time, under the name "*Gebackene Hähnel*," instructing the reader from slaughter to table.[38] Fried chicken also appears in the follow-up 1897 edition. Southern Germans in America did what immigrant cultures have done over and over: embedded their most cherished dishes in their most beloved social customs. Thus, we had fried chicken at weddings, church dinners, jubilees, or any occasion when we wanted to embrace the most cherished elements of our identity.

The Great Migration brought hundreds of thousands of Southern Blacks to Northern cities, and with them, they brought a taste for seasonings. While the German fried chicken I grew up with was simple, salted and rolled in flour and seasoned only with a little pepper, an ever-increasing number of Midwesterners, including myself, are developing a taste for fried chicken as it evolved in the South in the hands of African American cooks: with plenty of garlic and a hefty kick of spice. In cooking, sharing ideas builds a bigger table at which we can all sup.

The following recipe has plenty of flavor without getting too spicy. Even though I sell a lot of very good fried chicken at my restaurant, there is a high reward factor to making your own at home. When dining out, it is definitely worth taking the time to seek out your local Black-owned restaurant. The fried chicken of Black Southern heritage will bring more flavor. For dining in, I'm sharing one of my favorite highly seasoned recipes.

For one fried chicken; serves 2 to 4

FOR THE BRINE

1 small fryer chicken, about 3 pounds, cut at the joints—leg, thigh, breast, wing, plus the lower back (my favorite when I was a kid because it's all crispy skin!)

2 quarts iced water

2 tablespoons kosher salt

1 tablespoon celery salt

2 tablespoons granulated sugar

1 teaspoon freshly ground black pepper

2 tablespoons granulated onion

2 tablespoons white vinegar

2 bay leaves

3 or 4 sprigs fresh thyme, or 1 teaspoon dried

2 tablespoons Tabasco sauce

Place the chicken and all other ingredients in a large bowl with a tight-fitting lid, stir gently to disperse the seasonings, cover, and refrigerate at least 8 hours or overnight.

FOR THE DREDGE

5 cups all-purpose flour

2 teaspoons baking powder

2 tablespoons freshly ground black pepper

2 tablespoons fine sea salt

2 tablespoons celery salt

1 tablespoon granulated garlic

1 tablespoon ground sage

2 teaspoons dried thyme

1 teaspoon cayenne pepper

Mix all ingredients thoroughly and place in a large shallow pan.

FOR FRYING

6 large eggs

2 cups iced water

6 cups lard (3 pounds) or canola oil

3 strips smoked bacon

Fill a 2-gallon cast-iron dutch oven, stockpot, or Fry Daddy halfway with freshly ren-dered lard or canola oil, and heat to 375°F over medium-high heat, monitoring the temperature with a thermometer.

In the meantime, place your dredge in a large shallow pan, and fluff it with a fork. Beat the eggs and put them in a separate shallow pan with the water. Take your chicken, still dripping wet, and lay it in the dredge, turn gently to coat, and make sure all the chicken pieces are thoroughly coated, being careful that the skin stays in place. Shake off excess dredge, roll in the egg mixture, and return to the dredge, coating all sides again. Rest the chicken in the dredge until ready to fry.

Once the oil reaches 375°F, fry the bacon in the lard until just crispy, remove it, and drain on a paper towel. Save for later to use in salads or sandwiches, or enjoy a well-deserved snack.

Remove the breasts from the dredge and gently lay them skin side down in the hot oil. Cook the breasts for 3 minutes before adding the thighs. Gently add the thighs skin side down also. One minute later, add the legs and wings. Turn the heat down to 325°F and maintain that temperature. After 10 to 12 minutes, turn the chicken over. The skin should be crispy and golden brown. Continue cooking another 6 to 8 minutes, until the thickest part of the breast registers 155°F internally. Drain on a wire rack or towel and serve at once, pack your picnic basket, or refrigerate to serve cold.

Queen City Chili

During workday lunch hours, the line at the Camp Washington drive-through can easily stretch all the way around the restaurant and on down the street. It's quite a phenomenon, as is Cincinnati chili. Where else can you get a delicious plate of food crowned with a golden mane of shredded cheese so airy and cloud-like as to foster an air of mystery about what lies beneath?

The chili that retains its metaphorical grip on the Queen City is above all else an enduring testimonial to the idea that even in our heavily industrialized food system, regional foodways can emerge, take hold, and embed themselves among a people bound by place. Probably the most defamed food I've read about throughout my life, Cincinnati's chili is thus also perhaps the most felicitous exemplar of Midwestern cuisine: misunderstood and mischaracterized, a victim of closed minds unwilling to consider its virtues. Some even refuse to call it chili, but that's what it's called, so get used to it.

Unlike many of our Midwestern foodways, which are shrouded in mystery and lore, Cincinnati chili has a well-documented story. In the early 1920s, Macedonian immigrant Tom Kiradjieff spent some time in New York working coney dog stands before moving to Cincinnati and opening a chili parlor with his brother John, named Empress Chili after the burlesque revue next door.[39] Seeking a compelling and unique angle, he experimented with his coney topping, adding the seasonings of his Balkan heritage, cinnamon and allspice. His "chili spaghetti" was an adaptation of a traditional Macedonian meat stew served over pasta[40] and was boldly christened "chili" because American consumers would immediately recognize the name. It was a risky gambit that paid off.

In Empress Chili, Kiradjieff created an anchor for extended family and other Macedonian immigrants, offering jobs, connections, and a template for success in the New World that would foster a thriving Macedonian American community in the Cincinnati area.[41] He created an archetypal ecosystem for chain migration, which would lead to many more chili parlors and a culture of chili consumption.

The city's most famous chain, Skyline, was founded in 1949 by a former Empress employee, Nicholas Lambrinides. It now has over 150 locations. The Cincinnati style of chili is served in all kinds of restaurants, yet there are over 250 chili parlors that specialize in it. An astonishing 1988 study found that 80 percent of Cincinnatians ate chili at least once a week.[42] If those numbers have held (and given the proliferation of chili chains and independents, they probably have), today that's some 1.6 million servings of chili in metropolitan Cincinnati weekly.

Given the fierce competition, it's not surprising that chili quality is good to great across town, from the behemoth Skyline to other chains such as Gold Star, Empress, and Dixie, along with notable indies like Price Hill and Camp Washington. If one place misses a step, there's another on the next block ready to pick up the customers. In 2021, I found the service reliably fast and friendly and never paid more than about $7.50 for a 5-way (we'll get to that in a minute), so with a beverage you can have a sit-down lunch for twelve bucks (with tip), and your money stays in town instead of flowing up the corporate ladder to some far-off investors in a national chain.

In Cincinnati, a hot dog with chili topping is just called a coney, and it differs from a Michigan coney dog in its wardrobe. A coney is topped with Cincinnati chili, onions, a streak of mustard, and that majestic cloud of finely shredded mild cheddar cheese. The cheese and onions make it my favorite way, but that mustard just balances everything in a way that outdoes even a well-constructed 5-way. My only complaint about the coney is that the standard in Cincinnati is a skinless dog, which lacks the snap of a great wiener and renders it an afterthought to the chili and toppings, rather than a key player in the sandwich. One of these local chili parlors needs to get with the excellent local meat shop Avril-Bleh and get some natural-casing wieners for their coneys; then I might have to move to Cincinnati to be able to eat them every day.

Because there can be a long list of spices in a pot of Cincinnati chili, to avoid a cacophonous failure, a deft hand is needed to create a balance among them.

Available five ways (or more), Cincinnati chili is highly   Photo by Paul Fehribach.
customizable. That's hospitality!

Everything should combine to make one unified flavor. There are rumors that all or some chili parlors use chocolate in their recipes, and many printed recipes for "Cincinnati chili" include either unsweetened chocolate or cocoa powder, but every chili impresario denies the suggestion.[43] Is chocolate the secret ingredient? Possibly, but unlikely. I've tasted my way through Cincinnati on the alert for a whiff of chocolate and have never found one, or at least one has never whopped me over the head. To be fair, when tasting an unusually good Cincinnati chili such as the one at Camp Washington, it's easy to see why laypeople might think there is chocolate in there. The flavor is so deeply layered and complex that I do hear that clarion of Mesoamerican cuisine, mole, knocking at the door. It's time this chili got some of the respect it richly deserves.

FOR THE CHILI

Makes about 3 quarts, enough for 10 to 12 servings over pasta

2 tablespoons vegetable oil

2 cups Spanish onion, very finely diced

2 tablespoons garlic, minced

1 quart cold water

2 pounds ground beef, at least 80% lean

3 beef bouillon cubes

1 (6-ounce) can tomato paste

3 bay leaves

2 tablespoons chili powder

1 tablespoon ground cumin

2 teaspoons Hungarian paprika

½ teaspoon ground allspice

½ teaspoon ground Korintje or Mexican cinnamon

½ teaspoon ground cayenne pepper

¼ teaspoon ground cloves

2 tablespoons yellow mustard

1 tablespoon Worcestershire sauce

2 teaspoons Tabasco sauce

1 to 2 additional teaspoons salt, to taste

In a 4-quart saucepan or stockpot, heat the vegetable oil over medium-high heat until a piece of onion tossed in sizzles fiercely. Add the onion and garlic and sauté, stirring constantly, until the onions are rendered and just starting to brown, 4 to 6 minutes. Turn off the heat and add the cold water to stop the cooking. Crumble the beef into the pot and use a potato masher or spatula to work the beef in the water until it comes apart completely. Turn the heat back up to medium high and bring to a boil, working the beef constantly to keep breaking it up until it is a fine slurry. Skim any scum or foam that rises. Once it comes to a boil, add the bouillon cubes and tomato paste and return to a boil.

Reduce heat to maintain a low boil, and add the bay leaves, chili powder, cumin, paprika, allspice, cinnamon, cayenne, and cloves. Maintain a low boil to cook down to desired consistency, about 3 hours, skimming any fat as it rises. Stir more often as it thickens to prevent scorching. The chili is ready when a spoonful of it dolloped onto a plate doesn't bleed watery broth; it should hold up at about the consistency of a thick milkshake. Reduce heat to a simmer, add the mustard, Worcestershire, and Tabasco, simmer 15 more minutes, taste for seasoning, and add additional salt if desired.

This is best refrigerated overnight and reheated in a saucepan. When taking from the refrigerator, discard any fat from the surface.

MAKING A PLATE (OR BOWL) OF CHILI

The ordering key to a chili parlor is thus, and will guide you in your own kitchen as well:

1-way: Chili, plain in a bowl. Enough said.

2-way: Chili with beans to taste, or with spaghetti. With beans, it's served in a bowl. With spaghetti, about 2 cups of cooked spaghetti is topped with 1 cup of chili.

3-way: Chili with spaghetti and cheese. See 2-way for proportions of spaghetti and chili. Top with 2 ounces mild cheddar, grated on the smallest side of a box grater in long, smooth strokes to create long, cotton-like threads.

4-way: Chili with spaghetti, beans, and cheese. Heat canned kidney beans in the liquid they come in, then drain them well. Add ½ cup of beans to top the chili before adding the cheese.

5-way: Chili with spaghetti, beans, cheese, and onions. Add ¼ cup very finely diced yellow Spanish onion after the beans and before the cheese.

Many restaurants come up with other "ways" to order chili, such as adding **GOETTA** (p. 151) or hot dogs to the plate. My advice is to stick to a 5-way or a 3-way.

Pro tip: If your pasta isn't well drained, it will contribute to a watery plate of chili. This is the top, and worst, Cincinnati chili fail. Drain your pasta into a colander in a clean sink, and shake up and down until the pasta drips no more water.

Marty and Will Travis

———

Marty and Will Travis are two very busy guys. As the beating heart of Spence Farm and their aggregator project Down at the Farms, they are two central figures in the reimagination of farm economics in central Illinois, one thread in a global fabric that unites small farmers in common purpose: not just to survive but also to thrive.

Marty's fourth great-grandfather Valentine Darnall left Kentucky for Illinois, and first tilled this land outside Fairbury, in 1830, making it one of the oldest continually operating farms in Illinois. Marty himself left a comfortable tech career in 1999 when his grandmother Hazel Spence set up the farm in the care of her daughter Willa and Marty, Willa's son.

With Marty's son Will now running the bulk of the farm operation as Marty focuses more on aggregating small farmers into Down at the Farms, eight generations have worked the farm, and Will's kids are the ninth. They're doing this on just 160 acres, a prospect most industrialized farmers, drowning in debt and subject to a commodified market, would find preposterous. Yet Will sees nothing but potential, understands his responsibilities to the land and the farming community, and is committed to raising his kids to do the same.

Back in 1999, Marty thought they'd be able to make a happy living selling to a few of their chef friends, but it didn't take them long to observe that young people are leaving places like Livingston County and not coming back. Marty felt that his family had connections and relationships that would create opportunities for other folks and bring real economic change and development back to the county. "Their parents didn't want them to farm because they didn't want them to farm the way they were farming, and there wasn't enough farmland to farm conventional acres to support another family. So we started with some of these young kids, actually in 2005, we had twenty-five small family farms that were part of the Stewards [of the Land] group, and the majority of them were under eighteen. And that has perpetuated itself, and many of them are selling to the markets on their own now."

Many of those same farmers are part of Down at the Farms. Marty is recruiting new farmers all the time, and it's getting easier as word gets around that there are opportunities besides corn and beans. "We'd like to add twenty to twenty-five more farms by next year, and we might have more than that."

Currently, Down at the Farms aggregates seventy-five farms' products into one catalog, which is updated weekly. Orders from the catalog fill five trucks a week: two head to Chicago on Wednesdays, two to downstate markets on Thursdays, and one to Chicago on Fridays. Soon, two more trucks a week will be supplying the University of Illinois in Champaign. During peak season, the catalog is 18 to 20 pages long and is a tour de force of farm produce: dozens of varieties of corn, wheat from ancient emmer and farro plus the Midwestern-heritage standard Turkey Red wheat, all also processed into flours by Janie's Mill. Several varieties of rye and barley are available as well. One farm is nixtamalizing heritage corn into big hominy and masa flour. And those are just the grains. Creamline cream, milk, butter, cheeses, and yogurts from pasture-raised, grass-fed cows; a wide range of heritage poultry; rare breeds of pork such as red wattle and American Guinea; grass-fed beef; sausages; and then page after page of produce. Many farmers use high tunnels and greenhouses to extend the season, so a wide variety of lettuces and cooking greens is available throughout the year, and storage roots never bottom out in winter. It's a grocery store on wheels.

Even with the aggregator's impressive growth and current catalog, Marty sees gaps, and would like to continue to expand the season on both ends—for example, by adding fruit. Marty's son Will has taken the lead there and has added a huge and diverse orchard to the operations of Spence Farm. I tasted Winesap and Baldwin apples there, and they made me wistful for home. They'll have dozens of varieties of heirloom apples, peaches, nectarines, plums, and an oft-forgotten gem of the region, the **CHICAGO HARDY FIG** (see p. 81). As they open up the market for Illinois-grown orchard fruit, they will recruit and counsel more farmers, as they have done with growers of heritage grains and vegetables.

The experience of the farm community growing up around Spence Farm has come to countermand the standard narrative of rural decline and the flight of young people. New farmers joining Down at the Farms are of all ages, including one fourteen-year-old, whose Windy Knoll Farm supplies hundreds of pounds of tomatoes a week, along with peppers, spinach, and blackberries, to many of Chicago's top restaurants. Marty says Kyle's products are among the best produce they offer. "One of the key aspects of farming we try to get new farmers to understand is the importance of soil and plant health to making a great product, and he just gets it. For a teenager to be able to make $2,000 to $3,000 a week even before graduating from high school creates all kinds of opportunities. Kyle's older brother graduated from high school with over

$100,000 in the bank, just from selling vegetables and saving his money. Think of what kind of opportunity that creates." It's an appealing alternative to a life of debt, chemical inputs, and #2 Yellow Dent corn and soybeans, and other farmers, and their children, are taking notice. "That's my focus. I really want to offer more of those opportunities to young people."

Part of the joy in their work is training youngsters on their farm. "Right now we have these two high school girls working for us, and they are just tremendous workers, but the best part is the discovery process for them. We've been experimenting with passionfruit in the hothouse, and the other day they got their first taste. They get to taste and experience so many things, and it's always wonderful to hear them say, 'We've never tasted an apple like that,' or 'We've never tasted a strawberry like that.' They never knew what was possible with tomatoes, with lettuce. And the experience they've gotten learning about grafting trees and assessing plant health, whatever they decide to be in life, whether they farm or go into another line of work, they've developed a relationship to food which will always be with them."

"We've brought a great deal of economic development back to the community, and that's the sort of thing the financial leaders in the community take notice of, and it starts to change their thinking too." Marty and Will take this gospel on the road with them, helping farmers as far away as Nebraska, Brazil, and Kuwait develop strategies to change their local economic and cultural conditions.

The growth has been tremendous over the past fifteen years, but with twenty-five farms recently added to the group and as many more to be added in the next year, there's a lot of work to do just to keep up with the momentum. Sometimes, the best motivation is seeing results, and the Travises keep the results coming.

Based on a visit to Spence Farm (Fairbury, IL) and discussion with Marty Travis, owner, September 17, 2021.

7

BURGERLANDIA

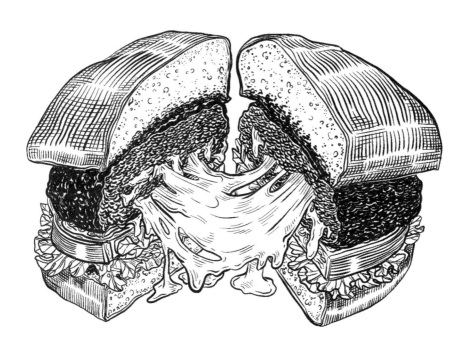

Break up the meat with a fork and scatter the garlic, onion and dry seasonings over it, then mix them into the meat with a fork or your fingers. Let the bowl of meat sit out of the icebox for ten or fifteen minutes while you set the table and make the salad. Add the relish, capers, everything else including wine and let the meat sit, quietly marinating, for another ten minutes if possible. Now make four fat, juicy patties with your hands. The patties should be an inch thick, and soft in texture but not runny. Have the oil in your frying-pan hot but not smoking when you drop in the patties and then turn the heat down and fry the burgers about four minutes. Take the pan off the burner and turn the heat high again. Flip the burgers over, put the pan back on the hot fire, then after one minute, turn the heat down again and cook another three minutes. Both sides of the burgers should be crispy brown and the middle pink and juicy.

Ernest Hemingway, on his favorite burger

As of 2023, it's fascinating to consider that what is perhaps America's favorite food has been with us for only about half the time we have been a nation. Hamburgers, of course, are considered an American dish and not uniquely Midwestern, yet we do have some delicious burger designs that are unique to our terroir. Some say the hamburger sandwich was first served in the Midwest. While we can't prove that, it is undeniable that our meat-processing industry made ground beef affordable, changing an upscale luxury, the Hamburg steak, into a totemic food of the working class.

I've never been satisfied with the origin stories of the humble hamburger because they're often vague or implausible, and in some cases dead wrong, so I decided to see what I could learn. When did people start cooking ground or chopped beef patties, and where? In Germany or, as some suppose, New York? Who first put one between two pieces of bread, making it a sandwich? Why is it called a hamburger?

Most origin stories correctly point to the trendy late nineteenth-century dish known as Hamburg steak, yet the stories of why Hamburg steak is thus named are often based on vague accounts of sailors and immigrants from Hamburg—a major port of departure for German emigrants to the United States—newly arrived in New York City. Some suggest that street vendors there were serving these beef patties. But it's highly unlikely that dockworkers and penurious immigrants were eating freshly broiled minced-beef patties; moreover, the Hamburg steak would have required the deft knife skills of a butcher or chef because the counter-top meat chopper hadn't yet been popularized. More likely the sailors and immigrants were eating Hamburg sausages[1] or *Rauchfleisch*,[2] smoked beef products that would have more aptly fit their budget and could have been ship rations.

In the German literature I was able to find a receipt for *Beefsteak auf andere Art* (Beefsteak in Another Way) in an 1845 cookbook from Hannover:

> You take really good, pure beef, knock and chop it up very finely, sprinkle it with black pepper, ground. Add onions and salt, shape it into a beefsteak and fry it in brown butter as described above. Then you cut an onion on it, but don't let it burn, add some sweetness, let the sauce thicken, and take the beefsteak to the table.[3]

This receipt, which perfectly describes the Hamburg steak as it would first appear stateside, pre-dates any credible appearance of it here by a few decades. (The oft-repeated legend of it first being offered at Delmonico's in 1834 has been thoroughly debunked.[4]) The cookbook's placement in Hannover, which shares the climes of the North German low plain with Hamburg, lends credibility to the suggestion that the dish arrived in America via the Port of Hamburg. I could find no corresponding dish from the High German literature of the South. It is worth noting that the book was intended for *die bürgerliche Küchen*, or bourgeois kitchens, and calls for good, pure beef: the Hamburg steak was an elite delicacy.

Hamburg steak appeared on menus in the States no later than 1873 at Anderson's European Hotel in Chicago[5] and Brooklyn's famed Dieter's.[6] The first printed receipt for it in America appears in Henriette Davidis's *Praktisches Kochbuch für die Deutschen in Amerika* in 1879. The Germans still weren't calling it Hamburg steak, however—Davidis calls it *gute Beefsteaks von gehackten Fleisch* (Good Beefsteaks from Chopped Meat) and mirrors Schwägermann's Hannover receipt, going further to admonish the reader that they be cooked very briefly "to remain red on the inside" lest they "become hard."[7] Yet the elegance of her receipt and requirement for the very best fresh beef continues to convey that this was an upscale dish, not yet fodder for the working class. But that would change soon, and with the harrowing speed of a freight train.

The increasing availability of commercial meat choppers during the last half of the nineteenth century would make ground beef affordable to the working class. By 1883, hamburgers, called by that name, were being sold cooked to go at a store serving factory workers on New York's Second Avenue.[8] An article in the *New York Sun* describes what sounds a lot like a carryout sandwich shop or deli and indicates it was a newsworthy and innovative business. Were the hamburgers it was selling on buns or bread? Sadly, there's no such claim. We have to wait until 1893 for a mention of an explicitly on-bread hamburger sandwich, when the *Indiana State Sentinel* states that it is common to use Hamburg steak in a sandwich with mustard-flavored butter.[9] So, besides presaging Wisconsin's popular butterburger, the short article indicates that the hamburger sandwich was already common.

The hamburger as a sandwich doesn't really take off in popular media until the first decades of the twentieth century. However, two interesting articles during the 1890s gush about the newest fixture of city life: the food wagon. In 1894, the *San Francisco Chronicle* refers to the proprietors of food wagons as "curbstone chefs" who "dispense fragrant food from their little carts," telling of "breezes pregnant with the hamburger."[10] A couple of years later, the *Chicago Tribune* is more matter of fact, describing their offerings of chicken sandwiches with pickle, green onion, and ketchup, as well as pork chops, ham, pigs' feet, fried fish, codfish cakes, hamburg steaks, and fried oysters, all in sandwich form, for 5 to 10 cents each.[11] Food wagons were as trendy as food trucks are today, and they helped take the hamburger to the masses.

It would be nice to have more descriptions of what was served with the meat on these early hamburger sandwiches, but over the ensuing hundred years, there would be plenty to discover. The Midwest claims several of the most delicious burger variations, starting with the cannibal, one that is not for the faint of heart.

Cannibal/Wildcat

Among the Eisenach ladies, whenever they have occasion to be away from home at so early an hour as to prevent their taking the 10 o'clock meal at their own house, it is by no means unusual for the sweet creatures to drop in at one of the butchers' shops, and bid the "*Fleischer*" chop up for them a groschen's worth of raw beef or pork (according to taste) with some raw onions which the damsels bring ready with them; and, when this has been done, they cram the lump of hacked meat into their pocket—often without even a piece of paper to cover it; and, then, having provided themselves with a halfpenny roll at the next baker's, proceed, with the meat in one hand, and the bread in the other, to take a bite, first at the chopped flesh and then at the "*Brödchen*"; or else, cutting the "*Semmel*" in twain, and spreading the mince of raw pork and onions between the slices, they munch the two together—laughing at those who shudder at the sight of the brutal meal, and declaring it, with a smack of the lips, to be "*pique fine.*"[12]

The Germans strike again. Henry Mayhew's account of the walking breakfast of Saxon women during the 1860s is curious on a few counts, but we're interested in the custom of eating raw ground meat for breakfast, and that mixture of meat and onions in split rolls, which were most certainly of rye. It doesn't take much of a leap to consider cooking the meat once back in a kitchen, so it is possible Germans were also eating what we know as hamburger sandwiches already in the 1860s, but without reading between the lines we can clearly see where Wisconsin's prized cannibal sandwich came from. A receipt for it was even printed in Milwaukee in Henriette Davidis's book in 1879:

Raw Beefsteaks

Good ox or beef from the cleft [round] is finely chopped with the necessary salt and onions, mixed with coarsely crushed pepper and given for breakfast.[13]

Commonly known as the cannibal sandwich, or alternatively as the wildcat, it's a fun topic of conversation to bring up with fellow food people of the Midwest because the response from the majority of folks is something like "Why the hell would people eat that?" and then I have my opening to convince them otherwise. A slim minority will answer "Yep! Every Christmas!" And then I know I'm talking with someone from Wisconsin.

Cannibals and wildcats are popular party and holiday fare. They typically consist of rye bread, onion, the most pristine of ground beef, and sometimes a smear of butter because, well, Wisconsin. Seriously, though, with the butter they go from filling and refreshing to filling, refreshing, and enchanting.

Truly, it's always fascinated me how people will happily eat sushi, in spite of (or perhaps out of lack of knowledge about) the long, underregulated supply chain of many sushi fish, yet they would eschew raw beef even from a reputable butcher in the highly regulated US meat industry. Raw beef has a light, refreshing taste that's perfect for a summer lunch or cocktail time at any party. And cannibals couldn't be easier to make.

Do choose beef from a reputable butcher shop or meat market, tell your butcher what you plan to do with it, and they should be happy to give you a special grind. Most Wisconsin meat markets keep such a grind around the holidays. They are extra cautious with sanitation steps, and the ground meat is laid in a tray or on a plate so it is loose and not packed down, as ground beef can be when stuffed into tubes or chubs. You definitely want the loose ground beef, in which you can see the individual threads from the meat-grinder apertures. Keep it very cold (below 40°F) and use it within 2 or 3 days. It will be safe to eat for several more days, but the flavor of the beef starts to change once ground.

This recipe makes four sandwiches of normal size. It is also common to set out the beef on a tray at parties with cocktail rye and sliced onion, pickles, cheese, and the works. Do not consume raw beef that's been sitting out at room temperature for more than 4 hours, as it can be spoiled by then. It's best to leave a tray out for an hour or, at most, two.

Serves 4

  8 slices rye bread
  16 ounces freshly ground beef, 80% lean, from the round or sirloin
  2 tablespoons shallot, minced
  1 teaspoon Worcestershire sauce
  4 tablespoons unsalted butter, softened
  Kosher salt and freshly ground black pepper, to taste
  Red onion, very thinly sliced, to taste
  Pickles to taste (optional)

Chill a mixing bowl in the freezer for 30 minutes or so before starting.

Toast the bread lightly and reserve; you'll want to use this at room temperature.

Gently spread the ground beef in the chilled mixing bowl and sprinkle with the shallot and Worcestershire. Season lightly with salt and a few twists of the peppermill. Use a rubber spatula to toss very lightly to combine, but don't overmix or pack the beef down—maintain an open, airy texture.

Spread 1 tablespoon of the butter on each of four slices of rye—these are the tops of your sandwiches. Divide the beef into four parts and form each into a ball quickly and very gently—your hands will warm the meat and it tastes best very cold. Place each ball on a dry piece of rye and use a table knife to spread the beef evenly across the bread. Add sliced onion to taste, then pickles if desired, and place the buttered slice on top, butter side down to marry with the onion and pickle.

Slice each sandwich diagonally and serve with potato salad or chips.

Loosemeat Burgers

Proudly claimed by Sioux City, Iowa, as its own, and popularized in surrounding states by Maid-Rite, a regional chain restaurant based in Urbandale, Iowa, since 1926, the loosemeat sandwich does indeed appear to have originated in Sioux City. It was created by Dave Heglin for his tavern at Fourteenth and Jackson, first called Tavern No. 1 and later Ye Olde Tavern. Heglin named his invention a Tavern Sandwich.[14] Maid-Rite calls it a loosemeat, and the chain's market presence, with over thirty restaurants in Iowa, Illinois, Minnesota, Missouri, and Ohio, may be why "loosemeat" seems to be the more popular name. Many even know it as a Maid-Rite.

At its essence, the loosemeat differs from a standard hamburger in that the meat is crumbled as it cooks with onion and other seasonings; it's similar to a sloppy joe, but dry. In order to hold the sandwich together, a bun firmer than the standard fast-food hamburger bun is used. Classic dressings are simply yellow mustard, onion, and pickle, although Iowans aren't known for being so fanatically anti-ketchup about their loosemeats as Chicagoans and Detroiters are about their hot dogs. Modern versions can be topped with a variety of cheeses and any number of other standard burger condiments.

There's a certain special pleasure that comes with attacking a loosemeat sandwich, holding it together with a clam-like grip and nibbling on the escaped bits that collect on your plate. Made correctly, it's a sandwich you can also feel good about eating: the technique of cooking the beef loose allows most of the fat to be drained away. Finishing it with a little added moisture in the form of Worcestershire sauce and water yields a meat that is still juicy on your palate. If this meat strikes you as similar to the filling of a **BIEROCK** (p. 103) from neighboring Nebraska, it's because it is!

Serves 4

1 pound ground beef chuck, 80% lean

1 cup yellow Spanish onion, very finely diced

1 cup cold water

2 teaspoons chili powder

1 teaspoon freshly ground black pepper

½ teaspoon kosher salt

½ cup tomato juice

1 tablespoon Worcestershire sauce

Place the beef and onion in a heavy cast-iron skillet, and break up into a mash with the square end of a steel spatula, then add the water and further mash into a thick slurry. Turn the heat on to medium high, add the chili powder and pepper, and cook to render the fat from the beef while you boil away the water, constantly turning and breaking up the beef with your spatula. Once the water is cooked out and the beef is frying in its own fat, about 10 minutes, brown the beef and onions lightly, turning regularly to prevent scorching or burning.

Once you have the level of browning you want, remove the pan from the heat and tilt it slightly, allowing the fat to drain to one side. Use the back of your spatula to press the meat against the pan to further squeeze out fat. Pour off the excess fat, or use a spoon to spoon it out.

Return the pan to the heat, add the salt, tomato juice, and Worcestershire, and stir to combine. Cook down until your beef crumbles are glazed in the juice but dry enough that the sauce doesn't run when the pan is tilted. Serve on firm buns with yellow mustard, sliced onion, and pickles.

Jucy Lucy

We're only covering the most prominent of regional Midwestern burgers in this chapter, and there are dozens more, but of all of them the Jucy Lucy might be the most significant. We're departing from our receipts-only research for a spell here because the creation story is a legend without receipts. The legend is that Jucy Lucys were first made in Minneapolis in 1954 at Matt's Bar. When a pleased customer exclaimed, "Wow, that's one juicy Lucy!," the burger soon appeared on the menu with the spelling *Jucy Lucy*. The 5-8 Club makes a counterclaim but doesn't offer a specific date, just the 1950s.[15] Both make a fine Jucy Lucy, and it's pointless to take sides because there are no news references or other possible citations until the 1970s—this burger quite literally looks like a local specialty that stayed local.

More recently, Jucy Lucys have popped up around the country, and they inspired people to start stuffing their burgers to the point of absurdity. Chefs in high-end restaurants have stuffed burgers with foie gras; others have used bone marrow, along with countless other ill-informed takes. The stuffed-burger debacle seems to have died down nationwide, but thankfully the Jucy Lucy endures. It's a perfect construction: fresh seasoned ground beef, American cheese.

I've always given the side-eye to stuffed burgers because I don't like my burgers cooked well, ever. The genius of the Jucy Lucy is the low melting point of American cheese, as low as 130°F, allowing a burger to be cooked to a beautiful medium around 140°F and still yield a molten core. The rendering juices in the center of the patty intermingle with the cheese and yield a one-of-a-kind treat: a beefy-cheesy explosion of juice that requires caution. Stuffing with other proteins requires a safe cooking temperature of 165°F, meaning your burger is overcooked and dry by the time the center is safe to eat. Harder "fancier" cheeses have higher melting temperatures as well. While soft cheeses such as brie or camembert would work, it's best to just embrace the good old American. Or go to Minneapolis and enjoy one at Matt's or the 5-8.

Makes 4 Jucy Lucys

4 medium-sized, soft egg hamburger buns, such as brioche

1½ pounds high-fat (70% to 75% lean) ground beef, for 6-ounce burgers

1 tablespoon Worcestershire sauce

1 teaspoon freshly ground black pepper

Lawry's Seasoned Salt

8 slices American cheese

Sliced onion and pickle, plus other condiments of your choice

Turn your oven to the lowest, or "warm," setting, and put your buns in it to warm while you make the burgers.

Mix the beef with the Worcestershire, pepper, and salt, and knead to combine well. Divide into four equal portions. Divide each portion in half and shape each half into a compact ball. I like to do this with a plate and two pieces of plastic wrap: Place a piece of plastic wrap on your work surface, and place one ball on the plastic wrap. Cover with the other piece of plastic wrap, then use the bottom of the plate to press the ball into a flat patty big enough to cover a slice of your cheese. Place two slices of American cheese in the center and set on a platter. Press another patty of equal size between the sheets of plastic. Place on top of the patty with the cheese, and pinch the patties together around the edges to seal the cheese in. Repeat with the remaining beef and cheese. Tuck the edges of the patties to make them a little more than 4 inches round and ½ inch thick.

Heat a large, heavy cast-iron skillet until a pinch of beef sizzles nicely but not furiously, about 400°F. Brown the patties on the first side for about 3 minutes, until a nice brown takes over the whole side. Gently turn and cook another 2 to 3 minutes on the second side, until the center of the patty registers 135°F to 140°F. Work in batches, and hold finished patties in the oven until all are done.

Classic Jucy Lucys place the condiments on the bottom bun. Use any sauce you like—mayonnaise, ketchup, Thousand Island dressing, and lettuce and tomato if you choose. Pickle and onion are virtually required. Eat right away, but proceed with caution: that explosion of juice is hot! French fries or onion rings are perfect sides, but since Jucy Lucys are a Minnesota thing, you can also go for Tater Tots, or, if you'd like some balance, a green salad with ranch dressing.

Butterburgers

You had me at butter—the burger is a bonus. Currently popularized by Culver's, a chain based in Prairie du Sac, Wisconsin, with over eight hundred locations, the butterburger is a natural descendant of the original Hamburg steak, although only some butterburgers are cooked in butter. In the broadest sense, these decadent sandwiches might also see the butter slathered on a cooked patty, or on the bun à la mayonnaise, or, as at Culver's, the bun itself may be buttered and toasted with no butter on the patty itself. Regardless, the combination of butter and beef is a natural one, and any butter added to a hamburger ups the decadent factor and piles on the delicious.

With Culver's taking the butterburger to a mass market, the earliest records I could find for it were in newspaper ads in Evansville and Muncie, Indiana, in 1938.[16] It is true that for every local establishment advertising in the newspaper, there could be several more spots serving similar products, but butterburgers start popping up in Midwestern states, including Wisconsin, during the 1940s. They continue to be a niche market, but many taverns in Wisconsin today offer one, and with the expansion of Culver's, they might become a nationwide phenomenon.

Always ready to take one for the team, I've tried several iterations of the butterburger and concluded the best is definitely an indulgence: bun toasted in butter, the burger hard-seared in the residual butter, and the bun given a little smear of softened butter right before serving. You can of course put cheese on a butterburger, but I have no idea why you would. Because of the richness of the buttery beef, "the works" are a must: Set your burger on top of a dressed salad on a buttered bun and it will refresh as it nourishes.

This recipe calls for what might seem like an odd quantity of beef, but I've found that a 5-ounce patty makes a perfect butterburger. The grind matters for this sandwich as well: as with the **CANNIBAL SANDWICH** (p. 202), look for a loose ground beef and not one that is packed into a tight cake or chub.

Serves 4

8 tablespoons unsalted butter, divided into pats and softened

4 buttery burger buns such as brioche

20 ounces ground beef

Salt and freshly ground black pepper, to taste

Mayonnaise, ketchup, yellow mustard, thick-sliced red onion, sandwich pickles,
  sliced tomato, iceberg lettuce

Using a 10- to 12-inch cast-iron skillet, heat until a speck of butter thrown in melts
quickly and sizzles without burning. Reduce heat to medium. Open the buns and butter
each half with ½ tablespoon of butter. Take two buns at a time, place buttered side
down in the skillet, and press them gently with your hands to make sure the open
crumb of the buns makes contact with the skillet. Toast until a nice light caramel color,
around 1 minute.

Once your buns are toasted, set them aside on a platter, turn the burner up to
medium high, and heat until a bit of beef sizzles rapidly, about 450°F. Divide the beef
into four portions and gently roll into balls. Place them in the skillet at the clock-face
positions of 10:30, 1:30, 4:30, and 7:30, spaced so that when you mash them they will
have room to spread.

Working quickly, wash your hands thoroughly, then use the back of a firm steel
spatula or meat turner to mash the balls into patties about ½ inch thick by about 3½
to 4 inches wide. Season with salt and a few twists of freshly ground black pepper. Cook
on the first side for 2 minutes, by which time you should have a beautiful hard sear on
the patty and it should easily separate from the skillet. Cook on the second side for 1 to
2 minutes, depending on whether you like a medium or well-done burger. Remove and
reserve on a platter while you build your burgers.

Classic butterburgers have the toppings on the bottom. Place your bottom buns on
four separate plates, spread each one with a smear of mayonnaise, and kiss with both
ketchup and mustard. Add a thick slice of red onion, topped with 2 or 3 slices of pickle,
a slice or two of tomato, and a couple of crisp open leaves of lettuce, concave side up.
Nest your patties in the lettuce. Spread each top bun with a tablespoon of butter, cap
the burgers, and serve right away. French fries are de rigueur accompaniment, but also
classic are **FRIED CHEESE CURDS** (p. 97), or serve with your favorite chips.

Horseshoes

Springfield, Illinois, lays claim to perhaps the most hyperlocal hamburger
variation in the Midwest, a stodgy yet resilient conglomeration known as the
horseshoe sandwich because of the shape of the deboned cut of ham originally
used in it. A proper horseshoe is served on a sizzle platter to represent an anvil
and flanked with french fries as stand-ins for the nails that would secure shoe
to hoof.[17] A fragrant cheese sauce ties it together. It's a clever construction,

even if it is lost on a consumer who may never have seen a horse in person. When I first read about the horseshoe and its invention by Joe Tomko and Joe Sweskia at the Leland Hotel in 1928, it seemed like a simplified copycat of the more famous Hot Brown from Louisville's famed Brown Hotel, which was invented in 1925.[18] It remains popular in Springfield today to the point of religiosity, but it is seldom seen outside the city that launched Abraham Lincoln's political career.

Locally, many variations on the horseshoe now exist, but the long-established standard is a sizzle platter, two slices of white toast, a substantial hamburger patty, cheddar-based cheese sauce, and french fries. It is heavy, but it is also delicious. You can lighten it up nicely by adding sliced tomato, onion, or pickles to the mix, but if you split the mountain of meat and potatoes with a friend, and have a cold beer or sparkling wine with it, it is pleasantly rich.

Serves 4

CHEESE SAUCE

2 cups whole milk

1 small onion, peeled whole, studded with 4 whole cloves

1 teaspoon dry mustard powder

1 bay leaf

A few grains cayenne pepper

3 tablespoons unsalted butter

4 tablespoons all-purpose flour

1 cup shredded sharp cheddar cheese

Salt to taste

Scald the milk with the onion, mustard, bay leaf, and cayenne. Maintain at a high simmer while you make a roux. In a separate saucepan, melt the butter and add the flour, cook to blond, and add the hot milk, discarding the onion, clove, and bay leaf. Bring to a boil while whisking constantly. Remove from heat and whisk in the cheese until melted and uniformly smooth. Taste for seasoning and add salt if desired. Cover tightly and hold on a very low burner until ready to use.

TO MAKE THE HORSESHOES

1 pound of your favorite brand frozen shoestring fries

2 tablespoons vegetable oil

Salt and freshly ground black pepper, to taste

8 slices Texas toast

1 pound ground beef, 80% lean, or 1 pound roast ham or turkey breast

1 tablespoon unsalted butter

2 cups cheese sauce

Preheat oven to 350°F.

Toss the frozen fries with the vegetable oil and a sprinkling of salt and pepper in a large bowl. Spread out on a 13-by-9-inch cookie sheet, making sure there is space between the fries for heat to circulate, and place on the top rack of the oven while you make the sandwiches. Keep an eye on the fries; they'll be done in about 20 minutes.

Toast the bread until golden brown on each side and set aside.

Shape the beef into four patties. Preheat a large cast-iron skillet until a bit of butter melts and browns quickly, about 450°F. Place the toast in the oven with the fries to reheat. Working quickly, add the butter to the skillet and swirl to coat the pan, add the beef patties, and season with salt and pepper. Cook on the first side for 2 minutes, by which time you should have a nice hard sear. Cook on the second side for 1 to 2 minutes, depending on your preferred doneness. Remove to a serving platter to assemble your horseshoes.

For each of four plates, slice two pieces of toast diagonally, and stack them. Pull the bottom slices out slightly, so that the upper slices tilt inward to make a trough. Fill the trough with fries, top with the burger, smother all with ½ cup cheese sauce, and strew fries around the edges, to mingle with any cheese sauce running over the sides. Garnish with pickles, hot peppers, or anything you like to temper the richness. Enjoy with cold beer or sparkling wine.

8

MIDWESTERN
BARBECUE

These are people who strictly deprive themselves of each and every eatable, drinkable, and smokable which has in any way acquired a shady reputation. They pay this price for health. And health is all they get for it. How strange it is. It's like paying out your whole fortune for a cow that has gone dry.

—**Mark Twain**

THE long, narrow gravel road crooked and bowed, rose and dipped through the hillocky woods north of Celestine, Indiana, eventually leading us into a fertile bottomland where Rich and Sue Schepers, dear family friends we called Uncle Rich and Aunt Sue, were putting on a pig roast for their extended family on their farm. Flanked by the woods on one side, modest cornfields on two, and a barn and feed yard for the hogs on the other with a forest beyond, where the hogs spent most of their time, the central grounds contained a large emerald lawn, a silo flanked by a timber loft that sequestered a grist mill and a hayloft, a chicken coop, and a grand 1890s timber farmhouse. Memories of the farm still paint a postcard in my mind.

Uncle Rich had set up a large steel barrel, split lengthwise and splayed end to end, over which he had positioned a seemingly ancient cast-iron spit. Adjacent to it was another steel barrel, cut in half crosswise, to serve as a fire pit in which oak and hickory from the woods were burned to coals before being shoveled into the barrel-trough. The spit above the coals impaled one of his hogs, which he'd had slaughtered and dressed by Sander Processing, the local meat processor and butcher to the town of a few hundred residents.

There was always a keg of beer at these fetes. The women brought covered dishes of every variety—potato salad, macaroni salad, egg salad, ham salad, pickles and relishes, deviled eggs, cabbage slaw, broccoli slaw, Jell-O salads both delightful and frightful. Corn on the cob was roasted over the coals with the pig as it neared completion, its skin glistening, blistering, a wondrous collage of golden to chestnut browns betraying the contours of the animal as the spit turned round and round. A mop and a bucket of cider and vinegar served to baste, or, as they say in the South, *mop*, the pig. Unadulterated blue-label Open Pit would be the sauce for those who didn't take their meat neat, and sliced supermarket white bread served as the carrier when eating out of hand. Some of the men had their nips of Early Times or Kessler nearby, but the watchful gaze of the women usually kept them from partaking even a little too much.

After a long break in the feasting, there would be peaches and ice cream; chocolate, yellow, and angel food cakes; and a summer's worth of joy served round. Marshmallows were skewered on freshly whittled green hickory branches, half the diameter of a pencil, and roasted over the dying embers, the more adventurous of us young'uns indulging innocent pyro fantasies by getting them close enough to the coals to ignite. We'd immediately blow the fire out and enjoy the char and crispy texture of the burnt edges and molten centers, lightly perfumed by the green hickory. The drive home was like waking up from a dream.

In spite of having experienced a few pig roasts growing up in the 1970s, I never really thought of the Midwest as having a barbecue tradition, at least not in the strictest sense, outside of Kansas City. Pig roasts were becoming increasingly rare as a social event; it was much easier and cheaper to do the burger and hot dog thing. I've missed those few rapturous days most of my life, and it's puzzled me why the Midwest would give up such a rich tradition while the South held fast to the occasional pig pickin'. That could be because the South has a longer and more intimate history with barbecue. Unlike fried chicken's multipronged foray into Midwestern foodways, barbecue, if we accept as its definition cooking meat (whole animals or parts) over wood coals in or on a pit, came strictly from the South.

We have accounts of whole deer being "roasted" for grand Fourth of July celebrations during pioneer times.[1] Nearly all these pioneers came from the Southern states of Kentucky, Virginia and Maryland, the Carolinas, and Tennessee, where barbecue culture had been well established during the early decades of the republic.[2] We don't have a description of the baking process for the deer, only that they were cooked whole, so they were undoubtedly put to the fire on a proper Southern pit.

The surprising vehicle of political campaign barbecues sprouted a great enthusiasm for barbecue north of the Ohio River. Campaign barbecues had been a thing since the early days of the country, but they grew in importance during the early nineteenth century.[3] Some of them were huge, though newspaper reports were fed by political operatives, so attendance numbers may have been exaggerated. Henry Clay, the prominent Whig politician from Kentucky, made regular forays into Ohio and Indiana. On one such occasion organizers claimed a crowd of 100,000 at an 1842 barbecue in Akron, which was a small town at the time.[4] By far the most mentions of these types of events during the 1830s and 1840s are in the areas near the Ohio River from Ohio west to Missouri.

Political barbecues spearheaded by Southern politicians exposed tens of thousands of Midwesterners to barbecue culture.

Midwesterners got the barbecue bug and found their own occasions to roast some meat over coals. A barbecue in honor of military volunteers returning home to Shelby County, Indiana, in 1847 featured a buffet of provisions "a half a mile in length" to regale its four thousand attendees.[5] For an 1887 gathering of the National Butcher's Association in Chicago, organizers roasted "fully 32,000 pounds of meat" consisting of fifty beeves and a hundred sheep. They dug six pits, each forty feet long and six feet deep, in Cheltenham Park on the south lakefront for the fires.[6] Perhaps there were that many butchers nationwide in 1887, but two things were clear: Midwesterners had embraced the barbecue as a community event, and their favored meats were beef and mutton.

The cookbook record doesn't offer much in the way of barbecue until well into the twentieth century, when a specialized trade was well developed. Lettice Bryan does inform us, in her *Kentucky Housewife*, how to barbecue a hind or forequarter of shoat (a fat young pig) by placing it between gridirons and roasting it slowly before "clear" coals for several hours, basting with nothing but salted water seasoned with a little pepper.[7] More interesting is "Barbecued Sheep" from *Buckeye Cookery and Practical Housekeeping*, published outside Columbus in 1877, which includes what might be the first formal cookbook receipt for true barbecue. Mrs. Ella Turner instructs readers to build a pit, erect a gridiron, maintain a side fire to supply the pit with clear-burning coals, and mop with a sponge soaked in a mixture of "ground mustard and vinegar, salt and pepper" and "let it drip over the meat until it is done."[8]

During the early twentieth century around the country, barbecue transitioned to a more commercial, restaurant-based culture. Urbanization also led to a regionalization of styles.[9] While most of the Midwest didn't come along for the ride, Kansas City became a leader and perhaps the best barbecue city in the country. Meanwhile, Black communities in Saint Louis and Chicago developed unique and exceedingly delicious local styles.

Barbecues were among the first events in the South that would, in certain communities, be integrated affairs. Kansas City's barbecue scene is well integrated, as White customers have long searched out the work of Black pitmasters and dined on their labors alongside Black customers. Sadly, in Chicago and Saint Louis, most White locals aren't even aware of their city's rich barbecue tradition because they won't venture into Black neighborhoods, where those traditions are kept in the hands of Black pitmasters who turn out delicious meat day in and day out. All I can say is that anyone who won't go to Chicago's South Side or East Saint Louis, Illinois, is missing out on some ridiculously good 'cue and some of our best local flavors.

In all three Midwestern barbecue towns, you can enjoy a variety of meats, but here I will share techniques for the meats most distinctive of each city: brisket and ribs for Kansas City, the rib tip & hot link combo for Chicago, and pork steaks and barbecued snoot for East Saint Louis. I'll also share recipes for each style of sauce. Since home barbecue rigs, smokers, and grills vary widely, I'll be as broad as possible, but barbecue really comes down to just temperature, moisture (baste or vapor), and time. I've made excellent barbecue in a range of smokers and even a Weber kettle grill, so pick the vehicle that works best for you.

Kansas City–Style Barbecue

Much has been written about Kansas City's barbecue culture. Kansas City was important in the emergence of barbecue restaurants, and as the meat-packing industry expanded westward in the late nineteenth century, giving pitmasters access to all manner of processed cuts of meat, it was equally important in inspiring the use of specialized cuts such as ribs and briskets, moving the culture away from whole roasted animals.

Henry Perry is widely acknowledged to be the father of Kansas City barbecue, boasting in 1911 that "I've never met a meat yet I couldn't barbecue. That goes for sheep, hogs, geese, chickens, fish, rabbits, squirrels, possums, oysters, and most everything you've heard of."[10] Perry also trained a generation of barbecue masters,[11] including Charlie Bryant, progenitor of one of the most famous barbecue restaurants, Arthur Bryant's, which Calvin Trillin called THE SINGLE BEST RESTAURANT IN THE WORLD [sic].[12] Gates, another one of Kansas City's top spots, also has a direct lineage from Perry through Arthur Pinkard and George Gates.

Today, Kansas City may well boast the most barbecue restaurants of any city in the country, rivaled only by Memphis. Its best barbecue shops, which still include Arthur Bryant's and Gates along with Joe's and Rosedale, boast a diverse and integrated clientele that harkens back to the heyday of Henry Perry's stand[13] and exemplifies barbecue's power to bring people together. Perhaps Kansas City's barbecue scene is as prosperous as it is because a well-heeled White clientele has been eager to support Black pitmasters, something we don't see elsewhere.

The Kansas City style is characterized by a somewhat wider range of meats than you'd traditionally see in the Southeast: beef brisket (and the resultant burnt ends), baby back ribs and spareribs, pulled pork, ham, turkey, and chicken. Its sauce is the thickest and sweetest of all the major regional styles of

Snow's Cut-Rate Market

1017 FREDERICK AVE.   PHONES, 968

Our Fresh and Smoked Sausages Are all Home Made.

Eggs, per dozen	15¢	Sausage, per pound	7 1-2¢
Dill Pickles, per dozen	8¢	Chuck Steak, per pound	7 1-2¢
Sour Pickles, per dozen	10¢	Rib Steak, per pound	8¢
Mutton Stews, per pound	5¢	Round Steak, per pound	9¢
Veal Stews, per pound	5¢	Sirloin Steak, per pound	11¢
Beef Stews, per pound	4¢	Porterhouse Steak, per pound, only	12 1-2¢
Beef to Boil, per pound	4¢	Pork Chops, per pound	10¢
Choice Beef to Boil	5¢	Sliced Ham Butts, per pound	9¢
Pot Roasts, per pound	6¢	Back Bones, per pound	3¢
Beef Roasts, heavy ribs, per pound, only	7¢	Neck Bones, per pound	3¢
		Pig Ears, per pound	3¢
Beef Roasts, per pound	6¢	Pig Tails, per pound	3 1-2¢
Prime Rib Roasts, per pound	9¢	Pig Snoots, per pound	3 1-2¢
Extra Short Rib Roasts, per pound only	10¢	Piggs Feet, per pound	3¢
		Pig Livers, per pound	3¢
Pork Loin Roasts, per pound	10¢	Pig Hearts, per pound	3¢
Ham Butts, per pound	9¢	Pig Brains, per pound	5¢
Shoulder Pork, per pound	8¢	Calf Brains, per pound	10¢
Spare Ribs, per pound	7 1-2¢	Beef Brains, per pound	5¢

WANTED—TWO EXTRA CUTTERS SATURDAY.

As meat markets began publishing their prices for specialized cuts, pitmasters mastered the cheaper cuts that would become Midwestern barbecue standards.

Source: *St. Joseph New-Press* (St. Joseph, MO), February 9, 1906, page 5.

barbecue, tomato-based but skewing brown, as it is usually goosed with brown sugar, molasses, or both.

BARBECUE RUB

Makes about 2 cups

- ½ cup kosher salt
- ½ cup dark brown sugar
- ¼ cup celery salt
- 3 tablespoons Spanish paprika
- 2 tablespoons freshly ground black pepper
- 3 tablespoons granulated onion
- 1 tablespoon ground mustard powder
- 2 teaspoons cayenne pepper
- 2 teaspoons ground sage

Mix thoroughly and store in an airtight container.

Serves 6 to 10

One 10-pound beef brisket
1 tablespoon Worcestershire sauce
1 cup **BARBECUE RUB** (above)

Set your brisket on a large cutting board and pat it dry with clean paper towels. Allow it to come up to room temperature while you build your fire, for at least 1 hour or, better yet, 2 hours.

Set up your smoker according to manufacturer instructions and use the vent controls to set the temperature to 250°F. Charcoal works perfectly. If using hardwood, you'll need to build a separate fire to burn the wood and supply clear coals to your smoker with a shovel.

Rub the Worcestershire sauce evenly all over your room-temperature brisket, and then the rub in three separate applications 10 to 15 minutes apart, until it is coated with a thin crust.

Place the brisket on the center rack of your smoker with the fat-veined side down. If your smoker doesn't have a vapor pan, place a shallow casserole-sized pan of water 6 to 8 inches below the cooking rack. Cover the smoker.

Maintain the fire with more coals as needed, and use the vent controls to maintain a temperature of 225°F to 250°F—try to keep it close to 250°F but don't go over— and cook for 5 hours. Turn the brisket over, and apply a thin sprinkling of rub. Cover and cook for another 6 to 8 hours at 250°F. At hour 6, begin monitoring the internal temperature of the brisket. Once it reaches 180°F to 185°F, you can let the fire temperature drop to 220°F to 230°F. Remove the brisket when the internal temperature reaches 195°F for toothsome, steak-like brisket, or 200°F if you like it softer. Don't let the internal temperature go any higher or you'll have beef hash!

Rest the brisket for at least 30 minutes or up to an hour before carving. Save the burnt ends for hash or your favorite barbecue guest if desired. Serve with **KANSAS CITY–STYLE BARBECUE SAUCE** (below) on the side.

BABY BACK RIBS

Serves 4 to 6

4 full racks baby back ribs, 1¾ down size
A few tablespoons Worcestershire sauce
6 tablespoons plus 4 teaspoons barbecue rub, divided

4 tablespoons molasses

½ cup **KANSAS CITY–STYLE BARBECUE SAUCE** (recipe follows)

Set your ribs on a large cutting board and pat them dry on all sides with clean paper towels. On the small-rib end of the rack, use a paring or utility knife to peel the silver skin on the back of the rack back from one corner ½ inch or so. Then, using a paper towel as a grip, pull the entire sheet of silver skin off. Rest the ribs until they reach room temperature, about 1 hour.

Build a fire according to your smoker's instructions and set the temperature to 225°F.

Sprinkle a few drops of Worcestershire sauce on each rack of ribs, both sides, and use a basting brush to mop it in. Rub each rack of ribs, spreading 1 tablespoon of rub over the top (convex) side and 1 teaspoon over the bottom (concave) side of the rack.

Place the ribs on the center rack of your smoker, and place a casserole-sized pan of water beneath them, unless you have a vapor pan. Place the lid on the smoker and cook at 225°F to 230°F for 2 to 2½ hours, until the ribs register 160°F to 175°F internal temperature.

Place each rack on a separate long strip of foil, lengthwise, with about 6 inches to spare on each side. Brush each with 1 tablespoon molasses, followed by 2 tablespoons of barbecue sauce, then sprinkle the last 2 tablespoons of rub evenly over the ribs.

Close up the foil over each rack individually by folding the sides up to form a tent. Close the ends of each tent. Return to the smoker and cook for an additional 1 to 2 hours, until the ribs register 185°F to 190°F internally. Rest for 15 minutes, then serve with additional barbecue sauce on the side.

KANSAS CITY–STYLE BARBECUE SAUCE

Makes about 4 cups

1 (14-ounce) can tomato puree

1 cup ketchup

½ cup apple cider vinegar

1 cup dark brown sugar

¼ cup molasses

2 teaspoons celery salt

2 teaspoons kosher salt

1 tablespoon Spanish paprika

1 tablespoon spicy brown mustard

1 tablespoon freshly ground black pepper

1 tablespoon chili powder

2 teaspoons granulated onion

1 teaspoon granulated garlic

½ teaspoon ground allspice

¼ teaspoon ground cloves

¼ teaspoon cayenne pepper

¼ cup bacon, ham, or barbecue drippings

Combine all ingredients except the drippings, whisk to combine well, and bring to a high simmer over medium heat, stirring regularly. Simmer to infuse for 15 minutes. Whisk the drippings in well to emulsify. Bottle while still hot for storage, or transfer hot to a serving bowl or boat to enjoy immediately.

Chicago-Style Barbecue

My favorite barbecue experience on earth is on Chicago's South Side. The amalgam of textures is positively symphonic: crispy-edged crinkle-cut fries buttress rough-cut chunks of smoked pork studded with gristle, the glistening cartilage of the rib tips themselves, toothsome rib meat, silken rendered fat, the rotund ends of peppery hot links and the angular edges of the chopped middles, the taut casing secreting the coarse-ground interior, all drenched in sauce and crowned with soft white bread.

Chicago-style barbecue does go beyond the rib tip & hot link combo to include ribs, chicken, and sauce-soaked fried chicken wings, but the hallmark of the style is the aquarium smoker, a sheet metal pit with a Plexiglas hood that adds a voyeuristic aspect to the barbecue experience. When the smoker is in view of the customers, as it is at Lem's (and was at Memphis's Cozy Corner before its 2017 fire), they can see the barbecue in the pit doing its thing. It was invented in 1951 by Leo Davis[14] and first deployed at Lem's, which also first popularized rib tips.

Lem's was opened by James P. Lemon and two of his brothers in 1952. Lem recounts that the Swift company used to throw out the chitterlings and rib tips in a barrel at its South Side plant, "and you'd take as many as you wanted. . . . We were the first barbecue house to sell them."[15] Lem's proved to be a sensation, so much so that today, if you want your tip & link on a summer holiday, you'd best be early or you'll wait in a line that wraps around the shop through the parking lot and tails off down the block.

One thing to keep in mind is that many Chicago barbecue shops don't have indoor seating, so be prepared to eat on the hood of your car, or inside your car, unless you espy a nearby park or parkway for a picnic. However, due to the composition of a tip & link, it doesn't travel well. Inside the box, the fries are steaming, the sauce is getting soaked up, and it is a matter of time before you're dealing with a still-delicious but texturally compromised mound of barbecue and starch. So, make quick work of finding a spot to picnic or do your reconnaissance ahead of time.

There really isn't an effective substitute for hot links, which may be impossible to find in your city (another fine reason to visit Chicago). A very peppery bratwurst, mettwurst, or hot Italian sausage can stand in.

CHICAGO-STYLE RIB TIPS AND HOT LINKS

Serves 4

4 racks rib tips (3 to 3½ pounds)
½ cup **BARBECUE RUB** (p. 218), divided
1 pound hot links in natural casings
1 pound of your favorite frozen crinkle-cut fries
CHICAGO-STYLE "HOT" BARBECUE SAUCE (recipe follows)
8 slices white sandwich bread

Prepare your grill or smoker for indirect cooking with a target temperature of 250°F. Place the rib tips in a large pan or casserole and pat them dry with clean paper towels. Rub them thoroughly with half the rub and let them rest for 15 minutes, until some moisture has been drawn to the surface. Then rub them with the rest of the rub; the moisture will allow more to stick. Once they are well coated, allow to rest and come to room temperature before cooking, about 30 minutes to 1 hour.

Arrange the tips on the center rack of your smoker or grill and cover. Allow the temperature to drop initially, then use the vents or temperature controls to maintain a steady 225°F. Feed the fire with prepared charcoal or clear coals only. You may flavor with hickory or applewood chips soaked well in cold water, but use only a few chips at a time. Cook for 3 to 4 hours, turning every 30 minutes. After 2 hours, arrange the hot links around the rib tips. Turn these every 15 minutes. Begin checking the temperature of the meats at the 3-hour mark. Remove the hot links when they register 170°F internally, and cook the tips until the thick end of the rack registers 190°F in the thickest part. Rest the meats for 15 minutes before serving.

Prepare your fries according to the manufacturer's instructions, either by deep-frying or oven-frying. Divide the fries between four plates. Chop the rib tips into 1- to

2-inch segments and arrange over the fries, then do the same with the hot links, chopping them into ½- to 1-inch segments. Smother in sauce, ¼ cup or more per plate to taste, then top with white bread.

CHICAGO-STYLE "HOT" BARBECUE SAUCE

Makes about 4 cups

    2 cups ketchup
    ½ cup distilled white vinegar
    ½ cup dark brown sugar
    ¼ cup soy sauce (cheap is better here—avoid the fancy tamaris, etc.)
    ¼ cup Louisiana-style hot sauce
    2 tablespoons yellow mustard
    1 tablespoon granulated onion
    1 teaspoon granulated garlic
    ½ teaspoon cayenne pepper

Combine all ingredients, whisk to combine well, and bring to a high simmer over medium heat, stirring regularly. Simmer to infuse for 15 minutes. Bottle while still hot for storage, or transfer hot to a serving bowl or boat to enjoy immediately.

East Saint Louis–Style Barbecue

Across the river from downtown Saint Louis, in the shadow of the great Cahokia Mound, named for a historic Illiniwek people, you'll find one of the most ingenious dishes in both the American barbecue and soul food canons. Crispy, crunchy, and succulent all at once, the humble snoot has been ensnaring addicts for a good century or more. Even though it's typically overshadowed by the barbecue monoliths of Memphis and Kansas City, East Saint Louis knows what it has.

The snoot is definitely the most eccentric offering of the province, but the real workhorses are Saint Louis–cut spareribs and pork steaks. Writer Elaine Viets got to the bottom of both cuts in a 1995 interview with retired butcher Robert F. Eggleston for the *Post-Dispatch*. Beginning in the 1930s, when the big national packers were cutting the ribs off the carcass and selling them with the brisket bone attached, along with the tips and a whole bunch of gristle, making for a huge, unwieldy rack, "the St. Louis packers took off about half that collar. It cost consumers a little more, but it was a better value. Rib lovers bought it."[16]

The new cut squared off the rack to make it more closely resemble baby back ribs—more or less rectangular in shape. The first record I could find for this cut, an ad by Council Oak Stores for "St. Louis style spare ribs" in the Sioux City, Nebraska, newspaper in 1953 corroborates Eggleston's account.[17] Under various names, such as Saint Louis cut, or Saint Louis style, spareribs, or just ribs, this squared-off cut is now the national standard—almost anywhere you order spareribs, it will be the Saint Louis cut, even if it's not advertised as such. The delicious side benefit of this style is that rib tips went unused—until they were adopted by urban Black pitmasters.[18]

Viets also recounted Eggleston's explanation of the pork steak phenomenon. We didn't always have the industrial freezer capacity that we developed in the late twentieth century, which virtually eliminated seasonal fluctuations in meat availability. Previously, around the Fourth of July, Saint Louis butchers would run out of ribs, so packers took the blade ends of pork butts and started making thick steaks out of them. As a pork lover myself, I gotta say it's a pretty dreamy idea to take the bones out of the equation. Pork steaks are usually cooked similarly to ribs, although they're often served swimming in sauce. I like them a little drier.

The dominant local sauce sits somewhere between Memphis and Kansas City on the thick-sweet scales, but an astute taster might deem it the most balanced and best for anything with a little bit of char.

Saint Louis–style barbecued spareribs and pork steaks will probably be more familiar to amateur barbecuers in terms of technique, with some basting going on over the coals, but the snoot is its own entity. It's worth the effort and can actually be cooked alongside ribs or steaks. Just don't baste a snoot; serve it dry with the sauce on the side for maximum crunch.

BARBECUED PIG SNOOT

Serves 4

4 to 6 pig snoots
2 quarts warm water
½ cup distilled white vinegar
2 tablespoons kosher salt
1 teaspoon cayenne pepper

Slice the nostrils off the tip of the nose flaps and discard. Turn each snoot skin side down, cut out any cartilage left from the sinus, and cut out the vein that runs through midway. Combine the remaining ingredients and mix to dissolve the salt. Submerge the snoots and soak for 1 hour, or better yet, overnight in the refrigerator.

Build a fire according to your smoker's instructions and set the temperature to 225°F. Clear coals are essential for snoots—you may flavor with a very few well-soaked apple or cherrywood chips during the last 30 minutes of cooking, but any more smoke or green wood will make your snoots taste like a forest fire. Feed your fire with prepared charcoal or build a side fire to transfer clear coals.

Place the snoots on the top rack of your smoker, at least 12 inches above the coals, where the heat will be even and steady. Close the cover. Turn the snoots every 10 minutes, rearranging them around the coals so they cook evenly. Cook at 225°F to 230°F for 2½ to 3 hours, until the snoots are puffy, brittle, and crunchy all over. Near the last hour, you'll see some parts of the snoot get that chicharrón kind of crunchy puffiness—these parts are done, so move the snoots at each turning so that the still-leathery parts are over the hot spots.

Your finished snoot with be puffy and crunchy throughout. Enjoy with **SAINT LOUIS–STYLE BARBECUE SAUCE** (recipe follows) on the side, or make sandwiches with barbecue sauce, onion, and pickles, and try not to become an addict!

SAINT LOUIS–STYLE BARBECUE SAUCE

Makes about 4 cups

    2 cups ketchup
    ½ cup apple cider vinegar
    ½ cup water
    ¾ cup dark brown sugar
    ¼ cup spicy brown mustard
    3 tablespoons Worcestershire sauce
    2 tablespoons soy sauce
    1 tablespoon granulated onion
    2 teaspoons granulated garlic
    ½ teaspoon cayenne pepper
    2 teaspoons kosher salt

Place all ingredients in a saucepan and bring to a low boil, stirring regularly. Simmer for 15 minutes to infuse. Bottle while still hot for storage, or transfer hot to a serving bowl or boat to enjoy immediately.

SAINT LOUIS–STYLE SPARERIBS

Serves 4 to 6

4 full racks Saint Louis–cut spareribs

½ cup **BARBECUE RUB** (p. 218), divided

1 cup **SAINT LOUIS–STYLE BARBECUE SAUCE** (above), plus more for the table

Set your ribs on a large cutting board and pat them dry on all sides with clean paper towels. On the small-rib end of the rack, use a paring or utility knife to peel the silver skin on the back of the rack back from one corner ½ inch or so. Then, using a paper towel as a grip, pull the entire sheet of silver skin off. Rub the ribs all over with ⅓ of the barbecue rub, let them rest 10 minutes, and rub in another ⅓ of the rub. Rest the ribs until they reach room temperature, about 1 hour. Rub in the final ⅓ of the rub.

Build a fire according to your smoker's instructions and set the temperature to 225°F.

Place the ribs convex side up on the center rack of your smoker, and place a casserole-sized pan of water beneath them, unless you have a vapor pan. Cook at 225°F to 230°F for about 3 hours, turning every 30 to 45 minutes, until the ribs register 170°F to 180°F internal temperature. Set the ribs concave side up and brush with sauce, just to lightly glaze. Turn back to convex side up and brush with sauce, just to glaze.

Cook the ribs another 45 minutes to 1 hour, glazing once more at the 30-minute mark, until the ribs register 190°F in the thickest part of the rack. Move the ribs directly above the coals, or bring the coals to underneath the ribs, about 4 to 6 inches below. Cook for a few minutes on each side to blister and caramelize the sauce and get some grill marks on them beauties. Glaze once more before serving, turn one last time on the grill, and rest for 15 minutes before serving.

BARBECUED PORK STEAKS

Serves 4 to 6

4 thick-cut pork blade steaks, about 1 pound each

6 tablespoons **BARBECUE RUB** (p. 218), divided

1 cup **SAINT LOUIS–STYLE BARBECUE SAUCE** (above), plus more for the table

Set your steaks on a large cutting board and pat them dry on all sides with clean paper towels. Rub the steaks all over with ⅓ of the barbecue rub, let them rest 10 minutes, and rub in another ⅓ of the rub. Rest the steaks until they reach room temperature, about 1 hour. Rub in the final ⅓ of the rub.

Build a fire according to your smoker's instructions and set the temperature to 225°F.

Under the center rack of your smoker, place a large casserole-sized pan of water 4 to 6 inches beneath where the main cooking will take place. Brown the steaks directly over the coals, about 3 to 4 minutes on each side. Then place them over the center rack, away from the coals, and cook at 225°F to 230°F for about 2 hours, until they register 160°F to 175°F internally. Brush each side with a thin glaze of sauce. Return to direct heat over the coals, but at 8 inches or more above them—you want a gentle cook on the steaks. Turn and brush with sauce every 10 to 15 minutes, adding sauce more liberally as the steaks get closer to done. Remove them at 185°F to 190°F internal temperature for a toothsome bite, or cook to 210°F for a more velvety steak. Slather with as much sauce as you desire and rest for 15 minutes before serving.

9

A PIZZA TOUR

He, like many people, tried to steal Pizzeria Uno's recipe. And the way
the fat person did it was this: he decided that he needed to watch it being
made. And there was a window in the kitchen in the alley running next
to Uno's. So the fat man got a volunteer sweetie to pretend to be necking
with him in the alley so that he could look in the window. Unfortunately,
he did not take into account the wind coming off the lake in February.
The volunteer sweetie had, was willing to undergo a little bit of spooning
with Goldberg, but she did not sign up for frostbite. So the two of them
were out of there before the pepperoni went on.

—**Calvin Trillin**

MIDWESTERNERS have long taken their pizza amid wood-paneled walls
and knotty pine booths, Formica tables lit by the eerie glow of neon beer
signs, mugs of suds and frosted plastic tumblers of pop fizzing with ice, and always with a well-stocked bar a few steps away. Far from the upscale experience
to be had in white-tablecloth Italian restaurants or the artisan pizza shops that
have popped up over the past few decades, eating pizza has been, and continues to be, a downscale affair of friendly neighborhood taverns or family restaurants that cater to workaday folks.

Chicago gets a lot of press for its famed deep-dish pies, and to their millions of fans these mammoth red sauce–laden disks of dough and cheese are
the very embodiment of indulgence, a perfect food for holiday vacations or
for fueling walking excursions on a visit to the big city. Delicious though they
are, over my decades in Chicago I've known few locals who would count deep
dish as everyday sustenance. With the notable exception of Detroit's excellent
slightly less deep-dish pies, which I still nonetheless classify as deep dish (because they are in fact baked in a deep dish), Midwesterners—and that includes
Chicagoans—take their everyday pizza with thin crust.

New York rivals, or perhaps even surpasses, Chicago for the press its floppy,
elephant-eared slices get, and New Haven deservedly gets its share of ink for
its coal-fired disks, but through a lifetime of pizza passion I've come to the conclusion that the Midwest is by far the most exciting region in which to go pizza
hunting. Within a few hundred miles, there are at least five distinct styles to be

had, some of them with micro-regional variations, all of them world-class if you know where to look.

Besides Chicago's deep dish, there is the deep-dish substyle of stuffed pizza, a leviathan round sliced into triangular bricks of cheese-stuffed, buttery crust slathered with red sauce on top. And there's the ubiquitous thin-crust style, often called "tavern style" (more on that later), found throughout the Ohio River Valley and extending to the north through Wisconsin and Minnesota, varying in thickness and topping technique. The standard is toppings to the edge, so there's no *cornicone*, and the pie is cut into small squares, not triangles as in most of the country. Saint Louis conforms to this construction as well, but with a unique crust recipe and cheese to set it apart.

In between the cities, pan pizza rules and expands upon the tavern-style standard. It usually has a somewhat thicker, airier crust and, characteristically, generous toppings. Typically baked in a well-oiled aluminum pan in a screaming-hot deck oven, these pies have a superfine crispness to the bottom of the crust, which gives way to a creamy crumb that convenes with the toppings and cheese to create a mouthful of textures to rival any pie on earth.

And there's the Detroit style, baked in heavy rectangular anodized-steel pans. The crust, fried crisp on the bottom by a pre-bake slathering of olive oil or (gasp) lard, has an airy, not-quite-as-soft-as-focaccia interior. It's topped with meats or vegetables and cheese, favoring Wisconsin brick cheese over mozzarella. And it's sauced after baking with "racing stripes" of red sauce, all so it remains slack and juicy. The cheese is sprinkled not only over the pie but around the edges of the crust so it caramelizes and creates a hard, toasty edge against the heavy steel pan. You have a choice of starting from the crunchy, cheesy edge and eating your way to the creamy, light center of your slice, or going the other way.

Not covered in the following recipes are some of the best and most interesting pizzas in the Midwest, because their styles are strictly Italian or unique to the approach of the chefs producing them. Chicago has long claimed one of the best examples of *pizza napoletana* outside of Italy in Jonathan Goldsmith's Spacca Napoli on the North Side. He bakes long-fermented dough from imported "oo" flour with artisanal toppings in voluntary but strict adherence to the rules for *pizza napoletana* set forth by Italy's Denominazione di Origine Controllata, finishing his pies in a wood-fired oven which burns at over 800°F.

Minneapolis chef Ann Kim also starts with a Neapolitan-style dough and bakes in a wood-fired oven, but her toppings might be Korean-style bulgogi short ribs and sesame with a soy chili vinaigrette bound by mozzarella and finished with a mound of pungent arugula; or Spanish chorizo, goat cheese, piquillo pepper, and preserved lemon; or potato and leek with gruyère, onion jam, and brown butter. The more innovative, genre-busting pies coexist on her menu at Young Joni with more familiar red sauce–based versions, but from the familiar to the avant-garde, the results are uniformly thrilling.

Iowa-based Fong's Pizza, with three locations, breaks all barriers with pizzas such as the crab Rangoon pizza, with a "crab Rangoon base" topped with surimi, mozzarella, asiago, scallions, crispy wontons, and sweet chili sauce. It also features a coconut curry pizza, with slow-roasted pork, curry sauce, red onion, mozzarella, and cilantro. And it doesn't stop there. If these pies sound like they just might work, it's because they do. They're masterpieces of East Asian–Italian fusion you would find only in the USA.

The future of pizza in the Midwest is provocative to ponder, so much so that a book of this type a generation from now might have a very different collection of recipes. But I'm eager to document the present, and wherever you are, you can easily make signature Midwestern-style pies in your home.

Saint Louis–Style Pizza

I love turning people on to Saint Louis–style pizza because many have never heard of it, and it's kind of a wild and interesting way to make a pizza. It uses a yeast-less crust and a processed-cheese product that's not available anywhere else. You literally have to go to Saint Louis to try it, because it's not possible to thoroughly replicate it without Provel cheese, and to my knowledge, there is no other pizza crust that doesn't employ yeast.

I couldn't find a clear source on who developed the Saint Louis style or when, but the introduction of pizza to Saint Louis is generally credited to Amedeo Fiore at his Melrose Café in 1947. While he was definitely using a very thin disk of dough as his base, it included yeast.[1] In 1953, Luca "Luigi" Meglio opened his iconic Luigi's, where he introduced Saint Louis to the thin-crust square-cut pizza, and incidentally, the conveyor belt–driven pizza oven.[2] Luigi's popularized Provel, processed cheese made from swiss and provolone cheeses and given a kiss of bacon flavor. Eventually expanding to four locations with 750 employees, Meglio established the style that holds the Gateway City in its thrall today.

Today's iconic name on the local pizza scene is Imo's, founded in 1964 and now operating about a hundred stores. Imo's pizza is a clear descendant of Meglio's: a crunchy hard crust that almost feels like a nacho chip at times, a highly seasoned sauce, and a judicious smothering of Provel. The crust is designed to bring the maximum topping game, and some take it to comical heights. I still like to keep the pie mostly about the crust, sauce, and cheese, but if you master the crust, you can pile as much topping on that plank of dough as your heart desires.

SAINT LOUIS–STYLE PIZZA SAUCE

Makes about 3 cups

> 1 (16-ounce) can tomato sauce
> 1 (6-ounce) can tomato paste
> 1 tablespoon plus 2 teaspoons sugar
> 1 teaspoon dried basil
> 1 teaspoon dried thyme
> 1 teaspoon granulated onion
> ½ teaspoon granulated garlic
> 1 teaspoon kosher salt

Whisk to combine thoroughly. No need to cook, but best made a day ahead. Refrigerate in a tightly sealed container until ready to use.

SAINT LOUIS–STYLE PIZZA DOUGH

Makes two 12- to 13-inch crusts

> 2 cups all-purpose flour, plus more for dusting
> 1 tablespoon brown sugar
> 1 teaspoon baking powder
> 1 teaspoon kosher salt
> 2 tablespoons olive pomace oil or vegetable oil
> ½ cup plus 2 tablespoons warm water, 90°F to 100°F

Combine dry ingredients in a mixing bowl, dig a well in the center, and add the oil and water. Stir with a wooden spoon until it's too stiff to work with a spoon, then switch to working with your hands. Press the dough together until it forms a ball. There is no need to knead the dough, but do work it enough that it comes together uniformly. Divide into two balls, and form each one into a hockey puck–shaped disk. Cover with plastic wrap and rest for 15 to 30 minutes before rolling out.

Makes two 12-inch pies

1 recipe (two pieces) **SAINT LOUIS–STYLE PIZZA DOUGH** (above)

4 teaspoons polenta cornmeal, divided

1½ cups **SAINT LOUIS–STYLE PIZZA SAUCE** (above)

Toppings of your choice, ½ to 1 cup each (the classics are sausage, pepperoni, mushroom, onion, green peppers, anchovy, bacon, black olives, and tomato)

3 cups shredded Provel, or 1½ cups each baby swiss and provolone cheese, shredded on the large side of a box grater and tossed with 1 tablespoon bacon grease

2 teaspoons Italian seasoning

Preheat oven, with a pizza stone on the center rack, to 450°F. Give the stone a good hour to heat while you prep the rest of the items. If you have two stones and two racks, you can bake both pies at once. Otherwise, do one at a time, using half of the ingredients on each pie.

Use an Italian rolling pin to roll out the dough to a minimum of 12 inches around—go for a little wider if you can. Use the pin to roll around the circumference of the dough, as well as up and down and sideways, to ensure a uniformly thin and even disk. Sprinkle half the cornmeal on your pizza peel, then lay the dough evenly across the dusted peel. Spread half the sauce over the dough all the way to the edges (you can use less than half if you prefer), then dress with toppings—generally speaking, place vegetables first, then meats. Cover evenly with cheese, 1½ cups per pie—this isn't an exceedingly cheesy pie! Sprinkle a little Italian seasoning over the top.

Transfer to the pizza stone and shut the oven door. Bake at 450°F, and begin checking for doneness at about the 12-minute mark. For maximum crunch, look for well-browned edges and deep golden cheese on top, up to 20 minutes total. Allow to rest and cool for 6 to 8 minutes before cutting into squares and enjoying.

Basic Midwestern Pizza Sauce

Pizza sauce varies slightly from place to place, but this sauce will tie most regional variations together, with the Saint Louis–style sauce being the outlier. Below, I'll refer to this recipe with instructions for modifying it by locale.

Makes about 3 cups

2 tablespoons extra-virgin olive oil

½ cup yellow Spanish onion, very finely minced

2 teaspoons garlic, very finely minced

1 (28-ounce) can San Marzano tomatoes

½ teaspoon dried thyme leaves

1 teaspoon dried oregano

1 teaspoon dried basil

½ teaspoon crushed red pepper

1 teaspoon kosher salt

Sauté the onion and garlic in the olive oil over medium heat to sweat, but do not brown. Puree the tomatoes in their juice thoroughly and add to the pot. Add remaining ingredients and simmer over low heat for 45 minutes to 1 hour. Stir the sauce regularly to prevent scorching. It is ready when a large dollop transferred to a plate holds it shape somewhat and doesn't bleed transparent juice. Refrigerate in a sealed container until ready to use.

Chicago-Style Deep-Dish Pizza

Easily the most famous of our homegrown Midwestern pies, Chicago's deep dish is a tour de force and not targeted at the calorie conscious. Whereas most of the Midwest didn't get to know pizza until after World War II, Chicago was home to a substantial Italian community and had at least one popular pizzeria by 1924: Granato's, on Taylor Street in the heart of Little Italy.[3] Granato's enjoyed a long lifespan; even after four decades it was cited as one of Chicago's best Italian restaurants.[4] We don't know much about the pizza it served, but can presume it was similar to the thin-crust styles that would appear around the country during the twentieth century.

The origins of Chicago's deep dish are fairly straightforward. During the 1940s, Ric Riccardo Sr., proprietor of the popular Riccardo's restaurant, made plans to open a new restaurant with Ike Sewell. Sewell, a former All-American football player with a big appetite, wanted to offer something more substantial than a traditional Italian pizza. In 1943, Pizzeria Uno opened with their deep-dish pizza, and the rest is history.[5]

Most legendary Chicago-style pizza operations have some history with Uno. The best example is Lou Malnati's, which many regard as the best of the local chains serving deep dish. Rudy Malnati was the manager of Riccardo's, and later of Pizzeria Uno, which he co-managed with his son Luciano "Lou" Malnati. The two went on to open Pizzeria Due (two) in 1955.[6] Lou would open the first location of his namesake chain in 1971, and today the company operates about sixty locations in Chicago and vicinity.

A quirky variation on deep dish popularized by the Giordano's chain is the "stuffed" pizza, which is a deep-dish pie filled with cheese and toppings (or, rather, fillings), then crowned with another disk of dough and sauced over the top before baking. While a deep-dish pie can take 40 minutes or so to bake, a stuffed pizza can push an hour. It's heavy and thus filling, but oh so delicious; just plan on waiting for a spell while they bake it.

The best deep dish has a laminated crust. The basics of constructing both pies are the same; to make a stuffed pie, increase the dough recipe by ⅓, then reserve ⅓ of the dough to make the lid. The other ratios remain the same. One essential step to being able to successfully build a deep-dish pie and have it bake to the right consistency is to retard the dough in the refrigerator after laminating it—don't skip this step. In fact, it's best to make the dough 1 to 3 days in advance. Likewise, have all the other ingredients refrigerated for successful construction—make the sauce ahead of time as well.

CHICAGO-STYLE DEEP-DISH DOUGH

Makes one 10-inch crust

2 cups all-purpose flour
¼ cup yellow cornmeal
1 teaspoon instant yeast
1 teaspoon kosher salt
¾ cup plus 2 tablespoons warm water (100°F to 110°F)
2 tablespoons extra-virgin olive oil
¼ cup (½ stick) unsalted butter, softened slightly

Combine the flour, cornmeal, yeast, and salt in a mixing bowl, dig a well in the center, and pour in the water and olive oil. Stir from the center with a wooden spoon, mixing thoroughly and bringing in more dry mix from the edges as the batter thickens to a dough. Finish working with your hands until you have a well-formed, uniform, and thick dough. No need to knead. Shape into a ball, oil on all sides, and set in a warm place to rise until doubled in bulk, about 1 hour. Degas the dough by rolling it out into a rough rectangle shape about 1 inch thick. Wrap in plastic and refrigerate for at least 2 hours before laminating.

Once the dough is well refrigerated, it will feel denser and stiffer. Working quickly, roll the dough out into a large rectangle about 12 by 8 inches spread lengthwise. Spread the softened butter over the left two-thirds of the rectangle, leaving about ½ inch around the edges unbuttered. Fold the unbuttered third at the right over the center third, and then fold the left, buttered third over the center as well to make three layers. Pinch well around all the edges to seal in the butter. Wrap in plastic and refrigerate for 30 minutes to 1 hour. Roll out into a 12-by-8-inch rectangle again, fold in thirds again, wrap in plastic, and refrigerate. The dough will be usable for up to 3 days. In the meantime, prepare and chill your sauce and other ingredients.

CHICAGO-STYLE PIZZA SAUCE

Make **BASIC MIDWESTERN PIZZA SAUCE** (p. 234), but substitute 1 tablespoon unsalted butter for 1 tablespoon of the olive oil. For deep-dish pizza, a chunkier sauce is nice, so pulse the tomatoes in your food processor instead of pureeing fully, until the average piece of tomato is the size of a pea.

CHICAGO-STYLE DEEP-DISH PIZZA WITH SAUSAGE AND MUSHROOMS

Makes one 10-inch pie

- 2 tablespoons unsalted butter
- 1 recipe **CHICAGO-STYLE DEEP-DISH DOUGH** (above)
- 12 ounces *whole-milk* mozzarella cheese, shredded on the large side of a box grater
- 2 links hot Italian sausage, cooked and crumbled (discard casings)
- ¾ cup button mushrooms, sliced
- 12 leaves fresh basil
- 3 cups **CHICAGO-STYLE PIZZA SAUCE** (above)
- ¼ cup parmesan or pecorino cheese, finely shredded
- A few twists freshly ground black pepper, to taste

Preheat oven to 425°F.

Grease a heavy 10-inch round cake pan with the butter. Remove the dough from the refrigerator and place on a dry, lightly floured surface. Working slowly at first, roll out into a large, 12- to 13-inch round at least ¼ inch thick—⅝ inch is better, but the dough will need to reach all the way up the sides of the pan. If necessary to help shape the round, you can fold the corners in toward the center and continue rolling out.

Roll the dough up on your rolling pin, and gently unroll it into the buttered cake pan, tucking the dough into the bottom and up the sides of the pan.

Spread ½ the mozzarella over the bottom of the crust and tuck in gently. Spread the sausage, mushrooms, and basil evenly over the cheese and tuck. Top with the remaining mozzarella and tamp everything down gently. Spread the sauce evenly over the pie, then lift the pie pan a couple inches off the counter and tap it flat on the counter a few times to help the ingredients settle. Sprinkle the parmesan over the top and season with a few twists of freshly ground black pepper.

Bake until the crust is a rich golden brown and the center of the pie registers 185°F, about 40 minutes. Allow to rest for 15 minutes before slicing and serving.

Detroit-Style Deep-Dish Pizza

Perhaps the last great regional pizza style to be "discovered," Detroit-style pizza has finally been having a bit of a moment the past few years, even if quietly so. Detroit-style anything stirs up a swirl of childhood good feelings in me, and the city's signature pizza never disappoints. Detroit's pizza delivers a wider range of textures and flavors than any other. It's that heavy anodized-steel pan and that hard, deeply caramelized crust of cheese, that creamy interior, that luscious slack sauce, the fine crispness of the bottom crust. Done right, it's a masterpiece nonpareil.

Looking to bring in a little extra income for his bar business, first-generation Italian American Gus Guerra first baked pizza pies in square pans in 1946 at the now-storied Buddy's Rendezvous at Six Mile Road and Conant. His mother, who was from Sicily, worked up a dough recipe for him.[7] His pizza was very different from any other: the dough was softer and thicker, and the square slices were framed in a hard crust formed by a long bake in a heavy, deep pan.

Gus Guerra and his wife, Anna, sold Buddy's Rendezvous in 1953 after a financial dispute with their business partner, and then opened the Cloverleaf Bar & Restaurant across town in Eastpointe, once again focusing on those increasingly popular square pies. Two Jimmys, Valenti and Bonacorsi, became the new owners of Buddy's, dropping Rendezvous from the name. Over the decades, various partnerships, management splits, and normal restaurant successions would lead to the formation of restaurants called Sorrento, Shield's, and Loui's. Buddy's has grown to sixteen locations in Metro Detroit, in addition to a handful of carryout-only spots.

Today, scores of restaurants in Detroit serve the style, and it's increasingly popular across the country. The more this pie gets around, the luckier we'll all be. While I could wax on about Detroit-style pizza, I'll let the recipe speak for itself.

Makes one 10-by-14-inch crust

1¼ cups warm water (100°F to 110°F)

1 tablespoon dry active yeast

1 teaspoon granulated sugar

1 tablespoon kosher salt

3 tablespoons extra-virgin olive oil

1¾ cups all-purpose flour, sifted before measuring, divided

¾ cup semolina flour

Place the warm water in a large mixing bowl and dissolve the yeast and sugar in it, along with ¼ cup of all-purpose flour. Cover and let the yeast activate until the mixture has a head of foam on it, about 15 minutes. Stir in the salt to dissolve, and mix in the remaining ingredients. Work the dough with your hands until it comes together in a rough ball, then knead it a few times to smooth the ball out, but don't work the dough excessively—it can make your pizza too chewy. Just form a smooth-ish ball.

Oil the ball on all sides and leave in the mixing bowl to rise, covered tightly with plastic wrap, until doubled in bulk. Knead the dough in the bowl for a few turns to degas it and shape it back into a ball. Cover tightly with plastic wrap and refrigerate for at least 4 hours or up to 3 days. Before using, set out at room temperature for 45 to 60 minutes so the yeast can wake up and the dough can rise again.

DETROIT-STYLE PEPPERONI PIZZA WITH "RACING STRIPES"

Makes one 10-by-14-inch pie

3 tablespoons extra-virgin olive oil, divided

1 recipe **DETROIT-STYLE PIZZA DOUGH** (above)

3 cups (about 12 ounces) Wisconsin brick cheese, shredded

6 ounces pepperoni slices

2 cups **BASIC MIDWESTERN PIZZA SAUCE** (p. 234)—⅔ cup cold, 1⅓ cups heated when the pie comes out of the oven

Preheat oven to 425°F.

Oil a 10-by-14-inch anodized Detroit-style pizza pan liberally with 2 tablespoons of olive oil. Gently turn out the dough into the oiled pan, being careful to degas it as little as possible. Use your fingers to stretch the dough across the bottom of the pan by pressing your fingers down into the dough and massaging it outward. Don't work it too much—just let it relax. If the dough isn't stretching all the way corner to corner, let it relax for 10 minutes to calm the gluten down, and finish the stretch. The dough should be a roughly even thickness end to end and side to side, but hills and valleys are fine—it's almost like making focaccia.

Drizzle the remaining tablespoon of olive oil over the dough. Sprinkle ½ of the cheese evenly over the dough, but pile extra along the edges. Tuck the cheese into the edges ever so gently. Dribble the cold pizza sauce (⅔ cup) over the cheese; try to cover most of the pie, but it doesn't have to be evenly spread. Dot the pie with half the pepperoni. Sprinkle the other half of the cheese over all, allowing a little extra on the edges, but don't tuck this time. Dot with the remaining pepperoni.

Bake on the bottom rack of the oven until the edges are a nicely caramelized deep, rich brown and the top of the pie is lightly browning. Have the remaining 1⅓ cups sauce hot and handy. Allow the pizza to rest for 10 minutes before unmolding. Use a knife to cut around the edge and separate the caramelized cheese from the pan. Use a large spatula to scoop under the pie and, tilting the pan toward a serving platter or cookie sheet, slide the pizza out. Add "racing stripes" of fresh sauce by ladling two streaks of sauce lengthwise across the pie, using ½ to ⅓ cup for each. Serve at once.

Tavern-Style Pizza

Tavern-style pizza is the favored style throughout much of the Midwest, although its variations could be the subject of an entire book itself. It's called tavern style because it was originally (and still is) bar food, offered to guests as an inducement to stay at the bar, which would usually lead to their buying more drinks.

The crust is typically very thin, with toppings spread all the way to the edge. To simplify dividing up the pies among many guests, they are cut into small squares, which some also know as the party cut. A small piece of pizza can be held in one hand without the care required of a flippity-floppity triangular slice, so the other is free to hold a beer, a hand of cards, or even a child. It also makes math simpler: if pies are cut into, say, eight wedges, how does that shake out for three people? Or six? With a tavern cut, everyone can simply eat until it's gone, no need to divvy up a set number of slices, so it's particularly handy for groups. Some folks like the crispy edges, others the gooey center. Win-win.

Thin-crust pizza has a longer history in Chicago than in most of the country; it was a postwar phenomenon in most locales. The Italian deli Pompei opened in 1909 on Taylor Street in Little Italy, serving the same thin-crusted sheet-pan pizzas that it still serves today. Granato's and Pizzeria Napolitana were operating by the 1930s, but perhaps the most seismic shift in our pizza culture came in 1947, when Vincent and Mary Grittani started serving pizza at their bar, which would become Home Run Inn.[8] Even today it might still be the most famous purveyor of tavern-style pizza, although subsequent versions at classic Chicago spots like the North Side's Pat's Pizza (opened in 1950) and the South Side's Vito & Nick's (which started serving pizza in 1965) are much thinner and more exemplary of the style today.

Notable examples outside of Chicago include Wells Brothers in Racine, Wisconsin, which serves the best example of tavern thin crust I've had, and Turoni's Pizzery & Brewery in Newburgh, Indiana, home of the thinnest crust on earth and a fresher, more modern take on toppings. Milwaukee's Maria's and Zaffiro's consistently satisfy. Cincinnati's local chain LaRosa's serves a fine tavern-style pie but stops just short of the edges when distributing the toppings, yielding a deliciously crisp yeasty crust around the edges.

Of all the pizza styles here, this is probably the hardest to pull off at home, but it's still not *that* hard and is worth the adventure. A screaming-hot pizza stone is essential to getting the crust properly crispy, a judicious hand with toppings is essential, and you should use one of the pizzerias' trade secrets: roll out your crust a day ahead and refrigerate it between layers of butcher paper, which will wick some moisture out of the crust, giving you a solid head start on that crispy pie.

TAVERN-STYLE PIZZA DOUGH

Makes two 12-inch crusts

- ¾ cup warm water (100°F to 110°F)
- 2 teaspoons dry active yeast
- 2 teaspoons granulated sugar
- 2 cups plus 1 tablespoon all-purpose flour, divided, plus more for dusting
- 2 tablespoons extra-virgin olive oil
- 1 teaspoon kosher salt

Place the warm water in a mixing bowl and stir in the yeast, sugar, and 1 tablespoon of the flour. Allow 10 to 15 minutes for the yeast to activate and form a sponge with a thick, foamy top. Add the remaining ingredients and work the dough into a ball, which will take a few minutes. Once the dough comes together, knead for 5 to 6 minutes, until the dough forms a smooth ball. Divide in two and form each half into a ball. Oil each ball on all sides and place them in separate bowls to rise, covered with plastic wrap, until doubled in bulk, about 45 minutes to 1 hour. Degas each by kneading for a few turns, put back in their covered bowls, and refrigerate for several hours or up to 3 days. The yeast will complete its second rise, and you'll have proofed balls of dough, well chilled and easier to handle.

Using extra flour as needed, roll out each well-chilled ball of dough into a round at least 12 inches in diameter, a little wider (and thinner) if you can—use an Italian rolling pin to keep the edges as slim as the center of the dough. Lay a piece of butcher paper on a cookie sheet, place one sheet of dough on it, top with another sheet of butcher paper, then place the other sheet of dough, and cap with another sheet of butcher paper, pressing down gently to be sure it is snug with the dough. Refrigerate overnight, uncovered, where nothing will drip or spill on it. The next day, go straight to building your pizza on the chilled dough.

TAVERN-STYLE PIZZA

Makes 2 pies—divide the toppings evenly between 2 crusts

- 2 tablespoons yellow cornmeal, divided
- 1 recipe **TAVERN-STYLE PIZZA DOUGH** (above) (2 prepared crusts)
- 1½ cups **BASIC MIDWESTERN PIZZA SAUCE** (p. 234)
- 3 cups part-skim low-moisture mozzarella, shredded on the large side of a box grater
- 1 to 2 cups toppings of your choice—classics are pepperoni, Italian sausage, anchovy, mushrooms, onion, green peppers, **CHICAGO-STYLE HOT GIARDINIERA** (p. 25), black olives, basil—limit toppings to 1 cup total per pie

Place your pizza stone on the bottom rack of the oven and preheat to 425°F for at least 1 hour.

For the first pie, sprinkle 1 tablespoon cornmeal evenly over your pizza peel and lay the first crust over it. Spread with ¾ cup sauce, working to distribute evenly and all the way to the edges. Sprinkle ¾ cup cheese evenly over the crust, then arrange your toppings as you wish: for the best results, place vegetables first, then meats. Sprinkle the other ¾ cup of cheese evenly over the toppings. Transfer via the peel to the pizza stone. Bake until crispy and well browned around the edges and lightly browned on top, 15 to 20 minutes. Place on a pan or cutting board and allow to rest for 10 minutes before cutting. Meanwhile, prep and bake your second pie. Cut both into 2-inch squares and serve hot.

Pan Pizza

From Chicago to Detroit and back around through Saint Louis, the Midwest has plenty of famous pizzas to go around, but I saved the small-town Midwest's most ubiquitous style for last, one that isn't exactly a precise style but rather an extended family of home-cooked pies. From Ohio stalwarts such as Geraci's in Cleveland, DiCarlo's in Steubenville, and the Youngstown-area Wedgewood Pizza, to the famed Mother Bear's Pizza of Bloomington, Indiana, and Jockamo's in Indianapolis, Harris Pizza in Iowa's Quad Cities, and Mama's in Saint Paul, plus too many mom-and-pop shops in between to mention, pan pizza is what most Midwesterners know as their perennial standard.

Pan pizza comes in many forms. It lives between tavern-style thin crust and deep dish, with a softer, creamier crumb yet with a smart crisp on the bottom. The pan is shallower than a deep-dish pan and often perforated to provide that crispness. The pie may be square, round, or rectangular, cut into wedges, strips, or squares, and it almost always employs a generous hand with toppings—this is the food of common folk, and value is paramount.

A deft hand with those toppings separates the best shops from the mundane. With a plusher crust than most, even a pan pizza that's piled high with toppings will have a light feel to it. Rather than forming the turgid, brick-like structure of a Chicago deep dish, the toppings will behave almost as a baked meat-and-vegetable salad atop the pillowy crust, usually with vegetables below meats, sprinkled about rather than matted down. The cheese floats across the top, waiting for your bite to marry everything into one whole.

My college days in Bloomington, Indiana, have embedded this middle-of-the-road, middle-of-the-country style in my consciousness as the most reliably satisfying pizza in America. (My favorite—many people's favorite—is Mother Bear's.) Most Midwesterners will count their own hometown standby as the most satisfying pizza in America; we have a uniquely outstanding pizza culture with deserving purveyors in every county.

When making pan pizza at home, look for a 15-inch round (or square if it's your speed) aluminum pan with a lip around the outside not more than ½ inch high—you're looking to frame the pizza as it rises during baking, not make a deep-dish pie. If you can find a perforated one (restaurant supply stores are good places to look), you'll have a head start on getting that crisp crust. You may oil the pan if it's a solid pan; it helps crisp the dough. If you're using a perforated pan, use a judicious amount of nonstick spray to avoid oil dripping through the holes into your hot oven.

You can go to town on toppings with pan pizza, as the thicker crust will stand up to them. Some pizza places go really heavy on the cheese, and if you're into that, go for it; nailing your exact taste is the best part of making your own pizza. Personally, I like to keep it to 1½ cups or less (about 8 ounces shredded) because more can cause the pizza to take on a matted, heavy texture. For a 15-inch pie, ½ to ¾ cup each for more flavorful toppings such as onion or olives is a good starting point; for mushrooms and peppers, maybe a cup or a touch more. With meats, go up to a cup or so each. Cook sausage and bacon before using. Crumbled sausage is best placed after the vegetables but before the cheese; pepperoni and bacon go on the pie last, after the cheese. Here's my favorite recipe.

PAN PIZZA SAUCE

Make **BASIC MIDWESTERN PIZZA SAUCE** (p. 234), but add:

1 extra teaspoon oregano, for 2 teaspoons total
½ extra teaspoon thyme, for 1 teaspoon total
1 teaspoon marjoram

PAN PIZZA DOUGH

Makes one 15-inch crust

1 cup plus 2 tablespoons warm water (100°F to 110°F)
1 tablespoon dry active yeast
1 tablespoon granulated sugar
2¾ cups all-purpose flour, divided
2 tablespoons extra-virgin olive oil
1 teaspoon kosher salt

Place the warm water in a mixing bowl and stir in the yeast, sugar, and ¼ cup of the flour. Allow 10 to 15 minutes for the yeast to activate and form a sponge with a thick, foamy top. Add the remaining ingredients and work the dough into a ball, which will take a few minutes. Once the dough comes together, knead for 5 to 6 minutes, until smooth. Oil the ball on all sides and place in a bowl to rise, covered tightly with plastic wrap, until doubled in bulk, about 45 minutes to 1 hour. Degas by kneading for a few turns, place again in a tightly covered bowl, and refrigerate for several hours or up to 3 days. The yeast will complete its second rise, and you'll have a proofed ball of dough, well chilled and easier to handle. Before using, set out at room temperature for 1 hour so the yeast can wake up and begin rising again.

"DELUXE" PAN PIZZA

Makes one 15-inch pie

1 tablespoon olive oil, or if using a perforated pan, use cooking spray
1 recipe **PAN PIZZA DOUGH** (above)

Extra flour for rolling the dough

1 cup **PAN PIZZA SAUCE** (above), chilled

1 cup red onion, cut into ½-inch dice

1 cup green bell pepper, cut into ½-inch dice

1 cup button mushrooms, thinly sliced

2 links sweet Italian sausage, cooked and crumbled (discard casings)

½ cup sliced black olives

8 to 10 fresh basil leaves, torn

½ pound whole-milk mozzarella, shredded on the large side of a box grater (about
   2 cups)

4 strips cooked bacon, crumbled finely

2 ounces pepperoni slices

Preheat oven to 425°F, without a pizza stone.

Oil or spray a 15-inch pizza pan.

Use as little extra flour as necessary to gently roll out the ball of dough to 15 inches in diameter; it should fit just inside the pan with ½ inch to spare around the edges. Try not to press down on the dough too hard and degas it. Transfer to the oiled pan. The disk should be evenly flat across, without any extra puffing around the edges. Ladle the sauce into the center of the pie and spread in a circular motion to cover the entire crust, leaving ½ inch or less to spare around the edges. Distribute the remaining ingredients evenly over the crust, one at a time and in order, taking care to have a light touch and not mat or weigh anything down. Just sprinkle them around, evenly edge to edge, leaving only a thin strip of dough visible around the edges.

Place the pizza in the pan directly on the bottom rack of the oven and bake until nicely browned around the edges and the cheese on top is just starting to caramelize, about 20 to 25 minutes. Allow to rest for 10 minutes before slicing and enjoying hot.

Stephanie Hart

One of Chicago's best food neighborhoods and easily its best-kept secret is a little corridor straddling the South Side's Grand Crossing and Chatham neighborhoods, a middle-class African American enclave with restaurants, cafés, and salons including two Chicago culinary landmarks, right across the street from each other: Lem's Bar-B-Q, the originator of Chicago-style 'cue and purveyor of world-class rib tips & hot links, and Brown Sugar Bakery, which is in the running for the absolute best cake bakery in America. Famous for her caramel cake, Detroit-born founder and CEO Stephanie Hart has her own favorites but quickly learned "you can't have a bakery in Chicago without having caramel cake." She has embedded Brown Sugar in Chicago's Black community and its culinary community at large, gaining fans nationwide as she has received recognition from the James Beard Foundation with multiple nominations for its Outstanding Baker award.

Hart was a longtime tech entrepreneur, and thus a seemingly unlikely baking impresario, but she found plenty of inspiration in her family, especially her daughter, who now has a successful career as an opera singer. "I was traveling too much. You have to understand, I was an entrepreneur, but also a mom, and a home-schooling mom." She had taken up baking trying to re-create a pineapple-coconut cake her grandmother used to make, and things took shape naturally, but not without struggles.

"Growing up I didn't really bake. I would cook but when I would go home to Michigan for the holidays, Grandma and my aunts would all have the cakes ready." Her favorite? "Pineapple-coconut. I would feel like such a queen when I would get that cake." But there was more. "For our birthdays we could have whatever cake we wanted, but I had to be twelve before I could have carrot cake, and fourteen years old to get the red velvet cake, and that was a really big deal."

Hart lights up with adulation when talking about her grandma, the product of a family migration from Yazoo City to Brooklyn to Detroit, and all the women in her family. "Those ladies could really cook. *Everything* was special." Her grandmother "had real power because of how she could cook. When she ever needed anything done, she'd have volunteers lined up down the block."

For herself, "I would literally sit at her feet for food." Learning to live up to those standards herself took some time.

"When I was trying to get that cake [pineapple-coconut] right, my daughter would tell you I was having a middle age crisis. But when I finally got that cake right, it was just like, wow." Brown Sugar Bakery would soon be off the ground, but there was more development to do. "Yellow chocolate was next, then lemon, strawberry. . . . I love a push pop, so we have dreamsicle, and I love frappes, so we have a rainbow sherbet cake. Then we did double chocolate, red velvet, and finally I had to go to Oklahoma on advice from a friend to learn this caramel cake from a woman who just made this cake, it was so simple, and it was ready."

Brown Sugar Bakery has grown to three outlets plus the occasional pop-up, and Hart has another project, too: in 2020, she purchased Chicago's legendary Cupid Candies—a multigenerational family business, birthplace of the Dove Bar, and longtime purveyor of elegant meltaway candies and a cumbersome line of generations-old customer favorites. While folding the brand into Brown Sugar Cakes and Candies, she focused the candy factory on a trim but sublime line of turtles and meltaways, which are selling briskly. "Now I just have to do a praline, people want a praline. And I'm really excited to be developing new ice cream flavors to sell under the Brown Sugar label." Everything Stephanie Hart touches is culinary gold, so we can definitely look forward to them.

Hart hired as many of the former Cupid Candies employees as she could and will keep the factory on the South Side, and she will continue developing her bakery business there. It's this type of commitment to Chicago's Black community that has garnered Brown Sugar an award from the Lupe Fiasco Foundation, which honors businesses with a demonstrated commitment to Chicago's underserved populations. As she continues her work, there will be more compelling reasons for North Siders and suburbanites to travel to the South Side for cakes, ice creams, and candies. The hope is that even small-scale culinary tourism will ignite more development and opportunity for Chicago's South Side. There is tremendous potential there, and for Black entrepreneurs, bakers, and chefs, Stephanie Hart is one of the brightest stars showing the way.

Based on a conversation with Stephanie Hart, CEO of Brown Sugar Bakery, April 17, 2022.

10

SWEETS

*Pies, Cakes, Cookies,
and Confections*

Then when the most hardy are still chewing away on chicken legs or wishbones, the cakes are cut—angel food, devil's food, banana, marble, sponge, coconut, orange, burnt sugar, and lazy daisy. These are followed by pumpkin, cherry, apple, mince, peach, blackberry, and custard pies.

—Nelson Algren, "Festivals in the Fields"

Pie, after all, is essentially a country product. It is one of the many very excellent gifts of America's farms and has antecedents in the pie-oneer days. And it's pretty hard to improve on the real farm pies as I've known them—both plain and with the additions which certain farm households make. For instance—vanilla ice cream on hot pie (a la mode to you city folks)—pie, hot or cold, with good American cheese—slip-on (mince or apple pie with cheese melted over it)—and hot fresh fruit pie with thick cream poured over it—these are pie ideas that come from the farms. And I'm awfully glad they came.

—George Rector, *Home at the Range with George Rector*

You don't have to spend too much time in the Midwest to learn that its inhabitants have quite a sweet tooth, from morning pastries to evening and late-night desserts with all the snacks in between. I've found it almost comical how dessert and confection recipes outnumber all others in many community cookbooks and even professional ones—especially those from the nineteenth century. For one example, which is a conservative one, *Your Happy Kitchen Cook Book* by the Michigan City, Indiana, *Evening Dispatch* (undated, probably 1920s) lists 194 savory recipes from canapés to entrées, and 211 for sweets.[1] *The Concordia Cook Book*, a church cookbook from Concordia, Missouri (1984, including a reprint of the 1928 edition) devotes 108 pages to savory dishes and breads, and a whopping 182 to sweets![2]

The variety of puddings and pies in Midwestern culinary literature isn't all that surprising in context. Recipes for meats, poultry, fish, and savory vegetables generally encompass a pretty narrow range of culinary techniques. Meats are roasted, fried, braised, and, with the increasing interest in backyard cooking over the course of the twentieth century, grilled. There is a great deal of creativity in the realm of protein, but the possibilities for creativity increase dramatically when it comes to sweets, which encompass all the fruits, plus many vegetables and a wide range of dairy products. And Midwesterners open up their spice cabinets much more readily when flavoring cakes and cookies than they do with savory dishes.

Church suppers, turkey shoots, and potluck events such as family reunions are always salient examples to me of the power of sweets to bring variety to the Midwestern table. There will ordinarily be one or two proteins, often something as mundane as burgers and hot dogs, or fried chicken, or a giant pot of chicken and noodles. But over along the side wall are the pie table and the cake table, each a prodigious display of the baking and pastry skills of the organization's women, with pies from mince to apple, strawberry rhubarb to cherry and blackberry, custard pies, lattice-topped and streusel-topped fruit pies, and cakes from devil's food to angel food, German chocolate to Lady Baltimore, and red velvet from every other baker who is out to prove hers is the best in town.

Holidays bring out the usual suspects in pies and cakes, from pumpkin or sweet potato to kuchen, coconut cake, and heady spice cakes, but the holidays are when the confections take center stage. Of course every household has a recipe for peanut brittle, some better than others. There are turtles, divinity, macaroons, Mexican wedding cookies, icebox cookies, springerle, spritz cookies, popcorn balls, and toffee, all present at Christmas parties and frequently given as gifts in decorative tins or boxes.

Even though no Midwestern cookbook would be complete without a recipe for cherry pie, they are easy enough to come by, so I've sought to bring out a collection of recipes that are either rarer or traditional ones that are commonly misrepresented. Some, like cranberry and bone marrow pudding pie, are new ideas that have been wildly successful at my restaurant, while others, like the mince pie recipe adapted from Lettice Bryan, are long-lost treasures that command another look. The fruit-based recipes should be made in season, while many others are good choices year-round. When they are traditional to a specific season, I'll note that.

The Midwest is often considered pie country, and I'd agree with that assessment, but when it comes to cakes and confections, we bow to no one.

Grandma Fehribach's Strawberry Custard Pie

I've heard this is the pie with which Frances Hauser stole Albert Fehribach's heart, and they went on to have eleven children and more than seventy grandchildren, in true German Catholic farm-family fashion. I love this pie because it represents a bygone approach to cooking that yields far more delicious results than our modern ways can muster. Considering the Swiss Brown dairy cow whose rich cream Grandma could skim for this pie, it would have been an absolute knockout.

The seasonality of dairy is never discussed anymore, since dairy products are now nearly universally produced by factory farms. Any character they might retain is processed out through prolonged pasteurization and homogenization, until a ruthlessly consistent but bland industrial product results.

Before mass dairy production, and still today on the dwindling number of family farms that keep dairy cows, dairy is as seasonal as anything else. During the late spring and early summer, the cattle are gorging on the rush of fresh growth. Spring rains and increasing daylight hours yield abundant green forage, and the milk shows it. Real spring cream is yellow, from all the beta-carotene and vitamin A in the grass. The cows literally milk what they eat, and the result is decadent, nutritious, and supremely delicious, with a hint of new-mown hay and the fragrance of spring pasture. It perfectly complements the first berries of the year, with their own intoxicating aroma of fresh green hay and red fruit. By winter, the cows are eating silage, or fermented hay, and the cream lightens in color and takes on a funkier, barnyard aroma that's fantastic with other winter flavors such as squashes, apples, and pears.

Here we're concerned with that thick, yellow cream of spring. Grandma knew what she was doing. When the strawberries in the garden were ripe, she had plenty of the year's richest cream to cook with them.

This pie works with any fruit you choose; I'm sharing strawberry because, well, it's strawberries and cream. Blackberries are another great choice. Use an unhomogenized creamline cream from a small local producer if you can find it. Real cream is worth asking around for, but this recipe will still be delicious with store-bought heavy whipping cream. I like to serve this warm with more of that spring cream, chilled and whipped, on the side.

Makes one 10-inch pie

1 prepared 10-inch pie shell, very well chilled

1/3 cup all-purpose flour

1 cup granulated sugar

3 large eggs

1 cup heavy whipping cream

1/2 cup sour cream

1/2 teaspoon kosher salt

4 cups fresh strawberries, quartered lengthwise

1 recipe **CRUMB TOPPING** (p. 265) from **CRANBERRY AND BONE MARROW PUDDING PIE**

Preheat oven to 350°F.

Sift the flour and sugar together. In a separate medium mixing bowl, beat the eggs until smooth, then whisk in the cream, sour cream, and salt. Add the flour mixture while whisking, and combine until a thick, smooth batter is obtained, just 20 to 30 seconds.

Spread the strawberries in the chilled pie shell, and carefully pour the batter over them. Tamp the berries down into the custard gently if necessary. Top with the crumb topping.

Place on the bottom rack of the oven, reduce heat to 325°F, and bake for 50 minutes to 1 hour. The pie is done when the center reaches 165°F. Cool to room temperature before serving or refrigerating. Serve with unsweetened whipped cream.

Sugar Cream Pie

Sugar cream pie has assumed legendary status in my home state, and it is most definitely a local specialty; it's a pie I have seen offered in many cafés and bake shops in Indiana, but seldom elsewhere. Properly made, it's a true delicacy because of its rarity. But, like pepperoni pizza, the magical thing about sugar cream pie is that even a bad one is pretty darn good. Make a good one, and it's astounding that something so ambrosial, so richly perfumed and luxuriously textured, could come out of such a crude roster of ingredients.

At first and second glance, it seems obvious that sugar cream pie is related to the vinegar pies, cider pies, and milk pies of Appalachia and the Pennsylvania Dutch. Many locals attribute the origins of sugar cream pie to the Shaker communities of eastern Indiana, but a true origin story with receipts has been hard to come by. One oft-cited claim is that a recipe shared in *The Hoosier Cookbook* was about 160 years old at the time of printing, dating roughly to the time of Indiana statehood.[3] Some cite 1816 specifically as the origin date on the basis of this recipe, but without any further evidence.[4]

The only problem with this cute legend is that it can't possibly be true. The name "sugar cream pie" doesn't pop up reliably or consistently until the end of the nineteenth century. But there are other serious problems. First, the *Hoosier Cookbook* recipe is written in modern recipe format with modern measurements—a format invented and popularized by the Boston Cooking School in the 1870s and 1880s. Perhaps more troublesome is its call for 2 teaspoons of vanilla, which we can only assume means vanilla extract. For one thing, vanilla was rare and expensive in 1816—the hand-pollination technique that allowed for mass cultivation of vanilla wasn't discovered until 1841 by an enslaved man on Réunion named Albius. Such an expensive ingredient would not have been used in a poverty pie. Furthermore, vanilla extract wasn't even invented until 1847.[5] The date claim in *The Hoosier Cookbook* is made up.

A far more likely scenario has the pie originating in Ohio, where Pennsylvania Dutch and Shaker communities were expanding their settlements during the first half of the nineteenth century. The earliest printed recipe that matches our description of sugar cream pie (an eggless cream pie gelled by wheat flour, with or without additional seasonings) appears in the Ladies' Department of the *Ohio Cultivator* in 1854:

> SUGAR PIE.—Cover your pan with good paste, spread over it a layer of sweet butter, then sugar enough to cover the bottom; then pour in a half pint of rich cream, in which a table spoonful of flour has been first stirred, and it is ready for the oven.[6]

Note the lack of vanilla. It is easy to imagine the pie winding up in Indiana soon thereafter, as the Amish and Shakers continued to settle westward.

The earliest printed recipe I could find in which the pie is otherwise flavored, in a home advice column syndicated out of Chicago, authored by the famed cooking instructor Lida Ames Willis,[7] called for a whopping whole tablespoon of cinnamon (still no vanilla), while a recipe shared in the *Indianapolis Star* in 1907 that includes vanilla, but no spices, is one of the earliest traceable recipes actually printed in Indiana.[8]

None of which is to deter Hoosiers: a true sugar cream pie is a masterpiece, and it is ours to claim. In fact, the Indiana state legislature voted to make it the official state pie in 2009.

This is such an easy recipe, and is best eaten soon after baking when still slightly warm but when the curd has set enough to cut yet retains a little jiggle. Alternatively, refrigerate for easy slicing and reheat slices in a low oven or toaster oven. Use low heat (225°F to 250°F) and heat just until the pie jiggles when tapped. Some serve this with whipped cream; I love it with any ripe fresh fruit.

Makes one 10-inch pie

    1 prepared 10-inch pie shell, very well chilled

    1 cup granulated sugar

    ⅓ cup all-purpose flour

1 teaspoon freshly grated nutmeg

½ teaspoon kosher salt

1 cup heavy whipping cream

1 cup half-and-half

Preheat oven to 350°F.

Sift the sugar, flour, nutmeg, and salt together into a mixing bowl. Add the cream and stir with a rubber spatula just to combine, taking care not to overstir or introduce much air. Stir in the half-and-half in similar fashion. Carefully pour into a well-chilled pie shell, taking care not to splash or slosh. Place on the bottom rack of the oven, shut the door, and reduce heat to 325°F. Bake for about 45 minutes, until the center of the pie is just set. You can tell it is set by tapping the side of the pan. The curd in the center of the pie should jiggle like jelly, rather than ripple like water. Cool to near room temperature before serving, or chill.

Cherry Delight

Lazy summer afternoons meant long-anticipated family reunions, ballgames, cookouts by the lake, and, for the Fehribach family, cherry delight. I don't recall when Mom first made this dainty, but when she did, it was an instant hit, forever after requested by the family for almost any event, especially during the summertime. Mom was happy to oblige because cherry delight was easy to make. In fact, it's little more than an assembly of ready-made industrial food products, making it an elegant metaphor for Midwestern food in general. Cherries are particularly apt in this context, as the modern cherry industry began in earnest during the mid-nineteenth century, and Michigan continues to be the center of the sour cherry industry.[9]

Cherry delight is an interesting study in how old recipes can be transformed into something entirely new as food manufacturers seek ways to sell their products by creating recipes that are easy to understand and execute. No need to make that cake, or whip that cream, or carefully temper the hot milk and eggs to make a pudding. Just buy the product and you're good to go!

We have what seems like a logical start to the current form of this recipe from the *Indianapolis Star* in 1900,[10] in which a pan is lined with sponge cake, then layered with hot custard and stewed cherries, to be thoroughly chilled before eating. Some decades later, we find a recipe in the 1962 Bloomington, Indiana, Evening Belles Home Demonstration Club cookbook, which calls for graham crackers and butter to make the bottom, and cream cheese lightened with whipped cream, topped with one can of Thank You brand cherries.[11] Just a few years later, in nearby Bedford, Indiana, the evolution to processed foods is complete with a concoction based on a layer of graham cracker crumbs and oleo, with layers of cream cheese, Dream Whip, and canned cherry pie filling topped with nuts.[12] This closely matches my mom's recipe. It's easy to assemble and a masterpiece of buttery-toasty whole-grain flavors with the signature crispness, light, fluffy whipped topping with the refreshing tang of cream cheese, and the acidic punch of toothsome pie cherries transcending the topping to dance with the graham cracker crust. Processed food genius. It's still a favorite of mine after all my training and high-end dining adventures.

Naturally, I'm not here to share favorite assemblages of processed food products, but to reverse-engineer this true delight back to something based on real, clean food. I'm not gonna lie, this recipe destroys the processed food version, and it isn't hard to make at all. It's now my summertime signature for the backyard.

Makes one 13-by-9-inch delight

FOR THE HONEY GRAHAM CRUST

2 cups whole wheat flour

6 tablespoons chilled butter, cut into bits

1 teaspoon ground cinnamon

¼ teaspoon salt

3 tablespoons honey

¼ cup milk or buttermilk

Preheat oven to 325°F.

Place the flour, butter, cinnamon, and salt in the food processor and pulse until the butter is incorporated and the mixture resembles a coarse meal. Add the honey and pulse a few times until incorporated. Add the milk a tablespoon at a time and pulse after each addition, just until the mix comes together into a coarse dough. Spread the dough evenly over a 9-by-13-inch casserole and bake until lightly browned and aromatic, about 15 to 20 minutes. Cool completely before filling.

TO ASSEMBLE

2 (8-ounce) packages cream cheese, softened

½ cup plus 2 tablespoons granulated sugar, divided

1 teaspoon pure vanilla extract

2 cups heavy whipping cream

2 quarts fresh sweet cherries, pitted

In a medium mixing bowl, use a hand beater to cream the cream cheese, ½ cup sugar, and vanilla together until fluffy. In a separate bowl, whip the cream and remaining 2 tablespoons sugar to stiff peaks.

Fold ½ of the whipped cream into the cream-cheese mixture and spread evenly over the crust. Spread remaining whipped cream over the top. Arrange pitted cherries in a single layer on top and refrigerate 1 hour or overnight before serving.

Sweet-Potato Pie

Sweet-potato pie, which fits into a category I call "orange pies," encompassing pies made from pumpkins and all the other squashes as well as sweet potatoes, is commonly thought of as a holiday pie. While it suits that role well, cured sweet potatoes can make a delicious pie any time of year. Strangely, although a dead-ringer sweet-potato pie recipe appears in Lettice Bryan's *Kentucky House-wife*,[13] and this pie is commonly mentioned in popular media throughout the late nineteenth and twentieth centuries, even appearing in a German-language cookbook for émigrés,[14] sweet-potato pie is unheard of in our community cookbook literature and doesn't even get represented in *The Joy of Cooking*.[15]

Cultivated mainly in the Southeast,[16] sweet potatoes were a rare and luxurious food in the North until the 1830s.[17] But a recipe appears in the Princeton, Indiana, newspaper in 1853,[18] and sweet-potato pies are winning awards at county fairs by 1869.[19] Still, the popularity of sweet-potato pie doesn't really take off in the Midwest until the early twentieth century, when it is established as part of the soul food canon of urban African Americans.[20] This is the sweet-potato pie most of us would recognize. A key distinction between sweet-potato pie and pumpkin/squash pies is that sweet-potato pie uses only white sugar, versus the white/brown sugar or molasses blend in most squash pies. It also usually has a much more austere spice profile, often relying solely on cinnamon. It's less common than pumpkin pie, but it shouldn't be, with farmers' markets making local sweet potatoes available across the Midwest—and there's a lot we can do with them besides pie, too.

The sweet-potato pie recipe mentioned in the *Princeton Clarion-Ledger* is an old-fashioned sliced-potato pie. Malinda Russell shares a more elaborate and exquisite recipe titled "Sweet Potato Slice Pie" in her *Domestic Cook Book*, which I'm adapting to share here.

Makes one 10-inch pie

1 prepared 10-inch pie shell with extra pastry for top crust, rolled out and
  thoroughly chilled

5 or 6 small sweet potatoes

1 cup granulated sugar

3 tablespoons all-purpose flour

2 teaspoons ground Korintje or Mexican cinnamon

Zest of 1 lemon, finely grated

Zest of ½ orange, finely grated

1 cup heavy whipping cream

¼ cup aged brandy or cognac

½ teaspoon kosher salt

Preheat oven to 350°F.

Bake the sweet potatoes until noticeably softened but still firm and not mushy, about 30 minutes. Allow to cool while preparing the crust.

Peel and slice the potatoes ¼ inch thick. You should have about 5 cups. Sift to-gether the sugar, flour, and cinnamon, then mix in the grated zests. Arrange a layer of sweet-potato slices on the bottom of the pie shell, sprinkle some sugar mixture over, then add another round of sweet potatoes, then sugar, layering until all the sweet potatoes and sugar mixture are used. Shuffle and press the sweet potatoes to settle them into the crust tightly.

Stir the whipping cream, brandy, and salt together and pour over the sweet potatoes. Place the top crust over and crimp carefully. Place on center rack of the oven, reduce heat to 325°F, and bake until sweet potatoes are thoroughly tender throughout, and the center of the pie reads at least 215°F, about 1 hour. Cool to room temperature or chill before slicing.

Coconut Cream Pie

Coconut cream pie might not seem Midwestern, unless you're from Indiana. In the *Café Indiana Cookbook* from 2010, Joanne Raetz Stuttgen, after years of surveying and studying Indiana's rich café culture, declares coconut cream the most popular pie there.[21] There is even a slice of it on the cover. When I was a boy, it was my absolute favorite pie, and also that of my godfather, Lee Gress. So I guess the question might be how a youngster in the southern Indiana woods would have had access to coconut cream pie. It certainly wasn't in my mom's repertoire, but she'd grown up in Texas, Tennessee, and Detroit.

In keeping with its trailblazing nature, *The Kentucky Housewife* contains three recipes for "cocoanut pudding" baked in a pastry shell,[22] but none of them has the telltale meringue or whipped cream topping. Maria Parloa appears to be the first author to call for a meringue topping, in 1872, directing readers to "frost immediately upon taking from the oven, with the whites of two eggs and one cup of sugar beaten to a stiff froth."[23] Aunt Babette would direct her readers to do the same. These days, you see coconut cream pie with either a meringue topping or a whipped cream topping. My favorite is the latter, but the most frugal (and common) method is to use the yolks of the eggs for the custard and the whites to top the pie. A proper coconut pie is always topped with a light dusting of toasted coconut.

Why is coconut cream pie so popular in Indiana? Maybe give it a try and find out.

Makes one 10-inch pie

> 1 prepared 10-inch pie shell, baked golden brown (can be baked up to 1 day in advance)
> 6 eggs, separated
> 1 large egg
> ¼ cup plus 1 tablespoon cornstarch
> 1½ cups sugar, divided
> 2½ cups whole milk
> 3 teaspoons vanilla extract, divided
> 2 tablespoons añejo rum
> ½ teaspoon kosher salt
> 1 cup plus 2 tablespoons shredded unsweetened coconut, divided
> 3 tablespoons unsalted butter, cut into small bits
> ½ teaspoon cream of tartar

Preheat oven to 350°F.

In a stainless-steel mixing bowl, whisk the 6 egg yolks, whole egg, cornstarch, and ½ cup sugar together until combined well and any lumps are worked out. In a small saucepan, heat the milk with ½ cup sugar, 2 teaspoons of vanilla, the rum, the salt, and 1 cup of the coconut. Just at the boil, pour the milk mixture into the egg-yolk mixture in a thin, steady stream, whisking constantly. Return the combined mix to the saucepan and bring to a boil over medium heat, stirring constantly with a wooden spoon or stiff rubber spatula. Boil for 15 seconds, remove from heat, and melt in the butter, stirring until thoroughly incorporated. Pour the boiled custard into the pie shell and smooth the top.

Beat the egg whites until soft peaks form, then sprinkle in the last ½ cup of sugar and beat to stiff peaks. Beat in the last teaspoon of vanilla and the cream of tartar during the last minute. Spread over warm custard and shape as you like, then sprinkle the last 2 tablespoons of coconut on top. Bake in the oven until lightly browned, about 10 to 12 minutes. Cool thoroughly before serving, and refrigerate any leftovers.

Persimmon Pudding

Proudly claimed by Hoosiers, especially in the southern part of the state, where the town of Mitchell has held an annual persimmon festival since 1947, persimmon pudding is one of the signature dishes of Indiana's country cooking. The tradition is shared by up-country North Carolina, where persimmon pudding probably originated.

Professor J. Troop of the Indiana Experiment Station stated in the *Richmond Item* of February 23, 1897, "There are few people who are not fond of sweet, well-ripened persimmons; they are good eaten out of hand, better with cream and sugar, but best of all when made into one of those good old North Carolina persimmon puddings."[24] The Hoosier was speaking some truth. Persimmon pudding starts popping up in county fair entries in North Carolina[25] decades before such mentions in Indiana. None of which makes the puddings made from our wild persimmons any less Midwestern; they've been part of our culinary lexicon for well over a century.

The wild American persimmon is a sorely underappreciated fruit, not for want of late nineteenth-century attempts to improve it as a crop.[26] The Midwest's wild persimmons aren't difficult to cultivate, and they store well without processing, but they are small, riddled with seeds, and have a thick skin and woody stem that must be dealt with. These properties have caused them to languish as a commercial crop.

In the wild, persimmon trees are absolutely spectacular. They are small and prefer woodland borders, meadows, or clearings. Their bright orange fruits linger even as the leaves of trees all around fall in autumn, dangling like ornaments of the angels on the black, skeletal branches. It's an enchanting sight on a bright fall morning or a positively ghoulish one at dusk, in the rusty light of sunset.

The pips and seeds can be easily removed by passing the fruits through a food mill, but many small producers sell frozen persimmon pulp locally and online. The fruit has a delightful light pulpy texture, not unlike a fruit smoothie, and a flavor that's hard to describe other than as "the woods during fall." Delightfully sweet with genteel aromas of spicebox and autumn leaves, persimmons make excellent ice cream, smoothies, mousses, and custards, but of course the famous traditional persimmon dessert is pudding. I like to go easy on the spices and eschew the heavy molasses flavor a lot of folks use in favor of letting the fruit's subtle brightness shine through.

Makes one 13-by-9-inch pudding

FOR THE CRUST

2 cups all-purpose flour

½ cup granulated sugar

½ cup (1 stick) salted butter, cut into ½-inch pats and softened to room
temperature

Preheat oven to 325°F.

Put the flour and sugar in the food processor with the S blade. Add the butter and pulse until the mixture forms a coarse dough, about 1 minute. Press into a greased 9-by-13-inch casserole pan and bake for 15 minutes. It won't be fully browned but will resemble a soft sheet cookie. Remove and cool while you make the filling.

FOR THE FILLING

1 cup granulated sugar

1 cup all-purpose flour

2 teaspoons baking powder

1 teaspoon kosher salt

1 teaspoon ground Mexican or Korintje cinnamon

1 teaspoon ground coriander

4 large eggs

Zest of ½ orange, grated

1 cup half-and-half

4 cups persimmon pulp

½ cup (1 stick) unsalted butter, melted

Preheat oven to 325°F.

Sift the sugar, flour, baking powder, salt, cinnamon, and coriander together twice. In a separate mixing bowl, beat the eggs well until smooth. Whisk in the orange zest, the half-and-half, and the persimmon pulp, combining well after each addition. Pour half of this wet mixture into the dry, stir until smooth, then stir in the remaining wet mixture. Finally, stir in the butter. Place on the bottom rack of the oven and bake for 1 hour. The pudding should be puffy and set in the center but will deflate as it cools. This is best eaten warm out of the oven (cooled for 45 minutes or so) with vanilla ice cream or whipped cream.

Pawpaw Chiffon Pie

After extolling the virtues of our native wild persimmons, I would be remiss to exclude our pawpaws, the largest true fruit native to the United States,[27] and a gem we need to stop overlooking. They do appear to be popping up more frequently at farmers' markets in Chicago, but perhaps the biggest obstacle to the fruit's popularity is its painfully short season of just a couple of weeks. Like the persimmon, however, the fruit does store well as frozen pulp, is versatile, and is wickedly delicious, so fragrant that it will shine righteously alongside any tropical fruit.

When ripe, the pawpaw is a beguiling fruit, with the texture of custard and aromas and flavors of banana, mango, strawberry, and forest floor, all rolled into something that fits in the palm of your hand. An 1831 guide for emigrants to Illinois, Missouri, and surrounding areas thought the fruit worth mentioning: "It is the favored region of the apple, the pear, and the peach tree. The persimmon is found throughout, and the pawpaw with its luscious fruit, is found in the southern part of this climate."[28] Of those fruits, the pawpaw is easily the most luscious while admittedly the hardest to obtain, but it's worth haunting your farmers' market during the last weeks of summer and first weeks of fall. In my experience, pawpaws peak right before the leaves begin changing colors. If a forager misses the mark, they'll be snapped up by all sorts of woodland critters. My dad, an experienced woodsman, always knew where and when to find them, and he showed me how to look when we would hunt for squirrels. We could reliably beat the critters to the fruit soon after the autumnal equinox, but climate change may have shifted that somewhat.

As much fun as tracking down your own pawpaws is, an increasing number of small shops are offering the cleanly processed and frozen pulp online. That makes it easy to get, and even easier to make this pie. Since pawpaws are so rich and fragrant in their raw form, I like to serve them in mousses, ice creams, panna cottas, and also chiffon, where we can lighten them and make the fragrance sing. They change color to brown under extensive cooking, so I'd caution against baking them. Quick, easy treatments that don't expose them to a lot of heat allow their complex flavors and aromas to shine. Try this pie—you'll be glad you did.

Makes one 10-inch pie or tart

FOR THE CRUST

14 graham crackers

2 tablespoons honey

½ teaspoon kosher salt

6 tablespoons unsalted butter, cut into ½-inch pats and softened

Preheat oven to 325°F.

Break up crackers into food processor bowl, then pulse until they are pulverized into a coarse meal. Add the honey, salt, and butter. Pulse until the butter is incorporated and a small amount of the mixture pressed between your fingers holds its shape. Press firmly into a 10-inch ungreased pie pan. Chill thoroughly before baking. Bake on the center rack of the oven until just browning and fragrant, about 20 minutes. Cool thoroughly before using. May be made ahead and stored in the pantry wrapped in plastic wrap for a day or two.

FOR THE FILLING

1 envelope Knox unflavored gelatin

1 cup sugar, divided

½ teaspoon kosher salt

1 cup whole milk

2 teaspoons pure vanilla extract

4 eggs, separated

2 cups pawpaw pulp, refrigerated

Put the gelatin, ¾ cup of the sugar, and the salt in a saucepan, mix, and add the milk, vanilla, and egg yolks, whisking to incorporate the yolks. Cook over medium heat, stirring constantly with a sturdy rubber spatula to prevent scorching, until the mixture thickens noticeably and coats the spatula well, 185°F on a food thermometer. Do not boil. Remove from heat, transfer to a large mixing bowl, and cool to lukewarm, 100°F to 110°F, before proceeding, about 20 minutes.

Stir in the pawpaw pulp. Whip the egg whites to soft peaks, add the remaining ¼ cup sugar, and continue whipping to just shy of stiff peaks. Fold the egg whites into the gelatin and pawpaw mixture in thirds, working out any pockets of unmixed egg white. Pour into the prepared graham cracker shell, and place in the refrigerator while you prepare the whipped topping.

FOR THE WHIPPED TOPPING

1 cup cream cheese
½ cup granulated sugar
3 cups heavy whipping cream
2 tablespoons brandy

Beat the cream cheese together with the sugar until light and fluffy. Add the heavy cream a little at a time, whipping constantly, until the cream cheese is fully incorporated into the cream without lumps, then add the remainder of the cream, and the brandy. Whip like whipped cream. Spread carefully with an icing knife, or use a piping bag to plant kisses over the entire pie. Refrigerate for at least 6 hours or overnight before serving. Will keep up to 1 week.

Cranberry and Bone Marrow Pudding Pie

Some years ago, inspired by a bone marrow custard pie recipe I found in an old Appalachian cookbook, I thought of combining the rich barnyard flavor of bone marrow with fruits in custard. The first attempt was with blackberries, and the results were astonishing. I then tried it with rhubarb in the spring, going after even more tart flavor to waltz with the marrow. Finally, without much optimism, I put cranberry and bone marrow pudding pie on a Christmas Eve Réveillon menu at my restaurant. To my great surprise, it was the hit of the evening, even outpacing the requisite bread pudding, and it has ever since been a staple of our Christmas Eve dinners.

Cranberries, of course, are not remotely Southern, as their presence at my restaurant might suggest; they stick to northern climes and bog ecosystems where a constant supply of decaying wood and effluent creates the acidic soil they require. They were an important food in early trade in Michigan,[29] where they are now a popular commercial crop.

Midwesterners haven't exactly done right by cranberries, one of our native fruits and one of the most versatile. They've been mostly relegated to kitschy holiday recipes and, in their dried form, to salads and granolas, in spite of their complex aromatics and bracing acidity, which allow them to pair with foods of all kinds. I share this recipe as one that is as earthy as a well-tilled Midwestern farm, yet elegant enough to serve at a buttoned-up dinner.

You can source marrow bones from any reliable butcher. Ask for canoe-cut marrow bones; this cut makes it much easier to scrape the marrow from the bones after giving them a short trip through the oven.

Makes one 10-inch pie

FOR THE CRUMB TOPPING

¼ cup (½ stick) unsalted butter, softened to room temperature

½ cup all-purpose flour

½ cup granulated sugar

½ teaspoon ground coriander

⅛ teaspoon kosher salt

Mix all ingredients in a small bowl, rubbing the flour and butter between the palms of your hands and fingers. Combine thoroughly, until no greasy spots remain and the mixture clumps easily when pressed together in your hands. Crumble onto a plate in a single layer. The average clump should be about the size of a marble, with some pea sized, some larger. Cover with plastic wrap or a clean towel and refrigerate until needed.

TO PREPARE THE BONE MARROW

8 to 10 canoe-cut marrow bones, about 4 to 6 inches long

Preheat oven to 425°F.

Place the marrow bones, cut side up, on a baking sheet with drip-proof sides, and place on the top rack of the oven. Roast for 6 to 8 minutes, until the edges of the marrow are cooking and loosening up from the bone, but the center of the marrow is still raw, solid, and uncooked. Remove from the oven and, using a clean towel to hold the hot bones, scrape the marrow onto a clean plate in a single layer. Cover with plastic wrap or a clean towel and refrigerate until needed.

TO PREPARE THE PIE

One prepared 10-inch pie or tart shell, very well chilled

3 cups fresh cranberries

1 cup granulated sugar

¼ cup plus 2 tablespoons all-purpose flour

½ teaspoon kosher salt

3 large eggs

¾ cup heavy whipping cream

Preheat oven to 375°F.

Evenly spread the cranberries in the prepared pie shell. Coarsely chop the chilled bone marrow and evenly disperse among the cranberries. In a mixing bowl, whisk together the sugar, flour, and salt, then add the eggs, beating well. Beat in the heavy cream a little at a time to form a smooth, thick batter. Pour over the cranberries and marrow, draping the batter evenly over the entire pie. Evenly sprinkle the crumb topping over the pie. Place it in the center rack of the oven and turn heat down to 325°F.

Bake for about 50 minutes, until the custard is set in the center, with a springy structure when touched. Cool and serve at room temperature with cold whipped cream.

Mince Pie

If I have felt one great, sorrowful loss in the evolution of Midwestern foodways, it is undoubtedly mince pie. Just a few years ago I would never have imagined saying that, having tried an example in my youth and deeming it offensive. At the Saint Mary's Church turkey shoot, I approached the dessert table with some of my paper-route money, looking to slay a sweet tooth. Seeing the dark, brooding filling of one of the pies, I asked the church lady what it was, and she replied, "Mince meat pie." I was naturally like, "You mean, like, *with meat?*" She replied that it was her favorite and gave me a forkful to taste. The smell was slightly reminiscent of pumpkin pie, so I bit. I was bowled over by a potent alcohol burn and a headful of spices that would take a liter of Sprite to simmer down. It was just so intensely rich, too much for my young blood.

Fast-forward a few decades, and the *Chicago Reader* featured a madly brilliant piece on its December 17, 2009, front page, titled "The Real American Pie," by Cliff Doerksen. It recounted the unbelievable history of mince pie in the United States. The article, which would later win a James Beard Foundation award for distinguished food writing, culminates in Doerksen making a mince pie and eating it. I had to do this myself. What was I, and America, missing, and why did mince pie disappear? Doerksen answers these questions as least partially:

Mince pie achieved and maintained its hegemony despite the fact that everyone—including those who loved it—agreed that it reliably caused indigestion, provoked nightmares, and commonly afflicted the overindulgent with disordered thinking, hallucinations, and sometimes death.[30]

Convinced that the anti-mince caterwauling was the type of sensationalized writing American media was known for at the time, I set out, as a responsible adult, to try a proper mince pie. It would take some years and quite a bit of research before I settled on "A Very Good Mince" from *The Kentucky Housewife*. Amazingly, Lettice Bryan provides not one, not two, or even three, but five recipes for mince,[31] clearly signifying its importance. When I made the mince and baked it in lard-based pastry, I was so gobsmacked that I would later prepare the same recipe when I had the chance to cook dinner at the James Beard House in New York. It had all those effects that had alarmed my young self, but as an adult, I found that the combination of alcohol, intense spices, and ridiculously unctuous texture yielded by curing suet, meats, and fruits together in alcohol and then baking them in pastry was quite unlike anything I had experienced before, and something I hope everyone gets to experience.

When they arrived from Great Britain, mincemeat pies were small, but they expanded to the larger pie-pan form in America. As early as the sixteenth century, they were associated with Christmas,[32] and the flavors certainly ring true, as does the seasonality of putting up meats and apples, as the mince would be ready to use for the holidays. This recipe I've adapted from *The Kentucky Housewife* is far more elaborate than later simplified versions. Even if it's only a once-in-a-lifetime pursuit, this mince pie is worthy of your bucket list.

"A VERY GOOD MINCE"

Makes mince for 3 or 4 pies

½ pound beef heart

½ pound lean veal

1 pound suet, chopped down to the size of peas

1 pound golden raisins

1 pound Granny Smith apples, cut into ¼-inch dice

½ pound dried currants

Zest and juice of 1 orange

Zest and juice of 1 lemon

2 cups dark brown sugar

1 teaspoon ground nutmeg

½ teaspoon ground mace

2 teaspoons ground cinnamon

1 teaspoon ground cloves

2 cups dry Madeira

1 cup fine brandy

2 teaspoons kosher salt

Brandy and granulated sugar, as needed

Boil the beef heart and veal in lightly salted water until quite tender, up to 2 hours. Cool and chop fine. Place all ingredients in a large mixing bowl. Toss to coat all with the liquor and fruit juices and dissolve the sugar. Transfer to a 1-gallon jar or bucket, tamp the dry ingredients down, then add just enough brandy to cover all. Sprinkle over sufficient granulated sugar to soak up the brandy and form a crust over the top. Cover with a tight-fitting piece of waxed paper, place an airtight lid on the container, and refrigerate for at least 2 weeks; 4 weeks is recommended. This mince will keep in the refrigerator indefinitely, but to be at its best, it should be used within a month or two after it's ready. Each time you use some, replace the top with brandy, sugar, and waxed paper as before.

TO MAKE A MINCE PIE

Makes one 10-inch pie

1 prepared 10-inch pie shell with extra pastry for top crust, rolled out and thoroughly chilled

4 to 5 cups **"VERY GOOD MINCE"** (above), with a proportional amount of the mince liquor juices

¾ cup sliced almonds

Dry white wine, if needed

Preheat oven to 375°F.

Put the mince in a mixing bowl and add the almonds, stirring to disperse them evenly but being careful not to break them. Add sufficient white wine, if necessary, to make the mince very moist; it should look and feel waterlogged, but not at all soupy. Transfer to the pie shell, place the top crust, and crimp well. Decorate as you will. Place in the center rack of the oven, reduce heat to 325°F, and cook for 50 minutes to 1 hour. The center of the pie should be at least 210°F. Best served warm with whipped cream or ice cream, it also makes a great breakfast.

Rhubarb Charlotte

Charlotte, trifle, icebox cake . . . this popular group of overlapping and often loosely defined layered refrigerator desserts is perfect for summertime, as they are generally best served chilled. The most famous of these is the charlotte russe, whose definition has long seemed malleable, but Lettice Bryan gives us an excellent example in *The Kentucky Housewife*, with slices of gingerbread, macaroons, and sponge cake neatly arranged as a decorative dome for an interior of strawberries in sweet custard.[33] Two more charlotte examples over the succeeding century provide a view into how varied the approach can be. Mrs. Gov. Osborn of Kansas shares a recipe calling simply for sponge cake slices arranged in a dish and filled with vanilla custard set with gelatin,[34] and the *Indiana Farmer's Guide Cookbook* shares a recipe for rhubarb charlotte that includes only buttered breadcrumbs layered with rhubarb, then baked.[35] That last one does sound delicious, but I say boo for calling it a charlotte.

A key factor defining a charlotte is the layering of ingredients, and most Midwestern charlotte recipes do involve either cake or ladyfingers and some type of sweet custard or mousse with some type of flavoring, which is often fruit. In *The Joy of Cooking*, Irma Rombauer declares, "Whether the mold is lined with ladyfingers, sponge or Genoise, it may still be called a Charlotte."[36] The fanciest versions, such as Lettice Bryan's, are elaborate multi-cake and cookie and filling affairs intended to be unmolded, revealing a cake or cookie dome in a showstopping presentation. More commonly, they are made in glass-bottomed trifle bowls for panache.

I'm going to share an easy, low-pressure spring version that you can make and enjoy without breaking a sweat. Rather than rhubarb, you can make this with strawberries, peaches, cherries, or any other fruit you favor.

Makes 1 large punchbowl-sized charlotte

FOR THE SPONGE CAKE

2½ cups all-purpose flour

1 teaspoon salt

1 teaspoon baking powder

½ teaspoon baking soda

1 cup (2 sticks) unsalted butter, at room temperature

1 cup granulated sugar

3 large eggs, at room temperature

2 teaspoons vanilla extract

1¼ cups buttermilk, at room temperature

Preheat oven to 325°F.

Butter a 10-inch cake pan and flour it well.

Sift together the flour, salt, baking powder, and baking soda, and reserve.

In a mixing bowl with an electric beater, cream the butter and sugar together until well combined and fluffy. Beat in the eggs one at a time, whipping until smooth after each. Beat in the vanilla extract. Using a rubber spatula, fold in ⅓ of the flour mixture, then ⅓ of the buttermilk, and repeat, alternating in thirds until all ingredients are incorporated. Turn out batter into the prepared pan and bake on the center rack of the oven until it passes to toothpick test, about 35 to 40 minutes. Cool on a wire rack.

TO MAKE THE CHARLOTTE

1 bunch rhubarb, about 1 pound

1 cup honey (clover is best), divided

2 pinches salt, divided

1 quart heavy whipping cream

Fresh mint leaves, for garnish

Wash and thinly slice the rhubarb and place in a medium saucepan with ¾ cup honey and a pinch of salt. Gradually bring to a boil and cook to reduce and thicken until it resembles a loose jam, about 30 minutes. Chill thoroughly.

Whip the cream with the remaining ¼ cup honey and pinch of salt until it forms soft peaks. Divide the cream in half. Gently fold 1 cup of the chilled rhubarb mixture into one of the halves.

Tear the cake up into coarse pieces averaging about 1 inch—or a nice bite size. Arrange the cake evenly in a large glass punchbowl or trifle dish. Gently sprinkle the rhubarb over, followed by the rhubarb whipped cream, followed by the plain whipped cream. If you're feeling playful, you can divide into even more layers. Top with fresh mint leaves to taste. Chill for 1 hour or overnight before serving.

Angel Food Cake

Such a heavenly name and such a heavenly cake, angel food was perhaps the last great cake to emerge in American baking before the widespread introduction of baking powder changed the art forever. Using only a few ingredients, and only the whites of the eggs, it is the very definition of elegance. It responds well to all manner of light icings or glazes and can be served with a wide range of sauces. My personal favorite is to glaze the cake with a light royal icing and serve it with the best fresh fruit of the moment.

Many food historians suggest that angel food cake was the invention of the Pennsylvania Dutch, but as we often see in such cases, that is more lore than history. It is speculated that frugal Pennsylvania Dutch cooks didn't want to waste egg whites left over from the making of noodles and thus invented the cake.[37] But it is just as likely (or perhaps more so) that a trained cookbook author and housekeeping guru was interested in demonstrating to her followers a great use for leftover egg whites. The most famous early recipe for angel food cake appears as "Angel Cake" in Mary Johnson Bailey Lincoln's influential *Boston Cook Book* from 1884,[38] though the earliest printed recipe for angel cake appears in *The Original Appledore Cook Book*, also out of Boston, in 1872.[39] Maria Parloa's *Appledore* recipe is also the first to specify pastry flour, a key ingredient when you want a cake with a refined and soft crumb.

Successful angel food cake baking got a huge boost in 1894, when the Igleheart Brothers mill in Evansville, Indiana, introduced Swans Down cake flour, now a bulwark for bakers who eschew cake mixes. Its promotional recipe booklet, titled *Cake Secrets*, sports angel food cake as its very first recipe, followed by Lady Baltimore, devil's food, jam cakes, and many others, including sugar pretzel and anise pretzel recipes,[40] which as sweet pretzel recipes might be considered unicorns in the United States.

When I was a kid, at any social event that involved a potluck and bakers bringing desserts, a perfect angel food cake was considered the holy grail, because it's a tricky beast. Using a nonstick angel food cake pan will greatly increase your chances of success. Beyond that, after reading dozens of recipes and testing several, I've got you covered with this one.

Makes 1 10-inch angel food cake

    1¼ cups Swans Down cake flour

    1½ cups granulated sugar

    ½ teaspoon fine sea salt

    1½ cups egg whites, completely free of traces of yolk or shell

    1 teaspoon cream of tartar

    1 teaspoon almond extract

    ½ teaspoon lemon extract

Do not preheat oven.

Sift the cake flour before measuring, then do the same with the sugar. Sift the cake flour, sugar, and salt together 5 times.

Beat the egg whites to soft peaks, then beat in the cream of tartar and continue beating to stiff peaks, beating in the almond and lemon extracts at the end. Sift the flour and sugar mixture into the egg whites ⅓ at a time, folding in gently with a rubber spatula until combined before each new addition. The egg whites will lose some volume during mixing, but be careful not to overmix and deflate the egg whites too much. Gently spoon the batter into an ungreased, parchment-lined 10-inch angel food cake pan and place on the center rack of the oven.

Turn the oven on and set to 325°F. Bake the cake without opening the oven door for 50 minutes. Then take a look at the cake by cracking the oven door; it should be nearly finished. Check it every 5 minutes until it is golden brown and set in the center. Do not use the toothpick test; simply tap the center of the cake. If it is springy, it is done; if it is soft and gooey, check back in 5 minutes.

When done, invert the cake, in the pan, on a wire cooling rack, but do not remove the cake or try to drop it out—let it cool completely in the pan. Once it's cooled to room temperature, use a dull knife to loosen the sides and remove the cake. It is now ready to glaze with royal icing or serve un-iced with your favorite dessert sauce or fresh fruit.

Devil's Food Cake

With angel food cake's exploding popularity during the last half of the nineteenth century, one would expect the devil himself to answer, and sure enough, a chocolate cake on steroids followed in just a few years. Chocolate cake was still a brand-new concept in the United States at the time, and the moment seemed perfect for a supercharged extra-chocolatey cake to take the Midwest, and the whole country, by storm.

Chocolate came late to the United States in the Columbian exchange. The first chocolate processor opened in Boston in 1780,[41] and Baker's Chocolate (named for founder Dr. James Baker) continues to produce culinary chocolate products today. Our early keystone cookbooks such as *The Virginia Housewife* and *The Kentucky Housewife* are bereft of chocolate receipts, and as late as 1856, even ambitious cookbooks such as *Widdifield's* treated chocolate solely as a beverage.[42]

The earliest chocolate cake recipe we have is for a sponge cake–like confection, *Ein Chocoladekuchen*, in the German-language *Die Hausmutter*, published in Leipzig in 1791, wherein author Christian Friedrich Germershausen advises that it is "one of the most expensive cakes" and admonishes the reader,

> You always have a guest with this cake. Food of the first rank, especially for certain sick people who have suffered a great loss of strength and who need a little strengthening of their vitality to recover.[43]

Medical science has come a long way since the eighteenth century, but who among us has never at least wished the doctor would just once prescribe a little (or a lot of) chocolate cake when we're feeling down?

We see multiple chocolate cake recipes published in Vienna during 1834,[44] yet it would still be a few decades before chocolate cake appeared stateside. America's first widely distributed printed recipe for chocolate cake was by S. Annie Frost in *The Godey's Lady's Book Receipts and Household Hints* (1870), for something called a chocolate drop cake, in which grated chocolate is folded into whipped egg whites and baked gently.[45] It was followed soon after by a receipt more closely resembling a classic chocolate sponge cake, by the highly influential Maria Parloa in the 1872 printing of *The Original Appledore Cook Book*, which called for Boston's own Baker's chocolate.[46] Remarkably, it appears to be a Mrs. L. A. Lewis of New Madrid, Missouri, who first called devil's food by its name, with "Black Chocolate or Devil's Food Cake," in the town weekly's recipe-sharing column in 1890.[47]

Recipes for devil's food cake vary wildly from baker to baker, but there is an unspoken standard of intense chocolate flavor. The following recipe uses an obscene amount of cocoa powder spiked with coffee and rum to obtain a chocolate flavor I've rarely experienced in cake; when we make this at my restaurant people are always bowled over. While in the pie versus cake battle I'm a pie guy, this is definitely a cake I'd switch teams for.

Makes one 9-inch three-layer cake

FOR THE CAKE

3 cups all-purpose flour

1 teaspoon kosher salt

1 teaspoon baking soda

½ teaspoon baking powder

1 cup plus 2 tablespoons cocoa powder

1 cup (2 sticks) butter, softened

3 cups granulated sugar

3 large eggs

½ cup vegetable oil

1½ cups whole milk

1 cup strong coffee, hot

½ cup añejo rum

1 tablespoon pure vanilla extract

Preheat oven to 325°F. Place a pie or casserole pan filled with water on the bottom of the oven, beneath the bottom rack.

Sift together the flour, salt, baking soda and powder, and cocoa powder, and set aside.

Cream butter and sugar together until smooth, then add the eggs one at a time, beating constantly and incorporating each egg thoroughly before adding the next. The mixture should become very fluffy and smooth. Continue beating while adding the vegetable oil in a thin, steady stream. The mixture will begin to take on the consistency of mayonnaise. Separately, combine the milk, coffee, rum, and vanilla. Add ⅓ of the flour mixture to the egg mixture and stir in gently until smooth, then add ⅓ of the milk mixture. Repeat, alternating in thirds until all ingredients are incorporated and you have a moderately loose, smooth batter.

Transfer batter to three buttered and floured 9-inch cake pans. Bake on the center rack of the oven until set, 25 to 30 minutes, when the cakes pass the toothpick test. Cool in pans on wire racks before turning the cakes out. Wrap in plastic wrap and re-frigerate or freeze before frosting. Pro tip: Freezing the cakes and icing them while very cold makes icing them much easier.

FOR THE FROSTING

2 cups milk

½ cup all-purpose flour

½ cup cocoa powder

½ pound bittersweet chocolate, about 70% cacao, cut into small bits

1 pound unsalted butter, cut into ½-inch pats and softened

2 cups sugar

1 tablespoon pure vanilla extract

In a small saucepan, whisk together the milk, flour, and cocoa powder, then bring to a boil, whisking constantly. Boil for 15 seconds. The mixture will be thick and pasty. Remove from heat and whisk in the chocolate until melted evenly. Chill mixture thoroughly. Cream the butter, sugar, and vanilla together until pale lemon colored. Adding

¹⁄₃ at a time, beat in the boiled milk mixture and continue beating until light, smooth, and fluffy, about 6 to 8 minutes. Use right away to frost well-chilled or frozen cakes.

Banana Caramel Cake

Caramel cake is one of the ultimate comfort food desserts. Like chocolate cake and angel food cake, it's a relative newcomer. The explosion of new cake recipes in the last half of the nineteenth century was probably due to the adoption of gas ranges and baking powder during that time, which gave cooks much better control over baking temperatures and leavening, respectively. Cakes could be more delicate and push boundaries of technique that were insurmountable when working with solid-fuel ranges and yeast or aerated egg leavening.

Commonly associated with soul food, and for good reason, caramel cake pops up in Midwestern culinary literature regularly beginning in the 1870s. The first printed recipe appears in 1872's *Common Sense in the Household* by Marion Harland,[48] a Southern-born writer working in New Jersey and New York. The book would go on to sell more than a hundred thousand copies,[49] cementing Harland's influence in American kitchens. A few years later, the cake pops up in the second edition of *Buckeye Cookery and Practical Housekeeping*, published in central Ohio in 1877, which appears to be the oldest surviving community cookbook.[50] The recipe was submitted by Mrs. George Bever. Aunt Babette offers up two versions in the first edition of *Aunt Babette's Cook Book*.[51] By the 1880s, the cake appears in cookbooks with increasing frequency, and by the 1890s, it is standard. Its rise to popularity may have been even faster than that of angel food or devil's food.

Most caramel cake recipes are for either a straightforward yellow cake or one made with brown sugar instead of white sugar and glazed with a caramel icing, but I'm interested in a variation mentioned by Nelson Algren—the burnt sugar cake. This recipe has the same base of yellow cake, but infused with caramel syrup made on the stovetop. The syrup imparts a much more complex aroma than brown sugar can alone and adds even more moisture to the cake. There seem to be as many recipes for caramel cake icing as there are food writers, but by channeling the Mexican kitchen, we can make a superior icing of dulce de leche. In dulce de leche, proteins from milk are added to the caramelization process, and the sugars can interact with these proteins and contribute to Maillard browning reactions, producing a larger range of aromas and a more complex flavor than caramelized sugar alone.[52]

Makes one 9-inch three-layer cake

FOR THE CARAMEL SYRUP

  1½ cups granulated sugar
  1¼ cups water, divided

Place the sugar in a small, heavy-bottomed saucepan and wet with ½ cup water. Beginning over low heat and gradually increasing it as the sugar dissolves, bring to a boil and cook over medium-high heat, not stirring, until the sugar begins to change color, 8 minutes or so. When the color begins to change, monitor very closely—don't walk away, it will burn fast! Swirling the pan gently to help it brown evenly, caramelize to a rich, deep golden color, 3 to 4 minutes, but stop shy of dark brown. Remove from heat and allow to cool for 10 minutes uncovered. Then, being very careful of splatter (stand back), add the remaining water and stir. Return to the heat and boil until the syrup is completely smooth and all chunks of caramel are dissolved. Cool completely to room temperature.

FOR THE CAKE

  5 cups cake or pastry flour, sifted before measuring
  1 teaspoon kosher salt
  1 teaspoon baking powder
  ¾ teaspoon baking soda
  ¼ teaspoon ground cloves
  1½ cups (3 sticks) unsalted butter, softened
  2 cups granulated sugar
  8 large egg yolks (save and freeze your whites to make ANGEL FOOD CAKE, p. 270),
     at room temperature
  6 large eggs, at room temperature
  2 cups very ripe banana, mashed
  ½ cup vegetable oil
  1½ cups low-fat buttermilk
  1¼ cups CARAMEL SYRUP (above)
  1 tablespoon vanilla extract

Preheat oven to 325°F.

Butter and flour three 9-inch cake pans, and line the bottoms with parchment paper. Sift the pastry flour with the salt, baking powder, baking soda, and cloves, and reserve.

Cream the butter and sugar together until fluffy and pale lemon colored. Add the egg yolks and then the eggs, one at a time, beating thoroughly between each addition to combine. Continue beating 3 to 5 minutes until batter is fluffy and beginning to take on the consistency of mayonnaise. Beat in the banana and vegetable oil thoroughly. Combine the buttermilk, caramel syrup, and vanilla in a separate pitcher. Fold ⅓ of the flour into the egg mixture, then ⅓ of the buttermilk mixture, and repeat, alternating in thirds until all ingredients are incorporated and you have a thick, lump-free batter. Divide among the three prepared cake pans and bake until the cakes pass the toothpick test, about 30 minutes. Rotate the pans halfway through baking for even browning. Cool for 10 minutes in the pan and turn out onto wire racks while still warm. Cool completely before icing.

FOR THE ICING

¾ cup (1½ sticks) unsalted butter, cut into ½-inch pats

2 (12-ounce) cans evaporated milk

2 cups granulated sugar

Any remaining caramel syrup from the cake

1 tablespoon pure vanilla extract

1 teaspoon kosher salt

Put the butter, milk, sugar, and syrup in a large, heavy-bottomed saucepan with high sides and bring to a boil, stirring regularly. Reduce heat to a low boil and reduce and caramelize over 1 to 2 hours (this will be closer to 2 hours than 1), stirring regularly and monitoring to prevent scorching (stir from the bottom of the pot with a heat-resistant rubber spatula, scraping the bottom to prevent buildup). Whisk periodically to keep the mixture smooth. The mixture will darken and thicken, and may curdle somewhat (which is ok, you can puree it in the food processor later to smooth it out). Cook until it is a rich, deep caramel color and heavily coats a spoon. Add the vanilla and salt when you remove it from the heat.

Cool the icing in the pan for about 10 minutes, and give it a spin in the food processor if needed to smooth it out, with a towel draped over the lid to protect you from any splatter. When too hot for your finger but not burning hot (about 130°F to 140°F), it's ready to ice your cake. Working quickly, spread each layer separately before stacking. Let the icing on the layers come close to setting, about 5 to 7 minutes, then stack up your layers. Pour the remaining icing over the top of the cake, allowing it to drape and drip around the sides. Enjoy after allowing the icing to cure for a few hours, or refrigerate, loosely wrapped in plastic, for up to 1 week.

Grandmother Hazel Spence's Black Walnut Spice Cake

Most people are so intimidated by chefs that we chefs consider it a rare blessing when someone cooks for us or shares a favorite recipe. Naturally, when Marty Travis of Spence Farm and Down at the Farms mentioned he'd like to share his grandma's spice cake recipe, I was thrilled.

For folks of a certain age who grew up in the Midwest, spice cake could be considered a metaphor for community life; its presence confirmed our own common bonds. Almost always a sheet cake with toothache-sweet white icing, it was everywhere people gathered: the dessert table at the turkey shoot, the cake table at the church supper, the Rotary Club bake sale, the county fair cake competitions. . . . Unlike the many varieties of chocolate cake or carrot cake or angel food cake, spice cake wasn't really talked about much, and certainly not in the same covetous manner. It was safe to assume that people loved spice cake because of its omnipresence. I, for one, am a huge fan.

Spice cake is in almost every old Midwestern cookbook; it might be considered our signature regional cake. Adding black walnuts to it is such a simple yet masterful stroke, I'm kinda jealous it never occurred to me. With the country's premier black walnut purveyor, Hammon's, based in Stockton, Missouri, and with my childhood having been spent in the woods foraging them, I consider black walnuts to be one of the most Midwestern of foods. Try this recipe from the oldest continually operating farm in Illinois, and you'll surely enjoy it!

One note: In most old recipes, "shortening" could mean any solid cooking fat: vegetable shortening, butter, or lard. For much of the mid-twentieth century, vegetable shortening was the most popular. I'd recommend a virgin-press palm oil or butter.

Makes one 9-by-13-inch sheet cake; double to make a three-layer 9-inch cake

FOR THE CAKE

  2 cups cake flour, sifted before measuring

  1 teaspoon baking soda

  ½ teaspoon ground cinnamon (best) or allspice

  ½ teaspoon ground nutmeg

  Dash of salt

  ½ cup shortening

  ¾ cup packed dark brown sugar

¾ cup granulated sugar

2 large eggs

1 teaspoon vanilla extract

1 cup buttermilk

⅔ cup black walnut pieces

Preheat oven to 350°F.

Grease and flour a 13-by-9-inch cake pan. Sift together the flour, baking soda, cinnamon or allspice, nutmeg, and salt. Sift a second time and reserve.

Cream the shortening together with the sugars until light and fluffy, about 6 to 8 minutes. Add the eggs one at a time, beating after each addition, then continue beating another 3 to 5 minutes until smooth, airy, and creamy. Beat in the vanilla at the end.

Using a sturdy rubber spatula, fold ⅓ of the flour mixture into the egg mixture, followed by ⅓ of the buttermilk, and repeat, alternating in thirds until all the ingredients are incorporated into a smooth, thick batter. Fold in the walnuts. Turn the batter out into the prepared cake pan and bake on the center rack of the oven for 35 to 45 minutes, until it passes the toothpick test. Cool completely before frosting with **VANILLA FROSTING** (recipe follows).

FOR VANILLA FROSTING

1 cup heavy cream

2 cups granulated sugar

1 teaspoon vanilla extract

1 teaspoon butter

In a medium saucepan, cook the cream and sugar until a spoon raked across the pan leaves a mark, 230°F to 235°F on a food thermometer. Add vanilla and butter. Use a hand beater to beat the mixture in the saucepan until it has a spreading consistency, 6 to 10 minutes. Frost cake while the frosting is still warm to the touch, but not hot.

Gooey Butter Cake

Many of our recipes are borrowed, shared, or claimed as our own when we adopt them, but the gooey butter cake is unquestionably a Midwestern original, native to Saint Louis. It has stubbornly remained local to Saint Louis and has been subject to its fair share of legends and lore.

Incredibly, even though gooey butter cake has been around only since the 1940s (some claim the 1930s, but there's no credible evidence of that), we still don't have a definitive origin story for it, but some stories are more credible than others. There are no receipts or recipes published before 1954.[53] The first one was a yeast cake topped with a gooey topping and crust, while many other recipes call for a pound cake–like base. Indeed, one of the most widely believed stories is that of Johnny Hoffman of Saint Louis Pastries Bakery, who in the early 1940s accidentally reversed the flour and sugar ratios while making a deep butter cake, a confection very similar to pound cake that did not include yeast. More recent recipes simply rely on yellow cake mix.[54]

The potential controversies surrounding the origin claims and the yeast dough versus cake batter question might be the source of endless debate in some locales, but people in Saint Louis take them in stride. It's easy to imagine that if Hoffman had introduced a product that was such a sensation, every bakery in town would have introduced its own version promptly, with the resulting frenzy creating a haze around the truth.

Contemporary gooey butter cakes, with their creamy cheese toppings, are just as likely to resemble a cheesecake as they are to resemble whatever we might choose to believe is the original. There are chocolate versions that aren't a far throw from a brownie, and versions that resemble fruit bars. As much as I've strived to focus on verifiable receipts in this book, we're going to have to leave a little bit to legend with this one. Personally, I like this yeast cake version, kind of like an extra sticky and, yes, gooey version of the stollen that German American bakers in Saint Louis were baking by the thousands during the 1940s.

Makes one 13-by-9-inch cake

FOR THE CAKE BASE

⅓ cup milk

1 teaspoon instant yeast

4 tablespoons granulated sugar, divided

6 tablespoons unsalted butter, cut into ½-inch pats and softened

Zest of 1 lemon, grated

¼ teaspoon ground Mexican or Korintje cinnamon

1 large egg

¼ teaspoon salt

1¾ cups all-purpose flour, sifted before measuring and resifted

Heat the milk to lukewarm, 110°F. Combine with yeast and 1 tablespoon sugar in a mixing bowl and stir to dissolve sugar. Allow to rest and bloom while you cream the butter.

In a separate mixing bowl, cream the butter with the remaining 3 tablespoons sugar until light and fluffy, about 4 to 5 minutes. Beat in the lemon zest, cinnamon, egg, and salt. Using a stiff rubber spatula, fold ⅓ of the flour into the egg mixture, then ⅓ of the milk mixture, and repeat, alternating in thirds, until all the ingredients are incorporated, using your hands to knead if the dough becomes too stiff for the spatula. Knead inside the bowl with your hands until the dough comes together into a smooth ball, 3 to 4 minutes. Press into a buttered 13-by-9-inch cake pan and allow to rise until doubled in height, 30 to 50 minutes.

MAKING THE TOPPING AND BAKING

- ¾ cup (1½ sticks) unsalted butter, cut into ½-inch pats and refrigerated
- 1½ cups granulated sugar
- ¼ teaspoon salt
- 1 large egg
- 1 tablespoon orange zest, finely grated
- 2 teaspoons pure vanilla extract
- ¼ cup light corn syrup or honey
- 3 tablespoons cold water
- 1¼ cups all-purpose flour

Preheat oven to 350°F.

Cream the butter and sugar together until light and fluffy, 4 to 5 minutes. Beat in the salt, egg, orange zest, and vanilla one at a time, beating to combine thoroughly with each addition. Beat in the honey, then add water in a thin, steady stream, beating constantly. Fold in the flour in thirds, using a stiff rubber spatula and scraping the bowl and turning the mixture over until you have a smooth, thick batter.

Gently spread over the risen yeast dough, taking care not to degas the dough. Bake on the center rack of the oven for about 45 minutes, until set and not fluid in the center. Cool thoroughly. Cut into squares and dust with powdered sugar to serve.

Spritz Cookies

One of the most common holiday cookies when I was growing up, these little gems were part of every Christmas cookie display, gift box, and gift basket.

Spritz cookies in various guises with colorful decorations were sold by the clamshell in bakeries and grocery stores during the holidays.

Translated as *syringe* from German, the word *spritz* appears in many historic to modern German recipes, from the churro-like spritz fritters of Philippine Welser's kitchen,[55] to the *Spritzkuchen*[56] (crullers) of Germershausen's eighteenth-century writings, to the *Plätzchen Spritz* we see on Christmas cookie displays. The cookies can easily be pressed and piped into myriad shapes—not only the classic star shape, but also rounds to be decorated as wreaths or even triangles to be decorated as trees.

I've always felt that spritz cookies, with their festive presentation, could also be cookies of distinctive taste, like springerle and lebkuchen, which would inevitably outflank spritz cookies on the dessert table with their delicious anise, honey, and spice flavors. In this recipe, I present a more flavorful spritz cookie that can stand on its own, with lemon zest and coriander. The ubiquitous maraschino cherry "nose" can easily be improved upon by using a high-quality maraschino such as those from the Italian company Luxardo, or any one of many dried or stewed fruits can be used in its place. Sanding sugars in festive colors are always a good idea. I like sprinkling about a third of the cookies each with red and green sugars before baking and dusting the last third with powdered sugar when they emerge from the oven. These cookies are supercharged with flavor and don't need a fruit filling, so don't feel obligated to use the maraschinos, but be creative in your own way.

Makes about 5 dozen cookies

2¼ cups all-purpose flour

¼ teaspoon baking powder

½ teaspoon kosher salt

1 teaspoon ground coriander

¼ teaspoon ground nutmeg

1 tablespoon lemon zest, finely grated

1 cup (2 sticks) unsalted butter, cut into ½-inch pats and softened

¾ cup granulated sugar

¼ cup beaten egg (1 large egg more or less; measure by volume, not by egg)

1 teaspoon almond extract

Whole unskinned salted almonds

1 jar Luxardo maraschino cherries

Red and green sanding sugar, and powdered sugar, as desired

Sift the flour twice before measuring, then resift with the baking powder, salt, spices, and lemon zest, and reserve. Cream the butter together with the sugar until light and fluffy, about 4 to 5 minutes. Beat in the egg in a thin, steady stream, then the almond extract, and continue beating until smooth and fluffy, 3 to 4 more minutes. Fold in the dry mixture in thirds, but be careful not to overmix the dough.

Fill a cookie press with the big star tip and pipe tablespoon-sized cookies onto an ungreased baking sheet, allowing the star shape to spread before pulling the press away from the pan. Sprinkle ⅓ with red sanding sugar, ⅓ with green, and leave the remainder plain. Press a salted almond into the center of each undecorated cookie, and a single maraschino into the center of each decorated cookie, both red and green. Refrigerate for 20 to 30 minutes before baking.

Preheat oven to 375°F.

Bake cookies on the center rack of the oven until set but not browned, about 10 to 12 minutes. Dust the almond-stuffed cookies with powdered sugar. Allow to cool before removing from the baking sheet, and store in a cookie tin.

Springerle

Little blessings and charms in the form of holiday cookies, springerle are one of the most rewarding baking projects you could ever undertake, and one for which my great-aunt Anne was a minor celebrity in the family. Embossed with striking designs imparted by specially carved molds made mostly in Switzerland, these precious confections make fantastic holiday greetings in edible form. Their boldly embossed designs can be made to reflect anything from holiday wishes or reflections to birthdays, betrothals, or any special occasion. Typically flavored with lemon zest and anise, they have an especially intoxicating aroma that pairs exceptionally well with either hot chocolate or mulled wine, both of which are excellent choices for dunking—and you will want to dunk. Springerle are very hard when fully cured and tailor-made for dipping in hot beverages.

Springerle date back to at least the fifteenth century in the Black Forest region of Swabia.[57] Because they were specialties of bakers who closely guarded their secrets, early receipts are hard to come by, but one from Eleonora Maria Rosalia in 1699 shows that the recipe was already pretty close to our modern take, although she uses cinnamon rather than anise.[58]

The picturesque springerle tradition came to the United States with German immigrants. They make appearances in Henriette Davidis's cookbook for German immigrants,[59] *The Settlement Cookbook*,[60] and *The Joy of Cooking*.[61]

The variety of shapes and designs of springerle cookies is limitless.   Photo by Paul Fehribach.

The art seemed to wane over the twentieth century, but as with many forms of artisanal cooking, there is a renewed interest in springerle baking. I for one can't tell you how much of a joy it is to spend a few hours turning these precious cookies out.

The relative ease of making springerle is complicated only by a few simple but key steps that need to be followed to achieve the unusually light and crunchy exterior and airy interior. Delicately spiced, they are receptive to your creativity, but I'm a huge fan of the traditional anise. If you don't like anise, substitute another favorite spice, but rather than using the pre-ground stuff, pulverize the whole spice in the blender until it has the consistency of cracked black pepper. This will preserve more of the oils and give you a more aromatic cookie.

It's a significant challenge to find purveyors of springerle molds among brick-and-mortar stores, but with a little sleuthing online, you can find molds to reflect Christmas, birthdays, Kwanzaa, Hannukah, and other occasions. Definitely go for wooden or wood composite molds; metal ones will not give you the relief you're after and are more likely to stick to your dough as well.

While I've mentioned often that certain pickles, preserves, and confections make great gifts, I'll say without hesitation that springerle lovingly embossed for the occasion are unequaled as a gift. Do take the time to plan ahead, so the dough has plenty of time to age and develop its fully complex flavor.

Makes about 3 dozen cookies

¾ cup beaten egg (about 3 large eggs—measure by volume, not by egg)

3 cups confectioners' sugar, sifted before measuring

2 teaspoons pure vanilla extract

2 teaspoons lemon extract

3 cups all-purpose flour, sifted before measuring

¼ teaspoon baker's ammonia

½ teaspoon kosher salt

2 to 3 tablespoons whole anise seeds (not star anise)

In a stand mixer with the wire whip attachment, beat the eggs on high until light and foamy, about 8 to 10 minutes. Reduce speed to medium low and add the sugar a little at a time, followed by the vanilla and lemon extracts. Continue beating on medium speed for another 8 to 10 minutes. Switch to the paddle attachment, and add the flour in thirds, mixing in each addition on low speed, then beating for a full 5 minutes on medium-high speed, for a total of 15 minutes from the first addition. With the last addition, add the baker's ammonia and salt.

Wrap tightly with plastic wrap and rest at room temperature for 3 days—don't worry, the sugar will prevent bacteria from taking over. After 3 days, refrigerate overnight before rolling out, or refrigerate for up to 1 week, tightly wrapped.

The day before you want to bake the cookies, roll the dough out into a rectangle ¼ inch thick, using as little flour as possible to prevent sticking. Once rolled out, dust the top very lightly with powdered sugar. Carefully press your molds into the top until the pattern is fully embossed. Use a shaped cookie cutter or crinkle cutter to finish separating the cookies. Cover your cookie sheet(s) with parchment paper, and lay the cookies out with at least ½ inch between them. Place the cookie sheets in a cool, dry place where it's safe to store them uncovered, and leave them to dry overnight.

The following day, preheat oven to 325°F.

Place the anise seeds in a small saucer. Wet a clean towel until it is thoroughly damp. Lift each cookie and gently press it, bottom side down, into the towel to just moisten the bottom; then tap it into the anise seeds so several stick to the moistened bottom, and return it to the cookie sheet. Place the cookies on the bottom rack of the oven, reduce heat to 300°F, and bake for 20 to 25 minutes. They should not brown, but remain somewhat pale. Cool thoroughly to room temperature before storing.

Place cookies in airtight tins, making room in each tin for a small shot glass stuffed with paper napkins wet with a little bit of white wine, damp but not sopping wet. Change out the shot glass once a week. Store cookies for 2 to 3 weeks before serving or giving away as good tidings.

Lebkuchen

Like springerle, lebkuchen have their origin in Germany centuries ago. Lebkuchen sprang from the Bavarian town of Nuremberg, where they were created by monks during the Middles Ages as special religious treats. They were made with honey, various nuts, and a dizzying quantity of spices, a combination of ingredients that was believed to have religious significance.[62] Their popularity increased dramatically in the sixteenth century, when we can find an intricate receipt in Sabina Welserin's manuscript cookbook that includes the requisite honey along with a mammoth clutch of spices and a delicate washing with rosewater but doesn't include any nuts.[63] Germershausen lumps lebkuchen together with honey cakes, or *Honigkuchen*, in *Die Hausmutter*, sharing a handful of receipts that display the full breadth of flavors in the lore of lebkuchen, with honey, cardamom, coriander, ginger, pepper, mace, citron, bitter orange, lemon peel, almond meal, and an exotic ingredient for Germans at the time: cornmeal. By the time lebkuchen arrive stateside, in Henriette Davidis's receipt,[64] they more closely resemble Germershausen's receipt than Welserin's. Davidis's receipt was one of the major inspirations for the recipe below, although she uses wheat flour, which I avoided.

Bertha Kramer, a.k.a. "Aunt Babette," of Cincinnati, printed the first English-language recipe, calling the cookies out as "German Lebkuchen" in 1889,[65] and the Milwaukeean authors of *The Settlement Cook Book* followed in 1903 with their own recipe.[66] As influential as these two cookbooks were in the early Midwest, their recipes for lebkuchen represent a considerable devolution from the elaborate German-language receipts, essentially appearing to be variations of another favorite holiday treat: gingerbread.

My favorite variant of this confection is the *Elisenlebkuchen* of Nuremberg, for its radical departure from other varieties, but even more so for the ecstasy of its aroma and its incredible crumb, at once chewy, creamy, mealy, and crispy. It's also made without flour, so folks who can't eat wheat can rejoice that one of the very best confections in our repertoire is naturally gluten free.

Christmas legends and traditions filled with stories of gingerbread houses and gingerbread men all help create a rich narrative, but the undisputed zenith of gingerbread is the lebkuchen. To glaze these holiday gems, use the same glazes as for **DONUTS** (p. 88), the best here being lemon or chocolate. I like to dust one-third in powdered sugar and glaze one-third each in lemon and chocolate.

Makes about 3 dozen 2½-inch lebkuchen

- 2/3 cup candied lemon peel (top quality from a specialty store)
- 2/3 cup candied orange peel (top quality from a specialty store)
- 1/2 cup candied ginger, chopped fine
- 1/4 cup almond meal
- 5 large eggs
- 1 cup dark brown sugar
- 1/2 cup honey (a bright honey such as clover is best)
- 2 teaspoons pure vanilla extract
- 1 teaspoon kosher salt
- 2 cups almond flour
- 2 cups hazelnut flour
- 1 teaspoon baking powder
- 1 teaspoon ground Mexican or Korintje cinnamon
- 1/2 teaspoon ground cloves
- 1/2 teaspoon ground mace (preferred) or nutmeg
- 1/2 teaspoon ground allspice
- 1/2 teaspoon ground coriander
- 1/2 teaspoon ground cardamom
- 1/2 teaspoon fresh cracked black pepper

Place the lemon and orange peels and ginger in the food processor with the 1/4 cup almond meal. Pulse until the peels are finely chopped. Reserve until needed.

In a stand mixer with the wire whip attachment, beat the eggs on high speed until foamy and frothy, 8 to 10 minutes. Reduce speed to medium high and whip in the brown sugar, honey, vanilla, and salt a little at a time, combining well after each addition.

Sift the almond and hazelnut flours together with the baking powder and spices.

Switch from the wire whip to the paddle attachment, reduce speed to low, and add the dry mixture to the wet in thirds, mixing in thoroughly after each addition until all the ingredients are incorporated. Transfer to a shallow casserole dish, cover tightly with plastic wrap, and chill for at least 4 hours or up to 3 days.

Preheat oven to 325°F.

Line your cookie sheet(s) with buttered parchment paper. Scoop the chilled batter onto the buttered paper, using about 3 tablespoons per lebkuchen, and shape the batter into a fat round shape a little more than ½ inch high and 2 inches around.

Place on the center rack of the oven and reduce heat to 300°F. Bake for 20 to 25 minutes, until set in the center, but don't give them too much time too brown—less browning is best in this case.

Cool to lukewarm before gently removing from the cookie sheets and glazing. Store in a cookie tin.

Black Walnut Rugelach

This delicate little pastry, something like a tiny filled croissant and pastry rolled into one, has gone from being a secret known only among Jewish communities to something so-called foodies seek out with semi-religious fervor during the holidays, when they are made in abundance in celebration of Hannukah. In a sure sign that rugelach are being creolized into macro Midwestern cooking, they are popping up in ostensibly nondenominational bakeries such as Amaranth Bakery in Milwaukee and Omega Artisan Baking in Columbus, Ohio.

Consisting of a delicate cream-cheese pastry filled with jam, candied nuts, or poppy seed, rolled and twisted into a crescent shape before baking, rugelach are the rare cookies that are at once light, decadent, elegant, and rich. The first time I had them in December 1996, I was smitten, and I now make regular trips to New York Bagel & Bialy in Skokie for apricot rugelach.

There is a history of rugelach in Poland, where some claim they originated, but the crescent shape probably originated in Austria. Without doubt, the rugelach came to the Midwest with Central European Jewish immigrants.[67]

Rugelach are fairly easy to make, although the dough can be somewhat delicate, so I recommend chilling it before rolling and filling, and chilling again before baking. You can fill a rugelach with almost anything; apricots, poppy seed, and raspberry jam are among the most common fillings, but nut filling is among my favorites. You can make these year-round or keep them as part of your holiday baking routine.

8 ounces cream cheese, softened to room temperature

1 cup (2 sticks) plus 3 tablespoons unsalted butter, softened to room temperature, divided

¼ cup granulated sugar

1 teaspoon pure vanilla extract

1 teaspoon kosher salt, divided

2¼ cups all-purpose flour

2 cups shelled black walnuts

½ cup plus 3 tablespoons maple sugar, divided

Zest of 1 lemon, very finely grated

½ teaspoon ground coriander

1 egg

¼ cup cold water

To make the dough, cream together the cream cheese and 1 cup butter until well combined. Add the granulated sugar, vanilla extract, and ½ teaspoon salt and beat until light and fluffy, 5 to 6 minutes. Fold in the flour with a sturdy rubber spatula. Knead with your hands when the dough becomes too thick for the spatula. Knead into a smooth ball, but don't overwork—once the dough is smooth, you are done. Divide the dough into four equal balls, roll each into a disk ¾ inch thick, wrap in plastic wrap, and refrigerate overnight.

Before shaping and baking, make the filling and egg wash. Place the black walnuts, ½ cup maple sugar, lemon zest, coriander, and the remaining ½ teaspoon salt in the food processor and pulse until ground into a coarse meal, with the largest bits of walnut smaller than a grain of rice. Separately, beat the egg with the cold water.

Melt the remaining 3 tablespoons of butter in a small saucepan. On a well-floured surface, roll each disk of well-chilled dough into a 9- to 10-inch circle (use a ruler). Brush each disk with butter, then spread the walnut filling evenly over the disks. Cut each disk pizza style into 12 equal wedges. Roll each wedge up into a croissant shape, starting with the thick outside end and rolling toward the point in the center. Turn the roll so the point is on the bottom and, pressing your thumb gently into the center from the side, twist the edges back toward one another to form a crescent shape. Place the cookies point side down on a cookie sheet lined with parchment paper. Brush with egg wash and sprinkle remaining 3 tablespoons maple sugar evenly over the cookies. Refrigerate for at least 30 minutes—1 hour is better—before baking.

Preheat oven to 350°F.

Bake cookies on the center rack of the oven until lightly browned, about 20 minutes.

Cool thoroughly to room temperature before removing from the parchment. Store in a cookie tin.

Mexican Wedding Cakes

When I first tasted a Mexican wedding cake, the hair stood on my neck and a shiver shot down my spine as I realized I might have just committed a mortal sin. The pharma-strength sweetness of the powdered sugar dusting, the explosive texture of the delicate crumb oozing the gamey scent of hog entwined with the equally potent aroma of oily nuts—it was all just too much, pornographic in its sensory stimulation. I took a deep breath, pensively looked around, and, reassured that I was at a church event, popped the rest of the delectable morsel into my mouth.

There are a lot of stories around these little delights, but early newspaper recipes yield a few clues. Mexican tea cakes appear as early as 1932 in Martinsville, Indiana,[68] in the exact form we know them today (butter, powdered sugar, nuts) in a recipe shared by Mrs. T. J. Lewis of the Morgan County Home Economists Club. I assume this means that they already enjoyed some degree of popularity at the time. From there, there is a steady stream of newspaper appearances throughout the Midwest before they emerge nationwide.

An alternative name, Russian tea cakes, appears in the first edition of the wildly influential *Betty Crocker's Picture Cookbook*,[69] and the recipe is on the nose as a proper nut shortbread. However, all the earlier recipes I could find for Russian tea cakes included at least some egg, which disqualifies them as proper Mexican wedding cakes. As a testimonial to the influence of Betty Crocker's brand and image, "Russian tea cakes" is nearly as popular a name for these cookies today, though that moniker predominates in the Southeast. The name "Mexican wedding cakes" predominates in the Midwest, especially in Indiana, where in some parts they are religion.

In Mexican baking, there is a shortbread cookie called a *polvoron*, descended from Spain, that often perfectly resembles the wedding cakes of Indiana and the Midwest. A straw poll of my Mexican and Mexican American friends found them all bemused by the idea they'd be called wedding cakes, because in Mexican culture they are sought for any celebration and are readily available in *panaderias* and *panificadoras*. I still scratch my head about how they would have come to the rural Midwest from Mexico by the 1930s.

We always knew these as Christmas cookies, but from now on, I'll take the cue from Mexican culture and enjoy them any time. Pecans are most commonly used, but if you'd like to give them an extra Midwestern touch, use black walnuts. I still like them with lard, but feel free to use butter or even palm oil if you wish. Delicious variations on this cookie substitute chickpea flour for some or all of the pastry flour.

Makes about 5 dozen cookies

> 1 cup pecan halves
>
> 1 cup lard
>
> 2½ cups confectioners' sugar, divided
>
> ½ teaspoon kosher salt
>
> 1 tablespoon vanilla extract
>
> 1½ cups pastry flour, or 1 cup all-purpose flour and ½ cup chickpea flour
>
> 1½ teaspoons ground Mexican or Korintje cinnamon, divided
>
> 1 cup granulated sugar

Preheat oven to 350°F.

Spread pecans in a single layer on a cookie sheet and toast until lightly browned and aromatic, about 15 minutes. Cool completely to room temperature before proceeding. Grind the pecans for several pulses in the food processor until they form a very coarse meal, with the average piece the size of a grain of rice.

Mix the ground pecans and the lard in the bowl of a stand mixer with the paddle attachment to combine, just about a minute. On low speed, mix in ½ cup of the confectioners' sugar, salt, and vanilla, then increase speed to medium and whip until fluffy, 3 to 5 minutes. Sift the flour, together with ½ teaspoon of the cinnamon, into the bowl, then mix on low speed just until combined. The dough will be somewhat fluffy, so don't overmix.

Grease your cookie sheet well. Mix the remaining teaspoon cinnamon with the granulated sugar. Scoop up the dough in 2-tablespoon (1-ounce, if you have a mechanical scoop) balls. Roll in the cinnamon sugar to coat lightly, then shape into slightly flattened balls. Space the cookies evenly, about 1 inch apart, on the cookie sheet.

Bake for about 20 minutes, until the edges just start to brown and the centers are set but still unbrowned. Cool for about 10 minutes until they are still hot but easy to handle. Roll each cookie in powdered sugar to coat thoroughly, and cool on wire racks. Store in cookie tins. These are good for a week or more when stored in a cool, dry place.

Erika Allen

———

For generations, the South Side of Chicago has been a destination for, and home to, dispossessed peoples, including generations of immigrants fleeing war and famine in Europe, political violence in China, and the Mexican Revolution, and in the greatest numbers, Southern Blacks looking for better opportunities outside the South. In many ways, the United States and the City of Chicago have failed to deliver those better opportunities, as Black residents have discovered in confronting the quieter, more insidious racism that festers in the Midwest (see Ta-Nehisi Coates, "The Case for Reparations").

Creating equity in communities of color has long been a struggle against the grain of the American banking system and a whole host of other structurally racist institutions that keep BIPOC (Black, Indigenous, and people of color) groups marginalized and vulnerable. Political and community activism have been the main vehicles for progress, but to Erika Allen and a growing movement of urban farmers, repairing the land and healing generations of trauma through growing nutrient-dense food is the foundation of a future in which everyone has equity.

Erika Allen's father is Will Allen, ex-professional basketball player and hero to the Good Food Movement for his work in founding and running the pioneering urban farming organization Growing Power. Will is the son of South Carolina sharecroppers who chased a dream north to Bethesda, Maryland, where Will was raised. While on scholarship at, and desegregating, the University of Miami (Florida), Will met Cynthia Bussler, daughter of German and Prussian immigrants, someone who, at first glance, wouldn't appear to have had anything in common with him. But the two became sweethearts and married, a family followed, and their revolution in urban agriculture lives on through Erika's Urban Growers Collective. UGC is a consortium of farmers and educators demonstrating the development of community-based food systems by operating eight urban farms, mentoring new growers and helping them incubate their own farms, and teaching schoolchildren about where food comes from and the healing power of naturally grown, unprocessed food. Through these activities, UGC helps create equity via productive local food systems and the land improvement that is a natural offshoot of good stewardship.

Erika received her BFA from the School of the Art Institute of Chicago, followed by an MA in art psychotherapy from the University of Illinois Chicago. She founded the Chicago branch of Growing Power in 2002 and ran it until Growing Power folded in 2017. After that, she and the longtime co-director of Growing Power Chicago, Laurell Simms, created Urban Growers Collective, whose motto is "Cultural Reclamation and Understanding."

She is quick to point out how her multicultural upbringing inspires her work. "My mom's family had a certain way of cooking cabbage and only her family would do it that way, except my dad's family would do it the same way. And there's a yellow squash she would make that only her family would make, yet my dad's family made it the same way. Food in our household is a creolization of these cultures and that's kind of how Urban Growers Collective works—we're a collective with all these different facets, but we work around these stories trying to repair some of the terror and racist infrastructures that remove the truth of how connected people really are."

The artist in Erika Allen is right on the surface at all times and is a source of her infectious enthusiasm. She attracts a steady stream of students to UGC's Farmers for Chicago, Youth Corps, and Activating Herbalism programs, where they will learn from the collective's knowledge base and carry the work forward. Over time, Allen believes, equity will grow, and through the three pillars of her learning philosophy—art, healing, and fun—the community will grow healthier.

Allen has also been busy with an even more ambitious project in which UGC is one of three partners: Green Era Chicago. Centered around an anaerobic "digester," which produces energy by composting food waste, Green Era Chicago will be able to realize one of Allen's longtime dreams of truly "closing the loop" between food production, food waste, and the energy required for growing food. With its seven-acre vegetable and herb farm on site increasing UGC's productive land by more than two-thirds, it also helps realize her vision of a more sustainable urban farming enterprise than Growing Power proved to be. "By closing the loop, and with the digester producing the energy needs while dealing with our waste stream, we are able to begin building that equity where Growing Power was dependent on philanthropy. We can self-sustain, and with the digester's energy available, engage in more of the emerging high-tech growing technologies which are based on a lot of my father's innovations." This means more fresh vegetables year-round, more revenue, and more food independence for the community.

Even with the multimillion-dollar Green Era launched and thriving, Allen is adamant about remaining a nonprofit even though UGC's education and mentorship programs will yield generations of for-profit urban growers. "You can't build a more equitable food system by profiting from solving social problems. We are trying to alleviate problems caused by structural racism, not perpetuate them."

Based on a discussion with Erika Allen, co-founder and CEO of operations, Urban Growers Collective; president, Green Era Educational NFP; co-owner, Green ERA Sustainability Partners, January 27, 2022.

11

WHAT NEXT, HEARTLAND?

So I began to teach young people from the projects and the inner city how to grow food. I conveyed the life lessons that agriculture teaches. Through trial and error, my staff and I developed new models for growing food intensively and vertically in cities. We found ways to make fresh fruits and vegetables available to people with little income. We created full-time agricultural jobs for inner-city youth. We began to teach people—young and old, black and white—how to grow vegetables in small spaces and reclaim some small control over their food choices. We found ways to redirect organic waste from the city's landfills, and to use it instead to create fertile soil. We connected small farmers in Wisconsin to underserved markets in inner-city communities. We provided a space where corporate volunteers could work alongside black inner-city youth, hauling dirt, planting seeds, and harvesting together.

—**Will Allen**

In the 350 years since Jacques Marquette and Louis Joliet first forayed into the Midwest, the way people eat here has been transformed as dramatically as the landscape. Today, it may be impossible to imagine a future in which people aren't sitting down to burgers and fries on a regular basis, but just 150 years ago, many folks would have had a hard time imagining a future without a regular plug of mince pie. No one had even heard of a hamburger. Since then, the Midwest has emerged as a breadbasket, a food industry hub, and the booming industrial heart of twentieth-century America. By the 1980s and 1990s, changes in technology and trade had inflicted a lot of pain on the Rust Belt, but urban redevelopment promises a prosperous future.

In some profound ways, the changes that have roiled Midwestern foodways for generations are coming full circle. A growing movement of Indigenous chefs, artisans, and scholars is reclaiming food sovereignty for their communities, with results both nourishing and delicious. The most famous of these chefs is James Beard Award–winning author Sean Sherman, whose 2017 cookbook *The Sioux Chef's Indigenous Kitchen* is as much a clarion call to Indigenous cooks to reclaim their food sovereignty as it is a memoir of his own discoveries, one delicious recipe at a time. In 2021, he opened his flagship restaurant Owamni in Minneapolis to critical acclaim and enthusiastic public support; reservations typically take weeks to acquire.

We should look forward to Sean Sherman's star turn inspiring a new generation of Indigenous chefs in restaurants, but closer-to-home chefs such as Elena Terry, through her nonprofit Wild Bearies, also serve as hubs for knowledge sharing and community building. Two chefs descended from displaced Midwestern tribes inspire from afar: Crystal Wahpepah (Kickapoo), of Wahpepah's Kitchen in Oakland, California, and Oklahoma-born Loretta Barrett Oden (Potawatomi), a writer and television personality. In 2021, Chicagoland got its first Indigenous restaurant when classically trained chef Jessica Pamonicutt (Menominee) opened Ketapanen Kitchen in suburban Stickney, where she is steadily building a following for her "expression of love in the Menominee language."

Just twenty years ago, Indigenous people weren't at the table when American food was discussed in the food media, so we can see today's publicity as progress, but there is a long way to go. Indigenous communities have experienced a generational trauma distinct from that of Black Americans, but just as significant. The concept of individual ownership of property was completely alien to America's First Nations, and what lands they did control were taken from them without compensation. They were moved to unsuitable places and given poor infrastructure and worse educational institutions. The investments required to give Indigenous Americans a way forward would be small (not to mention morally required) compared with what they have to teach us. But those investments need to be made on Indigenous people's own terms, supporting their visions without patriarchal intrusion.

We can see analogous signs of both progress and stagnation in the Black community. Finally, Black chefs, authors, and entrepreneurs are at the table, and many food writers actively pursue Black stories, but segregation continues to weaken the Midwest's potential. The evil ghost of redlining perpetuates the generational wealth gap, which makes it next to impossible for most Black Midwesterners to become an entrepreneur or restaurateur, or even to embark on the creative journey to become one. The Black farming community has been decimated by generations of bad USDA policy.

The comparative lack of opportunity in Black communities and the indifference of much of the White majority remain the most withering deficiencies in Midwestern economics and culture. All White consumers, particularly potential investors, should actively support Black-owned restaurants, beverage companies, and other businesses. Success isn't a zero-sum game; it begets more success. We are all leaving a bunch of money on the table when such a large portion of our population is left almost entirely out of the game. For Midwestern foodways to reach their full potential, Black communities must receive more investment in education, infrastructure, and institutions that support entrepreneurship. White consumers must seek out the work of Black chefs, pitmasters, bakers, and artisans.

Even before the COVID-19 pandemic, the food media had reached a reckoning with its history of racial exclusiveness and comical adulation of White male chefs at the expense of all others. During the pandemic, the murder of George Floyd further drove conscientious Americans to examine the culture and media landscape that devalues certain people while valorizing others. Food-related publications today seem keenly aware of their own intrinsic biases and are assembling more diverse writing and editing teams than ever. The quality and diversity of writing available is a gift to anyone who enjoys reading about food.

During my thirty-five years in the restaurant industry, I have had the privilege of working with people from over forty countries and every continent except Antarctica. For staff meals, family meals, and team treats, I have enjoyed *cuy*, marinated in achiote and spit-roasted before being lovingly packaged for the trip from Ecuador; Turkish coffee in elegant gilded glass cups, paired with pistachio *lokum*; *pad prik king* made with pigs' feet and fistfuls of Thai chilies and basil; *accara* fried in palm oil and served with a dip of tamarind, chilies, and palm sugar; *shakshouka* years before it became a hipster darling; *paczki* on Shrovetide; home-stewed menudo fragrant with guajillo peppers and studded with hominy; potato latkes during Hannukah; and so much more. I could fill pages with the gifts of food I've shared with people from all over the world. In spite of our different origins, we have had one thing in common: we call the Midwest home. I'll say it again: Success isn't a zero-sum game; there's so much to share, to learn, and to grow with. The more people—the more *different* kinds of people—we have at the table, the better we'll all eat, and live.

* * *

The Midwest has always been a dynamic place, as our food has shown. Many of the foods in this book are national and even international phenomena. But as I've mentioned, a book like this written a generation from now will look a lot different. What could the future of Midwestern food include?

If we first look to the past, the cuisines that most successfully transformed the way people here eat were first German, Mexican, Black, Southern, and Italian, followed by a second wave of Mexican, which is still underway. In each case, these immigrant cuisines were quickly co-opted by entrepreneurs and restaurateurs of other ethnicities. You didn't have to be German to cook hamburgers or make hot dogs, and you didn't have to be Italian to open a pizzeria, or Mexican to open a margarita bar or taco stand, or Black to cook Southern food, fried chicken, or barbecue. The twirling clash, and ultimately, the salubrious dance of cultures across America has long been our most unique attribute and the fount of ingenuity that powered the most formidable economic powerhouse in history.

In our recipes today, we see a foundation largely based on European cultural transfer. But our demographics are changing as rapidly as they ever have. Looking forward, it's hard not to imagine that the past will be prologue. Immigrant communities from all regions of China, Thailand, Vietnam, the Eastern Mediterranean and Persia, East and West Africa, the Caribbean, India, and South America from Peru to Brazil have been cooking here for at least a generation and in some cases two or three, while communities from Somalia and Burma are much more recent. All bring their most beloved recipes along with their most hopeful ambitions when they settle here and become part of who we all are.

But segregation will continue to pose needless challenges. It's not only geographic segregation but also the equally insidious cultural segregation that limits our possibilities for continued cultural evolution and renewal. When cultures come together and creolize, they can clash, but when that encounter happens with a sense of affinity, curiosity, and goodwill, the clash becomes a dance, in which all inevitably discover beautiful new moves.

Some of the most exciting eating experiences I've had in recent years have been the product of that cultural dance, such as fiery Korean fried chicken on a taco, with the chicken, sauce, and freshly griddled masa tortilla each exhibiting cultural passion. Seemingly ordinary pancakes become ethereal when soaked in *tres leches*, scented with Mexican cinnamon and vanilla from Veracruz, and mortared with painstakingly candied *cajeta*. Chicken noodle soup becomes a revelation when the shredded bird swims with ramen noodles in a *tom kha*-esque broth of coconut and lime leaves laced with just enough habanero pepper to give the whole thing an eerily smoky tang. *Pozole* and *tteokguk* become one when the chewy rice cakes swirl among nixtamalized corn kernels in a broth spiked with guajillo chilies, ginger, lime, and fish sauce. Don't segregate. Cook some food, set the table, pull up a chair.

* * *

Most Midwestern towns and neighborhoods are still blessed with that one spot that's been cooking food to local tastes for generations, but the encroachment of chains continues to be a threat to local culture. Even a city such as Cincinnati, which has been able to maintain a high degree of local food culture in its chili parlor chains, may suffer from their success because their ubiquitousness can also inhibit creativity. Cincinnati chili is delicious, but it's also seemingly preserved in amber.

The increasing power and influence of large independent restaurant groups has a similar if more muted effect: while most restaurant groups have one or more game-changing restaurants as flagships, as they become larger and more complex financially, defending and maintaining their position becomes a much higher priority than taking risks. Meanwhile, smaller independent operators face increasing competition from these much better funded companies.

In spite of these headwinds, immigrants continue to ply their trade. Chefs and entrepreneurs are willing to risk everything for their own businesses. Urban communities learn to regenerate brownfields to grow nourishment for their communities. And many rural families expand beyond the corn and beans business to grow fruits and vegetables for their neighborhoods and beyond. The renewed possibilities for ecological balance and food independence and sovereignty are more real now than they have been since colonization destroyed the First Nations. The great Midwestern incubator runs on.

The Midwest is at one of the most important turning points in its history, as is the nation as a whole. During the past generation, consolidation of capital has given more wealth to the richest 1 percent of the population than it has to the poorest 90 percent. This ridiculously lopsided distribution of wealth negatively impacts the ability of nine out of ten Midwesterners to participate fully in the economy, whether as consumers, potential farmers, entrepreneurs, or restaurateurs.

One of the most important questions for the future is who the Midwestern food economy will belong to. Black and Indigenous communities long ago learned not to wait around for the majority-White macro culture to do something. Their activists, community leaders, and entrepreneurs work diligently to create helpful food systems. But the food economy doesn't belong to the overwhelming majority of White people either, and if the rising tide of diet-related diseases over the past couple of generations is any indication, the food economy is hurting them, too. White Midwesterners are in the best position to effect policy changes that could benefit everyone, but the politics of division prevents the real progress on tax reform, education, community investment, and wealth redistribution that we need to allow everyone to participate fully in a vibrant food economy.

In lieu of meaningful political action, White Midwesterners would probably best be served by taking a course similar to that taken by Black and Indigenous people: checking out of the system. As we've seen, many have decided not to participate in the corn and bean economy and plant vegetables instead; others defiantly open restaurants or bakeries despite an economy that ruthlessly favors another Chipotle or Panera instead. Still others become entrepreneurs, tilting against international beverage groups as independent brewers, or taking on Unilever or Kraft Foods by starting a small chocolate or cheese company. Each risk taken is a point of light in a darkening sky dominated by equity capital and the chains it perpetuates, and each represents at least some chance that we'll soon have the next Vienna Beef, Imo's, or Graeter's. Those resounding entrepreneurial successes all decided that keeping things closer to home was the right thing for their brand. Midwestern food is as rich as it is partly because of companies like these that grew but remained regional.

The most ominous question about the future of Midwestern food is whether, in the face of economic inequality, the Amazons, Walmarts, Krafts, and Unilevers will eventually win all of our food dollars. Or will it be local grocery stores and farmers' markets and folks like Andy Hazzard, Urban Growers Collective, Carriage House Farm, and Brown Sugar Bakery? Unless we choose to put a little more effort into our food by seeking out local owners, local farms, and local producers, and taking a pass on national brands, we risk losing our uniqueness and a great deal of our identity. Life is a lot more fun when approached as Titus Ruscitti does it—go the extra couple of miles for that roast beef commercial at a local café and finish it off with a slice of coconut cream pie instead of surrendering to Arby's right by the highway interchange. The pursuit of your next great local meal can become a sport. You can discover treasures like Triple XXX Family Restaurant in Lafayette, Indiana; Rip's Tavern in Ladd, Illinois; or Rye in Leawood, Kansas. There's world-class food everywhere in the Midwest, but to keep it, we have to eat it.

We can't know what the next big change in Midwestern food will be—change is often sudden and disruptive—but by supporting our local food economies, including immigrant and BIPOC communities, we can be sure it will be something uniquely ours. Cultural change has never happened as quickly in the Midwest as it does on the coasts—Midwesterners are more likely to see the latest trend as a blithesome dalliance than as a real thing—but throughout our history, the Midwest has been the most consequential region in the development of American food and drink culture. That's one thing that is not likely to change.

Acknowledgments

This book is the fruit of many people's work, not just my own. Without these people, *Midwestern Food* would not be in your hands.

The scholarly and talented team at University of Chicago Press somehow made getting this book to you an absolute pleasure, even when the work was tedious. Extra-special thanks to my editors. Without the help of executive editor Timothy Mennel and senior production editor Tamara Ghattas, as well as freelance editor Norma Sims Roche, you very well might be reading gobbledygook. Special thanks to Isaac Tobin for designing a sharp volume, to Susannah Engstrom for keeping the project on the straight and narrow, and to Carrie Olivia Adams for a deft hand at getting the word out.

Thanks to Janice Shay of Pinafore Press for helping shape *Midwestern Food* from an unmarketable blob of a concept into what I hope you readers will find to be an engaging and informative read in addition to a great book to cook from.

It was intimidating to dive back into the German language after decades of letting it lapse on my tongue, especially when reading and translating antiquated texts and creating citations from them. Without Volker Bach's help researching and translating Reformation-era German, this book could easily have missed some of the most important research into the origins of Midwestern and, indeed, American food: the foods of our largest population by ancestry.

Telling the stories of Midwestern food through recipes works only if the recipes work, so special thanks to testers Stacey Ballis and Judy Shertzer for helping to make sure these recipes can grace your kitchen as they have so many others over generations.

Mark Armantrout has been a more steadfast and supportive partner than I could have ever hoped for, through years of silly travel adventures to try obscure foods or hidden restaurants, to months on end in which my schedule was work, write, research, repeat, travel, work, write, research, sleep, to over a year with dozens of books and periodicals I called research materials strewn throughout our home. Thank you, Mark, for everything.

Without a crackerjack team at my restaurant, Big Jones, I would not have been able to take the time away from operations to research and write this book. Special thanks to chef de cuisine Reynaldo Reyna for maintaining very high standards in my absence, sous chef Zachary Chamberlin for the same, and Quirino Juan Flores, Blake Davy, Keith Montanez, Garrett Allain, Eduardo Gonzalez, Chainida Phuthuphan, and Nathan Phuthuphan for seeing us safely out of the pandemic and into a bright future.

Benedictions to family both near and far, many of whom we have lost on this earth but who have left us the gifts of their inspiration. The grandmother I never knew, Frances Fehribach, née Hauser, and the man she wooed with her cooking, Albert Fehribach, served as the initial inspiration for this book, as the last generation of our family to truly live off the land. I learned my relentless work ethic from my parents, Sandra and Joseph Fehribach, but perhaps more importantly, the value of community and virtue and the innate value of all human beings. Also mentioned in the book were Rita and Lee Gress and Rich and Sue Schepers, all of whom fill my mind and heart with warmth at every recollection. And to my maternal grandmother, Melba Morelos, née Justice, who showed me a whole wide world beyond a Southern Indiana town and, most significantly, that life can be much more fulfilling when you are uncomfortable, because that is when you learn the most.

Notes

INTRODUCTION

Epigraph: Sixto Rodriguez, "Sandrevan Lullaby—Lifestyles," from the album *Coming from Reality*, Sussex Records SXBS 7012, 1972.

1. Daniel R. Black and Howard Rosing, *Chicago: A Food Biography*, 199.

2. Black and Rosing, *Chicago: A Food Biography*, 203.

3. Kurt Vonnegut, *If This Isn't Nice, What Is?* Commencement Address at Butler University, Indianapolis, Indiana, May 11, 1996 (RosettaBooks e-edition, 2020), 139.

4. Mark Kurlansky, *The Food of a Younger Land*, 200.

5. James Beard, introduction to *American Cooking: The Eastern Heartland*, by José Wilson and the editors of Time-Life Books, 6–7.

6. Census Reporter, table B02001, "Race," accessed July 24, 2022, https://censusreporter.org/data/table/?table=B02001.

7. Census Reporter, table B03002, "Hispanic or Latino Origin by Race," accessed July 25, 2022, https://censusreporter.org/data/table/?table=B03002.

8. Census Reporter, table B04006, "People Reporting Ancestry," accessed May 25, 2022, https://censusreporter.org/data/table/?table=B04006.

9. "Indiana's Amish Population," *INcontext* 13, no. 6 (November–December 2012), www.incontext.indiana.edu/2012/nov-dec/article2.asp, fig. 2.

10. William Woys Weaver, *As American as Shoofly Pie*, 3.

11. "Jewish Population in the United States by State," Jewish Virtual Library, updated 2021, https://www.jewishvirtuallibrary.org/jewish-population-in-the-united-states-by-state.

12. Nicholas Lehman, *The Promised Land: The Great Black Migration and How It Changed America*, 6.

13. Arwin D. Smallwood, *The Atlas of African-American History and Politics*, 111.

14. "Quick Facts: Cook County, Illinois," U.S. Census Bureau, https:census.gov/quickfacts/cookcountyillinois.

15. David E. Stannard, *American Holocaust: The Conquest of the New World*, x.

CHAPTER 1

Epigraph: Rachel Peden, "A Psalm of Grapes," in *Rural Free: A Farmwife's Almanac of Country Living* (Bloomington, IN: Quarry Books, 2009), 19.

1. Anne C. Rose, *Voices of the Marketplace: American Thought and Culture, 1830–1860*, 75.

2. Annie S. Frost, *The Godey's Lady's Book Receipts and Household Hints*, 65–72.

3. Karen Hess, introduction to *The Art of Cookery Made Plain and Easy*, by Hannah Glasse (1997, facsimile ed.), v–vii.

4. Irma S. Rombauer and Marion Rombauer Becker, *The Joy of Cooking*, 774–87.

5. Rombauer and Rombauer Becker, *Joy of Cooking*, imprint page.

6. "Livingston Realizes His Ambition," *Cincinnati Enquirer*, June 13, 1909, 8.

7. "Farmer's Reading: Chili Sauce," *Evansville Daily Journal* (Evansville, IN), August 30, 1867, 3.

8. "Chili Sauce," Household Department, *Boston Globe*, September 20, 1906, 12.

9. Marianne Postans, *Western India in 1838*, 18; Fitch W. Taylor, *The Broad Pennant: Or, A Cruise in the United States Flag Ship*, 32; Elizabeth Muter, *Travels and Adventures of an Officer's Wife in India, China, and New Zealand*, vol. 2, 16, 69, 110.

10. "McKenzie and McNeill," advertisement, *Charleston Daily Courier* (Charleston, SC), November 1, 1804, 3.

11. Malinda Russell, *Domestic Cook Book*, 19.

12. Andrew F. Smith, *The Tomato in America*, 3–24.

13. Christina Stapley, *The Receipt Book of Lady Anne Blencowe*, 85.

14. Richard Briggs, *The English Art of Cookery, a new edition*, 476.

15. Lettice Bryan, *The Kentucky Housewife*, 190.

16. *Evening Post* (New York), October 14, 1802, 1.

17. Bertha Kramer ["Aunt Babette"], *Aunt Babette's Cook Book*, 450.

18. Nick Kindelsperger, "How Giardiniera Crossed an Ocean to Become Chicago's Favorite Condiment," *Chicago Tribune*, May 19, 2017.

19. Alan Davidson, "Sauerkraut," in *The Penguin Companion to Food*, 834.

20. Volker Bach, *The Kitchen, Food, and Cooking in Reformation Germany*, 39.

21. Davidson, "Sauerkraut," 835.

22. Fanny Lemira Gillette, *The American Cook Book*, 167.

23. Rombauer and Rombauer Becker, *Joy of Cooking*, 785.

24. Presbyterian Church of LaPorte, *Many New and Reliable Recipes*, 43.

25. Indiana Farmers Guide, *The Indiana Farmers Guide New Cook Book*, 165.

26. Jonathan Carver and John Coakley Lettsom, *Travels through the Interior Parts of North America in the Years 1766, 1767, and 1768*, 511–12.

27. Huron E. Smith, "Ethnobotany of the Ojibwe Indians," *Bulletin of the Public Museum of the City of Milwaukee* 4, no. 3 (May 2, 1932): 369, 394; Smith, "Ethnobotany of the Monomini Indians," *Bulletin of the Public Museum of the City of Milwaukee* 4, no. 1 (December 10, 1923), 65–66.

28. "Apple Butter," *The Farmers' Cabinet; Devoted to Agriculture, Horticulture, and Rural Economy*, vol. 3, 103.

29. *Western Carolinian* (Salisbury, NC), March 8, 1834, 1.

30. Frances Wood, *The Silk Road*, 18.

31. Wood, *Silk Road*, 14.

32. Erika Monahan, "Locating Rhubarb: Early Modernity's Relative Obscurity," in *Early Modern Things: Objects and Their Histories, 1500–1800*, 234–35.

33. *New England Farmer* (Boston), April 4, 1828, 2.

34. Henriette Davidis, *Praktisches Kochbuch für die Deutschen in Amerika* (1897), 158.

CHAPTER 2

Epigraphs: Quoted in George R. Wilson, *History of Dubois County from Primitive Days to 1910*, 138–39; Wilson, *History of Dubois County*, 129.

1. William Hogeland, *The Whiskey Rebellion*, 66–67.

2. Henry Morley, *Early Papers and Some Memories*, 373.

3. Lettice Bryan, *The Kentucky Housewife*, 401.

4. Philomelia Hardin, *Every Body's Cook and Receipt Book*, 31.

5. Serhii Chruckey, "Tied Houses," last modified January 11, 2009, https://forgottenchicago .com/features/tied-houses/.

6. Brewers Association, "State Craft Beer Sales and Production Statistics," accessed June 16, 2022, https://www.brewersassociation.org/statistics-and-data/state-craft-beer-stats/.

7. Dann Woellert, *Cincinnati Wine*, 45–50.

8. Todd Kliman, *The Wild Vine*, 20–23.

9. Kliman, *Wild Vine*, 115–24.

10. "Rye," MGP Ingredients, accessed May 26, 2022, https://www.mgpingredients.com /distilled-spirits/beverage/product/rye.

11. "Cocktails," Bryant's Cocktail Lounge, accessed May 26, 2022, https://www .bryantscocktaillounge.com/cocktails.

12. Bryan, *Kentucky Housewife*, 390.

13. Bertha Kramer ["Aunt Babette"], *Aunt Babette's Cook Book*, 473.

14. Mrs. Simon Kander and Mrs. Henry Schoenfeld, *The Settlement Cook Book*, 14.

15. Kander and Schoenfeld, *Settlement Cook Book*, 469–72.

CHAPTER 3

Epigraph: Mimi Sheraton, "Cookery, Seen by Saul Bellow," *New York Times*, May 18, 1983, C1.

1. Polly Campbell, "How Cincinnati Became the Capital of Coffee Cake," *Cincinnati Enquirer*, April 9, 2017, 1AA.

2. Rae Katherine Eighmey, *Abraham Lincoln in the Kitchen*, 21.

3. Lettice Bryan, *The Kentucky Housewife*, 318.

4. "Cooking Hints," *Catoctin Clarion* (Mechanicstown, MD), June 17, 1880, 4.

5. "Delicious Fried Biscuit," *Indianapolis Star*, August 20, 1907, 9.

6. "Seasonable Dishes," *Bloomington Evening World* (Bloomington, IN), March 17, 1917, 2.

7. "Brown County's Nashville House," *Republic* (Columbus, IN), May 18, 1956, 10.

8. William Howitt, *The Rural and Domestic Life of Germany*, 91–93.

9. William Woys Weaver, *As American as Shoofly Pie*, 35.

10. Mark H. Zanger, "Pretzels," in *The Oxford Encyclopedia of Food and Drink in America*, 2nd ed., vol. 3, ed. Andrew F. Smith, 60.

11. Phyllis A. Trout Johanneman, *Ferdinand Life: How We Lived and Ate*, 27.

12. Manual Galvan Rivera, *Diccionario de cocina, o el nuevo cocinero Mexicano*, 571–78.

13. Salvador Novo, *Cocina Mexicana, o historia gastronomica de la Ciudad de Mexico*, 86. Translation by the author.

14. Robert Weis, *Bakers and Basques: A Social History of Bread in Mexico*, 40–41.

15. Eric Zolov, *Iconic Mexico*, 427–29.

16. Fannie Merritt Farmer, *The Boston Cooking-School Cookbook* (1896), 62

17. *Examiner* (London), April 21, 1839, 23.

18. Alan Davidson, *The Oxford Companion to Food*, 114.

19. "Cinnamon Rolls," *Edwardsville Intelligencer*, June 20, 1872, 7.

20. George Peltz, *The Housewife's Library*, 183.

21. Joh. Christ. Friedr. Báhrens, *Ueber das westphálische Grobbrod, genannt Pumpernickel*, 10. Translation by the author.

22. Elizabeth Coblentz, *The Amish Cook*, 82.

23. "Readers Share Turnip Kraut Recipes, Amish Bread," *Times-Mail* (Bedford, IN), September 23, 1987, 5.

24. "Art Colony Party," *Tri-County Banner* (Knightstown, IN), December 27, 1962, 9.

25. "'Friendship Bread' Name for Sourdough," *Nevada State Journal* (Reno, NV), January 14, 1968, 13.

26. "Serve 'Friendship Bread' for New Year," *Tennessean* (Nashville), December 28, 1951, 26.

27. Stefanson, D. H., "Friendship Bread," *Sioux City Journal* (Sioux City, IA), March 19, 1972, 88.

28. Weaver, *As American as Shoofly Pie*, 2.

29. Bertha Kramer ["Aunt Babette"], *Aunt Babette's Cook Book*, 326–35; Kander and Schoenfeld, *The Settlement Cookbook*, 22–26.

30. Maria Sophia Schellhammer, *Das Brandenburgische Koch=Buch*, 353–54.

31. Norma Jost Voth, *Mennonite Foods & Folkways from South Russia*, vol. 1, 36.

32. Voth, *Mennonite Foods & Folkways*, vol. 1, 14.

33. Volker Bach, *The Kitchen, Food, and Cooking in Reformation Germany*, 163.

34. Hannah Glasse, *The Art of Cookery Made Plain and Easy* (1805), 138.

35. Philomelia Hardin, *Every Body's Cook and Receipt Book*, 45.

36. Hannah Widdifield, *Widdifield's New Cook Book*, 279–80.

37. Henriette Davidis, *Praktisches Kochbuch für die Deutschen in Amerika* (1897), 379–82.

CHAPTER 4

Epigraph: Terra Brockman, "Green Corn Moon," in *The Seasons on Henry's Farm* (Evanston, IL: Agate, 2010), 231.

1. Don Walker, "Miller Park: Where the Sausage Is King," *Milwaukee Journal Sentinel*, April 2, 2010, accessed June 21, 2022, https://archive.jsonline.com/newswatch/89771437.html.

2. R. W. Apple Jr., "The Meat That Made Sheboygan Famous," *New York Times*, June 5, 2002, section F, 1.

3. Sabina Welserin, "Weltt jr gút prattwirst machen," in *Das Kochbuch der Sabina Welserin*, ed. Hugo Stopp, receipt no. 25. Translation by Ulrike Gießmann.

4. US Department of Agriculture National Agricultural Statistics Service, *Wisconsin Ag News—Specialty Cheese* (Madison: Wisconsin Field Office, April 28, 2020).

5. United States Census, "2020 Population and Housing State Data," accessed October 26, 2022, https://www.census.gov/library/visualizations/interactive/2020-population-and-housing-state-data.html.

6. Eliza Smith, *The Compleat Housewife*, 139.

7. "Figi's Certified Beer," advertisement, *Marshfield News-Herald* (Marshfield, WI), July 21, 1966, 15.

8. "Dave's Burger Shanty," advertisement, *Neenah Menasha Northwestern* (Oshkosh, WI), July 7, 1976, 14.

9. Jack Coffman, "Fair's Food Fare Flushes Freaky Feeders," *Star Tribune* (Minneapolis), August 28, 1976, 1.

10. "List of Premiums," *Somerset Herald* (Somerset, PA), September 30, 1874, 3.

11. "Great Meeting of Suffragists" *Republic* (Meyersdale, PA), June 29, 1916, 4.

12. *Kansas City Times* (Kansas City, MO), January 28, 1872, 1.

13. "Cold Pack," cheese.com, accessed May 26, 2022, https://www.cheese.com/cold-pack/.

14. Betty Wason, A Salute to Cheese, 97.

15. "Swedish Americans in Wisconsin," Swedish American Historical Society of Wisconsin, accessed May 26, 2022, https://sahswi.org/swedish-immigration-history/.

16. Lori McGinnis, "More People Are Driving In to More Runza Drive Inns," *Lincoln Journal Star* (Lincoln, NE), March 10, 1984, 4.

17. "Runza Firm Sues to Stop Use of Name," *Lincoln Journal Star*, August 12, 1993, 8.

18. James W. Long, *From Privileged to Dispossessed: The Volga Germans, 1860–1917*, 45–55.

19. "Meat Filled Yeast Rolls Easy to Serve and Eat," *Wichita Beacon* (Wichita, KS), February 21, 1957, 30.

20. "Who Invented Toasted Ravioli?," *St. Louis Magazine Online*, November 20, 2015, accessed October 26, 2022, https://www.stlmag.com/news/who-invented-toasted-ravioli/.

21. "Who Invented Toasted Ravioli?"

22. "Oldani's," advertisement, *St. Louis Star and Times*, February 20, 1943, 5.

23. Gustavo Arellano, *Taco USA: How Mexican Food Conquered America*, 31.

24. Mike Sula, "One the Trail of the Delta Tamale," *Chicago Reader*, May 15, 2008, Food and Drink, 1.

25. David J. Libby, *Slavery and Frontier Mississippi, 1720–1835*, 8–10.

26. Devon A. Mihesuah, "Sustenance and Health Among the Five Nations in Indian Territory, Post Removal to Statehood," *Ethnohistory* 62, no. 2 (April 2015), 263–84.

27. Priscilla Mullin Sherard, *Indian Recipes Collected from the Indian People I Love*, 6–7.

28. "Toothsome Tamales, How the Mexicans Make an Odd but Palatable Dish," *Grenada Sentinel* (Grenada, MS), March 27, 1886, 3.

29. "Isn't This Dish Worth Importing?" *Vicksburg Evening Post* (Vicksburg, MI), May 7, 1887, 5.

30. "Something Deserving Encouragement," *People's Vindicator* (Natchitoches, LA), August 14, 1880, 3.

31. "A Day in Queretaro," *Chicago Tribune*, June 21, 1867, 2.

32. "Tamale," *Chicago Tribune*, July 14, 1884, 9.

33. Arellano, *Taco USA*, 42.

34. "Hot Tamales Return with the Corn," *Chicago Tribune*, August 31, 1896, 7.

35. Mrs. W. L. Tabor, "Chicken Tamales: How to Prepare a Dish Which Is Esteemed Quite Highly," *Daily Free Press* (Carbondale, IL), May 27, 1899.

36. Phyllis Hammond, "Take a Tip from Old Mexico: Try a Hot Tamale!" *Chicago Tribune*, July 24, 1932, 34.

37. "Our Story," Nick's Kitchen, accessed June 23, 2022, https://www.nicksdowntown.com/.

38. "Nick's Kitchen Is the New Name," *Daily News-Democrat* (Huntington, IN), November 22, 1909, 8.

39. "Nick's Kitchen," advertisement, *Daily News-Democrat* (Huntington, IN), December 17, 1909, 8.

40. "Local and Personal," *Kansas Democrat* (Hiawatha, KS), October 17, 1906, 2.

41. "White's," advertisement, *Indianapolis Star*, September 28, 1908, 10.

42. "White's," advertisement, *Indianapolis Star*, May 1, 1908, 14.

43. John Mariani, *The Encyclopedia of American Food and Drink*, 273.

44. Cecil Adams, "The Straight Dope," *Chicago Reader*, February 19, 2009, 3.

45. Monica Eng, "Saga of a Sandwich," *Chicago Tribune*, June 18, 2003, section 2, 1.

46. "Consumption Stats," National Hot Dog and Sausage Council, accessed May 27, 2022, http://www.hot-dog.org/media/consumption-stats.

47. "Cristoforo Messisbugo, 1557," Mortadella Bologna, accessed May 27, 2022, https://mortadellabologna.com/blog/cristoforo-messisbugo-1557-le-ricette-forestiere/.

48. Maria Sophia Schellhammer, *Die wol unterwiesene Köchinn*, 507. Translation by Volker Bach.

49. Johann Wursthorn, *Wurstologia Novissima et Aucta*, 1690, accessed from the Bibliothek Universität Hamburg online May 27, 2022, https://resolver.sub.uni-hamburg.de/kitodo/PPN767145178.

50. Max Fuchs, *Xavier Krenkl's Leben, Anecdoten, und Sprüche*, post script advertisement for Hans Schwartz, *Die Wurstfabrikation für Wirtschaften*.

51. F. Eppner, *Die deutsche Wurstfabrikation*, 31–32.

52. "Chouteau Ave. Brauerei Salon," advertisement, *Mississippi Blätter* (St. Louis), December 2, 1866, 9.

53. "Splendid Sausage," *Intelligencer Journal* (Lancaster, PA), December 26, 1868, 2.

54. "Shifts to Live: Food for Two Weeks for the Impecunious for a Dollar," *Fort Wayne Daily Gazette* (Fort Wayne, IN), June 20, 1883, 2.

55. *Tennessean* (Nashville), November 14, 1886, 9.

56. "An Enterprising Nuisance Crushed," *Tennessean* (Nashville), October 27, 1886, 5.

57. "A Continuous Line," *Brooklyn Daily Eagle* (Brooklyn, NY), August 14, 1882, 3.

58. "Busy Merchants of Maxwell St., Chicago, Wonder," *El Paso Times* (El Paso, TX), December 5, 1920, 28.

59. Bruce Kraig, *Hot Dog: A Global History*, 77.

60. "History of the Chicago Hot Dog," Vienna Beef Company, accessed May 27, 2022, https://www.viennabeef.com/chicagos-hot-dog/history-of-the-chicago-hot-dog/.

61. Kraig, *Hot Dog*, 77–78.

62. "Second-Rate City," *Chicago Tribune*, May 22, 2000, 147.

63. "Suzie's Corner," advertisement, *Chicago Tribune*, March 26, 1953, 11.

64. "History," S. Rosen's Baking Company, accessed May 26, 2022, https://www.srosens.com/about/history/.

65. Phil Vettel, "Poppy Love? Why Seeds Adorn the Chicago-Style Bun," *Chicago Tribune*, August 30, 2017, section 6, 4.

66. Michael Stern and Jane Stern, *500 Things to Eat Before It's Too Late*, 235.

67. Katherine Yung and Joe Grimm, *Coney Detroit*, 6–7.

CHAPTER 5

Epigraph: Presbyterian Church of LaPorte, *Many New and Reliable Recipes*, title page.

1. Gil Marks, *The World of Jewish Cooking*, 63.

2. William Woys Weaver, *American as Shoofly Pie*. 21–22.

3. Andrea King Collier, "When Did Green Bean Casserole Become a Delicacy?" *Lansing State Journal* (Lansing, MI), April 20, 2006, 25.

4. Annabella P. Hill, *Mrs. Hill's New Cook Book*, 194.

5. Adrian Miller, *Soul Food: The Surprising Story of an American Cuisine*, 176.

6. "Perfection Salad Is an American Classic," *Philadelphia Enquirer*, February 20, 1964, 19.

7. Fannie Merritt Farmer, *The Boston Cooking-School Cookbook* (1911), 335, 337–38.

8. Marks, *World of Jewish Cooking*, 222.

9. Henriette Davidis, *Praktisches Kochbuch für die Deutschen in Amerika* (1879), 181–82.

10. "Local Fish Fry Recommendations," *Lake Geneva Regional News* (Lake Geneva, WI), February 20, 2020, D3.

11. Volker Bach, *The Kitchen, Food, and Cooking in Reformation Germany*, 33.

12. *Cincinnati Enquirer*, December 7, 1954, 18.

13. Dorothea Hake, "Goetta Drums Up A Real Argument," *Cincinnati Enquirer*, December 9, 1957, 27.

14. Henriette Davidis, *Praktisches Kochbuch für die Deutschen in Amerika* (1897), 457, receipt no. 22. Translation by the author.

15. Bach, *Kitchen, Food, and Cooking in Reformation Germany*, 41; W. R. Wilde, "On the Introduction and Period of the General Use of the Potato in Ireland." *Proceedings of the Royal Irish Academy (1836–1869)* 6 (1853): 357.

16. Gottlieb Sigmund Corvinus, *Frauenzimmer Lexicon*, 483–84.

17. Nathan Bailey, *Dictionarium Domesticum*, 497, 504.

18. Charlotte Mason, *The Lady's Assistant*, 322–25.

19. *Leicester Chronicle or Commercial and Leicestershire Mercury* (Leicester, England), May 15, 1858, 7.

20. Hill, *Mrs. Hill's New Cook Book*, 194.

21. Milton Reizenstein, *The Economic History of the Baltimore and Ohio Railroad, 1827–1853*, 13–14.

22. David Schley, *Steam City: Railroads, Urban Space, and Corporate Capitalism in Nineteenth-Century Baltimore*, 97–98.

23. John Wennersten, *The Oyster Wars of Chesapeake Bay*, 14.

24. Schley, *Steam City*, 186.

25. Buckeye Publishing, *Buckeye Cookery and Practical Housekeeping*, 2nd ed.

26. Hannah Glasse, *The Art of Cookery Made Plain and Easy* (1760), 186.

CHAPTER 6

Epigraph: Nelson Algren, "Festivals in the Fields," in *America Eats* (Iowa City: University of Iowa Press, 1992), 37.

1. "Life in the Pine Woods," *Sioux City Journal* (Sioux City, IA), November 27, 1891, 2.

2. *Junction City Weekly Union* (Junction City, KS), August 25, 1877, 5.

3. "Town and Neighborhood," *Junction City Tribune* (Junction City, KS), December 8, 1881, 3.

4. " Green Bay Booyah Change Name to Rockers," *Press Times* (Green Bay, WI), November 3, 2021, accessed May 27, 2022, https://gopresstimes.com/2021/11/03/green-bay-booyah-change-name-to-rockers/.

5. Grace Lutheran Ladies Aid, *Grace Lutheran Ladies Aid Cookbook*, 49.

6. Mary A. Dolve, *The School Lunch*, Cooperative Extension Circulars 1917–1950, no. 49.

7. Amy Bowen, "Legislative Hotdish," *Saint Cloud Times* (Saint Cloud, MN), February 16, 2011, 29.

8. Heid E. Erdrich, *Original Local: Indigenous Foods, Stories, and Recipes from the Upper Midwest*, 20.

9. Erdrich, *Original Local*, 35.

10. Sarah Rutledge, *The Carolina Housewife*, 48.

11. "Kennedy's Restaurant," advertisement, *Scranton Republican* (Scranton, PA), June 26, 1890, 4.

12. "A Pennsylvania Dinner," *Dixon Evening Telegraph* (Dixon, IL), March 10, 1897, 8.

13. "Fish Fry," *Readstown Special* (Readstown, WI), March 6, 1865, 2.

14. Korsha Wilson, "Celebrating the Fish Fry: A Late-Summer Black Tradition," *New York Times*, September 12, 2018, section D, 1.

15. Gottlieb Sigmund Corvinus, *Frauenzimmer Lexicon*, 54.

16. Hannah Glasse, *The Art of Cookery Made Plain and Easy* (1747), 86.

17. Bertha Kramer ["Aunt Babette"], *Aunt Babette's Cook Book*, 34–42.

18. "Complimentary Breakfast to Mr. Florence at the Lindell," *St. Louis Globe-Democrat*, December 4, 1876, 8.

19. "Grand Banquet," *Harrisburg Telegraph* (Harrisburg, PA), May 13, 1874, 3.

20. "Tartar Sauce for Meats," *Northern Ohio Journal* (Painesville, OH), October 19, 1878, 4.

21. "Oakland Items," *San Francisco Chronicle*, September 16, 1868, 3.

22. "Oyster Cocktail and Loaf," *St. Joseph Herald* (St. Joseph, MO), September 8, 1889, 9.

23. Leon Kientz, *The Fish and Oyster Book*, 1, 27.

24. John T. Edge, *Fried Chicken: An American Story*, 107–13.

25. Glasse, *The Art of Cooking Made Plain and Easy* (1747), 40

26. Joseph Wechsberg, *The Cooking of the Viennese Empire*, 49.

27. Eleonora Maria Rosalia, *Freiwillig aufgesprungener Granat-Apfel des Christlichen Samaritens*, part 2, "Koch Buch," 31. Translation by the author.

28. Corvinus, *Frauenzimmer Lexicon*, 904.

29. Conrad Hagger, *Neues saltzburgisches Koch-Buch* part 3, book 2, 43–44.

30. Michael Kelly, *Reminiscences of Michael Kelly*, 129.

31. Historic Jamestowne, National Park Service. "The Second Supply," accessed May 26, 2022, https://historicjamestowne.org/history/history-of-jamestown/the-second-supply/.

32. Günter Moltmann, *German Immigration to America: 300 Years of Immigration 1683–1983*, 27.

33. William Byrd, *The Secret Diary of William Byrd of Westover, 1709–1712*, eds. Marion Tinling and Louie Booker Wright, 242, 514.

34. Adrian Miller, *Soul Food: The Surprising Story of an American Cuisine*, 52–65.

35. "Refectory," *Evening Post* (New York), September 1, 1820, 3.

36. "The Run Up to Reading," *New York Daily Herald*, September 14, 1848, 3.

37. Edge, *Fried Chicken*, 98.

38. Henriette Davidis, *Praktisches Kochbuch für die Deutschen in Amerika* (1879), 145.

39. Timothy Charles Lloyd, "The Cincinnati Chili Culinary Complex," *Western Folklore* 40, no. 1 (1981): 28–40.

40. Dann Woellert, *The Authentic History of Cincinnati Chili*, 27–28.

41. Woellert, *Authentic History of Cincinnati Chili*, 40–41.

42. Susan Herrmann Loomis, "Fare of the Country: A City's Romance with a Bowl of Chili," *New York Times*, April 16, 1989, section 5, 6.

43. Catherine Hero, "Chocolate in the Chili? Well, We Asked," *Cincinnati Enquirer*, April 12, 2021, Z1.

CHAPTER 7

Epigraph: Helen Rosner, "A Writer's Beef," *Saveur* 166 (June–July 2014), 18.

1. Hannah Glasse, *The Art of Cookery Made Plain and Easy* (1763), 370.

2. F. Eppner, *Die deutsche Wurstfabrikation*, 59.

3. Wilhelmine Schwägermann, *Gründlich abgefasstes norddeutsches Kochbuch für die bürgerliche Küchen*, 68. Translation by the author.

4. Ellen F. Steinberg and Jack H. Prost. "A Menu and a Mystery: The Case of the 1834 Delmonico Bill of Fare." *Gastronomica* 8, no. 2 (2008): 40–50.

5. "Hotels: Anderson's European Hotel. Restaurant Bill of Fare," *Chicago Tribune*, July 6, 1873, 16.

6. "A Good Dinner, My Boy," *Brooklyn Daily Sun*, December 28, 1873, 6.

7. Henriette Davidis, *Praktisches Kochbuch für die Deutschen in Amerika* (1879), 80.

8. "Not Eaten on the Premises," *Sun* (New York), April 27, 1883, 3.

9. "Broiled Hamburg Steak," *Indiana State Sentinel* (Indianapolis), February 1, 1893.

10. "Odors of the Onion," *San Francisco Chronicle*, July 23, 1894, 7.

11. "In a Sandwich Car," *Chicago Tribune*, July 5, 1896, 16.

12. Henry Mayhew, *German Life and Manners as Seen in Saxony at the Present Day*, 34.

13. Davidis, *Praktisches Kochbuch* (1879), 80. Translation by the author.

14. Marcia Poole, "Sioux City's Signature Sandwich? The Loosemeat," *Sioux City Journal* (Sioux City, IA), October 19, 2005, E1.

15. Sharyn Jackson, "Who Invented Our Classic Burger?," *Star Tribune* (Minneapolis), July 8, 2017, E1.

16. "The Towers," advertisement, *Evansville Press* (Evansville, IN), September 17, 1938, 2; "The Idle Inn Sandwich Shop," advertisement, *Star Press* (Muncie, IN), October 2, 1938, 17.

17. Nancy J. Purdy, "Horseshoe: A Sandwich by Any Other Name," *Mattoon Journal-Gazette* (Mattoon, IL), February 18, 1981, 21.

18. Sarah Fritschner, "Three to Show," *Courier-Journal* (Louisville, KY), May 3, 1987, 166.

CHAPTER 8

Epigraph: Harriet Elinor Smith, ed., *The Autobiography of Mark Twain*, vol. 1 (Berkeley: University of California Press, 2010), 211.

1. George R. Wilson, *History of Dubois County*, 118, 115.

2. Robert F. Moss, *Barbecue: The History of an American Institution*, 24–29.

3. Moss, *Barbecue*, 42–48.

4. "The Dayton Barbecue," *Summit Country Beacon* (Akron, OH), October 5, 1842, 2.

5. "Shelby Barbecue," *Indiana State Sentinel* (Indianapolis), August 5, 1847, 2.

6. "The Butchers Have a Barbecue," *Champaign Daily Gazette* (Champaign, IL), May 27, 1887, 3.

7. Lettice Bryan, *The Kentucky Housewife*, 95–96.

8. Buckeye Publishing, *Buckeye Cookery and Practical Housekeeping*, 176.

9. Moss, *Barbecue*, 126–27.

10. Adrian Miller, *Black Smoke*, 123–24.

11. Moss, *Barbecue*, 156.

12. Calvin Trillin, "No! One of the Worlds' Foremost Authorities on Ribs, Cheeseburger, French Fries and Frosty Malts Takes a Gourmet Tour of Kansas City," *Playboy Magazine* 19, no. 4, April 1972, 209.

13. Moss, *Barbecue*, 156.

14. Lolis Eric Elie, *Smokestack Lightning: Adventures in the Heart of Barbecue Country*, 96.

15. Elie, *Smokestack Lightning*, 97–98.

16. Elaine Viets, "Cutting Us In on St. Louis Cut Ribs," *St. Louis Post-Dispatch*, July 20, 1995, 108.

17. "Council Oak Stores," advertisement, *Dakota County Star* (South Sioux City, NE), September 17, 1953, 5.

18. Miller, *Black Smoke*, 155.

CHAPTER 9

Epigraph: Calvin Trillin, "Calvin Trillin Discusses His Book *Third Helpings*," *The Studs Terkel Program*, Chicago: WFMT, April 22, 1983, https://studsterkel.wfmt.com/programs/calvin-trillin-discusses-his-book-third-helpings.

1. Frances Dawson, "Favorite Dish: Pizza, A New Arrival in St. Louis," *St. Louis Post-Dispatch*, April 13, 1947, 116.

2. "Luca 'Luigi' Meglio," Obituaries, *St. Louis Post-Dispatch*, August 31, 2014, A025.

3. Bruce Kraig, Carol Haddix, and Colleen Taylor Sen, eds., *The Chicago Food Encyclopedia*, 197.

4. Evangeline Mistaras, "Chicago Restaurants and Nightlife," *ALA Bulletin* 57, no. 6 (1963), 565–70.

5. "Ike Sewell, 87, Creator of 'Chicago-Style' Pizza," *Chicago Tribune*, August 21, 1990, 55.

6. Kathryn Loring, "Have You Heard?," *Chicago Tribune*, April 8, 1956, 370.

7. Sylvia Rector, "Detroit's Old-School Pizza: It's Hip to Be Square," *Detroit Free Press*, June 4, 2009, 70.

8. Nicole Schnitzler, "From Little Italy to the World: Pizza's Place in Chicago History," *For the Love of Pizza*, supplement, *Chicago Tribune*, 10–11.

CHAPTER 10

Epigraphs: Nelson Algren, *America Eats*, 37–38; George Rector, *Home at the Range with George Rector* (New York: Rector, 1939), 135.

1. *Evening Dispatch* (Michigan City, IN), *Your Happy Kitchen Cookbook*.

2. Sunshine Circle of Bethel Evangelical Church, *The Concordia Cook Book: Tried and Tested Recipes*.

3. Elaine Lumbra, ed., *The Hoosier Cookbook*, 236.

4. Jenny Lewis, *Midwest Sweet Baking History*, 106.

5. Rosa Abreu-Runkel, *Vanilla: A Global History*, 56–59.

6. M. B. Bateham and S. D. Harris, eds., "Sugar Pie," *Ohio Cultivator*, vol. 10, 301.

7. "Table and Kitchen," *Daily Times* (Davenport, IA), April 23, 1902, 7.

8. "Sugar Cream Pie," *Indianapolis Star*, December 25, 1907, 7.

9. Andrew Mariani, "Cherries," in *The Oxford Encyclopedia of Food and Drink in America*, 2nd ed., vol. 1, ed. Andrew F. Smith, 360.

10. "A Chapter on Cherries," *Indianapolis Journal*, June 24, 1900, 18.

11. Evening Belles Home Demonstration Club of Bloomington, Indiana, *Favorite Recipes*, 100.

12. "Luscious Cherry-Filled Desserts for February," *Times-Mail* (Bedford, IN), February 9, 1969, 18.

13. Lettice Bryan, *The Kentucky Housewife*, 268.

14. Henriette Davidis, *Praktisches Kochbuch für die Deutschen in Amerika* (1897), 361.

15. Irma S. Rombauer and Marion Rombauer Becker, *The Joy of Cooking*, 702.

16. Harold McGee, *On Food and Cooking*, 304.

17. Andrew F. Smith, "Sweet Potatoes," in *The Oxford Encyclopedia of Food and Drink in America*, 2nd ed., vol. 3, ed. Andrew F. Smith, 400.

18. "Sweet Potato Pie," *Princeton Clarion-Ledger* (Princeton, IN), October 15, 1853, 2.

19. "The County Fair: Bread, Cakes and Pickles," *Daily Kansas Tribune* (Lawrence, KS), October 24, 1869, 3.

20. Adrian Miller, *Soul Food: The Surprising Story of an American Cuisine*, 248–50.

21. Joanne Raetz Stuttgen, *The Café Indiana Cookbook*, 114.

22. Bryan, *Kentucky Housewife*, 239–40.

23. Maria Parloa, *The Original Appledore Cook Book*, 158.

24. "The American Persimmon," *Richmond Item* (Richmond, IN), February 23, 1897, 3.

25. "Randolph County Agricultural Fair: Food, Condiments, and C." *Fayetteville Weekly Observer* (Fayetteville, NC), November 5, 1860, 2.

26. James Troop and O. M. Hadley, "The American Persimmon," *Purdue University Agricultural Experiment Station Bulletin* 7, no. 60 (April 1896); "The American Persimmon," *Richmond Item* (Richmond, IN), February 23, 1897, 3.

27. K. W. Pomper, D. R. Layne, and R. N. Peterson, "The Pawpaw Regional Variety Trial," in *Perspectives on New Crops and New Uses*, ed. J. Janick, 353–57.

28. J. M. Peck, *Guide for Emigrants, Containing Sketches of Illinois, Missouri, and the Adjacent Parts*, 38.

29. Jay K. Wesley, *Kalamazoo River Assessment*, Michigan Department of Natural Resources, Fisheries Division, Special Report no. 35 (September 2005), 7.

30. Cliff Doerksen, "The Real American Pie," *Chicago Reader*, December 17, 2009, 1.

31. Bryan, *Kentucky Housewife*, 271–74.

32. Alan Davidson, *The Oxford Companion to Food*, 507.

33. Bryan, *Kentucky Housewife*, 328–29.

34. Buckeye Publishing, *Buckeye Cookery and Practical Housekeeping*, 85.

35. Indiana Farmer's Guide, *The Indiana Farmer's Guide Cookbook*, 66.

36. Rombauer, and Rombauer Becker, *Joy of Cooking*, 643–44.

37. Evan Jones, *American Food: The Gastronomic Story*, 2nd ed., 93.

38. Mrs. D. A. Lincoln [Mary Johnson Bailey Lincoln], *Mrs. Lincoln's Boston Cook Book*, 374.

39. Parloa, *Original Appledore Cook Book*, 119.

40. Inglehart Brothers, *Cake Secrets*, 1–27.

41. Andrew F. Smith, "Chocolate," in *The Oxford Encyclopedia of Food and Drink in America*, 2nd ed., vol. 1, ed. Andrew F. Smith, 396.

42. Hannah Widdifield, *Widdifield's New Cook Book*, 317, 319.

43. Christian Friedrich Germershausen, *Die Hausmutter in allen ihren Geschäfften*, 3rd ed., vol. 2, 53. Translation by the author.

44. Anna Dorn, ed., *Neuestes universal oder großes wiener Koch Buch*, 285–86.

45. Annie Frost, *The Godey's Lady's Book Receipts and Household Hints*, 362–63.

46. Parloa, *Original Appledore Cook Book*, 121.

47. "Household Recipes Contributed: Black Chocolate or Devil's Food Cake," *Weekly Record* (New Madrid, MO), November 16, 1890, 24.

48. "Marion Harland" [Mary Virginia Terhune], *Common Sense in the Household*, 322.

49. "Marion Harland, Author, Dies at 91," *New York Times*, June 4, 1922, 28.

50. Buckeye Publishing, *Buckeye Cookery and Practical Housekeeping*, 49.

51. Bertha Kramer ["Aunt Babette"], *Aunt Babette's Cook Book*, 303–4.

52. McGee, *On Food and Cooking*, 657.

53. Dorothy Brainerd, "Use Bright Settings for Your Table," *St. Louis Post-Dispatch*, May 23, 1954, 82.

54. Daniel Neman, "Gooey Love," *St. Louis Post-Dispatch*, February 10, 2016, page L04.

55. Volker Bach, *The Kitchen, Food, and Cooking in Reformation Germany*, 161.

56. Germershausen, *Die Hausmutter in allen ihren Geschäfften*, 33–35.

57. Alan Davidson, *The Penguin Companion to Food*, 898.

58. Eleonora Maria Rosalia, *Freiwillig aufgesprungener Granat-Apfel des Christlichen Samaritens*, part 2, "Koch Buch," 114.

59. Henriette Davidis, *Praktisches Kochbuch für die Deutschen in Amerika* (1879), 284–85.

60. Kander and Schoenfeld, *The Settlement Cook Book*, 151.

61. Rombauer and Rombauer Becker, *Joy of Cooking*, 663.

62. Davidson, *Penguin Companion to Food*, 535.

63. Sabina Welserin, *Das Kochbuch der Sabina Welserin*, ed. Hugo Stopp, receipt no. 153, translation by Ulrike Gießmann.

64. Davidis, *Praktisches Kochbuch* (1897), 285.

65. Bertha Kramer ["Aunt Babette"] *Aunt Babette's Cook Book*, 360.

66. Kander and Schoenfeld, *Settlement Cookbook*, 150.

67. Gil Marks, *The World of Jewish Cooking*, 326.

68. "Exchange of Ideas: Mexican Wedding Cake," *Reporter-Times* (Martinsville, IN), November 17, 1932, 3.

69. *Betty Crocker's Picture Cookbook*, 1st ed., 206.

CHAPTER 11

Epigraph: Will Allen, with Charles Wilson, *The Good Food Revolution* (New York: Gotham Books, 2012), 9.

Bibliography

ORAL INTERVIEWS

Allen, Erika, co-founder & CEO of operations, Urban Growers Collective; president, Green Era Educational NFP; co-owner, Green Era Sustainability Partners. Interview by author on Zoom, January 27, 2022.

Connoley, Rob, chef and owner of Bulrush. Interview by author on Zoom, October 19, 2021.

Dean, Justin, co-owner, Mad House Vinegar. Visit and discussion with author at Carriage House Farm (North Bend, OH), September 9, 2021.

Hart, Stephanie, CEO, Brown Sugar Bakery. Interview on Facetime by author, April 17, 2022.

Hazzard, Andy, owner, Hazzard Free Farm. Visit and discussion with author at Hazzard Free Farm (Pecatonica, IL), September 2, 2021.

Ruscitti, Titus, blogger, chibbqking.blogspot.com. Telephone interview by author, April 13, 2022.

Travis, Marty, owner, Spence Farm. Visit and discussion with author at Spence Farm (Fairbury, IL), September 17, 2021.

DEMOGRAPHIC SOURCES

Census Reporter. Table B02001. "Race." Data from American Community Survey 5-year, 2020. Accessed July 24, 2022. https://censusreporter.org/data/table/?table=B02001.

Census Reporter. Table B03002. "Hispanic or Latino Origin by Race." Data from American Community Survey 5-year, 2020. Accessed July 25, 2022. https://censusreporter.org/data/table/?table=B03002.

Census Reporter. Table B04006. "People Reporting Ancestry." Data from American Community Survey 5-year, 2020. Accessed May 25, 2022. https://censusreporter.org/data/table/?table=B04006.

German Roots." U.S. Census Bureau, 2016. Accessed July 25, 2022. https://www.census.gov/library/visualizations/2016/comm/german-roots.html.

"Indiana's Amish Population." *INcontext* 13, no. 6 (November–December, 2012), fig. 2. www.incontext.indiana.edu/2012/nov-dec/article2.asp.

"Jewish Population in the United States by State." Jewish Virtual Library. Updated 2021. https://www.jewishvirtuallibrary.org/jewish-population-in-the-united-states-by-state.

"Quick Facts: Cook County, Illinois." U.S. Census Bureau. https:census.gov/quickfacts/cookcountyillinois.

Schomburg Center for Research in Black Culture, Jean Blackwell Hutson Research and Reference Division, The New York Public Library. "The Great Migration, 1900–1929." New York Public Library Digital Collections. Accessed July 27, 2022. https://digitalcollections.nypl.org/items/85f0908d-8265-f747-e040-e00a18062131.

United States Census. "2020 Population and Housing State Data." Accessed October 26, 2022. https://www.census.gov/library/visualizations/interactive/2020-population-and-housing-state-data.html.

SECONDARY SOURCES

Abreu-Runkel, Rosa. *Vanilla: A Global History*. London: Reaktion Books, 2020.

Adams, Cecil. "The Straight Dope." *Chicago Reader*, February 19, 2009, 3.

"The American Persimmon." *Richmond Item* (Richmond, IN), February 23, 1897, 3.

"Ancestry in the United States." Statistical Atlas. Updated September 4, 2018. https://statisticalatlas.com/United-States/Ancestry, figs. 4 and 179.

Apple, R. W., Jr. "The Meat That Made Sheboygan Famous." *New York Times*, June 5, 2002, section F, 1.

"Apple Butter." *The Farmers' Cabinet; Devoted to Agriculture, Horticulture, and Rural Economy*, vol. 3, 103. Philadelphia: Prouty, Libbey, and Prouty, 1839.

Arellano, Gustavo. *Taco USA: How Mexican Food Conquered America*. New York: Scribner, 2012.

"Art Colony Party." *Tri-County Banner* (Knightstown, IN), December 27, 1962, 9.

Bach, Volker. *The Kitchen, Food, and Cooking in Reformation Germany*. Lanham, MD: Rowman & Littlefield, 2016.

Báhrens, Joh. Christ. Friedr. *Ueber das westphälische Grobbrod, genannt Pumpernickel*. Dortmund and Leipzig: H. Bloth and Comp., 1798.

Bailey, Nathan. *Dictionarium Domesticum, being a new and compleat household dictionary, for the use of city and country*. London: C. Hitch and C. Davis, 1736.

Bateham, M. B., and S. D. Harris, eds. "Sugar Pie." *Ohio Cultivator*, vol. 10. Columbus, OH: M. B. Bateham, 1854.

Betty Crocker's Picture Cookbook. 1st ed. Minneapolis: General Mills, 1950.

Black, Daniel R., and Howard Rosing. *Chicago: A Food Biography*. Lanham, MD: Rowman and Littlefield, 2015.

Bowen, Amy. "Legislative Hotdish." *Saint Cloud Times* (Saint Cloud, MN), February 16, 2011, 29.

Brainerd, Dorothy. "Use Bright Settings for Your Table." *St. Louis Post-Dispatch*, May 23, 1954, 82.

Brewers Association. "State Craft Beer Sales and Production Statistics." Accessed June 16, 2022. https://www.brewersassociation.org/statistics-and-data/state -craft-beer-stats/.

Briggs, Richard. *The English Art of Cookery, a new edition*. Dublin: P. Byrne, 1798.

"Broiled Hamburg Steak." *Indiana State Sentinel* (Indianapolis), February 1, 1893.

"Brown County's Nashville House." Advertisement. *Republic* (Columbus, IN), May 18, 1956, 10.

Bryan, Lettice. *The Kentucky Housewife*. Cincinnati: Shepard and Stearns, 1839.

Buckeye Publishing. *Buckeye Cookery and Practical Housekeeping*. 2nd ed. Marysville, OH: Buckeye Publishing, 1877.

"Busy Merchants of Maxwell St., Chicago, Wonder." *El Paso Times* (El Paso, TX), December 5, 1920, 28.

"The Butchers Have a Barbecue." *Champaign Daily Gazette* (Champaign, IL), May 27, 1887, 3.

Byrd, William. *The Secret Diary of William Byrd of Westover, 1709–1712*. Edited by Marion Tinling and Louie Booker Wright. Richmond, VA: Dietz Press, 1941.

Campbell, Polly. "How Cincinnati Became the Capital of Coffee Cake." *Cincinnati Enquirer*, April 9, 2017, 1AA.

Carver, Jonathan, and John Coakley Lettsom. *Travels through the Interior Parts of North America in the Years 1766, 1767, and 1768*. Dublin: S. Price, 1779.

"A Chapter on Cherries." *Indianapolis Journal*, June 24, 1900.

"Chili Sauce." Household Department, *Boston Globe*, September 20, 1906, 12.

"Chouteau Ave. Brauerei Salon." Advertisement. *Mississippi Blätter* (Saint Louis), December 2, 1866, 9.

Chruckey, Serhii. "Tied Houses." Forgotten Chicago. Last modified January 11, 2009. https://forgottenchicago.com/features/tied-houses/.

Cincinnati Enquirer. December 7, 1954, 18.

"Cinnamon Rolls." *Edwardsville Intelligencer*, June 20, 1872, 7.

Coates, Ta-Nehisi. "The Case for Reparations." In *The Best American Magazine Writing*, edited by Sid Holt for the American Society of Magazine Editors, 3–49. New York: Columbia University Press, 2015.

Coblentz, Elizabeth. *The Amish Cook*. Berkeley, CA: Ten Speed Press, 2002.

"Cocktails." Bryant's Cocktail Lounge. Accessed May 26, 2022. https://www .bryantscocktaillounge.com/cocktails.

320

Coffman, Jack. "Fair's Food Fare Flushes Freaky Feeders." *Star Tribune* (Minneapolis), August 28, 1976, 1.

"Cold Pack." Cheese.com. Accessed May 26, 2022. https://www.cheese.com/cold-pack/.

Collier, Andrea King. "When Did Green Bean Casserole Become a Delicacy?" *Lansing State Journal* (Lansing, MI), April 20, 2006, 25.

"Complimentary Breakfast to Mr. Florence at the Lindell." *St. Louis Globe-Democrat*, December 4, 1876.

"Consumption Stats." National Hot Dog and Sausage Council. Accessed May 27, 2002. http://www.hotdog.org/media/consumption-stats.

"A Continuous Line." *Brooklyn Daily Eagle* (Brooklyn, NY), August 14, 1882, 3.

"Cooking Hints." *Catoctin Clarion* (Mechanicstown, MD), June 17, 1880, 4.

Corvinus, Gottlieb Sigmund. *Frauenzimmer Lexicon*. Leipzig: Johann Fredrich Gleditch, 1712.

"Council Oak Stores," advertisement, *Dakota County Star* (South Sioux City, NE), September 17, 1953, 5.

"The County Fair: Bread, Cakes and Pickles." *Daily Kansas Tribune* (Lawrence, KS), October 24, 1869, 3.

"Cristoforo Messisbugo, 1557." Mortadella Bologna. Accessed May 27, 2022. https://mortadellabologna.com/blog/cristoforo-messisbugo-1557-le-ricette-forestiere/.

"Dave's Burger Shanty." Advertisement. *Neenah Menasha Northwestern* (Oshkosh, WI), July 7, 1976, 14.

Davidis, Henriette. *Praktisches Kochbuch für die Deutschen in Amerika*. Milwaukee, WI: Georg Brumder's Verlag, 1879.

Davidis, Henriette. *Praktisches Kochbuch für die Deutschen in Amerika*. Milwaukee, WI: Georg Brumder's Verlag, 1897.

Davidson, Alan. *The Oxford Companion to Food*. Oxford, England: Oxford University Press, 1999.

Davidson, Alan. *The Penguin Companion to Food*. New York: Penguin Group, 2002.

Dawson, Frances. "Favorite Dish: Pizza, a New Arrival in St. Louis." *St. Louis Post-Dispatch*, April 13, 1947.

"A Day in Queretaro." *Chicago Tribune*, June 21, 1867, 2.

"The Dayton Barbecue." *Summit County Beacon* (Akron, OH), October 5, 1842, 2.

"Delicious Fried Biscuit." *Indianapolis Star*, August 20, 1907, 9.

Doerksen, Cliff. "The Real American Pie." *Chicago Reader*, December 17, 2009, 1.

Dolve, Mary A. *The School Lunch*. Cooperative Extension Circulars, 1917–1950, no. 49. Brookings: South Dakota State University, 1922.

Dorn, Anna, ed. *Neuestes universal oder großes wiener Koch Buch*. Vienna: Franz Tendler, 1834.

Edge, John T. *Fried Chicken: An American Story*. New York: G. P. Putnam's Sons, 2004.

Eighmey, Rae Catherine. *Abraham Lincoln in the Kitchen*. Washington, DC: Smithsonian Books, 2013.

Elie, Lolis Eric. *Smokestack Lightning: Adventures in the Heart of Barbecue Country*. Berkeley, CA: Ten Speed Press, 2005.

Eng, Monica. "Saga of a Sandwich." *Chicago Tribune*, June 18, 2003, section 2, 1.

"An Enterprising Nuisance Crushed." *Tennessean* (Nashville), October 27, 1886, 5.

Eppner, F. *Die deutsche Wurstfabrikation*. Weimar: Bernard Friedrich Voight, 1870.

Erdrich, Heid E. *Original Local: Indigenous Foods, Stories, and Recipes from the Upper Midwest*. Saint Paul, MN: Minnesota Historical Society Press, 2013.

Evening Belles Home Demonstration Club of Bloomington, Indiana. *Favorite Recipes*. Kansas City, MO: North American Press, 1962.

Evening Dispatch. Your Happy Kitchen Cookbook. Michigan City, IN: Evening Dispatch, n.d.

Evening Post (New York). October 14, 1802, 1.

Examiner (London). April 12, 1839, 23.

"Exchange of Ideas: Mexican Wedding Cake." *Reporter-Times* (Martinsville, IN), November 17, 1932, 3.

Farmer, Fannie Merritt. *The Boston Cooking-School Cookbook*. New York: Weathervane Books, 1896.

Farmer, Fannie Merritt. *The Boston Cooking-School Cookbook*. Boston: Little, Brown, 1911.

"Farmer's Reading: Chili Sauce." *Evansville Daily Journal* (Evansville, IN), August 30, 1867, 3.

"Figi's Certified Beer." Advertisement. *Marshfield News-Herald* (Marshfield, WI), July 21, 1966, 15.

"Fish Fry." *Readstown Special* (Readstown, WI), March 6, 1865, 2.

"'Friendship Bread' Name for Sourdough." *Nevada State Journal* (Reno, NV), January 14, 1968, 13.

Fritschner, Sarah. "Three to Show." *Courier-Journal* (Louisville, KY), May 3, 1987, 166.

Frost, Annie S. *The Godey's Lady's Book Receipts and Household Hints*. Philadelphia: Evans, Stoddart, 1870.

Fuchs, Max. *Xavier Krenkl's Leben, Anecdoten, und Sprüche*. Post script advertisement for Hans Schwartz, *Die Wurstfabrikation für Wirtschaften*. Regensburg: Stahl's Verlagsbuchhandlung, 1825.

Germershausen, Christian Friedrich. *Die Hausmutter in allen ihren Geschäfften*. 3rd ed. Vol. 2. Leipzig: Johann Friedrich Junius, 1791.

Gillette, Fanny Lemira. *The American Cook Book, a Selection of Choice Recipes Original and Selected During a Period of Forty Years' Practical Housekeeping*. Chicago: H. J. Smith, 1889.

Glasse, Hannah. *The Art of Cookery Made Plain and Easy*. London: Printed for the Author and sold at Mrs. Ashburn's, a China-Shop, the Corner of Fleet-Ditch, 1747.

Glasse, Hannah. *The Art of Cookery Made Plain and Easy*. London: A. Millar, J. and R. Tonson, W. Strahan, P. Davey, and B. Law, 1760.

Glasse, Hannah. *The Art of Cookery Made Plain and Easy*. 8th ed. London: A. Millar, J. and R. Tonson, W. Strahan, T. Caslon, B. Law, and A. Hamilton, 1763.

Glasse, Hannah. *The Art of Cookery Made Plain and Easy*. Alexandria, VA: Cottom and Stewart, 1805.

Glasse, Hannah. *The Art of Cookery Made Plain and Easy*. With introduction by Karen Hess. Facsimile edition. Bedford, MA: Applewood Books, 1997.

"A Good Dinner, My Boy." *Brooklyn Daily Sun* (Brooklyn, NY), December 28, 1873, 6.

Grace Lutheran Ladies Aid. *Grace Lutheran Ladies Aid Cookbook*. Mankato, MN: n.p., 1930.

"Grand Banquet." *Harrisburg Telegraph* (Harrisburg, PA), May 13, 1874, 3.

"Great Meeting of Suffragists." *Republic* (Meyersdale, PA), June 29, 1916, 4.

"Green Bay Booyah Change Name to Rockers." *Press Times* (Green Bay, WI), November 3, 2021. Accessed May 27, 2022. https://gopresstimes.com/2021/11/03/green-bay-booyah-change-name-to-rockers/.

Hagger, Conrad. *Neues saltzburgisches Koch-Buch*, part 3, book 2. Augsburg: Lotter, 1719.

Hake, Dorothea. "Goetta Drums Up a Real Argument." *Cincinnati Enquirer*. December 9, 1957, 27.

Hammond, Phyllis. "Take a Tip from Old Mexico: Try a Hot Tamale!" *Chicago Tribune*, July 24, 1932, 34.

Hardin, Philomelia. *Every Body's Cook and Receipt Book, But More Particularly Designed for Buckeyes, Hoosiers, Wolverines, Corncrackers, Suckers, and all Epicures Who Wish to Live with the Present Times*. Cleveland, OH: Printed for the author by Sanford and Co., 1842.

Harland, Marion [Mary Virginia Terhune]. *Common Sense in the Household*. New York: Charles Scribner, 1872.

Hero, Catherine. "Chocolate in the Chili? Well, We Asked." *Cincinnati Enquirer*, April 12, 2021, Z1.

Hill, Annabella P. *Mrs. Hill's New Cook Book*. New York: Carleton, 1870.

Historic Jamestowne, National Park Service. "The Second Supply." Accessed May 26, 2022. https://historicjamestowne.org/history/history-of-jamestown/the-second-supply/.

"History." S. Rosen's Baking Company. Accessed May 26, 2022. https://www
.srosens.com/about/history/.

"History of the Chicago Hot Dog." Vienna Beef Company. Accessed May 27, 2022.
https://www.viennabeef.com/chicagos-hot-dog/history-of-the-chicago-hot-dog/.

Hogeland, William. *The Whiskey Rebellion: George Washington, Alexander Hamilton,
and the Frontier Rebels Who Challenged America's Newfound Sovereignty*. New
York: Scribner, 2006.

"Hotels: Anderson's European Hotel. Restaurant Bill of Fare." *Chicago Tribune*,
July 6, 1873, 16.

"Hot Tamales Return with the Corn." *Chicago Tribune*, August 31, 1896, 7.

"Household Department: Chili Sauce." *Boston Globe*, September 20, 1906, 12.

"Household Recipes Contributed: Black Chocolate or Devil's Food Cake." *Weekly
Record* (New Madrid, MO), November 16, 1890, 24.

Howitt, William. *The Rural and Domestic Life of Germany*. London: Longman,
Brown, Green, and Longmans, 1842.

"The Idle Inn Sandwich Shop." Advertisement. *Star Press* (Muncie, IN), October 2,
1938, 17.

"Ike Sewell, 87, Creator of 'Chicago-Style' Pizza." *Chicago Tribune*, August 21,
1990, 55.

"In a Sandwich Car." *Chicago Tribune*, July 5, 1896, 16.

Indiana Farmer's Guide. *The Indiana Farmer's Guide New Cook Book*. Huntington,
IN: The Indiana Farmer's Guide, 1945.

Inglehart Brothers. *Cake Secrets*. Evansville, IN: Inglehart Brothers, 1915.

"Isn't This Dish Worth Importing?" *Vicksburg Evening Post* (Vicksburg, MI), May 7,
1887, 5.

Jackson, Sharyn. "Who Invented Our Classic Burger?" *Star Tribune* (Minneapolis),
July 8, 2017, E1.

Johanneman, Phyllis A. Trout. *Ferdinand Life: How We Lived and Ate*. Ferdinand, IN:
Phyllis A. Trout Johanneman, 2008.

Jones, Evan. *American Food: The Gastronomic Story*. 2nd ed. New York: Vintage
Books, 1981.

Junction City Weekly Union (Junction City, KS), August 25, 1877, 5.

Kander, Mrs. Simon, and Mrs. Henry Schoenfeld. *The Settlement Cook Book*. Milwaukee: A. R. Shepard, 1903.

Kansas City Times (Kansas City, MO). January 28, 1872, 1.

Kelly, Michael. *Reminiscences of Michael Kelly, of the King's Theater, and Theatre Royal
Drury Lane, Including a Period of Nearly Half a Century*. New York: J. & J. Harper,
1826.

"Kennedy's Restaurant." Advertisement. *Scranton Republican* (Scranton, PA),
June 26, 1890, 4.

Kientz, Leon. *The Fish and Oyster Book*. Chicago: Hotel Monthly Press, 1906.

Kindelsperger, Nick. "How Giardiniera Crossed an Ocean to Become Chicago's Favorite Condiment." *Chicago Tribune*, May 19, 2017.

Kliman, Todd. *The Wild Vine*. New York: Broadway Paperbacks, 2010.

Kraig, Bruce. *Hot Dog: A Global History*. London: Reaktion Books, 2009.

Kraig, Bruce, Carol Haddix, and Colleen Taylor Sen, eds. *The Chicago Food Encyclopedia*. Champaign: University of Illinois Press, 2017.

Kramer, Bertha ["Aunt Babette"]. *Aunt Babette's Cook Book*. Cincinnati: Bloch, 1889.

Kurlansky, Mark. *The Food of a Younger Land*. New York: Riverhead Books, 2009.

Lehman, Nicholas. *The Promised Land: The Great Migration and How It Changed America*. New York: Alfred A. Knopf, 1992.

Leicester Chronicle or Commercial and Leicester Mercury (Leicester, England). May 15, 1858, 7.

Lewis, Jenny. *Midwest Sweet Baking History*. Charleston, SC: History Press, 2011.

Libby, David J. *Slavery and Frontier Mississippi, 1720–1835*. Jackson: University Press of Mississippi, 2008.

"Life in the Pine Woods." *Sioux City Journal* (Sioux City, IA), November 27, 1891, 2.

Lincoln, Mrs. D. A. [Mary Johnson Bailey Lincoln]. *Mrs. Lincoln's Boston Cook Book*. Boston: Robert Brothers, 1884.

"List of Premiums." *Somerset Herald* (Somerset, PA), September 30, 1874, 3.

"Livingston Realizes His Ambition." *Cincinnati Enquirer*, June 13, 1909, 8.

Lloyd, Timothy Charles. "The Cincinnati Chili Culinary Complex." *Western Folklore* 40, no. 1 (1981): 28–40.

"Local and Personal." *Kansas Democrat* (Hiawatha, KS), October 17, 1906, 2.

"Local Fish Fry Recommendations." *Lake Geneva Regional News* (Lake Geneva, WI), February 20, 2020, D3.

Long, James W. *From Privileged to Dispossessed: The Volga Germans, 1860–1917*. Lincoln: University of Nebraska Press, 1988.

Loomis, Susan Herrmann, "Fare of the Country: A City's Romance with a Bowl of Chili." *New York Times*, April 16, 1989, section 5, 6.

Loring, Kathryn. "Have You Heard?" *Chicago Tribune*, April 8, 1956, 370.

"Luca 'Luigi' Meglio." Obituaries. *St. Louis Post-Dispatch*, August 31, 2014.

Lumbra, Elaine, editor. *The Hoosier Cookbook*. Bloomington: Indiana University Press, 1976.

"Luscious Cherry-Filled Desserts for February." *Times-Mail* (Bedford, IN), February 9, 1969, 18.

Mariani, Andrew. "Cherries." In *The Oxford Encyclopedia of Food and Drink in America*, 2nd ed., vol. 1, edited by Andrew F. Smith. New York: Oxford University Press, 2013.

Mariani, John. *The Encyclopedia of American Food and Drink*. New York: Blooms-
    bury, 2013.

"Marion Harland, Author, Dies at 91." *New York Times*, June 4, 1922, 28.

Marks, Gil. *The World of Jewish Cooking*. New York: Simon & Schuster, 1996.

Mason, Charlotte. *The Lady's Assistant for Regulating and Supplying Her Table*. Dub-
    lin: Robert Burton, 1778.

Mayhew, Henry. *German Life and Manners as Seen in Saxony at the Present Day*. Lon-
    don: Wm. H. Allen, 1865.

McGee, Harold. *On Food and Cooking*. New York: Scribner, 2004.

McGinnis, Lori. "More People Are Driving In to More Runza Drive Inns." *Lincoln
    Journal Star* (Lincoln, NE), March 10, 1984, 4.

"McKenzie and McNeill." Advertisement. *Charleston Daily Courier* (Charleston,
    SC), November 1, 1804, 3.

"Meat Filled Yeast Rolls Easy to Serve and Eat." *Wichita Beacon* (Wichita, KS),
    February 21, 1957, 30.

Mihesuah, Devon. "Sustenance and Health among the Five Nations in Indian Terri-
    tory, Post Removal to Statehood." *Ethnohistory* 62, no. 2 (April 2015), 263–84.

Miller, Adrian. *Black Smoke*. Chapel Hill: University of North Carolina Press, 2021.

Miller, Adrian. *Soul Food: The Surprising Story of an American Cuisine*. Chapel Hill:
    University of North Carolina Press, 2022.

Mistaras, Evangeline. "Chicago Restaurants and Nightlife." *ALA Bulletin* 57, no. 6
    (1963), 565–70.

Moltmann, Günter. *German Immigration to America: 300 Years of Immigration 1683–
    1983*. Stuttgart: Institute for Foreign Cultural Relations, 1982.

Monahan, Erika. "Locating Rhubarb: Early Modernity's Relative Obscurity." In
    Early Modern Things: Objects and Their Histories, 1500–1800, edited by Paula
    Findlen, 227–51. London: Routledge, 2013.

Morley, Henry. *Early Papers and Some Memories*. London: George Routledge and
    Sons, 1891.

Moss, Robert F. *Barbecue: The History of an American Institution*. Tuscaloosa: Uni-
    versity of Alabama Press, 2010.

Muter, Elizabeth. *Travels and Adventures of an Officer's Wife in India, China, and New
    Zealand*. Vol. 2. London: Hurst and Blackett, 1864.

Neman, Daniel. "Gooey Love." *St. Louis Post-Dispatch*, February 10, 2016, L04.

New England Farmer (Boston). April 4, 1828, 2.

"Nick's Kitchen." Advertisement. *Daily News-Democrat* (Huntington, IN), Decem-
    ber 17, 1909, 8.

"Nick's Kitchen Is the New Name." *Daily News-Democrat* (Huntington, IN), Novem-
    ber 22, 1909, 8.

"Not Eaten on the Premises." *Sun* (New York), April 27, 1883, 3.

Novo, Salvador. *Cocina Mexicana, o Historia Gastronomica de la Ciudad de Mexico*. Paris: Libreria de Ch. Bouret, 1979.

"Oakland Items." *San Francisco Chronicle*, September 16, 1868, 3.

"Odors of the Onion." *San Francisco Chronicle*, July 23, 1894, 7.

"Oldani's." Advertisement. *St. Louis Star and Times*, February 20, 1943, 5.

"Our Story." Nick's Kitchen. Accessed June 23, 2022. https://nicksdowntown.com/.

"Oyster Cocktail and Loaf." *St. Joseph Herald* (St. Joseph, MO), September 8, 1889, 9.

Parloa, Maria. *The Original Appledore Cook Book*. Boston: Charles E. Brown, 1872.

Peck, J. M. *Guide for Emigrants, Containing Sketches of Illinois, Missouri, and the Adjacent Parts*. Boston: Lincoln and Edmands, 1831.

Peltz, George. *The Housewife's Library*. Philadelphia: Hubbard Bros., 1883.

"A Pennsylvania Dinner." *Dixon Evening Telegraph* (Dixon, IL), March 10, 1897, 8.

"Perfection Salad Is an American Classic." *Philadelphia Inquirer*, February 20, 1964, 19.

"Piggly Wiggly." Advertisement. *Cincinnati Enquirer*, November 12, 1921, 12.

Pomper, K. W., D. R. Layne, and R. N. Peterson. "The Pawpaw Regional Variety Trial." In *Perspectives on New Crops and New Uses*, edited by J. Janick. Alexandria, VA: American Society for Horticultural Science Press, 1999.

Poole, Marcia. "Sioux City's Signature Sandwich? The Loosemeat," *Sioux City Journal* (Sioux City, IA), October 19, 2005, E1.

Postans, Marianne. *Western India in 1838*. London: Saunders and Otley, 1839.

Presbyterian Church of LaPorte. *Many New and Reliable Recipes*. LaPorte, IN: LaPorte Printing, 1887.

Purdy, Nancy J. "Horseshoe: A Sandwich by Any Other Name," *Mattoon Journal-Gazette* (Mattoon, IL), February 18, 1981, 21.

"Randolph County Agricultural Fair: Food, Condiments, & C." *Fayetteville Weekly Observer* (Fayetteville, NC), November 5, 1860, 2.

"Readers Share Turnip Kraut Recipes, Amish Bread." *Times-Mail* (Bedford, IN), September 23, 1987, 5.

Rector, Sylvia. "Detroit's Old-School Pizza: It's Hip to Be Square." *Detroit Free Press*, June 4, 2009, 70.

"Refectory." *Evening Post* (New York), September 1, 1820, 3, column 5.

Reizenstein, Milton. *The Economic History of the Baltimore and Ohio Railroad, 1827–1853*. Baltimore: The Johns Hopkins Press, 1897.

Rivera, Manuel Galvan. *Diccionario de cocina, o el nuevo cocinero Mexicano*. Mexico: I. Cumplido, 1845.

Rombauer, Irma S. and Marion Rombauer Becker. *The Joy of Cooking*. New York: Plume, 1973.

Rosalia, Eleonora Maria. *Freiwillig aufgesprungener Granat-Apfel des Christlichen Samaritens*. Part 2, "Koch Buch." Vienna: Leopold Boight, 1699.

Rose, Anne C. *Voices of the Marketplace: American Thought and Culture, 1830–1860*. New York: Rowman & Littlefield, 2004.

"The Run Up to Reading." *New York Daily Herald*, September 14, 1848, 3.

"Runza Firm Sues to Stop Use of Name," *Lincoln Journal Star* (Lincoln, NE), August 12, 1993, 8.

Russell, Malinda. *Domestic Cook Book: Containing a Careful Selection of Useful Receipts for the Kitchen*. Paw Paw, MI: Printed for the author by T. O. Ward at "The True Northerner," 1866.

Rutledge, Sarah. *The Carolina Housewife*. Charleston, SC: W. R. Babcock, 1847.

"Rye." MGP Ingredients. Accessed May 26, 2022. https://www.mgpingredients.com /distilled-spirits/beverage/product/rye.

Schellhammer, Maria Sophia. *Das Brandenburgische Koch=Buch*. Berlin: Johann Andreas Rudiger, 1723.

Schellhammer, Maria Sophia. *Die wohl unterwiesene Köchin, Das ist: Unterricht, Wie man alle Speisen, so nur in Teutschland bekant seyn mögen, aufs füglichste zubereiten*. Braunschweig Helmstät: Gruber Hesse, 1697.

Schley, David. *Steam City: Railroads, Urban Space, and Corporate Capitalism in Nineteenth-Century Baltimore*. Chicago: University of Chicago Press, 2020.

Schnitzler, Nicole. "From Little Italy to the World: Pizza's Place in Chicago History." *For the Love of Pizza*. Supplement, *Chicago Tribune*, September 18, 2016, 10–11.

Schwägermann, Wilhelmine. *Gründlich abgefasstes norddeutsches Kochbuch für die bürgerliche Küchen*. Hannover, Germany: A. L. Pockwitz, 1845.

"Seasonable Dishes." *Bloomington Evening World* (Bloomington, IN), March 17, 1917, 2.

"Second-Rate City." *Chicago Tribune*, May 22, 2000, 147.

"Serve 'Friendship Bread' for New Year." *Tennessean* (Nashville), December 28, 1951, 26.

"Shelby Barbecue." *Indiana State Sentinel* (Indianapolis), August 5, 1847, 2.

Sherard, Priscilla Mullin. *Indian Recipes Collected from the Indian People I Love*. Oklahoma City: Priscilla Mullin Sherard, 1975.

"Shifts to Live: Food for Two Weeks for the Impecunious for a Dollar." *Fort Wayne Daily Gazette* (Fort Wayne, IN), June 20, 1883, 2.

Smallwood, Arwin D. *The Atlas of African-American History and Politics*. New York: McGraw Hill, 1998.

Smith, Andrew F. "Chocolate." In *The Oxford Encyclopedia of Food and Drink in America*, 2nd ed., vol. 1, edited by Andrew F. Smith. New York: Oxford University Press, 2013.

Smith, Andrew F. "Sweet Potatoes." In *The Oxford Encyclopedia of Food and Drink in America*, 2nd ed., vol. 3, edited by Andrew F. Smith. New York: Oxford University Press, 2013.

Smith, Andrew F. *The Tomato in America: Early History, Culture, and Cookery*. Columbia: University of South Carolina Press, 1994.

Smith, Eliza. *The Compleat Housewife, or Accomplish'd Gentlewoman's Companion*. London: R. Ware, S. Birt, F. Longman, C. Hitch, J. Hodges, J. and J. Rivington, J. Ward, W. Johnston, and M. Cooper, 1750.

Smith, Huron E. "Ethnobotany of the Monomini Indians." *Bulletin of the Public Museum of the City of Milwaukee* 4, no. 1 (December 10, 1923): 65–66.

Smith, Huron E. "Ethnobotany of the Ojibwe Indians." *Bulletin of the Public Museum of the City of Milwaukee* 4, no. 3 (May 2, 1932): 369, 394.

"Snow's Cut-Rate Market." Advertisement. *St. Joseph New-Press* (St. Joseph, MO), February 9, 1906, 5.

"Something Deserving Encouragement." *People's Vindicator* (Natchitoches, LA), August 14, 1880, 3.

"Splendid Sausage." *Intelligencer Journal* (Lancaster, PA), December 26, 1868, 2.

Stannard, David E. *American Holocaust: The Conquest of the New World*. New York: Oxford University Press, 1992.

Stapley, Christina. *The Receipt Book of Lady Anne Blencowe: Seventeenth Century Cookery and Home Medicine*. Basingstoke, England: Heartsease Books, 2004.

Stefanson, D. H. "Friendship Bread." *Sioux City Journal* (Sioux City, IA), March 19, 1972, 88.

Steinberg, Ellen F., and Jack H. Prost. "A Menu and a Mystery: The Case of the 1834 Delmonico Bill of Fare." *Gastronomica* 8, no. 2 (2008), 40–50.

Stern, Michael, and Jane Stern. *500 Things to Eat Before It's Too Late and the Very Best Places to Eat Them*. Boston: Houghton Mifflin Harcourt, 2009.

Stuttgen, Joanne Raetz. *The Café Indiana Cookbook*. Madison, WI: Terrace Books, 2010.

"Sugar Cream Pie." *Indianapolis Star*, December 25, 1907, 7.

Sula, Mike. "On the Trail of the Delta Tamale." *Chicago Reader*, May 15, 2008, Food and Drink, 1.

Sunshine Circle of Bethel Evangelical Church. *The Concordia Cook Book: Tried and Tested Recipes*. Concordia, MO: Lohoefer House Museum, 1984.

"Suzie's Corner." Advertisement. *Chicago Tribune*, March 26, 1953, 11.

"Swedish Americans in Wisconsin." Swedish American Historical Society of Wisconsin. Accessed May 26, 2022. https://sahswi.org/swedish-immigration-history/.

"Sweet Potato Pie." *Princeton Clarion-Ledger* (Princeton, IN), October 15, 1853, 2.

"Table and Kitchen." *Daily Times* (Davenport, IA), April 23, 1902, 7.

Tabor, Mrs. W. L. "Chicken Tamales: How to Prepare a Dish Which Is Esteemed Quite Highly in Some Parts of the West." *Daily Free Press* (Carbondale, IL), May 27, 1899.

"Tamale." *Chicago Tribune*, July 14, 1884, 9.

"Tartar Sauce for Meats." *Northern Ohio Journal* (Painesville, OH), October 19, 1878, 4.

Taylor, Fitch W. *The Broad Pennant: Or, a Cruise in the United States Flag Ship*. New York: Leavitt, Trow, 1848.

Tennessean (Nashville). November 14, 1886, 9.

"Toothsome Tamales: How the Mexicans Make an Odd but Palatable Dish." *Grenada Sentinel* (Grenada, MS), March 27, 1886, 3.

"The Towers." Advertisement. *Evansville Press* (Evansville, IN), September 17, 1938, 2.

"Town and Neighborhood." *Junction City Tribune* (Junction City, KS), December 8, 1881, 3.

Trillin, Calvin. "No! One of the World's Foremost Authorities on Ribs, Cheeseburger, French Fries and Frosty Malts Takes a Gourmet Tour of Kansas City." *Playboy* 19, no. 4 (April 1972), 209.

Troop, James, and O. M. Hadley. "The American Persimmon." *Purdue University Agricultural Experiment Station Bulletin* 7, no. 60 (April 1896).

United States Department of Agriculture National Agricultural Statistics Service. *Wisconsin Ag News—Specialty Cheese*. Madison: Wisconsin Field Office, April 28, 2020.

Vettel, Phil. "Poppy Love? Why Seeds Adorn the Chicago-Style Bun." *Chicago Tribune*, August 30, 2017, section 6, 4.

Viets, Elaine. "Cutting Us In on St. Louis Cut Ribs." *St. Louis Post-Dispatch*, July 20, 1995.

Vonnegut, Kurt. *If This Isn't Nice, What Is?* Commencement Address at Butler University, Indianapolis, Indiana, May 11, 1996. RosettaBooks e-edition, 2020.

Voth, Norma Jost. *Mennonite Foods & Folkways from South Russia*. Vol. 1. Intercourse, PA: Good Books, 1990.

Walker, Don. "Miller Park: Where the Sausage Is King." *Milwaukee Journal Sentinel*, April 2, 2010. Accessed June 21, 2022. https://archive.jsonline.com/newswatch /89771437.html.

Wason, Betty. *A Salute to Cheese*. New York: Hawthorn Books, 1966.

Weaver, William Woys. *As American as Shoofly Pie*. Philadelphia: University of Pennsylvania Press, 2013.

Wechsberg, Joseph. *The Cooking of the Viennese Empire*. New York: Time-Life Books, 1968.

Weis, Robert. *Bakers and Basques: A Social History of Bread in Mexico*. Albuquerque: University of New Mexico Press, 2012.

Welserin, Sabina. *Das Kochbuch der Sabina Welserin*, edited by Hugo Stopp, translation by Ulrike Gießmann. Heidelberg: Universitätsverlag C. Winter Heidelberg, 1980. Accessed October 26, 2022. https://www.unigiessen.de/fbz/fb05/germanistik/absprache/sprachverwendung/gloning/tx/sawe.htm.

Wennersten, John. *The Oyster Wars of Chesapeake Bay*. Washington, DC: Eastern Branch Press, 2007.

Wesley, Jay K. *Kalamazoo River Assessment*. Michigan Department of Natural Resources, Fisheries Division. Special Report no. 35 (September 2005).

Western Carolinian (Salisbury, NC). March 8, 1834, 1.

"White's." Advertisement. *Indianapolis Star*, May 1, 1908, 14.

"White's." Advertisement. *Indianapolis Star*, September 28, 1908, 10.

"Who Invented Toasted Ravioli?" *St. Louis Magazine Online*, November 20, 2015. Accessed October 26, 2022. https://www.stlmag.com/news/who-invented-toasted-ravioli/.

Widdifield, Hannah. *Widdifield's New Cook Book*. Philadelphia: T. B. Peterson and Brothers, 1856.

Wilde, W. R. "On the Introduction and Period of the General Use of the Potato in Ireland." *Proceedings of the Royal Irish Academy* 6 (1853–1857), 356–72.

Wilson, George R. *History of Dubois County from Primitive Days to 1910*. Mt. Vernon, IN: Published by the author, 1910. Reprint, Mt. Vernon, IN: Windmill Books, 1992.

Wilson, José, and the editors of Time-Life Books. *American Cooking: The Eastern Heartland*. Foods of the World. New York: Time-Life Books, 1971.

Wilson, Korsha. "Celebrating the Fish Fry: A Late-Summer Black Tradition." *New York Times*, September 12, 2018, section D, 1.

Woellert, Dann. *The Authentic History of Cincinnati Chili*. Charleston, SC: American Palate, 2013.

Woellert, Dann. *Cincinnati Wine: An Effervescent History*. Charleston, SC: American Palate, 2021.

Wood, Frances. *The Silk Road: Two Thousand Years in the Heart of Asia*. Berkeley: University of California Press, 2002.

Wursthorn, Johann. *Wurstologia Novissima Et Aucta, Das ist: Neu-vermehrte / wahr- und eigentliche Beschreibung Aller Arten Würste / Dabey vielerley Geschlechter und Nationes, anderer Sonder- und Wunderbahrer Mißgebuhrten und Ketzerischen Würste*. Westphalia, 1690. Accessed from the Bibliothek Universität Hamburg Online, May 27, 2022. https://resolver.sub.uni-hamburg.de/kitodo/PPN767145178.

Yung, Katherine, and Joe Grimm. *Coney Detroit*. Detroit, MI: Wayne State University Press, 2012.

Zanger, Mark H. "Pretzels." In *The Oxford Encyclopedia of Food and Drink in America*, 2nd ed., vol. 3, edited by Andrew F. Smith. New York: Oxford University Press, 2013.

Zolov, Eric. *Iconic Mexico: An Encyclopedia from Acapulco to Zocalo*. Santa Barbara, CA: ABC-CLIO, 2015.

Index

Abraham Lincoln in the Kitchen (Eighmey), 60
Achatz, Grant, 161
acorn-flour donuts, 162–63
Acorns and Cattails (Connoley), 161
affordable foods, 95, 141–42, 200–201, 254.
    See also Depression-era foods
African American communities and food,
    10–11, 108–9, 163, 176, 188–89, 216, 246–
    47, 257, 292. *See also* Black communities
    and food; Southern communities and
    food
A&J Comfort Foods, Rheinland label (Cin-
    cinnati, OH), 152
alcoholic beverages, 40. *See also* beer; ciders;
    cocktails; liqueurs; wine
Algren, Nelson, 117, 166, 250, 275
Alinea restaurant (Chicago, IL), 161; as mod-
    ernist cuisine, 7
Allen, Cynthia, 292
Allen, Erika, 292–94, 317
Allen, Will, 292, 296
Al's (Chicago, IL), 116–17
Althea's White cornmeal, 55
Amaranth Bakery (Milwaukee, WI), 288
American Cook Book, The, 28
Amish communities and food, 8–9, 10, 75–
    76, 174, 254
Anderson, C. W., Mrs., 170
Anderson's European Hotel (Chicago, IL),
    201
angel food cake, 215, 250, 251, 275, 276, 278;
    recipe, 270–72
apfelkuchen (apple cake), recipe, 78–81
Appalachian communities and food, 2–3, 30,
    253, 264
Appel, Todd, 46
Appel's Cordials (Chicago, IL), 46
apple butter: and fried biscuits, 5, 32, 61–62,

64; recipe, 31–33; as sweetener, 150,
    152–53
apples, 23, 29–30, 32–34, 76, 79, 197, 252, 267;
    apple cake (apfelkuchen), recipe, 78–81;
    apple cider pecan cheese ball, recipe,
    101–3; apple cider vinegar, in potato
    salad, 155; in pies, 251; and quince, 30;
    varieties of, 79
applesauce, 150
Arthur Bryant's restaurant (Kansas City,
    MO), 217
Art of Cookery Made Plain and Easy, The
    (Glasse), 17, 86, 176, 186
As American as Shoofly Pie (Weaver), 76
Asian communities and food, 9, 59, 232
Aunt Babette. *See* Kramer, Bertha (a.k.a.
    Aunt Babette)
Aunt Babette's Cook Book (Kramer), 6, 13, 22,
    24, 28, 51–52, 79, 86–87, 176, 259, 275, 286
Avril-Bleh meat market (Cincinnati, OH),
    152, 192

Babette, Aunt. *See* Kramer, Bertha (a.k.a.
    Aunt Babette)
Backhendl (Viennese fried chicken), 187–88
Bailey, Nathan, 154
baked goods and bakeries, 12, 58–60, 71,
    75, 79, 81, 282, 288, 301; artisan, 59–60;
    Asian, 59; European, 66; and grain pro-
    ducers, 59–60; Mexican, 59, 66–67, 290;
    Middle Eastern, 59; Scandinavian, 59. *See
    also* breads; desserts; donuts; pastries;
    rolls; sweets
Baker, James, Dr., 272
Baker's Chocolate, 272, 273
Balkan (Macedonian) communities and
    food, 128, 191–92
Baltimore and Ohio Railroad, 158

bananas, 262; banana caramel cake, recipe, 275–77

Banchet, Jean, 6

banh mi, 59

bao, 59

barbecue, 5, 20–21, 29, 58–59, 94, 143, 213–27, 299; and Black Southern migrant influence, 10–11; cherry barbecue relish, recipe, 18–19; Chicago-style barbecue, 216–17, 246; Chicago-style barbecue, recipe, 221–23; and cornbread, 32; cornbread with, 32; East Saint Louis–style, 216–17, 223–24; East Saint Louis–style, recipe, 223–27; Kansas City–style, 166, 215–18, 223–24; Kansas City–style, recipe, 217–21; Memphis, 217, 221, 223–24; mutton in, 216; and political events, 215–16; rub, 222, 226; rub, recipe, 218; sauces, 20, 59, 220–23, 225–26; Southern, 215

barley: availability, 197; in booyah, 167; purple, 55; wine, 42

bars [place], 45, 46, 48, 113, 143. *See also* German beer halls; pubs; saloons; taverns

beans: beans and knefles, recipe, 142–43; and corn, 196, 198, 300–301. *See also* green beans

Bear, The (FX/Hulu series), 117

Beard, James, 7–8, 246, 266–67, 296

Beauregard sweet potatoes, 147

beef: affordable, 116, 200; in borscht, 139; brisket, 217; and butter, 208; drippings, 104, 152; dry-aged, 166; grass-fed beef, 152, 197; Italian, 25, 91, 105, 107, 116–17; Italian beef sandwich, recipe, 116–19; in mince pie, 267–68; in ravioli, 105; roast, 25, 142, 143, 154, 166, 301; stew, 142; tallow or lard, 97–99, 130, 187. *See also* barbecue; beefsteaks; hamburgers; hot dogs; sausages

beefsteaks: beefsteak, good, from chopped meat (*gute Beefsteaks von gehackten Fleisch*), 201; beefsteak, in another way (*Beefsteak auf andere Art*), 201; beefsteak, raw (cannibal or wildcat sandwich), recipe, 202–4

beer, 51–52; and brats, 27, 95–97; breweries, 42–43; craft, 37, 42–43, 161; Figi's Cer-
tified Beer, 98; in fish fry, 179; German beer halls, 42, 64; and horseradish, 101; London Porter, 41–42; macro culture of larger breweries, 42; malt companies, 43; microbreweries, 37, 42–43, 161; and tavern culture, 42. *See also* ciders; cocktails; distilleries; wine

beer brats: recipe, 95–97; and sauerkraut, 27

beets, 139, 166; borscht, recipe, 139–41; pickled or preserved, 16–17; roasted or sautéed, 137; in salad, 148; syrupy candied beets, 4

Behrens, Rosa, 41

Bell, Charles, Mrs., 62

Bellow, Saul, 58, 72

Bell's Brewery (Kalamazoo, MI), 42

Belonische Würste, recipe, 123

Berg, David, 125

Better Homes & Gardens, 148

Betty Crocker's Picture Cook Book, 6, 13, 290

Bever, George, Mrs., 275

bierocks, or Runzas, 95, 205; recipe, 103–5

Big Jones Cookbook, The (Fehribach), 18, 24, 137–38

Big Jones restaurant (Chicago, IL), 24, 28, 30, 55, 60, 189, 251, 264, 273, 303–4

BIPOC (Black, Indigenous, and people of color) communities, 292, 301

biscotti. *See* zwiebach rolls

biscuits, as sides, 136

biscuits, fried: and apple butter, 5, 32, 61–62, 64; Maryland, as possible origin of, 62; recipe, 61–64

bison, 131–32, 152

Black, Indigenous, and people of color. *See* BIPOC (Black, Indigenous, and people of color) communities

blackberries: cordial, 34; cordial, recipe, 51–53; foraging, 5; frozen, 136; jam, quick, 52; jam, quick, recipe, 34–35; jelly, 4, 62; pies, 5, 251, 252, 264; quick blackberry jam, 52; quick blackberry jam, recipe, 34–35; three doyennes blackberry cordial, recipe, 51–53; wild cherry and blackberry wine, recipe, 49–51; wine, 4, 40–41, 43, 49–51

Black communities and food, 9–11, 108, 146, 155, 167, 176–77, 186, 189, 215–16, 224,

246–47, 292, 297–301. *See also* African American communities and food; Southern communities and food
Black Walnut Bakery (Minneapolis, MN), 59
black walnuts: black-walnut-sap sorghum sauce, 163; rugelach, recipe, 288–90; spice cake, recipe, 278–79
Blencowe, Anne, Lady, 23
Bloody Butcher cornmeal, 55
blueberry donut glaze, recipe, 89
Bohemian immigrants, 86
bologna: mortadella, 122–23; sandwich, 163
Bon Appetit magazine, 6
bone marrow: cranberry and bone marrow pudding pie, 251, 253; cranberry and bone marrow pudding pie, recipe, 264–66; in hamburgers (Jucy Lucys), 206
booyah (stew), recipe, 167–69
Borinquen restaurant (Chicago, IL), 119
borscht, recipe, 139–41
Boston Cook Book (Lincoln), 271
Boston Cooking-School Cookbook, The, 69, 146, 148
Boston Globe (Boston, MA), 19–20
boudin. *See* goetta (meat-and-grain sausage)
bouillon, 167–68
bratwurst, 5, 91, 125, 222; beer brats, and sauerkraut, 27; beer brats, recipe, 95–97; German bratwurst, recipe, 95–96
breadcrumbs, panko, 114–16
bread pudding, 264
breads, 2, 57–90; artisan, 59; conchas chocolates, recipe, 66–68; fried, 13; friendship bread, recipe, 75–78; friendship bread, starter, 79; Italian, 25, 116–17; Japanese, 163; Mexican, 66–67; milk, 129, 163; plantains, fried as, 119; pone, 108; potato-scented, 59; pretzels as, 58, 64; pumpernickel, 58, 72; pumpernickel, recipe, 71–75; quick, 78; rye, 58, 59, 72, 140, 152–53, 176, 203–4; rye sourdough starter, 73; rye sourdough starter, recipe, 74–75; *shokupan*, 163; sourdough, 74–76; stuffed, 103; sweet, 84; virtues and civilization of, 72; wheat, 58, 72; white, 55, 72, 177, 181, 214–15, 221–23; yeast, 2, 76, 129, 136. *See also* burgers; cornbread; sandwiches

Bretzel, 64
breweries and brewing. *See* beer
Briggs, Richard, 23
brisket, 59, 217; barbecued brisket, recipe, 219
British communities and food, 9, 22, 35, 154–55
Brockman, Terra, 94
Brown County fried biscuits: and apple butter, 32, 62; recipe, 61–64
Brown Hotel (Louisville, KY), 210
Brown Sugar Bakery (Chicago, IL), 246–47, 301
Brühwurst, 122
Bryan, Lettice, 23–24, 41–42, 51–52, 60, 186–87, 216, 251, 257, 267, 269
Bryant, Arthur, 217
Bryant, Charlie, 217
Bryant's Cocktail Lounge (Milwaukee, WI), 49
Buckeye Cookery and Practical Housekeeping, 158–59, 216, 275
bulgogi, 59, 231
Bulrush Land Partnership (Saint Louis, MO), 162
Bulrush STL restaurant (Saint Louis, MO), 161–63
burgers, 94–95, 114, 199–211; butterburgers, recipe, 208–9; horseshoes (hamburger), recipe, 209–11; Jucy Lucy, recipe, 206–7; loosemeat burgers, recipe, 204–6. *See also* hamburgers
burgoo. *See* booyah (stew)
Bussler, Cynthia, 292. *See* Allen, Cynthia
butter, 166; and beef, 208. *See also* apple butter
Byrd, William, 188

cabbage, 23, 103–4, 148, 167, 293; fermented and preserved, 4, 27, 163; oxheart, 162; slaw, 214; sour, 27; stew, 137; tomato-cabbage relish, 24. *See also* sauerkraut
Café Indiana Cookbook (Stuttgen), 258
cafés, 12, 59, 92–94, 113, 176, 246, 253, 258, 301
cajeta, candied, 299
Cajun boudin, 151, 152
cake flour, Swans Down, 271

cakes, 249–51, 272; angel food cake, recipe, 270–72; apfelkuchen (apple cake), recipe, 78–81; banana caramel cake, recipe, 275–77; black walnut spice cake, recipe, 278–79; caramel cake, 246–47; carrot, 246, 278; chocolate, 215, 251, 272–73, 275, 280; coconut cake, 250, 251; coffee cakes, 58, 79; devil's food (chocolate) cake, 250–51, 271; devil's food (chocolate) cake, recipe, 272–75; gooey butter cake, recipe, 279–81; pineapple-coconut cake, 246–47; pound cake, 280; red velvet, 246–47, 251

Cake Secrets (Swans Down), 271

California Chicken Tamale Co. (Chicago, IL), 109

Campbell's soup, 145

Campbell's Soup Test Kitchen, 144

candied: beets, 4; *cajeta*, 299; nuts, 288; yams, recipe, 146–47

caramel: banana caramel cake, recipe, 275–77; caramel cake, 246–47

Carolina Housewife, The, 159, 174

Carriage House Farm (North Bend, OH), 37–38, 301

carrot cake, 246, 278

casseroles, 5, 170; green bean casserole, recipe, 144–45. *See also* hotdish

catfish, 176–77, 179; catfish fiddlers, 5, 177; catfish fiddlers, recipe, 181–83; cornbread with, 181; cornmeal-crusted catfish, recipe, 180–81

Charlie Trotter's restaurant (Chicago, IL), 6–7

cheese: apple cider pecan cheese ball, recipe, 101–3; cheese curds, 91; cheese curds, fried, 209; cheese curds, fried, recipes, 97–99; cheese sauce, for horseshoes (burgers), recipe, 209–11; cold-pack cheese, 66; cold-pack cheese, recipe, 100–101; cottage cheese, 166; harder, fancier cheeses, higher melting temperatures of, 207; in latkes, 149; on pies, 250. *See also specific cheese(s)*

cheesecake, 81, 94, 280

Chelsea buns, 69

cherries: cherry barbecue relish, recipe, 18–19; cherry delight, recipe, 255–57; in pies, 251; wild cherry and blackberry wine,

recipe, 49–51; in wine, 4, 40–41, 43, 49–51

Chez Panisse restaurant (Berkeley, CA), 7

Chicago, Illinois: apples in, 79; German immigrants in, 8; Indigenous communities and food in, 297; as railroad hub for nationwide food industry, 6, 158

Chicago Chow King (blogger), 91

Chicago Hardy figs, 197; kringle, recipe, 81–84

Chicago Reader (Chicago, IL), 266–67

Chicago-style: barbecue, 216–17, 246; barbecue, recipe, 221–23; deep-dish pizza, 230–31; deep-dish pizza, recipe, 235–38; egg rolls, peanut butter, 91; hot dogs, 26–27, 125–27, 130; hot dogs, recipe, 125–28; hot giardiniera, 118, 242; hot giardiniera, recipe, 25–26; pizza, 5, 26, 230–31, 236, 240–41; *pizza napoletana*, 231; thin-crust pizza, 240–41

Chicago Tribune (Chicago, IL), 109, 126, 202

chicken: chicken and dumplings, 142; chicken and noodles, 11, 251; chicken and noodles, recipe, 173–75

chicken, fried, 5, 13, 59, 94, 96, 143, 144, 167, 185–89, 215, 251, 299; breast, 163; Korean, 299; recipe, 185–91; as southern soul food, 10–11; wings, 221

chicken noodle soup, 174, 299

Chicken Place (Ireland, IN), 42, 157

chili: chili con carne, 107–8; chili spaghetti, 191–92; chocolate in, 193; Cincinnati-style chili, 5, 20, 122, 129, 192–93, 300; Detroit-style Coney Island chili, recipe, 130–31; Macedonian (Balkan) descent, 191–92; and mole, 193; Queen City (Cincinnati) chili, recipe, 191–95

chili sauce: on coney dogs, 128; history of as major staple, 20; recipe, 19–21; sweet, on crab Rangoon pizza, 232; in tamales, 108, 110; as ubiquitous, 17

Chloe's Eatery (North Bend, OH), 38

chocolate: cakes, 215, 251, 272, 275, 278, 280; cakes, German chocolate, 251; in chili, 193; conchas chocolates, 85; conchas chocolates, recipe, 66–68; hot (beverage), 283; rich double chocolate glaze for donuts, recipe, 88–89; tamales, 109 chophouses, 6, 166. *See also* steakhouses; supper clubs

chow-chow, 17–19; and piccalilli, 23–24; recipe, 21–23

church suppers, 166, 185, 251, 278

churros, 59, 86, 282

cider, 43; apple cider pecan cheese ball, recipe, 101–3; apple cider vinegar, in potato salad, 155; cider and vinegar for barbecue prep, 214; cider pies, 253; in sauerkraut, 27, 143. *See also* beer

Cincinnati, Ohio, 6–8; as brewing city, 6, 37, 40; chili, 5, 20, 122, 129, 192–93, 300; chili, recipe, 191–95; as coffee-cake capital, 58; coney dogs, 128, 129, 192; German immigrants in, 8, 151, 186, 286; as river town, 9

Cincinnati Enquirer (Cincinnati, OH), 17–18, 20

Clay, Henry, 215

Cleveland, Ohio: bakeries in, 58; Black Southerners in, 10; pizza, 243

cocktails, 39–53; blackberry cordial, recipe, 51–53; brandy Manhattan, recipe, 46; brandy old-fashioned, recipe, 46–47; craft, 45, 47; elderflower collins, recipe, 48; ice cream in, 48–49; Midwestern, 52; Moscow mule, 45; Old Tom gin, 38; pink squirrel, recipe, 48–49; three doyennes blackberry cordial, recipe, 51–53; whiskey industry, 40. *See also* beer; wine

cocktail sauce (for fish), 19; recipe, 184–95

coconut, 2; cakes, 250, 251; coconut and lime broth, 299; coconut cream pie, 301; coconut cream pie, recipe, 258–60; pineapple-coconut cake, 246–47; pudding, 259

coffee cakes, 58, 79

cold-pack cheese, 66; recipe, 100–101

coleslaw, 59, 166, 176

Columbian Exposition (1893), 125

Common Sense in the Household (Harlan), 275

conchas, 59; conchas chocolates, 85; conchas chocolates, recipe, 66–68. *See also* pan dulce (Mexican sweet bread)

Concordia Cook Book, The, 250

condiments, 17–18, 20, 23, 25, 119, 184–85, 205. *See also* giardiniera; relishes; *specific condiment(s)*

Coney Detroit (Young and Grimm), 129

coney dogs, 5, 94–95, 109, 124–26; buns, 125–27, 129; chili sauce on, 128; Cincinnati-style, 128, 129, 192; Detroit-style, 92, 122, 128–30; Detroit-style Coney Island chili, recipe, 130–31; Macedonian descent, 128, 191; Michigan-style, 128–33, 192; recipe, 128–33; sauce, 122, 130; sauce, recipes, 132–33; sausage, 129–30; styles, 128; toppings, 130. *See also* hot dogs

Coney Island hot dogs. *See* coney dogs

Coney Island Kalamazoo (Kalamazoo, MI), 128

confections, 62, 249–51, 272, 280, 283, 285, 286–87. *See also* desserts

Connoley, Rob, 7, 161–63, 317

conserves, 17, 29. *See also* preserves

Cooke, John E., Mrs., 148

cookies, 249; lebkuchen, recipe, 286–88; Mexican wedding, 251; Mexican wedding cake, recipe, 290–91; shortbread cookie (*polvoron*), 290; springerle, 284; springerle, recipe, 283–86; spritz cookies, recipe, 281–83

Cool Whip, 145

corn: and beans, 196, 198, 300–301; co-opted from Indigenous peoples, 12; as cultural and economic icon, 12; as side dish, 135. *See also* sweet corn

cornbread, 55; with barbecue, 32; with catfish, 181; Lincoln family frontier cornbread, recipe, 60–61

cornmeal, 54–55, 176, 286; Althea's White, 55; Bloody Butcher, 55; cornmeal-crusted catfish, recipe, 180–81; in tamales, 108–9

corn on the cob, 13, 137, 214. *See also* sweet corn

cottage cheese, 100, 148, 166

county fairs, 100, 166, 257, 260, 278. *See also* state fairs

COVID-19 pandemic, 38, 170, 298, 304

cranberries: cranberry and bone marrow pudding pie, recipe, 264–66; cranberry pear preserves, recipe, 29–30; cranberry sweet corn relish, recipe, 33–34

Creamette brand macaroni, 170

crock cheese, 100

Crocker, Betty, 6, 13, 290

crullers (*Spritzkuchen*), 86–87, 282

Cubano sandwich, 91

cuisine: and culture, 95; handheld food as, 95; hot dogs as, 95; tamales as, 95

Cupid Candies (Chicago, IL), 247

custard: desserts, 261, 269; donuts, 88; pies, 250–53, 262, 264

Czech immigrants, 81

Daily Gazette (Fort Wayne, IN), 124

dairy, 252. *See also* butter; milk

dandelions: dandelion greens, 137; in wine, 41

Danish communities and food, 59, 81

Dave's Burger Shanty (Oshkosh, WI), 98

Davidis, Henriette, 149, 189, 201, 203, 283, 286

Davis, Leo, 221

Dean, Justin, 7, 37–38, 317

Dearborn Meat Market restaurant (Dearborn, MI), 92

Depression-era foods, 116, 126. *See also* affordable foods

desserts, 30, 49, 136, 250, 266, 271, 272, 275, 278, 282; cherry delight, recipe, 255–57; custard, 261, 269; persimmon pudding, recipe, 260–62; puddings, 154, 261; rhubarb charlotte, recipe, 269–70. *See also* baked goods and bakeries; cakes; confections; cookies; pies; puddings; sweets

Detroit, Michigan, 2–3, 66; Black Southerners in, 10; as creative large urban center, 130; as food city, 92; Mexican communities and food in, 59

Detroit-style: coney dogs, 92, 122, 128–30; Coney Island chili, recipe, 130–31; deep-dish pizza, 230; deep-dish pizza, recipe, 238–40; pizza, 92, 230–31; pizza, recipe, 238–40

deviled eggs, 166, 214

devil's food cake, 250–51, 271; recipe, 272–75

Diccionario de cocina (Rivera), 66

Dieter's (Brooklyn, NY), 201

distilleries, 38, 40, 45, 47

Dixon Evening Telegraph (Dixon, IL), 174

Doerksen, Cliff, 266–67

Domestic Cook Book (Russell), 257

donuts, 62, 188, 287; acorn-flour donuts, 162–63; custard, 88; filled and fillings, 32, 58,

86–87, 298; German, 86; Polish paczki, 58, 86–87, 298; recipe, 86–90

Dove Bar, Chicago as birthplace of, 247

Down at the Farms, LLC (Fairbury, IL), 196, 278

Dream Whip, 256

dressing, oyster, recipe, 158–60

dressing, salad: ranch, 16; ranch dressing, recipe, 99–100

Drexler, Abe, 126

duck and manoomin (wild rice) hotdish, recipe, 170–73

dumplings, 97, 103, 105, 136, 141–43. *See also* knefles, knephflas, knoephlas (dumplings)

Dutch communities and food. *See* Pennsylvania Dutch communities and food

Eastern European communities and food, 27, 59, 71, 125

Eastern Heartland: Illinois as, 7–8; Indiana as, 7–8; Michigan as, 7–8; New Jersey as, 7–8; New York State as, 7–8; Ohio as, 7–8; Pennsylvania as, 7–8

East Saint Louis (IL)-style barbecue, 216–17; recipe, 223–27

Edge, John T., 186

edible plants, 162

Eggleston, Robert F., 223–24

egg rolls, peanut butter (Chicago-style egg rolls), 91

eggs, deviled, 166, 214

Eighmey, Rae Katherine, 60

elderflower collins cocktail, recipe, 48

Elisenlebkuchen (confection), of Nuremberg, 286–87

El vocero newspaper (Puerto Rico), 119

Empress Chili (Cincinnati, OH), 191–92

English communities and food, 8

Eppner, F., 123

Erdrich, Heid E., 171

Evansville Courier (Evansville, IN), 20

Evansville Daily Journal (Evansville, IN), 19

Evening Belles Home Demonstration Club cookbook (Bloomington, IN), 255–56

Evening Dispatch (Michigan City, IN), 250

Everett, Donald, Jr.; Donald, Sr.; and Sarah (Sally), 103

fairs. *See* county fairs; state fairs

fakelore. *See* foodlore, and fakelore

family reunions, 251

Farkas Pastry Shoppe (Cleveland, OH), 58

Farmer, Fannie, 69, 146, 148

Farmers' Cabinet, The, 31–32

Fassbender, Hubert, 101

fast food, 6, 49, 109, 114–15, 184, 205

fastnachts, 86–87

Fehrenbach, Anna and George [great-grandparents], 3

Fehribach, Albert Paul [grandfather], 4, 40–41, 43, 49–50, 251–52, 304

Fehribach, Frances [grandmother], 4, 136, 251–52, 304

Fehribach, Raymond [great-great-grandfather], 3

Fehribach, Rita. *See* Gress, Rita [aunt]

Fehribach, Sandra and Joseph [parents], 2–3, 259, 304

Ferdinand Life: How We Lived and Ate (Johanneman), 64

Ferreri, Al, 116

Ferreri, Frances. *See* Pacelli, Frances

"Festivals in the Fields" (Algren), 166, 250

Field & Fire (Grand Rapids, MI), 59

Figi's Certified Beer (Marshfield, WI), 98

figs: Chicago Hardy fig kringle, recipe, 81–84; Chicago Hardy figs, 197

Figueroa, Juan, 119

Fiore, Amedeo, 232

fish: catfish fiddlers, *177*; catfish fiddlers, recipe, 181–83; cocktail sauce, 19; cocktail sauce, recipe, 184–95; cornmeal-crusted catfish, recipe, 180–81; fish fries [event], 150, 166, 176–86; fried, 11, 176–86; tartar sauce, recipe, 183–84; Wisconsin-style fish fry, recipe, 177–80

flour milling and mills, 6

Floyd, George, 298

Fluky's (Chicago, IL), 126

foie gras, in hamburgers (Jucy Lucys), 206

foodlore, and fakelore, 12–13, 42, 76

Foods of the World (Time-Life Books), 7–8

Formusa, Vincent, 25

Franken, Al, Senator, 170

frankfurters and wieners, 122–26, 128, 130, 192. *See also* hot dogs

Frauenzimmer Lexicon, 154, 176, 187

Freienstein, Nick, 114

French communities and food, 9, 59, 72, 146, 166, 168

French remoulade, 183

fried chicken. *See* chicken, fried

Fried Chicken: An American Story (Edge), 186

Frischmann, Ignatz, 125

fritters, 86, 282

Frost, S. Annie, 273

fruits: in ciders, 43; in jams and jellies, 17, 34; in liqueurs, 34; in mince pie, 267; in piccalilli, 23; preserved, 4, 17, 51; in wine, 38, 40–41, 45. *See also specific fruit(s)*

Garagiola, Joe and Mickey, 105

Gates, George, 217

Gates and Son restaurant (Kansas City, MO), 217

Gateway City. *See* Saint Louis, Missouri

gelatin, 147–48, 269. *See also* Jell-O

Geraci's pizza (Cleveland, OH), 243

German communities and food: baked goods, 58–59; beer halls, 42, 64; bratwurst, recipe, 95–96; chocolate cakes, 251; coney dogs, 128; cookbooks, 35, 123, 157; cookies, 282–84, 286; dough-nuts, 86; fried chicken, 186–89; fries/fried potatoes, recipe, 157–58, 181; hamburgers, 200–203; home distilleries, 38, 40; immigrants in Midwest, 3, 8–9, 40, 58–59, 79, 81, 84, 86, 103, 113–14, 123, 149, 151–52, 154–55, 157, 176, 186, 189, 251–52, 280, 283–84, 286, 292, 298–99; knefles, 141–43; lager, 41; liqueurs, 38; potato pancakes, 176; potato salad, warm, 154–56; pretzels, 64; sauerkraut, 27, 143; sausages, 95–96, 122–23

Germershausen, Christian Friedrich, 272–73, 286

giardiniera, 16–17, 117; Chicago-style hot, 118, 242; Chicago-style hot, recipe, 25–26; Marconi brand (V. Formusa), 25

gingerbread, 269, 286–87

Glasse, Hannah, 17, 86, 159, 176, 186

Glier's goetta, 152

Godey's Lady's Book, 17

340

Godey's Lady's Book Receipts and Household Hints, The, 17, 22, 273
goetta (meat-and-grain sausage), 195; recipe, 151–54
Good Food Movement, 292
Gopher State. *See* Minnesota
Gorham, George C., 184–85
graham cracker crust, recipe, 256
Granato's pizzeria (Chicago, IL), 235, 240
Great Lakes, 7, 9, 29, 81, 167
Great Plains, 3, 103–4, 141; states as Midwest, 9
Greek hot dogs and coney dogs, 125, 128–29
green beans, 4, 17, 136, 166–67, 170; green bean casserole, recipe, 144–45
"Green Corn Moon" (Brockman), 94
Green Era Chicago (Chicago, IL), 293–94
Green Era Educational NFP (Chicago, IL), 294
Green ERA Sustainability Partners (Chicago, IL), 294
Grenada Sentinel (Grenada, MS), 108
Gress, Lee [godfather], 136, 258, 304
Gress, Rita [aunt], 5, 136, 304
Grimm, Joe, 129
Grittani, Vincent and Mary, 240–41
Growing Power Chicago (Chicago, IL), 292–93
G&R Tavern (Waldo, OH), 42
Grüzewurst, 152
Guerra, Gus and Anna, 238

Hagger, Conrad, 187
hamburgers, 94–95, 114, 199–211; butterburgers, recipe, 208–9; horseshoes (hamburger), recipe, 209–11; Jucy Lucy, recipe, 206–7; loosemeat burgers, recipe, 204–6; as sandwiches, 202; steaks, 200
Hamburg steak, 200–202, 208
Hamel, Glennadene, 159
Hammon's black walnut purveyor (Stockton, MO), 278
handheld food, 93–133; as cuisine, 95. *See also* burgers; sandwiches
Harland, Marion, 275
Harrison, William Henry, 40
Hart, Stephanie, 246–47, 317
Hartzell, James, 95

Hauser, Frances. *See* Fehribach, Frances
Hazzard, Andrea (Andy), 54–55, 301, 317
Hazzard Free Farm (Pecatonica, IL), 54–55
Heartland, 42; Eastern, 7–8; and Midwestern food changes, 295–301. *See also* Midwest (US)
Heglin, Dave, 205
Hemingway, Ernest, 200
Hermann, Missouri, as historic wine town, 44
Hill, Annabella, 22, 146, 155
Hispanic Americans. *See* Latin American communities and food; Mexican communities and food; Puerto Rican communities and food
History of Dubois County (Wilson), 40
Hoffman, Johnny, 280
Home at the Range with George Rector (Rector), 250
honey: on biscuits, 76; on bread, 75; in ciders, 43; in cookies, 282; honey cakes (*Honigkuchen*), 286; in liqueurs and spirits, 38; quince honey, recipe, 30–31; as topping, 75, 76, 86
Honigkuchen (honey cakes), 286
Hoosier Cookbook, The, 253–54
Hoosiers. *See* Indiana
horseradish, 22, 144, 185; and beer, 101
hot chocolate (beverage), 283
hotdish, 94, 170; duck and manoomin (wild rice) hotdish, recipe, 170–73; ground beef and macaroni, 170; Taconite Tater Tot hotdish, 170. *See also* casseroles
hot dogs, 94–95, 122–28; Chicago-style, 26–27, 125–27, 130; Chicago-style, recipe, 125–28; as cuisine, 95; Michigan-style, 129–30. *See also* coney dogs; sausages
Household Dictionary (Bailey), 154
Hughes, J. L., Colonel, 40
Hungarian communities and food, 58, 86, 125

ice cream, 30, 136, 183, 215, 247, 261–62; in cocktails, 48–49; on pies, 250, 268
Igleheart Brothers mill (Evansville, IN), 271
Illinois: as Eastern Heartland, 7–8; farm economics in, reimagined, 196; German immigrants in, 186; and horseshoe sandwich, 209–11; and Indiana Territory, 40; Mexican communities and food in,

11, 290; as Midwest, 7; oldest continually
operating farm in, 278
Imperial Baking Company (Chicago, IL), 58
Indiana, 33, 243; as Eastern Heartland, 7–8;
German immigrants in, 186; immigrants
in, 3; and Indiana Territory, 40; as
Midwest, 7; southern, 2–3, 25, 60–61, 141,
157, 166, 258–59, 304; sugar cream pie, as
official state pie, 254
Indiana Farmer's Guide Cookbook, 269
Indiana Farmer's Guide New Cook Book, The,
28, 30–31
Indianapolis, Indiana, Black Southerners
in, 10
Indianapolis Star (Indianapolis, IN), 62, 254,
255
Indiana State Sentinel (Indianapolis, IN), 202
Indiana Territory, 40
Indigenous (Native American) communities
and food, 5, 11–12, 29, 108, 170–71, 296–
97, 300–301
Intelligencer Journal (Lancaster, PA), 76,
123–24
Inter-Ocean (Chicago, IL), 124
Iowa: and loosemeat burgers, 204–5; as
Midwest, 7, 8
Iraqi Kabob restaurant (Dearborn, MI), 92
Irish pubs, 42
Italian beef sandwich, recipe, 116–19
Italian communities and food, 9, 25, 116,
298–99

Jackson, Andrew, 40
James Beard Foundation Awards, 246, 266,
296
James Beard House (New York, NY), 267
jams and jellies, 29, 72, 166; blackberry, 4,
62; in donuts, 87; fruit in, 17, 34; quick
blackberry, recipe, 34–35; strawberry,
and biscuits, 62. *See also* marmalades;
preserves
Janie's Mill (Ashkum, IL), 59–60, 197
jellies. *See* jams and jellies
Jell-O, 145; salads, 147–49, 214. *See also*
gelatin
Jewish American communities and food,
9–10, 125–26, 139, 149, 176, 288
jibarito sandwich, recipe, 119–22

Johanneman, Phyllis A. Trout, 64
Johnson, Jeff, 25
Joliet, Louis, 296
Jolly Pumpkin brewery (Michigan), 42
Joy of Cooking, The (Rombauer), 6, 17, 19, 28,
257, 269, 283
Jucy Lucy hamburgers, recipe, 206–7
Junction City Weekly Union (Junction City,
KS), 168
Justice, Melba. *See* Morelos, Melba [grand-
mother]

Kander, Simon, Mrs., 51–52
Kansas, as Midwest, 7
Kansas City-style barbecue, 166, 215–21, 223–
24; recipe, 217–21
Kansas zwieback rolls, recipe, 84–86
Kegel's Inn (Milwaukee, WI), 42
Keller & Sons (Indianapolis, IN), advertise-
ments for pork tenderloin, 114
Kelly, Michael, 187–88
Kennedy's Restaurant (Scranton, PA), 174
Kentucky: barbecue, 215; fried chicken, 186;
whiskey industry, 40; wine, 38
Kentucky Housewife, The (Bryan), 51, 60, 186–
87, 216, 257, 259, 267, 269, 272
Keros, William and Constantine, 128–29
Ketapanen Kitchen (Stickney, IL), 297
ketchup, 16, 19–20, 98, 126, 128, 130, 205,
207, 209
Kim, Ann, 7, 231–32
Kiradjieff, John and Tom, 191–92
Klobuchar, Amy, Senator, 170
knefles, knephflas, knoephlas (dumplings),
141–43; basic knefles, recipe, 142; beans
and knefles, recipe, 142–43; as noodles in
soup, 142
Knob Hill Tavern (Newburgh, IN), 177, 181,
182
Knox gelatin, 147–48
kolaches, 58–59
Kool-Aid, 145
Korean communities and food, 59, 231, 299
Kramarczuk's Sausage Company (Minneapo-
lis, MN), 71–72
Kramer, Bertha (a.k.a. Aunt Babette), 6, 51–
52, 176, 286. See also *Aunt Babette's Cook
Book* (Kramer)

342

kringles, 5, 59; Chicago Hardy fig kringle, recipe, 81–84; as official state pastry of Wisconsin, 81

kuchen, 58, 251, 282; apfelkuchen, recipe, 78–81; lebkuchen, recipe, 286–88

Ladany, Samuel, 125

Lady's Assistant, The (Mason), 154

La Gloria Bakery (Detroit, MI), 2, 66

Lambrinides, Nicholas, 192

Land of 10,000 Lakes. *See* Minnesota

LaRosa's pizza (Cincinnati, OH), 6, 241

Latin American communities and food, 108, 137. *See also* Mexican communities and food; Puerto Rican communities and food

latkes (potato pancakes): Ashkenazi Jewish, 149, 298; recipe, 149–51

lebkuchen cookies, 282; recipe, 286–88

Le Francais restaurant (Wheeling, IL), 6

Leland Hotel (Springfield, IL), 210

Lemon, James P., 221

lemon donut glaze, recipe, 89

Lem's Bar-B-Q (Chicago, IL), 221, 246

Lentz, Mary Lou, 148

Lewis, L. A., Mrs., 273

Lewis, T. J., Mrs., 290

Libertus, Ron, 171

Lincoln, Mary Johnson Bailey, 271

Lincoln family frontier cornbread, recipe, 60–61

Lin Zexu, 35

liqueurs, 34, 38, 45, 51–52, 162

Lithuanian American communities and food, 59

Lithuanian Baking Company (Omaha, NE), 59

livermush. *See* goetta (meat-and-grain sausage)

London Porter beer, 41–42

Longworth, Nicholas, 44

loosemeat burgers, recipe, 204–6

Lost Bridge Beverage Company (North Bend, OH), 38

Louisville, Kentucky, as river town, 9

Luigi's pizza (Saint Louis, MO), 232–33

macaroni: Creamette brand, 170; ground beef hotdish, 170; salad, 177, 214. *See also* noodles

macaroni and cheese, 10–11, 136, 177

Macedonian (Balkan) communities and food, 128, 191–92

Mader's restaurant (Milwaukee, WI), 42

Mad House Vinegar, 37–38

Madison Sourdough (Madison, WI), 59

Maid-Rite (Urbandale, IA), 204–5

Maillard browning reactions, 275

main street cafés, 93

Maisonette restaurant (Cincinnati, OH), 37

Malnati, Luciano "Lou," 235–36

Malnati, Rudy, 236

Mama's pizza (Saint Paul, MN), 243

manoomin. *See* wild rice

Many New and Reliable Recipes (Presbyterian Church of LaPorte), 136

Marconi Foods (Des Plaines, IL), 25

Marina's market (Cincinnati, OH), 71–72

marmalades, 72; rhubarb marmalade, recipe, 35–36. *See also* jams and jellies

Marquette, Jacques, 296

Marshfield News-Herald (Marshfield, WI), 98

Maryland: barbecue, 215; fried biscuits, 62

Mason, Charlotte, 154

Matt's Bar (Minneapolis, MN), 206–7

Mawby, Larry, 44–45

Mayhew, Henry, 203

McKenzie and McNeill importers (Charleston, SC), 22

meat: goetta (meat-and-grain sausage), recipe, 151–64; and potatoes, 6, 165–95. *See also specific meat(s)*

meatloaf, 166

Meglio, Luca "Luigi," 232–33

Melrose Café (St. Louis, MO), 232

Memphis, Tennessee, barbecue, 217, 221, 223–24

Mennonites, 8, 84–85

Merkley and Sons hot dogs (Jasper, IN), 128

Mesoamerican foodways and cuisine, 137, 193

mettwurst, 96, 125, 222

Mexican communities and food, 2, 11, 59, 66–67, 86, 108–10, 126, 251, 275, 290–91, 298–99. *See also* Latin American communities and food

Mexican wedding cakes (cookies), 251; recipe, 290–91

MGP Ingredients distillery (Atchison, KS), 38, 40, 45

Michigan: coney dogs, 128–33, 192; and cranberries, 264; as Eastern Heartland, 7–8; hot dogs, regional, 129–30; and Indiana Territory, 40; as Midwest, 7; and sour cherry industry, 255; wines of, 44–45

microbreweries. *See under* beer

Middle Eastern communities and food, 59

Midwest (US), 7–12; as booming industrial heart of twentieth-century America, 296; as "Breadbasket of America," 58, 296; demographics of, 299; demographics of, sources, 317–18; diversity in, 5, 7–11, 292, 297, 299, 301; as dynamic, 298; as "flyover country," 7; German ancestry in, 8–9; and Great Migration (1900–1929), 8, 10, 11, 108, 186, 189; immigrants in, 3, 5, 8, 11; and Indigenous cultures, 5, 11–12; as most exciting pizza region in America, 13; racism and segregation in, 292, 299; states defined as, 7–9. *See also* Great Lakes; Great Plains; Heartland

Midwestern food: and archetypal foods, 13; august importance of in America's national diet, 14; and BIPOC communities, 292, 301; and "Breadbasket of America," 58, 296; and changes, 295–301; and culinary memoir, 3; and culture(s), 8, 14, 100–101, 299; as dynamic, 298; and European cultural transfer, 299; and farm-to-table movement, 5; and fast-food enterprises, 6; and food industry hub, 296; foodways, 5, 9–13, 18, 27, 49, 60, 66, 91, 94, 108, 116, 125, 137, 163, 191, 215, 266, 296, 298; future of, 295–301, 304; and heritage, 8; and identity, 5, 8; and immigrant communities, 3–4, 5, 8, 11, 13–14, 298–301; independents vs. chains, 299–301; and industrialization, 5, 18, 100–101, 170; and innovation, 5; and local food economies, 301; and Mississippians, 10–11; and modernist cuisine, 7; and Native American civilization, 5, 11–12; patchwork quilt of, 3–4; racial biases and exclusiveness, 298; and regionalization, 216, 301; and suburbanization, 170; success of, 298; taken seriously, 6, 13, 14; and tavern

culture, 42; and tradition, 5; and urban farming, 5; and urbanization, 170, 216; world-class, 301

"Midwestern nice," 12

milk: milk breads, 129, 163; milk pies, 253

Milwaukee, Wisconsin, 6; as brewing city, 6, 40; German beer halls in, 42; German immigrants in, 8

mince pie, 251, 296; recipe, 266–68

Minneapolis–Saint Paul, Minnesota, 7; Black Southerners in, 10; and flour milling, 6

Minnesota: and hotdish, 170; and Indiana Territory, 40; as Midwest, 7, 8

Minnesota State Fair, 98

Missouri: as Midwest, 7; wines of, 44

Missouri Baking Company (Saint Louis, MO), 58–59

morel mushrooms *(Morchella)*, pan-fried, recipe, 137–38

Morelos, Melba [grandmother], 2, 4–5, 66–67, 128, 304

mortadella bologna, 122–23

mother-in-law sandwich, 109–10

Mrs. Hill's New Cook Book (Hill), 146, 155

mushrooms, 4, 136–37; breaded, 166; morels, pan-fried, recipe, 137–38; on pizza, 237–38, 244; quick cream of mushroom soup, 145, 173; quick cream of mushroom soup, recipe, 171–72; in tamales, 110–11

mutton, in barbecue, 216

Nashville, Indiana, 61–62

Nashville House (Nashville, IN), 61–62

National Butcher's Association (Chicago, IL, 1887), 216

Native Americans. *See* Indigenous (Native American) communities and food

Nebraska: German immigrants in, 8; as Midwest, 7

Neues saltzburgisches Koch-Buch (Hagger), 187

Never Put Ketchup on a Hot Dog (Schwartz), 126

New England Farmer (journal), 35

New Jersey, as Eastern Heartland, 7–8

New System of Domestic Cookery (Rundell), 17

New York Bagel & Bialy (Skokie, IL), 288

New York State: as Eastern Heartland, 7–8; German immigrants in, 8; as Midwest, 9

New York Sun, 201–2
New York Times, 7
Nick's Kitchen (Huntington, IN), 114
noodles: chicken and noodles, 11, 251;
  chicken and noodles, recipe, 173–75. *See
  also* macaroni; pasta
North Carolina: barbecue, 215; persimmon
  pudding, 260
North Dakota: German immigrants in, 8; as
  Midwest, 7
Norton, Daniel, Dr., 44
Novo, Salvador, 66
nuts: candied, 288. *See also* pecans; walnuts

Ocean Spray cranberries, Massachusetts-
  based, 29
Oden, Loretta Barrett, 297
Ohio: as Eastern Heartland, 7–8; as Midwest,
  7; wine, 38, 44
Ohio Cultivator (newspaper), 254
Ohio River Valley, 37, 44, 51–52, 60, 158, 167,
  181, 231
Oldani's (St. Louis, MO), 105–6
Omega Artisan Baking (Columbus, OH), 288
Omnivore's Dilemma, The (Pollan), 161
Original Appledore Cook Book, The (Parloa),
  271, 273
*Original Local: Indigenous Foods, Stories, and
  Recipes from the Upper Midwest* (Erdrich),
  171
Osborn, Gov., Mrs., 269
Owamni restaurant (Minneapolis, MN),
  296–97
oysters: in barbecue, 217; fried, 202; oyster
  cocktails, 184–85; oyster cocktail sauce,
  185; oyster dressing, recipe, 158–60; scal-
  loped/scallop of, 159; shooters, 185

Pacelli, Chris, Sr., and Frances, 116
paczki (filled donuts), 58, 86–87, 298
Pamonicutt, Jessica, 297
pan dulce (Mexican sweet breads), 2, 66–67.
  See also conchas
panaderias, 59, 66, 290
panificadoras, 290
pandemic. *See* COVID-19 pandemic
panko breadcrumbs, 114–16
Parloa, Maria, 259, 271, 273

parsnips, 137, 139, 144. *See also* borscht,
  recipe
passionfruit, 198
pasta, 137, 191–95. *See also* macaroni;
  noodles; ravioli
pastries, 29, 59, 86, 250; black walnut rugelach, recipe, 288–90; Chicago Hardy fig
  kringle, recipe, 81–84; Mexican, 66–67
Pat's Pizza (Chicago, IL), 241
pawpaws (fruit), 4, 162–63; pawpaw chiffon
  pie, recipe, 262–64; pawpaw vinaigrette,
  163
peanut butter egg rolls (Chicago-style egg
  rolls), 91
pears: cranberry pear preserves, recipe, 29–
  30; and quince, 30; in wine, 38
pecans: apple cider pecan cheese ball, recipe,
  101–3; in Mexican wedding cookies, 290–
  91; sorghum pecan sticky rolls, recipe,
  69–71
Peden, Rachel, 16
Pennsylvania: as Eastern Heartland, 7–8;
  German immigrants in, 8; as Midwest, 9;
  Swabian immigrants in, 64
Pennsylvania Dutch communities and food,
  8, 13, 31, 76, 100, 174, 188, 253–54, 271
Perry, Henry, 217
persimmons, 38, 162–63; persimmon pudding, recipe, 260–62; vinegar, 38
piccalilli, 17–18, 22, 127, 184; and chow-chow,
  23–24; recipe, 23–25
pickles, 15–17, 136, 214, 285; bread-and-
  butter, 4, 114, 115, 156, 184; on burgers,
  205; dill, 4; India, 23–24; watermelon
  pickles, recipe, 28–29. *See also* chow-
  chow; giardiniera; piccalilli; preserves;
  relishes
pies, 249–51; blackberry, 5; cheese on, 250;
  cider pies, 253; coconut cream pie, 301;
  coconut cream pie, recipe, 258–60;
  cranberry and bone marrow pudding
  pie, recipe, 264–66; custard, 250–53, 262,
  264; fruit, 251; graham cracker crust,
  recipe, 255–56; ice cream on, 250, 268;
  milk pies, 253; mince pie, recipe, 266–68;
  orange, 257; pawpaw chiffon pie, recipe,
  262–64; strawberry custard pie, recipe,
  251–53; sugar cream pie, recipe, 253–55;

sweet-potato pie, recipe, 257–58; vinegar pies, 253
pigeons, fried, recipe, 187
Piggly Wiggly grocery store advertisement, 20
pig snoots, barbecued, 5; recipe, 224–25
pineapple-coconut cake, 246–47
Pinkard, Arthur, 217
pizza, 14, 229–45; basic Midwestern pizza sauce, 242; basic Midwestern pizza sauce, recipe, 234–35; Chicago-style, 5, 26, 230–31, 236; Chicago-style deep-dish, recipe, 235–38; coconut curry, 232; crab Rangoon, 232; Detroit-style, 92, 230–31; Detroit-style deep-dish, recipe, 238–40; Midwestern, 231, 237, 241–43; pan, recipe, 242–45; *pizza napoletana*, Chicago-style, 231; Saint Louis–style, recipe, 232–34; stuffed, 236; and taverns, 42, 231, 240–42; tavern-style, recipe, 240–42; thin-crust, 240–41
Pizzeria Due (Chicago, IL), 236
Pizzeria Uno (Chicago, IL), 235–36
plantains, fried, 121–22; as bread, 119
plants, edible, 162
Poeschel, Michael, 44
polenta, 55
Polish communities and food, 3, 9, 58, 71–72, 86–87, 126, 139, 176, 298
Pollan, Michael, 161
polvoron (shortbread cookie), 290
ponthaus. *See* goetta (meat-and-grain sausage)
pork: tenderloin, breaded, 5, 92; tenderloin, breaded, recipe, 113–16
potatoes: creamy potato salad, recipe, 156–57; German fries, 181; German fries, recipe, 157–58; Irish, 154; mashed, 143; potato pancakes (latkes/*Rosti*), 298; potato pancakes (latkes/*Rosti*), recipe, 149–51; potato pancakes, German, 176; potato salad, recipes, 154–57; potato wedges, deep-fried, 181; warm German potato salad, 154; warm German potato salad, recipe, 155–56. *See also* meat and potatoes; sweet potatoes; Tater Tots
potlucks, 154, 251, 271
poverty foods. *See* affordable foods; Depression-era foods

Praktisches Kochbuch für die Deutschen in Amerika (Davidis), 149, 189, 201
Presbyterian Church of LaPorte (LaPorte, IN), 136
preserves, 4, 15–18, 51, 143, 285; and condiments, 17–18; cranberry pear, recipe, 29–30; fruit, 16–17; sweet corn in, 29, 33. *See also* giardiniera; jams and jellies; pickles; relishes
pretzels: anise, 271; as breads, 58, 64; pretzel salad, recipe, 147–49; "everything" rye pretzels, recipe, 64–66; sugar/sweet, 271
Price, Ellen, 109
Prima Cider (Long Grove, IL), 43
Princeton Clarion-Ledger (Princeton, IN), 257
probiotics, 27
Prussian communities and food, 84, 292
"Psalm of Grapes, A" (Peden), 16
pub cheese, or cold-pack cheese, 100–101
Publican Quality Bread (Chicago, IL), 59
pubs, 42. *See also* bars; saloons; taverns
puddings, 250; bread pudding, 264; coconut pudding, 259; cranberry and bone marrow pudding pie, 251, 253; cranberry and bone marrow pudding pie, recipe, 264–66; desserts, 154, 261; persimmon pudding, recipe, 260–62
Puerto Rican communities and food, 119
pumpernickel: black Russian, 58; bread, recipe, 71–75; origin of name (folktale), 72; Westphalian, 72
purple barley, 55
Putnam, Robert, 109

Queen City. *See* Cincinnati, Ohio
quinces, 17; quince honey, recipe, 30–31

ranch dressing, 16; as National Everything Dressing of the Midwest, 99; recipe, 99–100
Randolph, Mary, 186–87
Rauchfleisch (Hamburg sausages), 201
ravioli, toasted, 105–7
recipes: and cookbook sources, 12–13; and methods, 12–14; receipts as, 12; "salvage," 34
Rector, George, 250
Rector's seafood house (Chicago, IL), 185

346

Refectory restaurant (New York, NY), 188
Reichl, Emil, 125
Reilly, Dorcas, 144
Reitz, Glennadene. *See* Hamel, Glennadene
relishes, 15, 17, 136, 214; cherry barbecue,
    recipe, 18–19; cranberry sweet corn,
    recipe, 33–34; sweet corn in, 29, 33;
    tomato-cabbage, 24. *See also* condiments;
    giardiniera; pickles; preserves
remoulade, French, 183
Republic, The (Columbus, IN), 62
rhubarb: marmalade, recipe, 35–36; pies,
    251; charlotte, recipe, 269–70; walleye,
    rhubarb-poached, 163; wine, 41
ribs: baby back, 217, 224; baby back, recipe,
    219–20; Kansas City-style, 217; Korean-
    style short ribs, 231; Saint Louis-style
    spareribs, 223–24; St. Louis-style spare-
    ribs, recipe, 226. *See also* spareribs
rib tips, 95, 224; and hot link combo, 5, 217,
    221, 246; and hot link combo, recipe,
    222–23
Riccardo, Ric, Sr., 235–36
Riccardo's restaurant (Chicago, IL), 235–36
rice, wild. *See* wild rice
Richmond Item (Richmond, IN), 260
Rivera, Manuel Galvan, 66
rivvels (dumplings), 136
Rodriguez, Sixto, 2
rolls: Chelsea buns, 69; Kansas zwiebach,
    recipe, 84–86; sorghum pecan sticky
    rolls, recipe, 69–71; Swedish rolls, 69
Rombauer, Irma, 6, 17, 269
Rosalia, Eleonora Maria, 187, 283
Rosen, Sam, 125–27
Rosti (potato pancakes), recipe, 149–51
rugelach: apricot, 288; black walnut, recipe,
    288–90
Rundell, Maria, 17
Runzas, or bierocks, recipe, 103–5
Russell, Malinda, 22, 257
Russian tea cakes. *See* Mexican wedding
    cakes (cookies)
Rutledge, Sarah, 174
rye: pretzels, recipe, 64–66; whiskey, 45. *See
    also under* breads

Saint Louis, Missouri, 6, 7; Black commu-
    nities in, 216; as brewing city, 6, 40;
    German immigrants in, 8, 58–59, 280; as
    river town, 9
Saint Louis Pastries Bakery, 280
Saint Louis-style: gooey butter cake, 279–80;
    hot dogs, 123–24; pizza, 231; pizza, recipe,
    232–34; spareribs, 223–24; spareribs,
    recipe, 226; toasted ravioli, 105–7
Saint Louis (East)-style: barbecue, 216–17,
    223–24; barbecue, recipe, 223–27
Saint Paul, Minnesota. *See* Minneapolis-
    Saint Paul, Minnesota
salad dressings. *See* dressings, salad
salads: Jell-O, 147–49, 214; macaroni, 177,
    214; potato, recipes, 154–57; pretzel,
    recipe, 147–49
saloons, 124. *See also* bars; pubs; taverns
salsa, 16, 145
"salvage" recipes, 34
sandwiches, 93; beefsteak, raw (cannibal
    or wildcat), recipe, 202–4; bologna, 163;
    Cubano, 91; Italian beef, recipe, 116–19;
    jibarito, recipe, 119–22. *See also* burgers
San Francisco Chronicle (San Francisco, CA),
    202
sauerkraut, 4; basic recipe, 26–28; and beer
    brats, 27; ciders in, 27, 143; prepared,
    recipe, 143–44; stew, 137
sausages: for coney dogs, 129–30; goetta,
    recipe, 151–54; for hot dogs, 122–27. *See
    also* bratwurst; hot dogs
Scandinavian communities and food, 9, 27,
    59, 86
Schellhammer, Maria Sophia, 84, 123
Schepers, Rich and Sue, 304
Scherer, John, 44
Schlitz tied houses, 42
schmaltz (rendered fat, lard), 149–50, 157
Schmierkase (cheese), 100
Schoenfeld, Henry, Mrs., 51–52
Schwägermann's Hannover Hamburg steak
    receipt, 201
Schwartz, Bob, 126
Scranton Republican (Scranton, PA), 174
scrapple. *See* goetta (meat-and-grain sau-
    sage)

Second City. *See* Chicago, Illinois

Settlement Cook Book, The (Kander and Schoenfeld), 22, 28, 51–52, 79, 86–87, 283, 286

Sewell, Ike, 235

Shakers, 253–54

Sherman, Sean, 7, 296–97

shortbread cookies, 290

shortening (cooking fat), 278

shrimp: fried, 11; cocktails, 184–85

side dishes, and vegetables, 135–60

Simms, Laurell, 293

Sioux Chef's Indigenous Kitchen, The (Sherman), 296

slaws, cabbage, 214. *See also* coleslaw

Smith, Eliza, 97–98

Smokin' Chokin' and Chowing (blog), 91

Snider, T. A. (Thomas A.), 17–18, 185

Snider's condiments (Cincinnati, OH), 185

Snow's Cut-Rate Market (Saint Joseph, MO), advertisement, 218

sorghum: black-walnut-sap sorghum sauce, 163; molasses, 65, 70, 146–47, 247; pecan sticky rolls, recipe, 69–71

soul food, 11, 146, 223, 257, 275

soups: borscht, recipe, 139–41; chicken noodle soup, 174, 299; quick cream of mushroom soup, 145, 173; quick cream of mushroom soup, recipe, 171–72. *See also* stews

sour cabbage. *See* sauerkraut

sours, 15

South Carolina, barbecue, 215

South Dakota: German immigrants in, 8; as Midwest, 7

Southern communities and food, 5, 9–11, 17–18, 54, 108–10, 112–13, 146, 167, 168, 176–77, 186, 189, 215–16, 275, 292, 298–99. *See also* Black communities and food

Southern Foodways Alliance, 186

spareribs, 143, 217; Saint Louis-style, 223–24; Saint Louis-style, recipe, 226

Spence Farm (Fairbury, IL), 196–98, 278

spice cake, 251; black walnut, recipe, 278–79

springerle cookies, 282, 284; recipe, 283–86

spritz cookies, recipe, 281–83

squeeze cheese, or cold-pack cheese, 100

S. Rosen's, poppy-seed buns (Chicago, IL), 125–27

state fairs, 93, 94, 98, 114–15. *See also* county fairs

steak, Hamburg, 200–202, 208. *See also* beefsteaks

steakhouses, 6. *See also* chophouses; supper clubs

stews: booyah, recipe, 167–69; cabbage, 137. *See also* soups

sticky rolls. *See* rolls

St. Joseph New-Press (Saint Joseph, MO), 218

St. Louis. *See* Saint Louis, Missouri

St. Louis Post-Dispatch (Saint Louis, MO), 223

St. Louis Star and Times (Saint Louis, MO), 106

stollen (German coffee cake), 58, 79, 280

Stone Hill Winery (Hermann, MO), 44

St. Paul. *See* Minneapolis–Saint Paul, Minnesota

strawberries: jam, and biscuits, 62; strawberry custard pie, recipe, 251–53

stuffing, oyster dressing, recipe, 158–60

Stuttgen, Joanne Raetz, 258

Sullivan, Howard, 98

Summit Brewing (Saint Paul, MN), 42

supper clubs, 45–48, 176. *See also* chophouses; steakhouses

Swabian communities and food, 3, 64, 283

Swans Down cake flour, 271

Swedish communities and food, 69, 76, 81, 100–101

sweet corn, 139; cranberry sweet corn relish, recipe, 33–34; in preserves and relishes, 29, 33. *See also* corn on the cob

sweetmeats, 17, 29

sweet potatoes, 147; sweet-potato pie, recipe, 257–58. *See also* yams

sweets, 15, 60, 249–50. *See also* baked goods and bakeries; cakes; confections; cookies; desserts; ice cream; pies; puddings

Taconite Tater Tot hotdish, 170

tacos, 13–14, 25, 92, 94, 299

tailgates and tailgating, 93, 96

tamales, 14, 94–95, 107–13; chocolate, 109; cornmeal in, 108–9; as cuisine, 95; Delta-style hot, 108–10; Delta-style hot, recipe, 112–13; fillings, 108; folklore and history of, 107–10; Mexican-style, 108–10, 113; Mexican-style, recipe, 110–11; in mother-in-law sandwich, 109–10

tartar sauce, recipe, 183–84

tasting menus, 161

Tater Tots, 145, 170, 207

taverns: and beer, 42; and loosemeat burgers, 205; and pizza, 42, 231, 240–42. *See also* bars; pubs; saloons

tenderloins, 94–95; pork, breaded, 5, 92; pork, breaded, recipe, 113–16

Tennessean (Nashville, TN), 124

Tennessee barbecue, 215

Terkel, Studs, 117

Terry, Elena, 297

tied houses. *See* taverns

tomatoes, 23, 139

Travis, Marty, 196–98, 278, 317

Travis, Will, 196–98

Treemont Coffee House, 162

Trillin, Calvin, 217, 230

Troop, J., Professor, 260

Trotter, Charlie, 6–7

turkey shoots, 251, 266

Twain, Mark, 214

Twin Cities. *See* Minneapolis–Saint Paul, Minnesota

UGC. *See* Urban Growers Collective (Chicago, IL)

Upland Brewing (Indiana), 42

Urban Growers Collective (Chicago, IL), 292–94

Vander Mill ciders (Grand Rapids, MI), 43

vegetables: preserved, 4; and sides, 135–60. *See also* giardiniera; *specific vegetable(s)*

V. Formusa Co. (Chicago, IL), 25

Vicksburg Evening Post (Vicksburg, MI), 108–9

Vienna Beef (Chicago, IL), 122–26, 301

Vienna Sausage Mfg. Company (Chicago, IL), 125

Viennese communities and food, 187–88, 273

Viets, Elaine, 223–24

vinegars: apple cider vinegar, in potato salad, 155; cider and vinegar for barbecue prep, 214; pawpaw vinaigrette, 163; vinegar pies, 253

Violet Hour bar (Chicago, IL), 45

Virginia: barbecue, 215; fried chicken, 186

Virginia Housewife, The, 159, 186–87, 272

Virtue Cider (Fennville, MI), 43

Vizetelly, Henry, 44

Vonnegut, Kurt, 7

Voth, Norma Jost, 84

Wahpepah, Crystal, 297

Wallace, Wm. T., 184–85

Wally's grocery store (Chicago, IL), 72

walnuts: black walnut rugelach, recipe, 288–90; black-walnut-sap sorghum sauce, 163; black walnut spice cake, recipe, 278–79

watermelon pickles, recipe, 28–29

Weaver, William Woys, 13, 76

Weekly Union (Junction City, KS), 168

Wells Brothers pizza (Racine, WI), 241

Welser, Philippine, 86, 282

Welserin, Sabina, 95–96, 286

whiskey: barrels, 4–5, 40–41, 49–50; cocktails, 45–46, 48, 51, 64; corn, 40; industry, 6, 40, 45; rye, 45

Widdifield's New Cook Book, 272

Wiener schnitzel, 113–14

wieners and frankfurters, 122–26, 128, 130, 192. *See also* hot dogs

wild cherries: wild cherry and blackberry wine, recipe, 49–51; wine, 4, 43, 49–51

wild rice: duck and manoomin (wild rice) hotdish, recipe, 170–73; manoomin, 170–71

Willingly Cracked-Open Pomegranate of the Christian Samaritans (Rosalia), 187

Wilson, George R., 40

Windy Knoll Farm (Fairbury, IL), 197

wine, 40–45, 49–52; barley, 42; blackberry, 4, 40–41, 43, 49–51; Catawba grapes, 44; fruits in, 38, 40–41, 45; Midwestern, 44–45; mulled, 283; Norton grapes, 38, 44–45; rhubarb, 41; wild cherry and blackberry, recipe, 49–51; wild cherry, 4, 43, 49–51. *See also* beer; cocktails

Wisconsin: and Cheeseheads, 97; fish fry, recipe, 177–80; and Indiana Territory, 40; kringle as official state pastry of, 81; as Midwest, 7, 8

Würste, Belonische, 123

yams, candied, recipe, 146–47. *See also* sweet potatoes

Yiddish cooking, 149

Young, Katherine, 129

Young Joni pizza (Minneapolis, MN), 231–32

Your Happy Kitchen Cook Book, 250

zwiebach rolls, recipe, 84–86